The Beginning Guide to
Microsoft Access 2010
Microsoft Office Specialist Exam 77-885 Study Guide

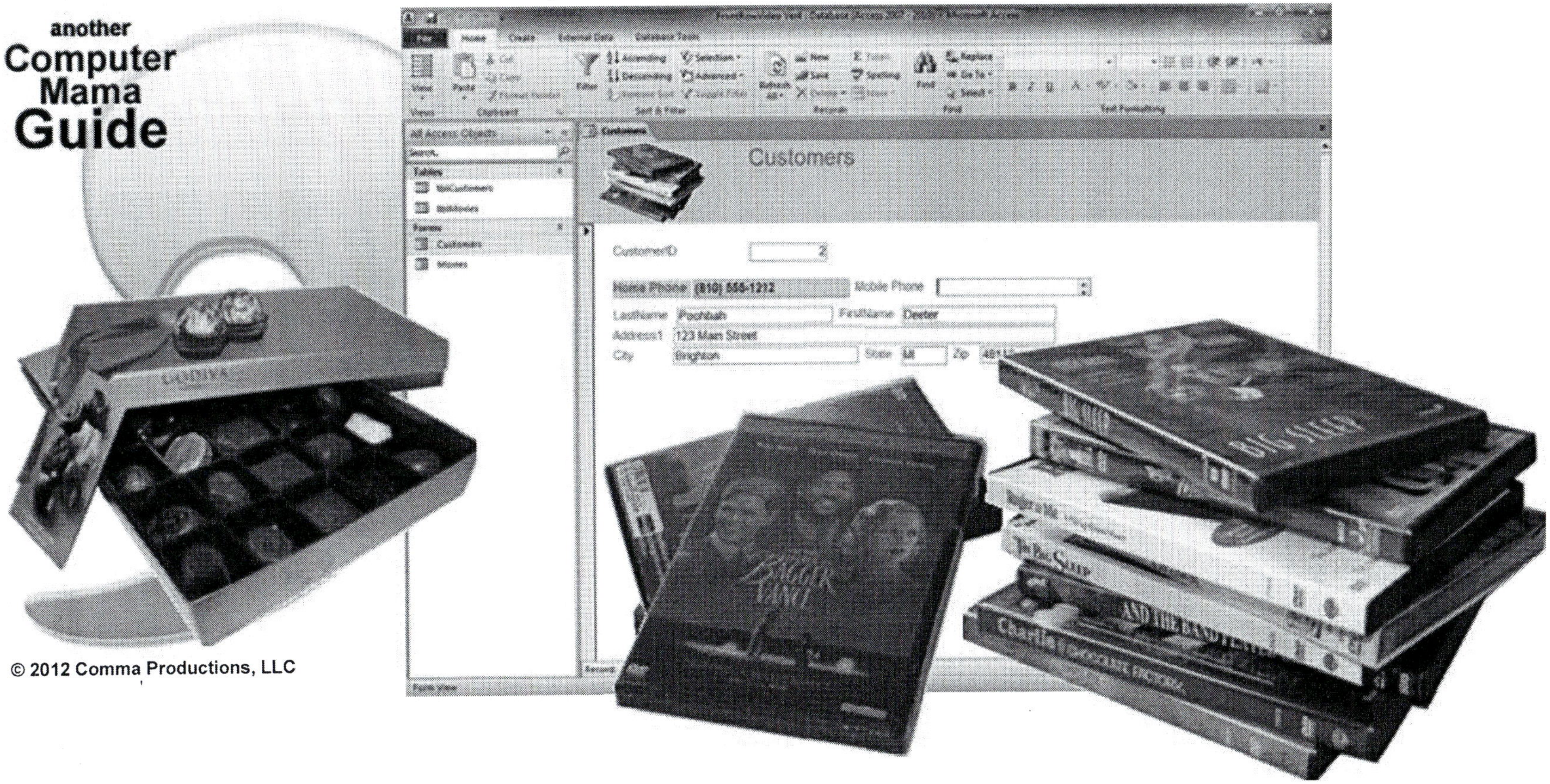

another
Computer
Mama
Guide

another
Computer Mama
Guide

The Beginning Guide to Microsoft Access 2010

© 2012 Comma Productions, LLC
9090 Chilson Road
Brighton, MI 48116
978-0-9838917-8-9

Trademark and Copyright

Limit of Liability/Disclaimer of Warranty:

⊙ The Beginning Guide to Microsoft Access 2010

Microsoft Office Specialist Certification

What is the Microsoft Office Specialist Certification?

The Microsoft Office Specialist certification validates through the use of exams that you have obtained specific skill sets within the applicable Microsoft Office programs and other Microsoft programs included in the Microsoft Office Specialist Program. The candidate can choose which exam(s) they want to take according to which skills they want to validate.

CertiPort is the premier provider for validating technology skills.

The **Microsoft Office Specialist** tests are offered at authorized testing centers.

For more information on the MOS exam topics or to find a testing center near you please contact: **www.certiport.com**

What is the Microsoft Office Specialist Certification Program?

The **Microsoft Office Specialist (MOS) Certification Program** enables candidates to show that they have something exceptional to offer – proven expertise in Microsoft Office programs. Recognized by businesses and schools around the world, millions of certifications have been obtained in over 100 different countries. The **Microsoft Office Specialist (MOS) Certification Program** is the only Microsoft-approved certification program of its kind.

The Microsoft Office Specialist Certification Series

Core Certification: Pass any 1 test:
Word 2010 Core: Exam 77-881
Excel® 2010 Core: Exam 77-882
PowerPoint® 2010: Exam 77-883
Access® 2010: Exam 77-885
Outlook® 2010: Exam 77-884

Expert Certification: Pass either test:
Word 2010 Expert: Exam 77-887
Excel® 2010 Expert: Exam 77-888

Master: Pass 3 required and 1 elective test:
Required
Word 2010 Expert: Exam 77-887
Excel® 2010 Expert: Exam 77-888
PowerPoint® 2010: Exam 77-883

Elective
Access® 2010: Exam 77-885 or
Outlook® 2010: Exam 77-884

The Benefits of Certification

Why Get Certified?

For employers, the certification provides skill-verification tools that not only help assess a person's skills in using Microsoft Office programs but also the ability to quickly complete on-the-job tasks across multiple programs in the Microsoft Office system. (http://www.microsoft.com/learning/en/us/certification/mos.aspx). Certification proves a certain level of advanced competency with the programs in question. Employers don't have to wonder if the skills stated on the resume are honest and without exaggeration. This can lead to further employment opportunities and increased pay.

A person holding Microsoft Office Certification shows not just a level of skill, but an ability to quickly complete tasks, due to familiarity with the program and it's many time-saving features. The hard work that goes into learning Microsoft Office programs to the level of proficiency necessary for successful completion of the Certification Exams also indicates a desire on behalf of the student to learn and succeed.

The Benefits: Earn More, Find Jobs Quicker

Research indicates that employees with Microsoft Certification earn more and find jobs quicker than those employees without certification. Furthermore, employees with certification report a greater feeling of confidence. These things translate into greater job satisfaction. (http://www.microsoft.com/learning/en/us/certification/mos.aspx)

Research also shows that individuals with certification make up to 12% more than those without certification. In addition, 82% of Microsoft Office Specialists report a salary increase after receiving certification. Managers like the skills proven and the ability demonstrated by those with Microsoft Office Certifications.
http://www.certiport.com/Portal/desktopdefault.aspx?page=common/pagelibrary/mos2003.html

For More Information:
www.certiport.com
www.microsoft.com

About Our Certification Program

Books in this Series:
Beginning Guide to
Microsoft® Access 2010

Intermediate Guide to
Microsoft® Access 2010

Advanced Guide to
Microsoft® Access 2010

Microsoft Office Specialist (MOS) Certification for Access 2010

Overview: Our Microsoft Office Specialist certification program for Access 2010 covers all of the exam objectives for the Access certification exam. Microsoft Office Specialist exam 77-85 for Access is an <u>elective</u> exam that demonstrates expert knowledge of database programming and Microsoft Office automation. <u>It is not required for MOS certification</u>.

Our Approach: In designing these Guides, we found that it made more sense to write the lessons based on the Ribbons and Tasks. The beginning of each lesson provides an overview of the Ribbons and Tasks covered.

The Beginning Guide to Microsoft Access 2010 demonstrates the following Ribbons: **Home, Create, Table Tools, Form Layout Tools: Arrange and Format, Query Tools, and Report Layout Tools.** The lesson activities focus on basic database objects: Tables, Forms, Queries and Reports.

The Intermediate Guide to Microsoft Access 2010 demonstrates the following Ribbons: **Table Tools, Form Design Tools: Arrange and Format, Query Tools, Report Design Tools and the Macro Tools.** The programming focuses on representing one-to-many relationships: Form and Subform, Report and Subreport. The lessons show how to design for Real Users that includes creating a Switchboard that opens when the database is launched.

The Advanced Guide to Microsoft Access 2010 begins with a discussion of how to design a database in Third Normal Form to minimize repeat data and reduce errors. The programming focuses on using Key data to create relationships between Tables. The projects include a Receipt Form that calculates the total amount owed and a Receipt Printout formatted for a small Point of Sale (POS) printer.

Course Prerequisites: Students who enroll in the Microsoft Access 2010 program should have strong computer skills including how to use an Internet browser and how to select commands from a menu. Students should know how to save files and send attachments by email as well. In addition, students should have good skills with spreadsheets.

Microsoft Access 2010 Study Guide

Microsoft Office Specialist (MOS): Exam 77-885 for Access 2010

Microsoft Access 2010 Study Guide

Microsoft Office Specialist (MOS): Exam 77-885 for Access 2010

❾ About the Authors

Microsoft Office Specialist (MOS): Exam 77-885 for Access 2010

Elizabeth Ann Nofs

Elizabeth is the Computer Mama. She developed the teaching methodology in the Complete Computer Guide series using breakthrough research in gender balanced training. Elizabeth has taught several thousand men and women from government, manufacturing, small business, and education in both online and hands-on classrooms.

She is the author of the Complete Computer Guides as well as a Microsoft Certified Office Specialist. She earned a BA in Biology from the University of Michigan.

Alex Sergay, Senior Instructional Designer

For more than 20 years, Alex has made complex technology easy to understand. Alex has developed instructional multimedia software for educational websites including the Sounds of English, a linguistics-training tool that earned a ComputerWorld/Smithsonian Laureate.

Alex earned his Masters of Educational Technology from the University of Michigan, Ann Arbor.

Clair Dickson, Student Services

Clair works with adult learners in online, face-to-face and hybrid classroom settings. She is considered "highly qualified" to teach introductory computers, including Microsoft Office.

Clair has a Graduate Certificate in Educational Media and Technology, a program that explored ways to infuse technology into the learning experience so that learning is interactive. She has earned Microsoft Office 2007 Master Certification. She also holds a BS in Secondary English Education from Eastern Michigan University.

Leo Michael Nofs, Technical Writing and Quality Control

Leo is a Microsoft Certified Professional and an Access database designer. He uses his exemplary attention to detail for copy editing the computer instructions for accuracy and clarity.

Traci Nofs, Photography and Photo Editing

Traci has been photographing children and nature since 2000. She works freelance out of her home, including weddings, engagements, and particularly children's photography. She has further enhanced her photos by use of image manipulation, focusing on light and color.

M. Jeanette McCrickard, Office Manager

Jeanette has years of experience as an office manager, including the increasing use of computer-related tasks. Her excellent attention to detail has lead her to work as an Access database administrator and a copy editor.

All of my books

are dedicated to

Fr. Paul Cummings

who taught me

computers.

Love, eBeth

How To Use This Guide
Microsoft Office Specialist Certification Training

The Comma Method

Observation is a perceptual strategy that asks: why am I doing this and which tools would be most effective? Each lesson begins with a discussion of the purpose and the objectives.

Orientation helps students start at the right place. The screen shots in the *Complete Compute Guides* show the entire window as well as a close up of the particular button or command.

Notation There are "breadcrumbs" above each screen image. Like Hansel and Gretel, the breadcrumbs show the pathway to a button or option. Our notation uses the following convention:

Ribbon->Group->Button->Options

Menu Maps

The Comma Method recognizes that there is a difference in how men and women navigate the menus. Men typically have the ability to see the map first. This method of acquiring knowledge is called *Breadth-first*. [1] Women tend to work with the details first. They learn several commands, such as copy, cut, and paste, then they put those concepts under the label, "edit." This method of learning is called *Depth-first*.

The Comma Method uses menu mapping to assist men and women to see both the Breadth and the Depth. An example of the menu map is can be seen here.

[1] Ford, Nigel, Sherry Chen, Matching/mismatching revisited: An Empirical Study of Learning and Teaching Styles. British Journal of Educational Technology v.32 no1 (Jan. 2001)

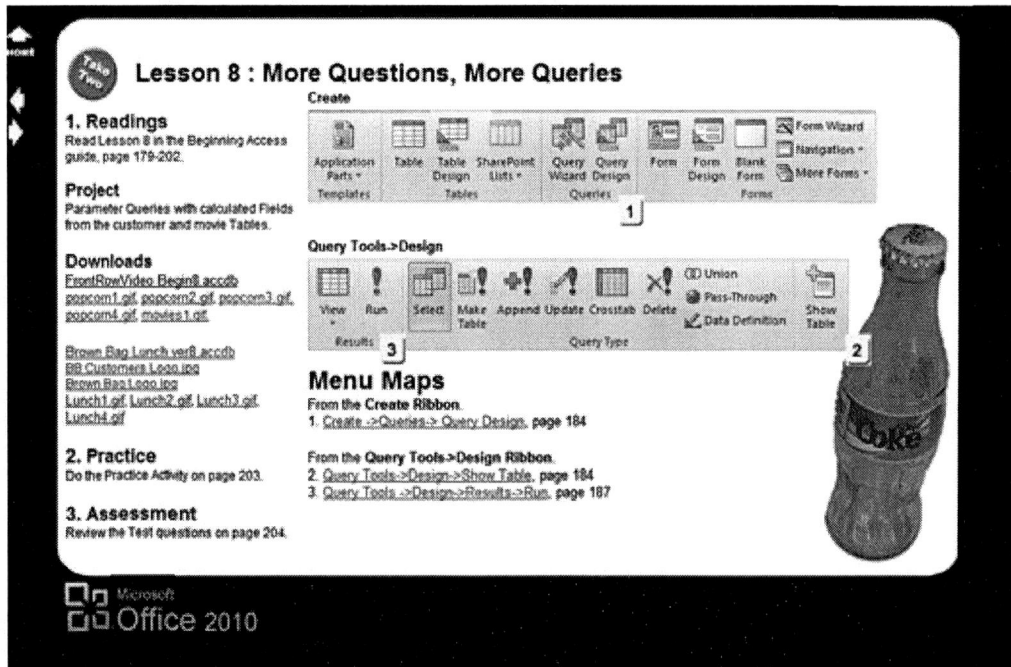

Query Tools->Design

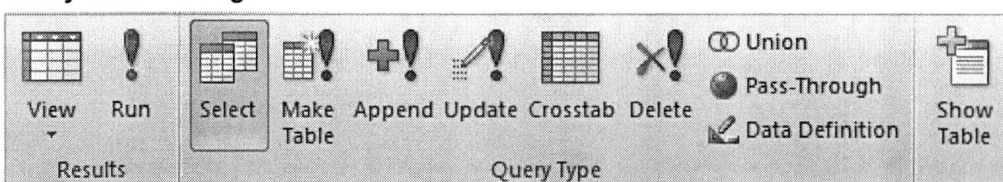

Excel 2010: Getting Started
Welcome!

Course Objectives
Students will be able to:

1. Log in to the online course
2. Navigate the outline and lessons
3. Take quizzes online
4. Submit assignments online
5. Participate in the Forums and Chat

Welcome

This course presents a practical, hands-on approach to computers. The lessons are based on what you see on the screen, what you can do with the options, and what works on the job. The goal is to enable you to use Microsoft Windows and Office 2010 effectively, even creatively.

Use this *Guide* as part of your professional development plan to prepare for the Microsoft Business Certification exams, Microsoft Office Specialist (MOS) or as a reference book to solve problems as they come up.

This introduction provides information on:
• Navigation
• Practice
• Sample Documents
• Assessments

Log into the course

This online course requires a User Name and Password. You probably received an email with your username and password when you enrolled.

How to Login
Go to the website for your course.
1. Click on the (Login) link.
2. You will be prompted for your Username and Password.

What If This Doesn't Work?
First, look at the keyboard and make sure the Caps Lock is off (no light.) Passwords may include both upper and lower case letters.

Second, check the spelling. Your user name may not be exactly the same as your email address.

Third, you can click on the Live Chat and get immediate assistance.

Memo to Self: It's OK if your computer does not match exactly. The logon screen may show a logo or it may be a different color.

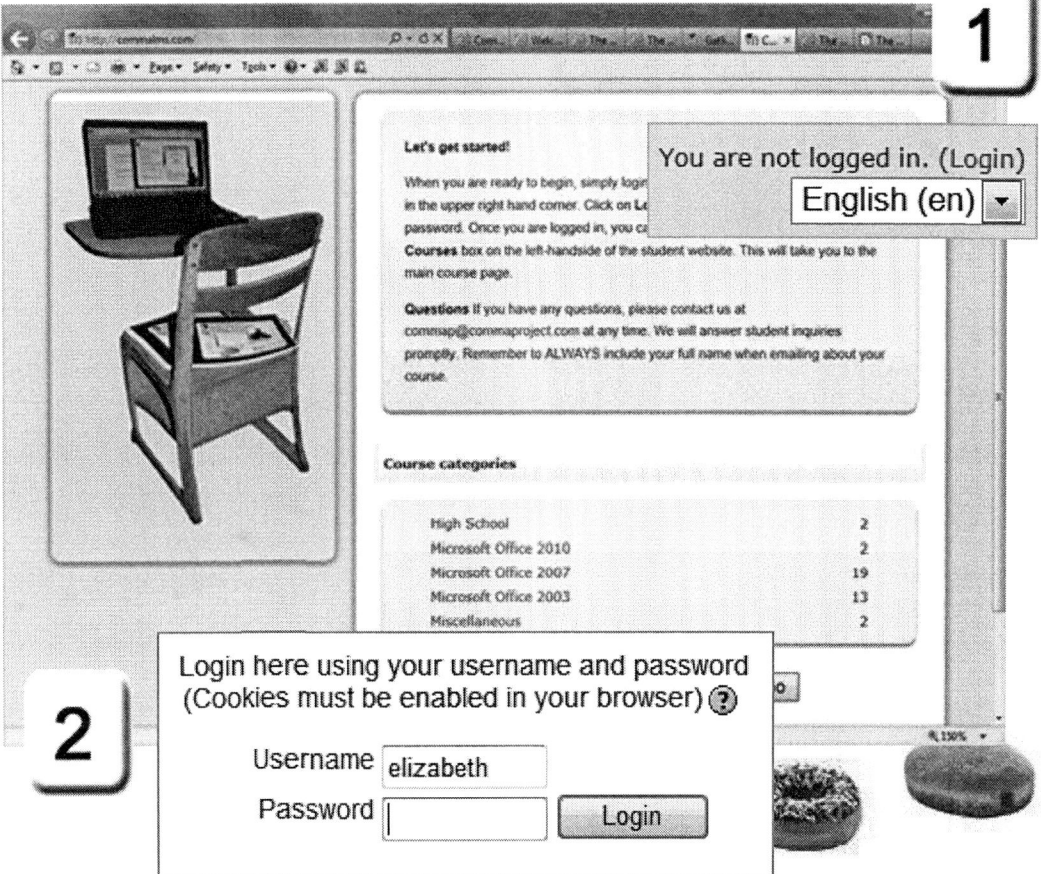

You are not logged in. (Login)

English (en) ▾

Let's get started!

When you are ready to begin, simply login in the upper right hand corner. Click on L_ password. Once you are logged in, you c_ **Courses** box on the left-handside of the student website. This will take you to the main course page.

Questions If you have any questions, please contact us at commsap@commaproject.com at any time. We will answer student inquiries promptly. Remember to ALWAYS include your full name when emailing about your course.

Course categories

High School	2
Microsoft Office 2010	2
Microsoft Office 2007	19
Microsoft Office 2003	13
Miscellaneous	2

Login here using your username and password
(Cookies must be enabled in your browser) ⑦

Username | elizabeth

Password | | Login

The Topic Outline

When you log into your course, you should see the **Topic Outline**. The Topic Outline is a course syllabus: it lists your lessons, practice and quizzes.

Each Level has Lessons and Assessments. The lesson links are short discussions that demonstrate the options on a particular Ribbon. The lessons links may also list the page number where these pages can be found in the print version of the computer guides.

Many students prefer to read the lessons on a second monitor or in print, rather than switch from the lesson screens to Microsoft Office to practice the options.

Memo to Self: It's OK if your computer does not match exactly. The important part is learning the steps. Please contact your facilitator if you have any questions

My Course ->Topic Outline

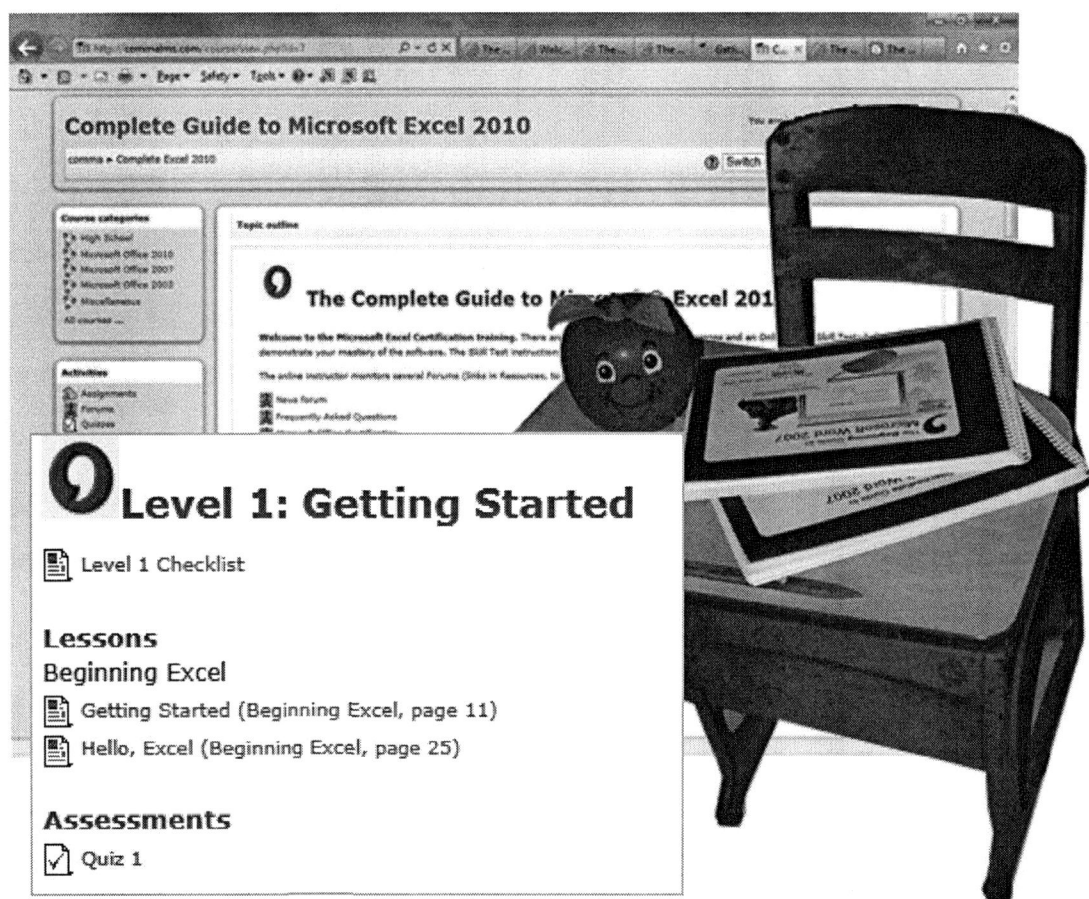

Lesson Links

When you click on a hyperlink to read a lesson, a new window will open.

What Do You See? On the left side of each screen you should see the white navigation arrows: Next, Previous, and Home

What Else Do You See? When you are done with a lesson, you can close the browser window. Go to the upper right corner of the lesson window and click on the X to Exit.

The Topic Outline should be there, the window was left open behind the lesson screen.

My Course ->Topic Outline ->Lesson

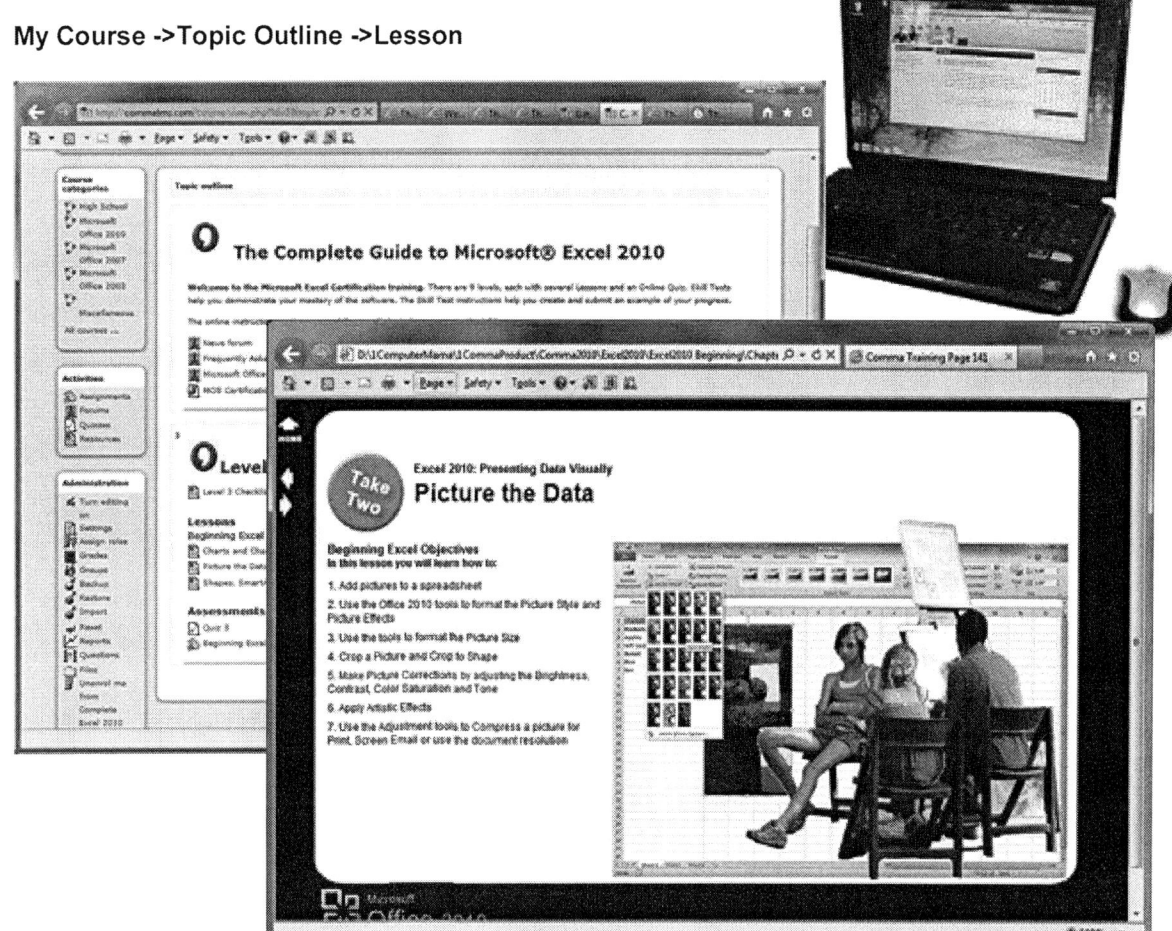

Level Checklists

Each Level has many lessons, sample files and practice sheets, depending on which course you are in. The **Level Checklists** offer a complete list of the lessons, download, practice and quizzes.

Downloads

When you click on a link to a Download, you will be prompted to **Open** or **Save** this file.

Click on **Save.**

Browse to your Documents folder. This will save a copy of the file on your computer.

Memo to Self: It's OK if your Checklist does not match exactly. Please contact your facilitator if you have any questions

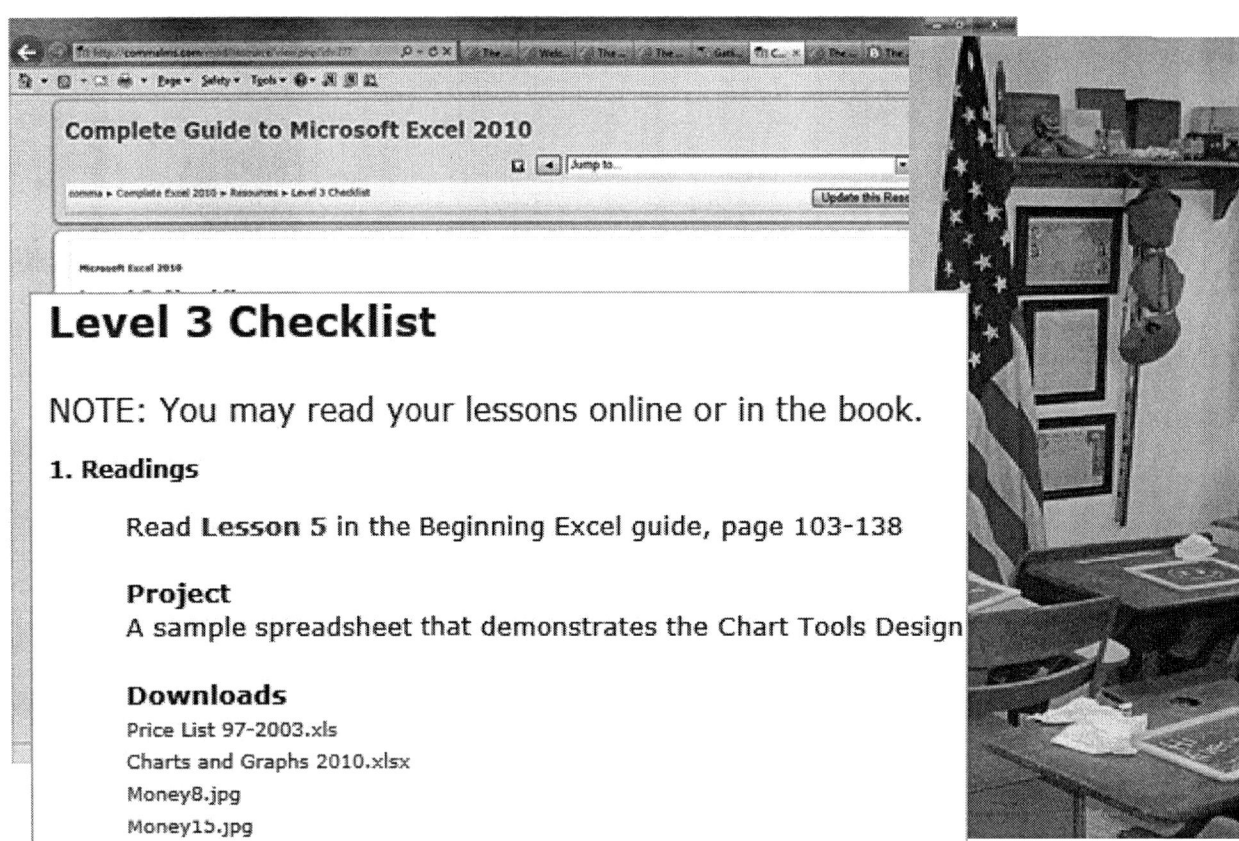

Complete Guide to Microsoft Excel 2010

Level 3 Checklist

NOTE: You may read your lessons online or in the book.

1. Readings

Read **Lesson 5** in the Beginning Excel guide, page 103-138

Project
A sample spreadsheet that demonstrates the Chart Tools Design

Downloads
Price List 97-2003.xls
Charts and Graphs 2010.xlsx
Money8.jpg
Money15.jpg

2. Practice

Take a Quiz Online

After you review the materials online or with the *Guides*, you can log into the course online and take a **Quiz**. This is an open book quiz. You are allowed to look up the answers in your notes, online, or in the computer *Guides*.

Review the Quiz Buttons
Submit: This button posts your answer for the current question.

Save without submitting: This button saves your answers. You can leave the quiz and finish it later.

> Save without submitting

Submit page: This button sends your answers to all questions on the page.

Submit all and finish: Use this button to finish the quiz and submit your quiz online. When you Submit all and finish, you cannot go back and print your answers. So, print first!

> Submit all and finish

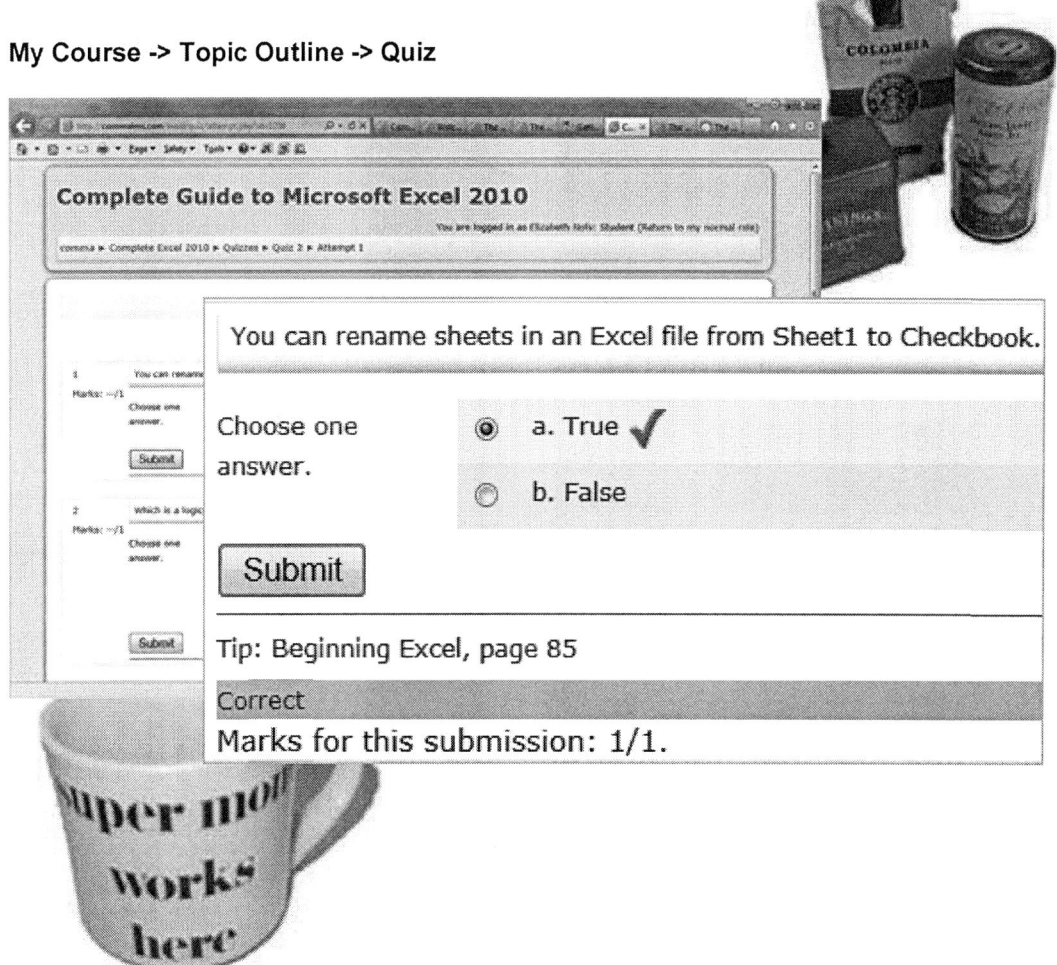

Complete Guide to Microsoft Excel 2010

You can rename sheets in an Excel file from Sheet1 to Checkbook.

Choose one answer.

⦿ a. True ✓

○ b. False

Submit

Tip: Beginning Excel, page 85

Correct

Marks for this submission: 1/1.

Submit Your Work

Most of our online courses ask you to upload a document or a spreadsheet. Here are the steps you can take when you are ready to submit your work.

Review This: Upload a file
1. Go to the **Topic Outline**.
Click on **Beginning Excel Skill Test.**

What Do You See? You will be taken to the Upload screen. The instructions should be available.

2. Click on **Browse** to select the file you want to upload. Navigate to your file, then click **Open**. The path and file name will appear in the upload box.

3. Click **Upload this file** to submit your Skill Test online. Your instructor will be notified automatically.

My Course -> Topic Outline -> Upload a file

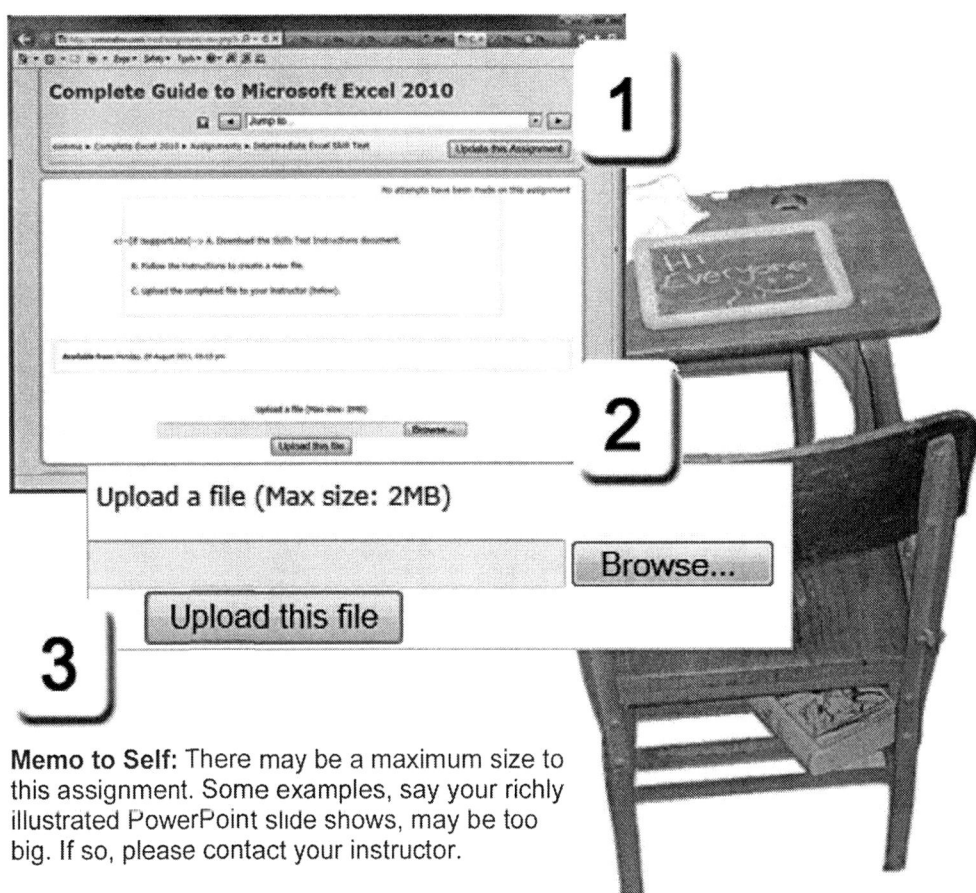

Memo to Self: There may be a maximum size to this assignment. Some examples, say your richly illustrated PowerPoint slide shows, may be too big. If so, please contact your instructor.

Use the Forums

In an online class, a **Forum** is similar to raising your hand and asking a question. When you post a question to a Forum anyone can reply with a suggestion or comment. Some of the answers are very creative and useful.

Your instructor may also post an explanation or offer additional links.

Edit | Delete | Reply

Live Chats

Many instructors keep Office Hours. Chat allows you to type questions online and get an answer immediately from your instructor when your instructor is in the office.

Don't Explain and Don't Complain:
Please keep your posts professional and on topic!

My Course ->Topic Outline -> Forums

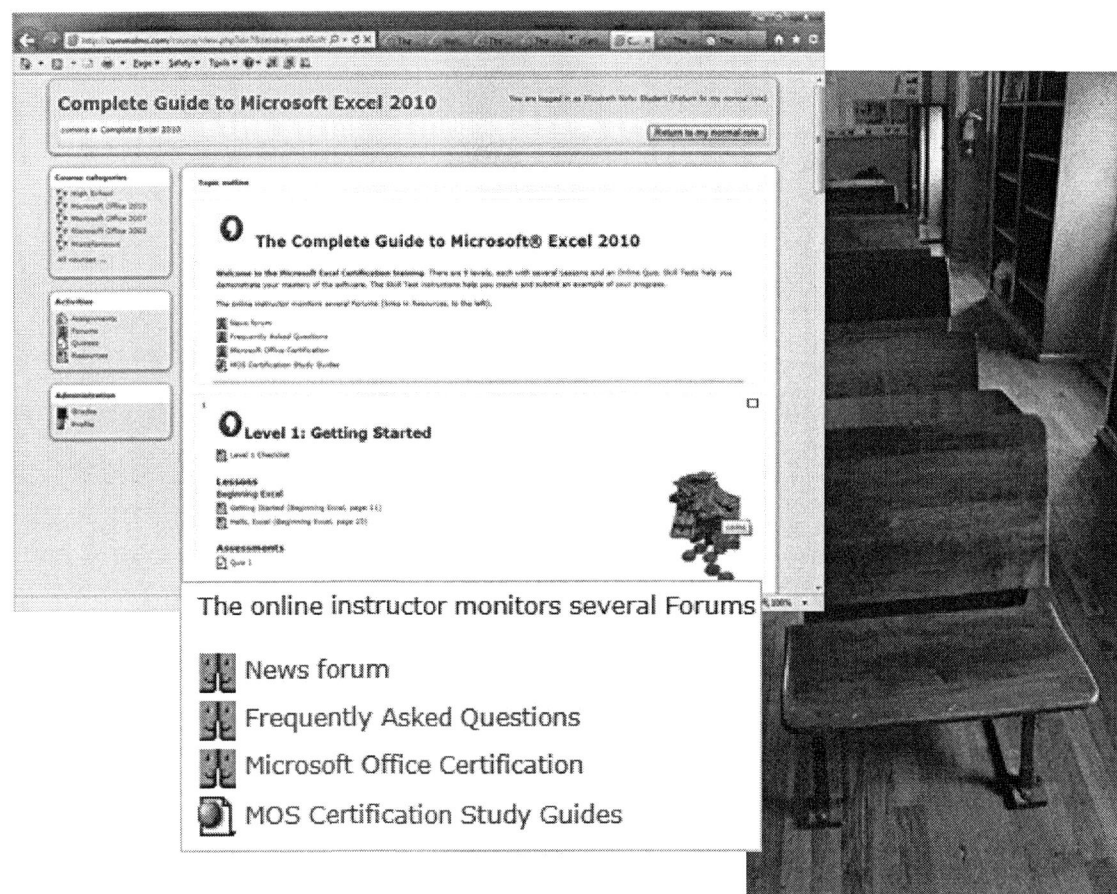

The online instructor monitors several Forums

News forum

Frequently Asked Questions

Microsoft Office Certification

MOS Certification Study Guides

Practice

This *Guide* offers additional reference materials and practice certification tests. You can use the multiple choice quizzes and skill tests to practice if you wish. When you are ready, please log into the course and do the assessments online.

The Microsoft certification tests are timed: you have to perform the process steps very quickly and efficiently in order to pass. **That takes practice!**

More practice

If you have a question about a document or file you are working on you are always welcome to email a copy of your work to your instructor as an attachment.

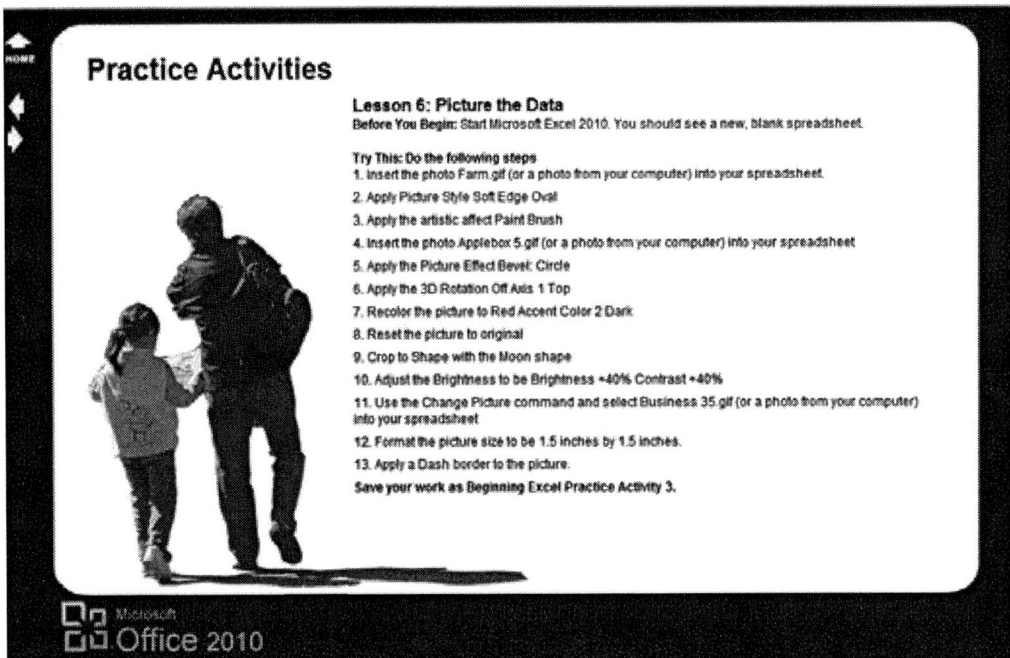

Practice Activities

Lesson 6: Picture the Data
Before You Begin: Start Microsoft Excel 2010. You should see a new, blank spreadsheet.

Try This: Do the following steps
1. Insert the photo Farm.gif (or a photo from your computer) into your spreadsheet.
2. Apply Picture Style Soft Edge Oval
3. Apply the artistic affect Paint Brush
4. Insert the photo Applebox 5.gif (or a photo from your computer) into your spreadsheet
5. Apply the Picture Effect Bevel: Circle
6. Apply the 3D Rotation Off Axis 1 Top
7. Recolor the picture to Red Accent Color 2 Dark
8. Reset the picture to original
9. Crop to Shape with the Moon shape
10. Adjust the Brightness to be Brightness +40% Contrast +40%
11. Use the Change Picture command and select Business 35.gif (or a photo from your computer) into your spreadsheet
12. Format the picture size to be 1.5 inches by 1.5 inches.
13. Apply a Dash border to the picture.

Save your work as Beginning Excel Practice Activity 3.

Microsoft Office 2010

Microsoft Business Certification

The course prepares you to pass the **Microsoft Office Specialist (MOS)** exams. This credential recognizes the business skills needed to get the most out of Microsoft Office 2010.

Microsoft Certification Exams are available through authorized testing centers. They are not included as part of the certification training program in the same way that taking the Bar Exam is not included with getting a degree in Law from a college or university.

More Information Online.
Certiport provides the official Microsoft certification tests. You can download the Microsoft certification topics and study guides. Here is their address: www.certiport.com

Please Note: Comma Productions, LLC. is independent from Microsoft Corporation, and not affiliated with Microsoft in any manner. While the Complete Computer Guides may be used in assisting individuals to prepare for a Microsoft Business Certification exam, Microsoft, its designated program administrator, and Comma Productions, LLC. do not warrant that use of these Complete Computer Guides will ensure passing a Microsoft Business Certification exam.

Can Microsoft Office 2010 Starter be used for Microsoft Office certification training?

Yes and No. The Microsoft Excel 2010 Starter software has all of the features required to practice and prepare for the Microsoft Excel 2010 CORE certification test. The Microsoft Word 2010 Starter software is missing several key features that are part of the Microsoft Office 2010 CORE certification requirements.

Compare the MOS CORE certification topics
The Microsoft Word 2010 Starter:
Word 2010 MOS CORE certification topics (PDF)

The Microsoft Excel 2010 Starter:
EXCEL 2010 MOS CORE certification topics (PDF)

With the Office 2010 Starter evaluation:
Office 2010 Starter evaluation (PDF)

More information on Office Starter software:
View an image of Word 2010 Starter
View an image of Excel 2010 Starter

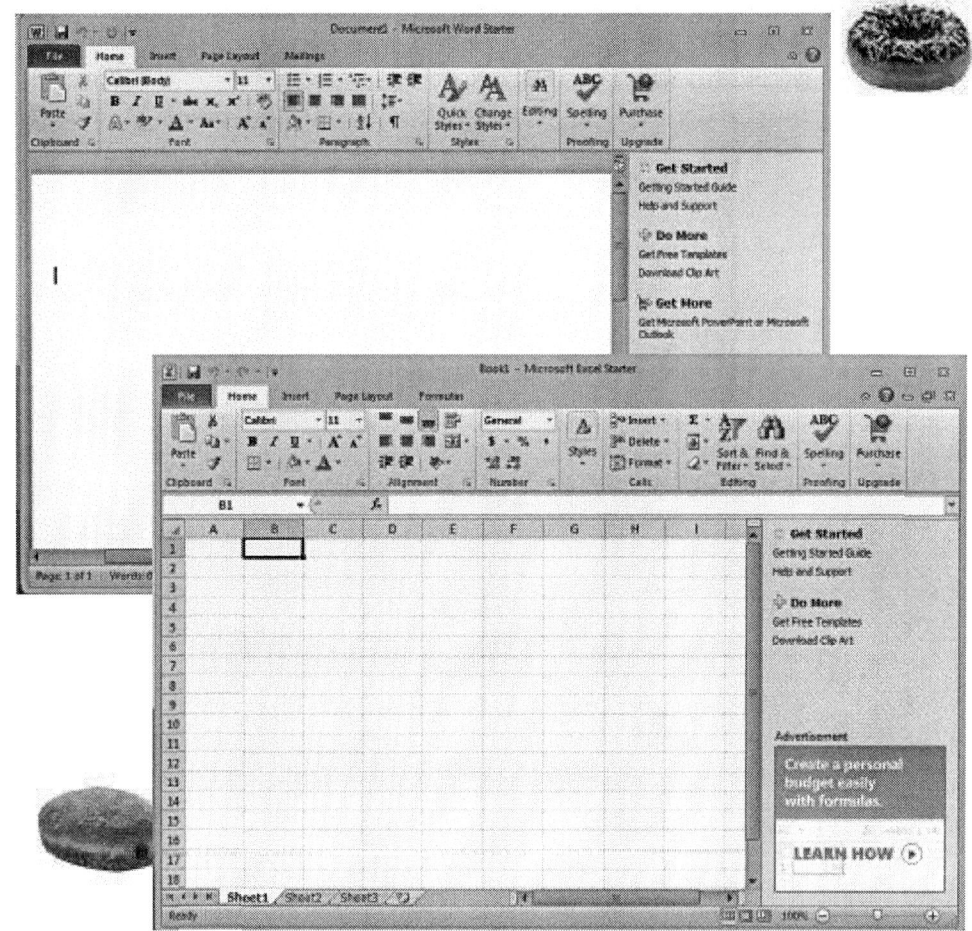

Self-Assessment

Skill Level-Beginning Excel	Mastered	Needs Work	Required for my job
Select rows, columns, and cells			
Edit text and numbers in a cell			
AutoFill a series			
Create a graph with the Chart Wizard			
Add numbers with the AutoSum tool			
Calculate a simple equation "by hand"			
Sort data in a list			
Print a spreadsheet			

Beginning Excel is recommended if you selected "needs work" on three or more skills.

Skill Level-Intermediate Excel	Mastered	Needs Work	Required for my job
AutoFill data and formulas			
Link Spreadsheets			
Use Relative and Absolute cell references			
Use conditional formatting			
Create a drop down list			
Use the auditing toolbar			

Intermediate Excel is recommended if you selected "needs work" on three or more skills.

Skill Level-Advanced	Mastered	Needs Work	Required for my job
Create a Pivot Table for data analysis			
Format, group and graph Pivot Tables			
Use the What If tool			
Use Goal Seeking			
Import from Access or another database			
Use HLOOKUP and VLOOKUP			

Advanced Excel is recommended if you selected "needs work" on three or more skills.

Using an eReader

Now you can download our Microsoft Office certification training books to your eReader. In addition to being available online as a webpage we have included the materials , within the course as **Adobe PDF files** for download to your computer, eReader or Tablet of choice!

eReaders provide full color pages, zoom control, search, bookmarking and other great features. You can prop the eReader beside your mighty desktop or laptop computer as you read the lessons and practice the steps.

This is a simple, easy to use process. Our books work best on the **iPad** or other similarly sized tablets because of the large format of the pages. When a PDF is accessed online, such as in our courses, the iPad automatically offers to put that PDF file into the iBooks app.

Any **Kindle** with a web browser should be able to download the PDF to the Kindle, then open it with either a PDF app or in the Kindle App. Another option with the Kindle is to download the files to a desktop, email them to your Kindle account, then send them to the Kindle.

How Do You Practice?

80.6% I have the book beside my computer so I can look at both.

16.7% I read the lessons online on the the same computer I am working on, switching between screens.

Which way do you prefer for reading the lessons?

54.1% In print (books)

37.8% Online (web pages)

8.1% eReader/Tablet (PDF pages)

If your course did not include books you can buy them on Amazon.com if you wish

Access 2010: Getting Started

Hello, Microsoft Access

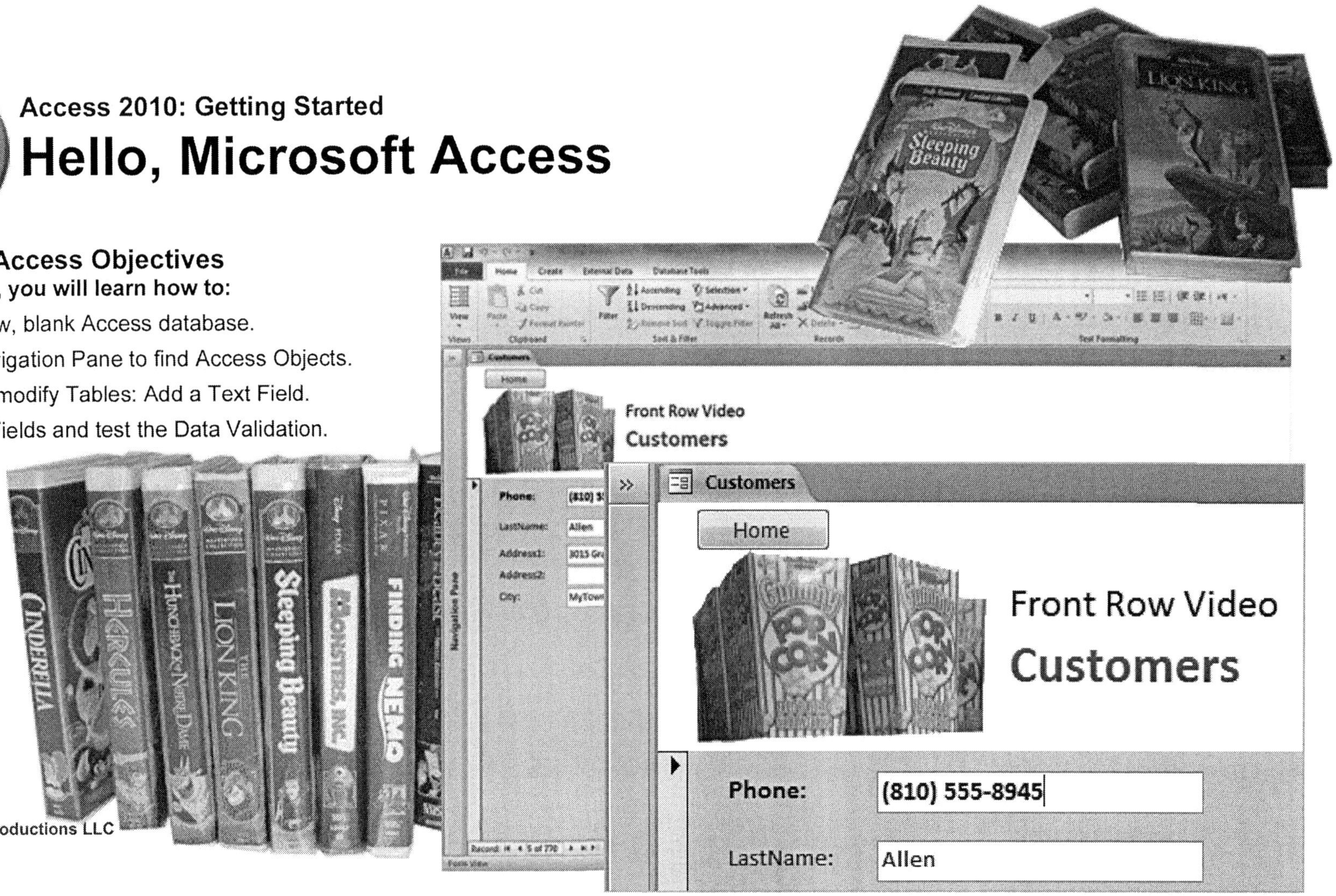

Beginning Access Objectives
In this lesson, you will learn how to:

1. Create a new, blank Access database.
2. Use the Navigation Pane to find Access Objects.
3. Create and modify Tables: Add a Text Field.
4. Modify the Fields and test the Data Validation.

© 2012 Comma Productions LLC

Lesson 2 : Hello, Microsoft Access!

1. Readings
Read Lesson 2 in the Beginning Access guide, page 25-50.

Project
Introduction to Access database objects. Create and modify a customer Table.

Downloads
There are no downloads for this lesson.

2. Practice
Complete the Practice Activity on page 51.

3. Assessment
Review the Test questions on page 52.

Table Tools->Fields

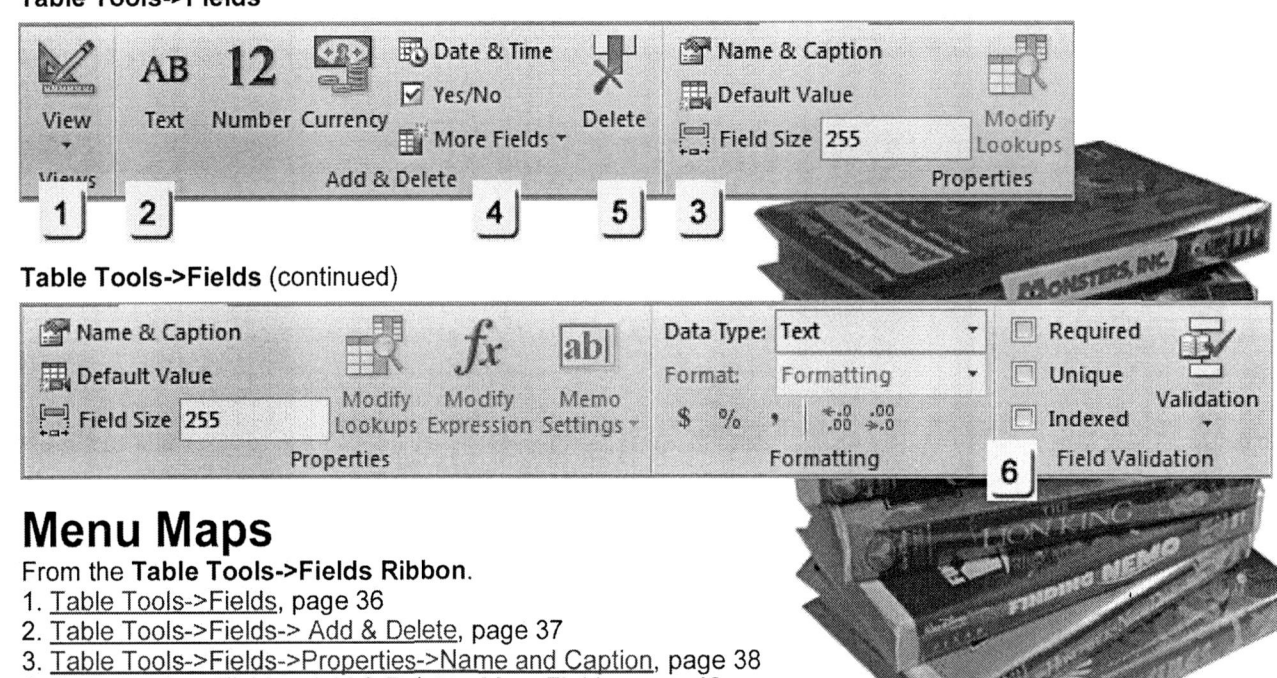

Table Tools->Fields (continued)

Menu Maps

From the **Table Tools->Fields Ribbon**.
1. Table Tools->Fields, page 36
2. Table Tools->Fields-> Add & Delete, page 37
3. Table Tools->Fields->Properties->Name and Caption, page 38
4. Table Tools ->Fields->Add & Delete->More Fields, page 43
5. Table Tools ->Fields->Add & Delete->Delete, page 45
6. Table Tools ->Fields->Field Validation->Required, page 46

From the **Home Ribbon**.
1. Home ->Records->Delete, page 40

Who Bought What?

Every business needs to record and track the goods and services that they provide.
It is a fundamental question:
Who (our customers)
Bought (receipt)
What (our products)

Many offices manage this information with Microsoft Excel Spreadsheets.
For example, here is a list of customers in Excel. The data includes the name and address.

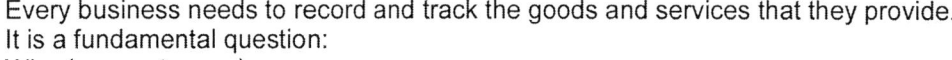

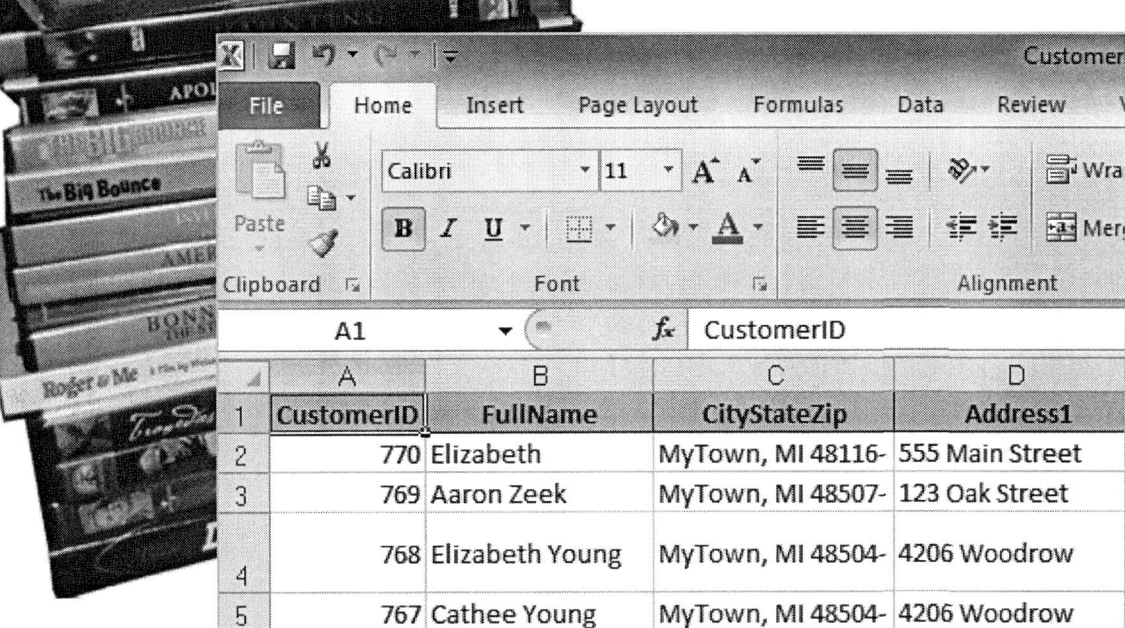

	A	B	C	D
1	CustomerID	FullName	CityStateZip	Address1
2	770	Elizabeth	MyTown, MI 48116-	555 Main Street
3	769	Aaron Zeek	MyTown, MI 48507-	123 Oak Street
4	768	Elizabeth Young	MyTown, MI 48504-	4206 Woodrow
5	767	Cathee Young	MyTown, MI 48504-	4206 Woodrow

Our Business

In this course, we will use a simple business model: a movie rental store. There will be three rental prices: new movies, yesterday's movies and old movies.

This business model uses the date the movie was released to calculate the rental price. It also uses the date on the receipt to determine if the movie rental is overdue.

Say What, Now?

Most offices enter customer and product information separately. There may be a spreadsheet for the customers (who) and another spreadsheet for the products (what). In our sample business the customers rent movies, so there will be a list of movies.

Who Bought What?

A receipt lists who bought what.
Question: how do you show that in Excel?

A spreadsheet can record one-to-one relationships. Picture the receipt spreadsheet. Each row would have <u>one</u> answer in each column: receipt no, date, customer, movie, price. So far, so good.

However one customer may get many movies, say 3 or 5 titles. At some point you need to document that <u>many</u> customers bought <u>many</u> products on <u>many</u> days.

Databases do many-to-many relationships.

Keep going, please.

Microsoft Excel 2010: Sample Customer and Movie Data

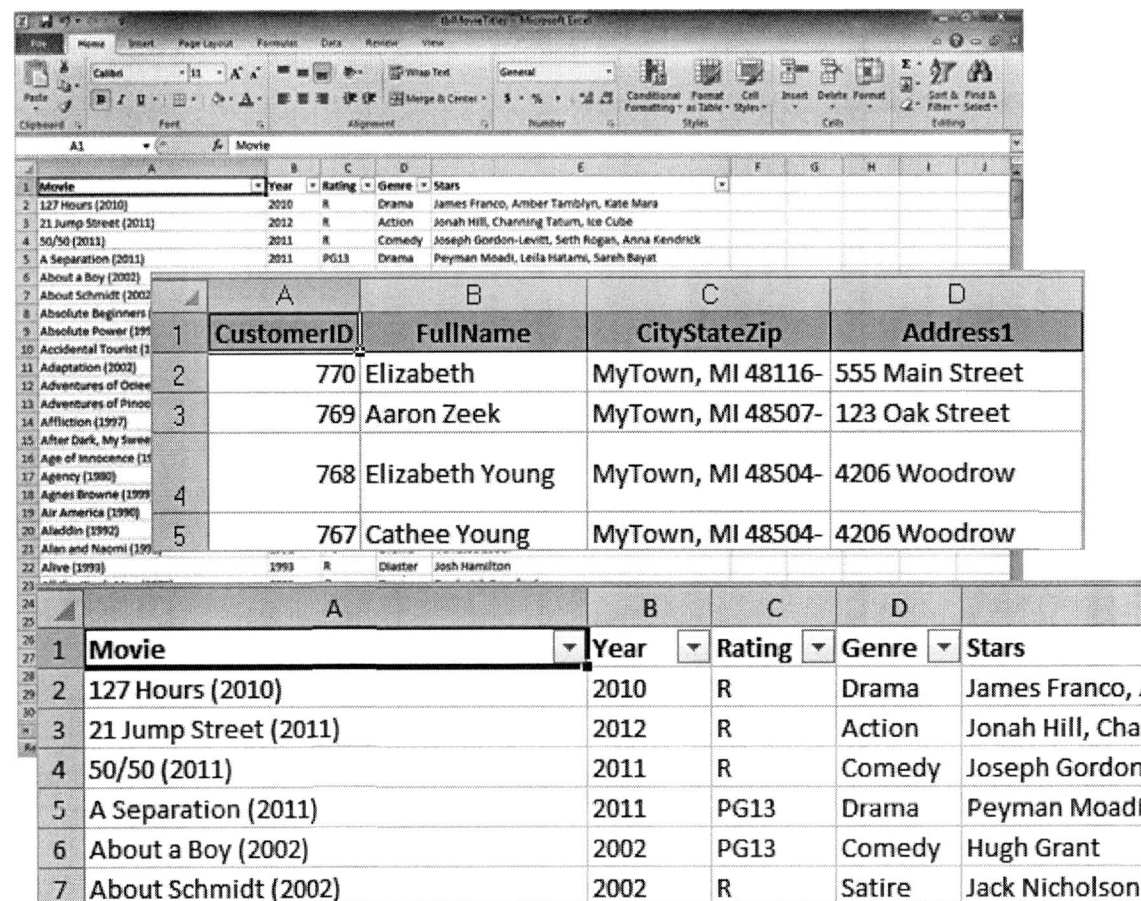

Access Objects: Tables

What is a database? All databases begin with the Tables. Data entry forms, queries, and reports just use the information in the Tables.

Table Views: Design and Datasheet
The **Datasheet View** looks like an Excel spreadsheet. The Header Row at the top of the Datasheet has filters that you can use to Sort, Select and Find if you wish. The **Design View** lets you create the Table by adding Fields and defining what kind of data these Fields will store. The Fields can be Text, Numbers, Date/Time, Yes/No.

Table Options: Unique Information
Each Table has a unique collection of data. For example, tblCustomers has customer names and addresses...it does not include any information about movies. tblMovieTitles lists products... no customer phone numbers.

Keep going...

Microsoft Access 2010: Sample Database Table

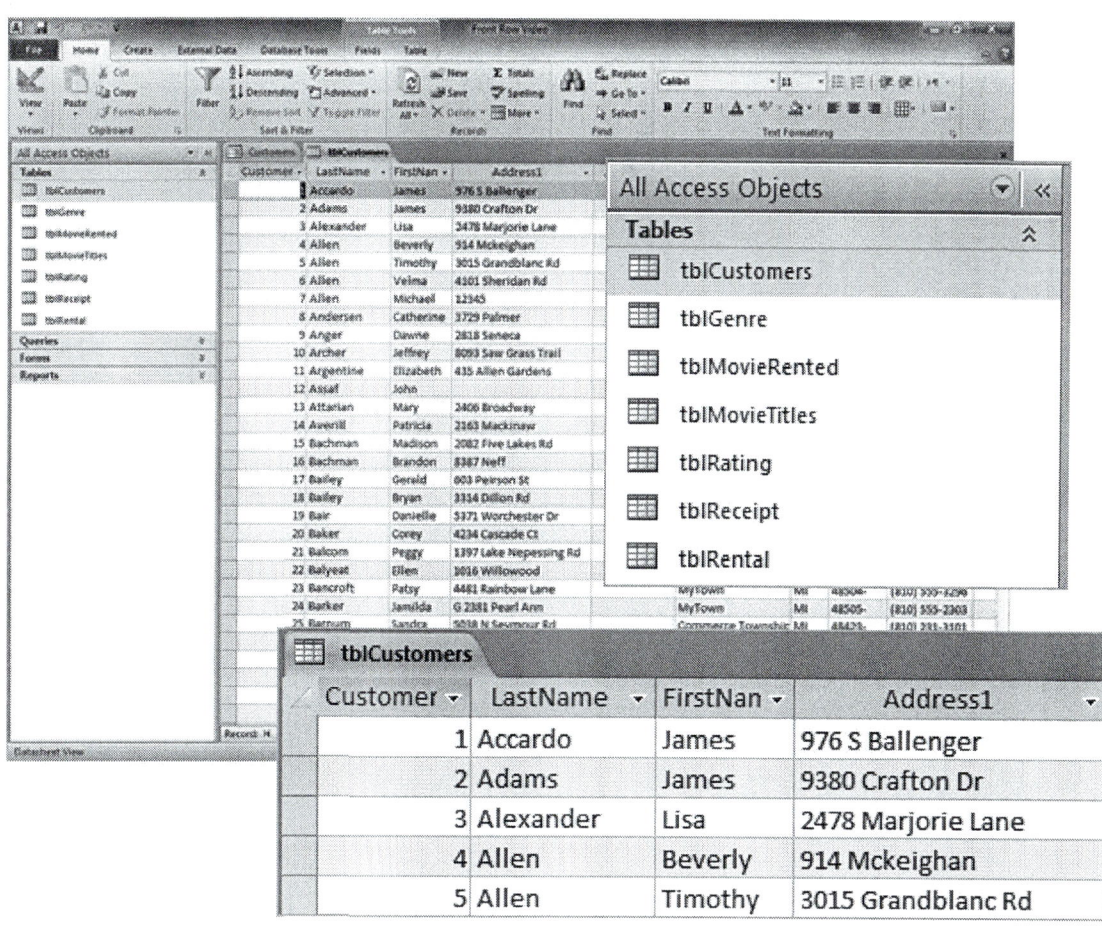

Database Objects: Queries

Queries ask questions. Queries can lookup information as well as manipulate the data in the Tables. For example, a query can search for and modify the rental price for all the old movies.

Query Views: Design and Datasheet
The **Design View** helps you select the tables and working with the data. For example, the query on this page looks at the Movies table and counts the movies by the Genre. The **Datasheet View** displays the records in the Movie Table.

Query Options: Query Types
Select Queries look for records that match your criteria. Say you wanted to find the movies released before 1999.

Action Queries change or update the data.
The Action queries include:
Make Table
Append (Add new records)
Update (Modify the records)
Crosstab (Analyze the records)
Delete

Keep going...

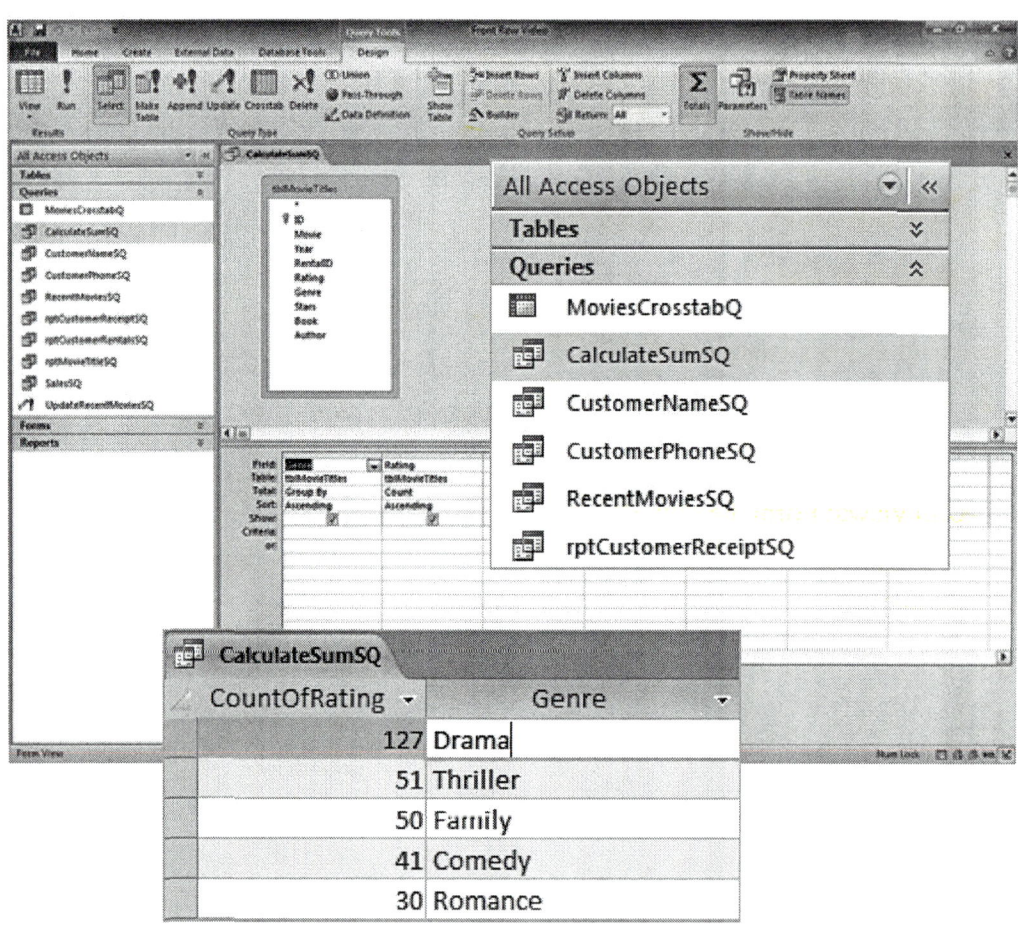

CountOfRating	Genre
127	Drama
51	Thriller
50	Family
41	Comedy
30	Romance

Database Objects: Forms

Forms put a pretty face on the Tables. Whatever is typed into a Form is saved in the Table that goes with the Form.

Forms can prompt Users to enter all of the necessary information. In this example the Customer Form includes a phone number Field, which is required. Forms can also include Command Buttons that save the data, close the Form and return to the Home screen.

Form Views: Form, Layout, Design
The **Design View** is a wonderful form editor with rich tools. The **Layout View** is a quick and efficient form editor. There are three Ribbons in the Design View: Design, Arrange and Format.

The **Normal View** shows the Form as a User would see it when they are entering data. Each Table may have a Form for data entry.

Keep going...

Microsoft Access 2010: Sample Database Form

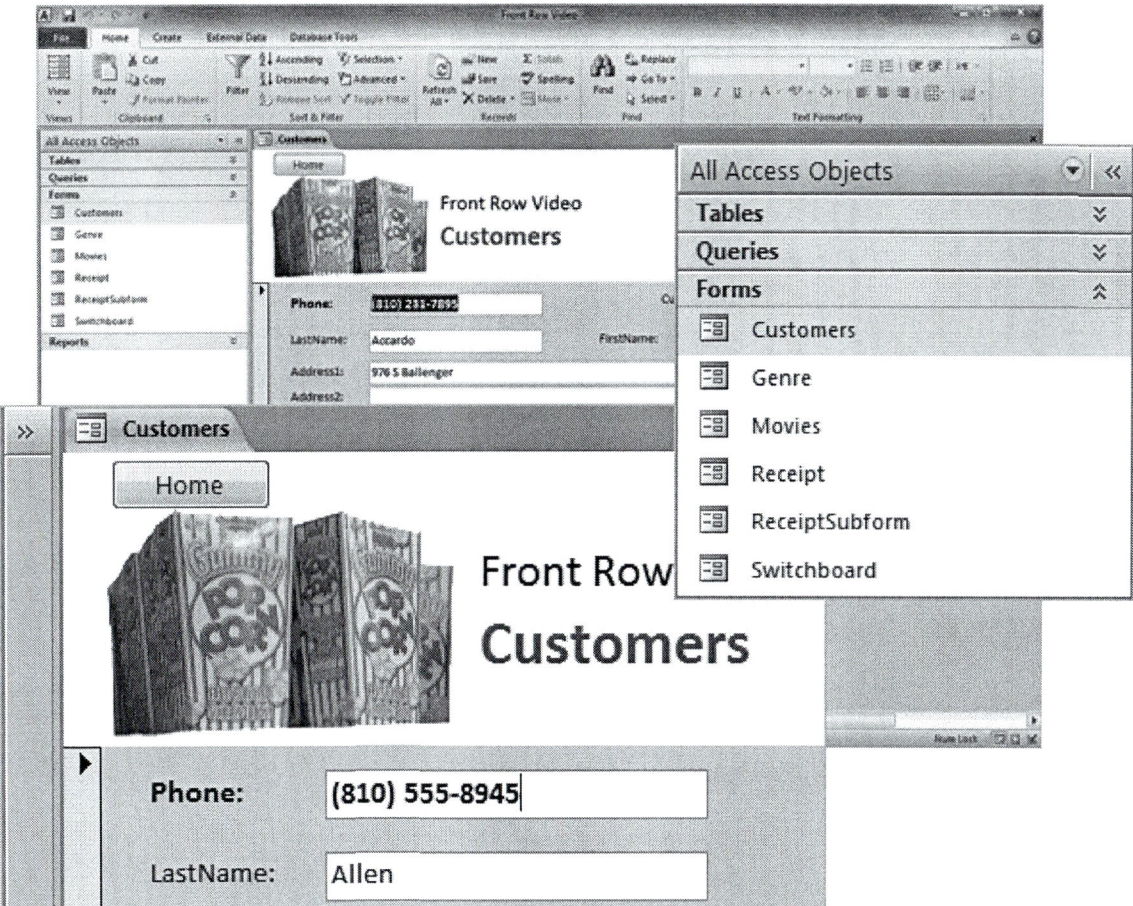

Microsoft Access 2010: Sample Database Report

Database Objects: Reports

A Report can be anything you want to print. A Report can be a little 2" receipt that is printed and handed to the customer. A report can also sort and group all of the movies that are currently rented.

Report Views and Report Design Tools
There are four **Report Views**: Report, Print Preview, Layout and Design View. The **Report Design Tools** include: Design, Arrange, Format and Page Setup.

Keep going...

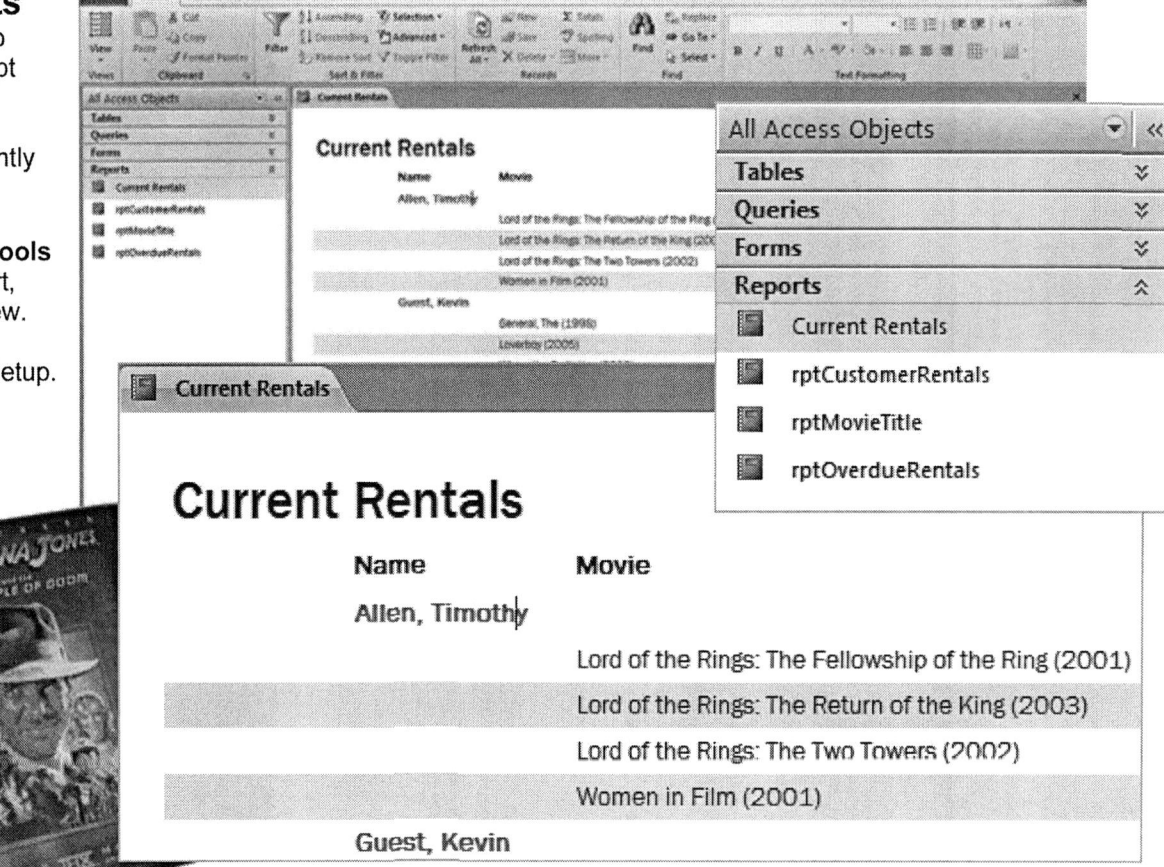

Database Programming

Every aspect of the Tables, Forms, Queries and Reports can be programmed to make it easier to enter data and print the results.

Command Buttons can be added to Forms and Reports for quick steps (Save, Print, Add a Record) or navigation.

Macros can automatically update Forms and Reports. Access uses Embedded Macros that are easy to program. Macros can pretty much automate anything in Microsoft Access!

Visual Basic for Applications (VBA) is the legacy code for Microsoft Office applications.

Keep going...

Microsoft Access 2010: Sample Database Property Sheet

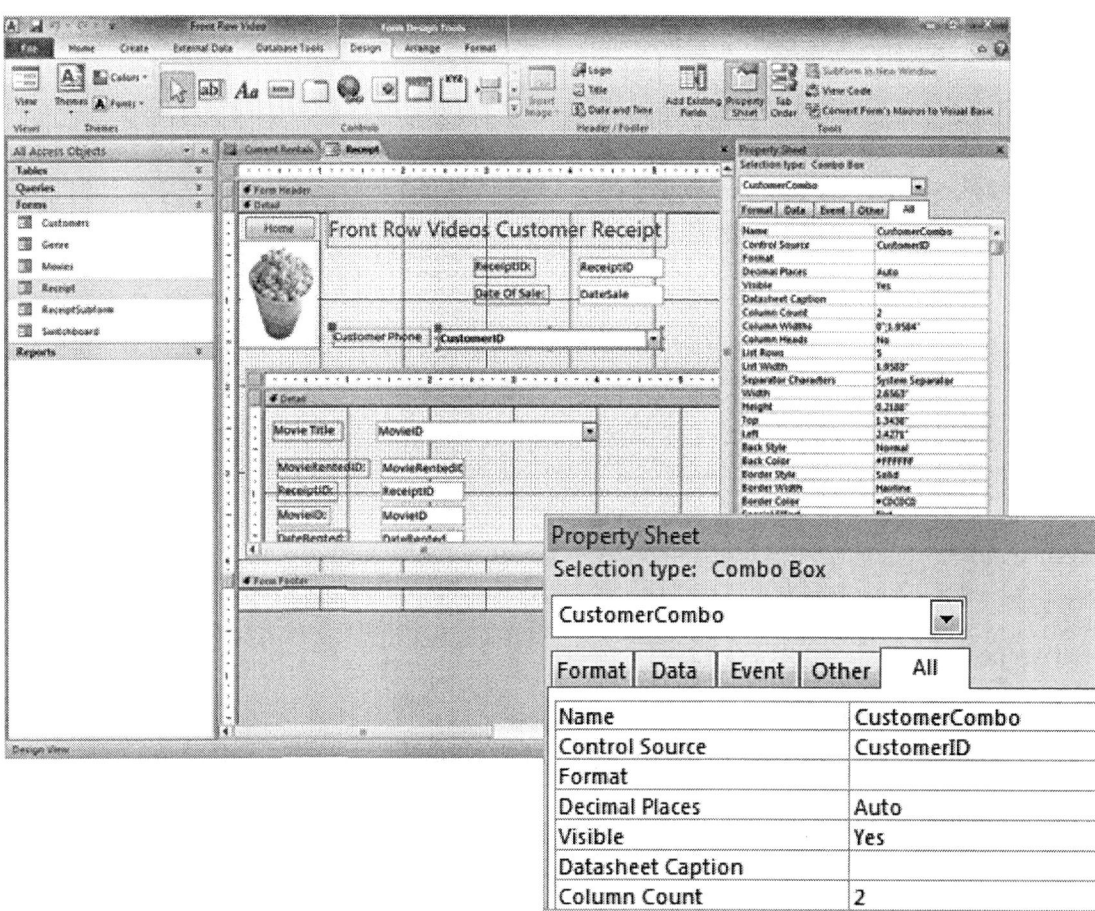

Property Sheet

Selection type: Combo Box

CustomerCombo

Format	Data	Event	Other	All

Name	CustomerCombo
Control Source	CustomerID
Format	
Decimal Places	Auto
Visible	Yes
Datasheet Caption	
Column Count	2

Database Relationships

The Tables in a database can be linked by key data. For example, a receipt includes key data on who (tblCustomers) bought (tblReceipt) what (tblMovies).

Beginning Access Teaches One-to-One
The beginning lessons show how to create and modify Tables. One Table will be used for each Form.

Intermediate Access Teaches One-to-Many
The intermediate lessons teaches how to capture one-to-many relationships. In our little video store, one customer may rent many movies. In Access, one-to-many is captured with a Form and Subform.

Advanced Access Teaches Many-to-Many
In a good business, many customers would return many times and rent many movies. The Advanced Access lessons show how to create Search Forms and how to analyze the data.

OK, that's enough for the introduction.
Let's get started with Microsoft Access 2010.

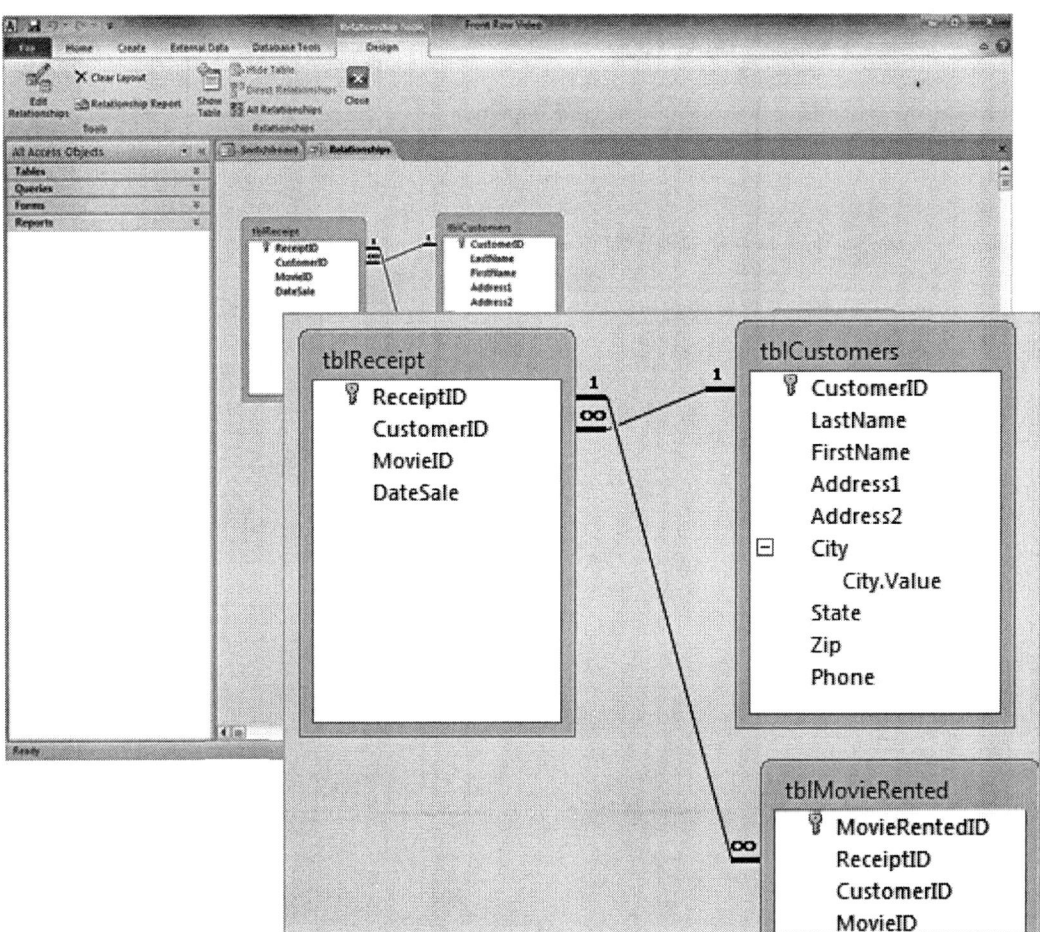

Create a New Database

When you start Microsoft Access 2010, you will be greeted by the Backstage and prompted to select a database.

The options include **Available Templates** as well as database templates online through Office.com

1. Try It: Create a New, Blank Database
Go to **Available Templates**.
Select **Blank database**.

Look for the **File Name** on the far right side of the Backstage. It is not immediately obvious because of the division in the screen.

Enter a **File Name**: FrontRowVideo Begin1
"Begin1" is for numbering the different versions as we complete the lessons.

What Do You See? The new database will be saved to your **Documents** folder. You can choose a different folder if you wish. This Guide will refer to the default location, the Documents folder.

Click **Create**. Keep going...

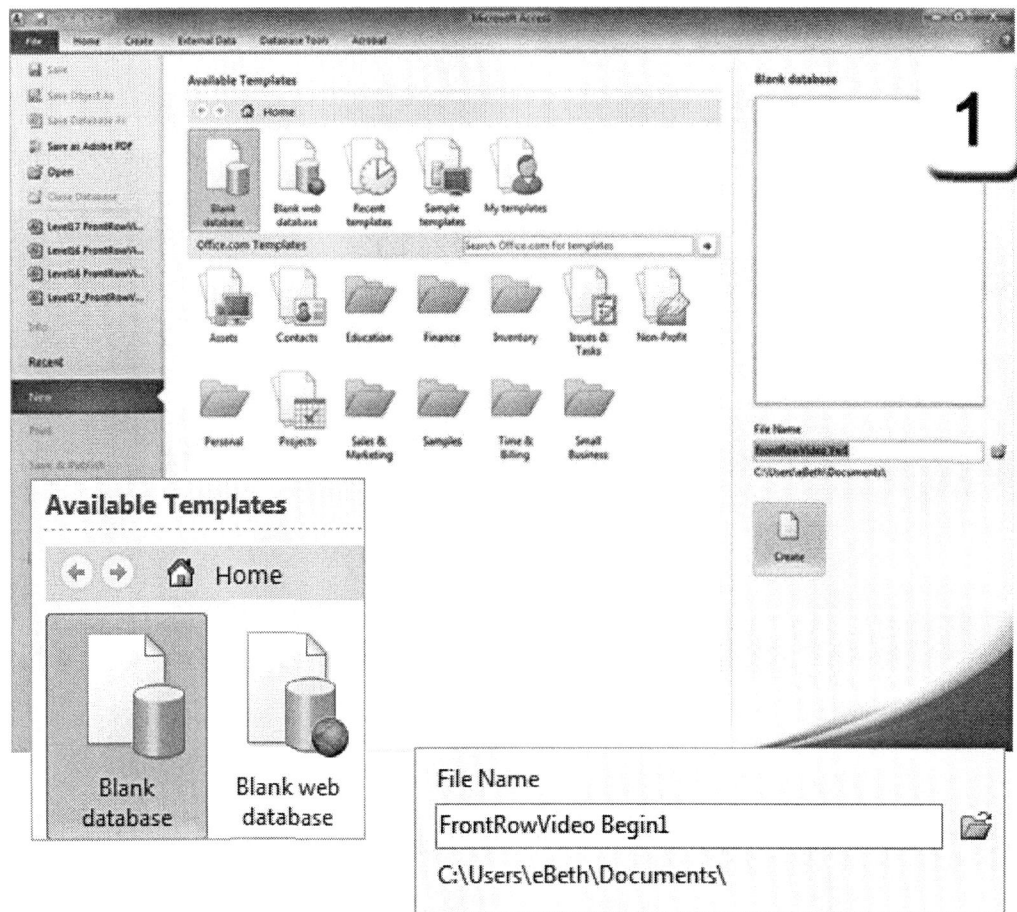

Hello, Access Database

All databases begin with the data. Data is saved in Tables. Microsoft Access 2010 opens a new, blank database with a Table.

2. Try it: Review the Ribbons
The Access Ribbons, from left to right are:
File
Home
Create
External Data
Database Tools

The **Table Tools, Fields** and **Table,** are available. A new Table, Table1, is open.

What Do You See? On the left side of the database is the **Navigation Pane**. The Navigation Pane is showing **All Access Objects**. Table1 is in the Tables.

Keep going...

Microsoft Office Access 2010

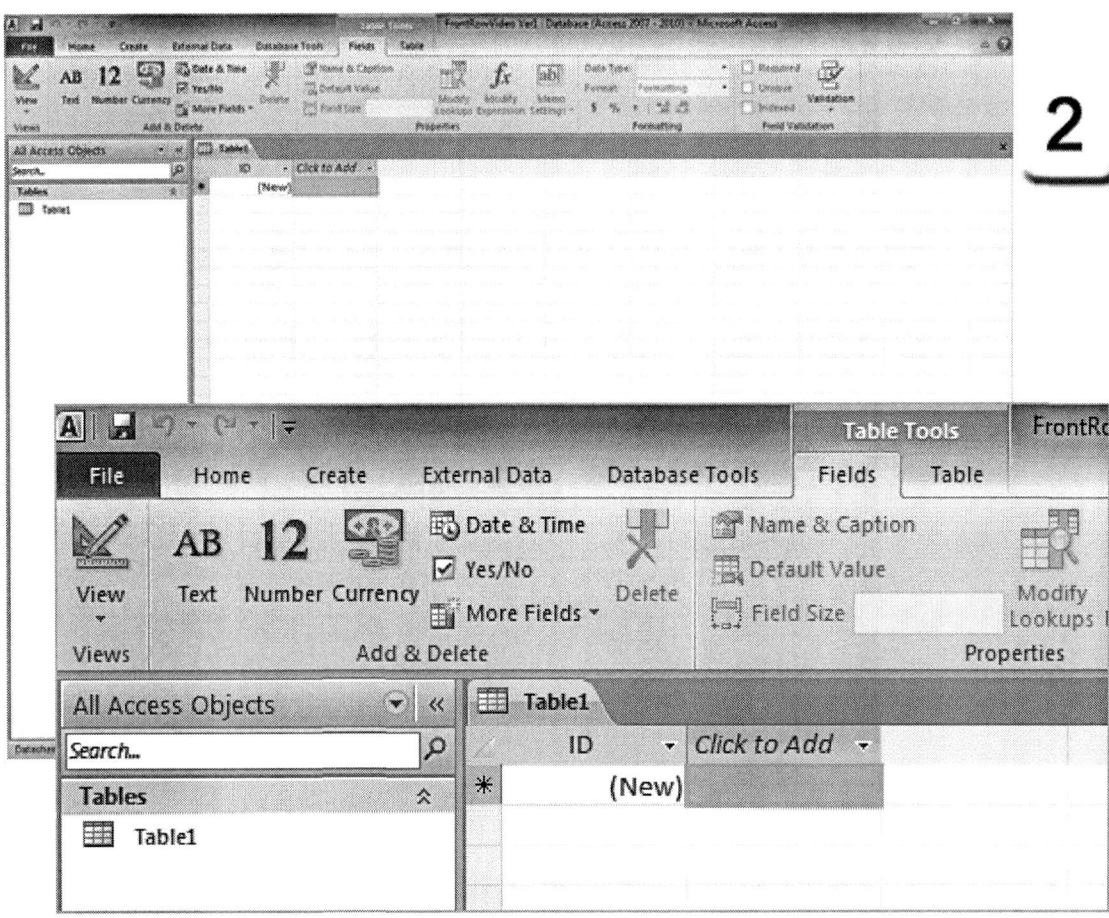

Exam 77-885: Microsoft Access 2010
1. Managing the Access Environment
1.2. Configure the Navigation Pane

Click to Add a Field

A Table in Access looks like a spreadsheet in Microsoft Excel. At the top there is a Header Row with the labels. The first Column in this Table is the ID, an Autonumber, which we will discuss in a minute. You can **Click to Add** a Field.

3. Try it: Click to Add a Field
Go to **Click to Add**.
Select a Field Type: **Text**

What Do You See? The Field Types are:
Text
Number
Currency
Date & Time
Yes/No
Lookup & Relationship
Rich Text
Memo
Attachment
Hyperlink
Calculated Field

At the bottom of the list is Paste as Fields.
Keep going...

Click to Add

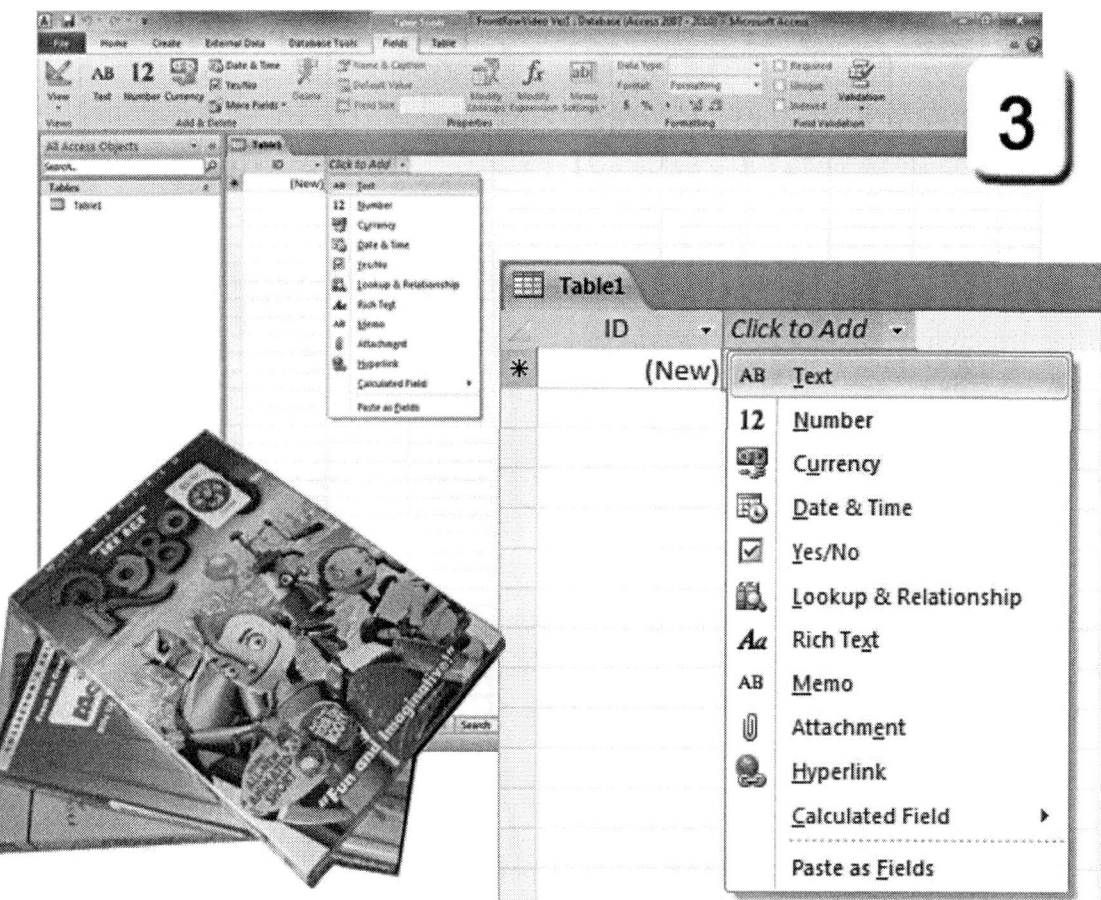

Exam 77-885: Microsoft Access 2010
2. Building Tables
2.2. Create and Modify Fields: Add a Text Field

Add the Text Fields

4. Try it: Edit the New Text Field
Select the Field Name: Field1
Go to **Table Tools->Fields->Properties**.
Click on **Name and Caption**.
Edit the Name: FirstName

Try This, Too: Add Another Text Field
There are several ways to add Fields to a Table.
The previous page used Click to Add. The next
Field will be added with the Table Tools.

Go to **Table Tools->Fields**.
Go to **Add & Delete->Text**.
Edit the Field Name: LastName

Thoughts to Consider: Should the Field names
include spaces? It is usually better to skip the
spaces in a Field name. When Microsoft Access
finds a Field name with spaces, the database will
alter the name with an underscore like this:
Last_Name.

Table Tools->Fields->Add & Delete->Text

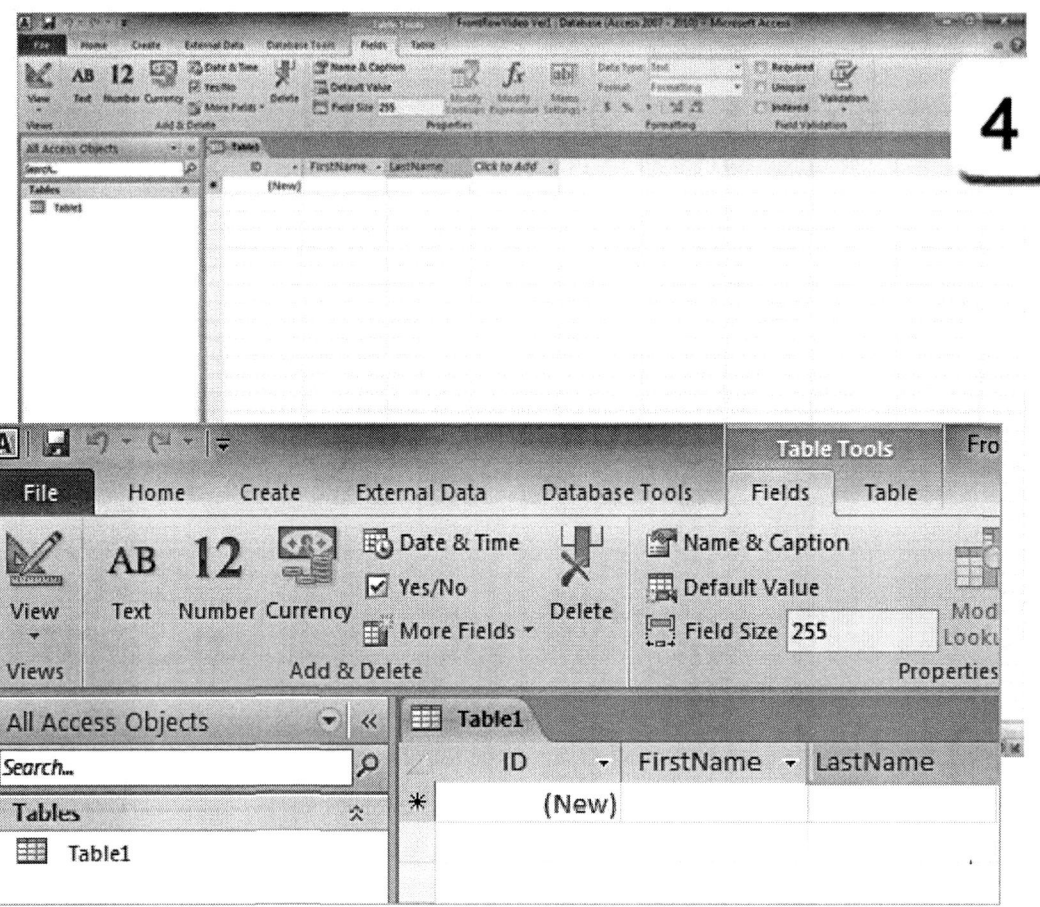

Exam 77-885: Microsoft Access 2010
2. Building Tables
2.2. Create and Modify Fields: Modify the Field Description (Name and Caption)

Add a Couple of Records

5. Try it: Add a New Record
Go to Row 2 and Tab to the second
column. Add the following:
FirstName: Alpha
LastName: Beta

Try This, Too: Add Another Record
Enter the following in Row 3.
FirstName: Deeter
LastName: Poohbah

What Do You See? There should be a
pencil on the **Record Selector** as you are
entering data. When you go to the next
record, your data will be saved
automatically and the pencil will be gone.

Please keep going.

Table Tools->Fields

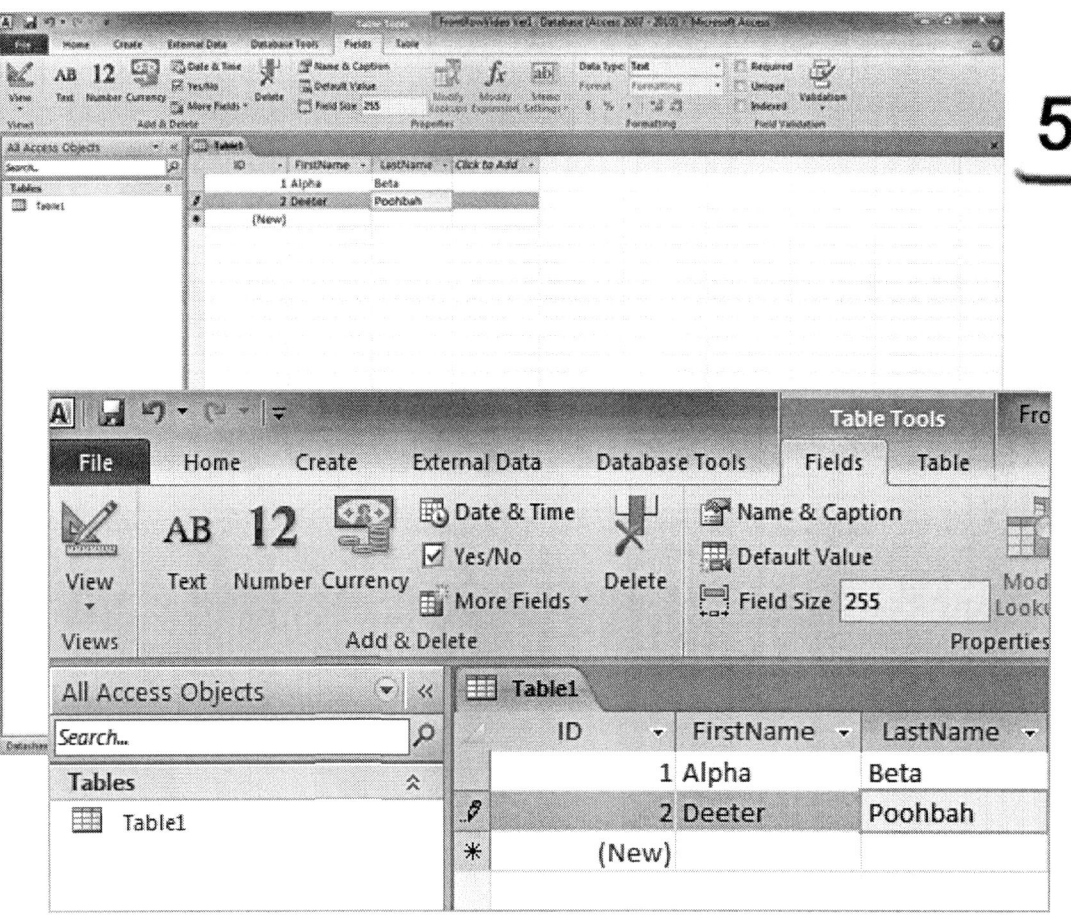

5

Delete a Record

You can use the **Record Selector** to delete a record from a table.

6. Try it: Delete a Record

Select Record 1, the sample customer named Alpha Beta.

The row will be highlighted blue, the same as it would be in Microsoft Excel.

Go to **Home ->Records->Delete**.

Note: You can also click Delete on your keyboard if you wish.

What Do You See? A database has only one job: Save the data. A database is <u>supposed</u> to keep the data. You will be prompted to confirm whether you really wanted to delete this record.

Click **Yes**. Record 1 will be permanently deleted from this Table. Keep going.

Memo to Self: There is NO undo after you click **Yes** to delete a record!

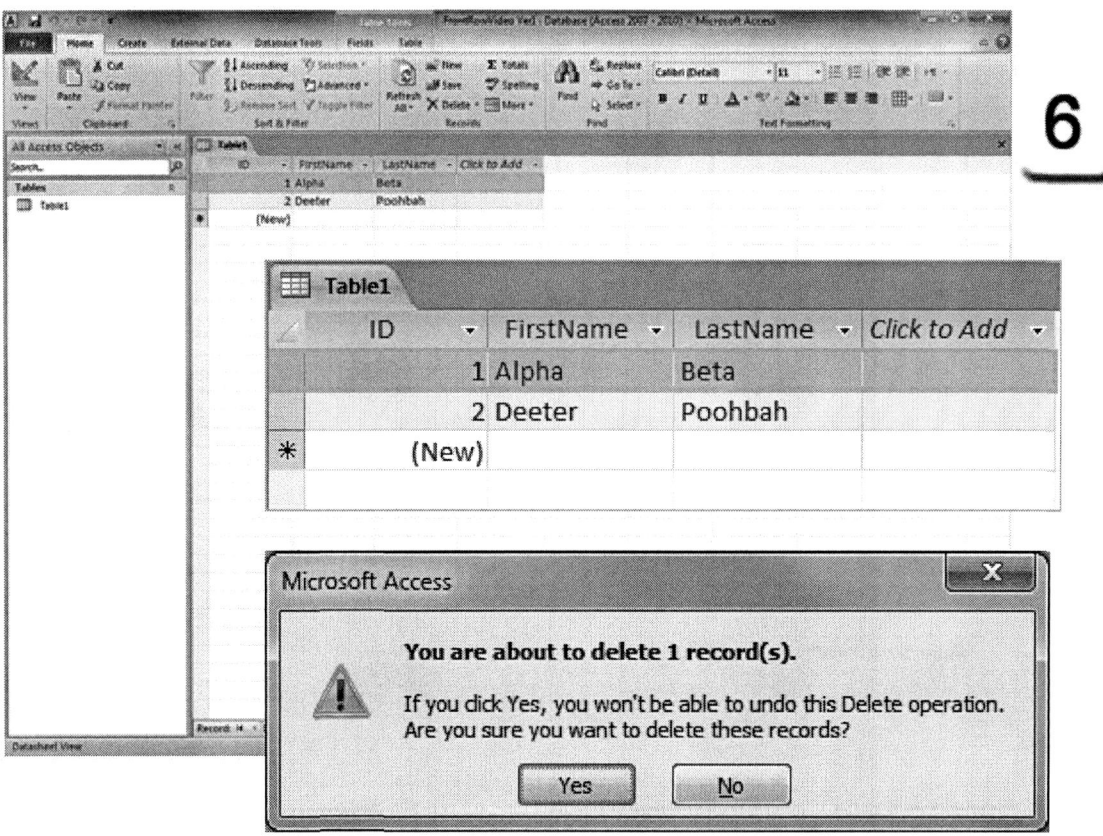

Save the Table

So far so good. You can add and delete data in this little Table. It is always a good idea to saves things that work.

7. Try it: Save the Table
Go to **File->Save**.
You will be prompted by a Save As box.
Enter a Table Name: tblCustomers
Click **OK**.

The tab at the top of the Table1 should say tblCustomers, now.

Memo to Self: One key to working with databases is naming objects consistently. The Tables, Forms, Queries and Reports should be named according to the object they use. For example, tblCustomers has customer data, not movie data.

File ->Save

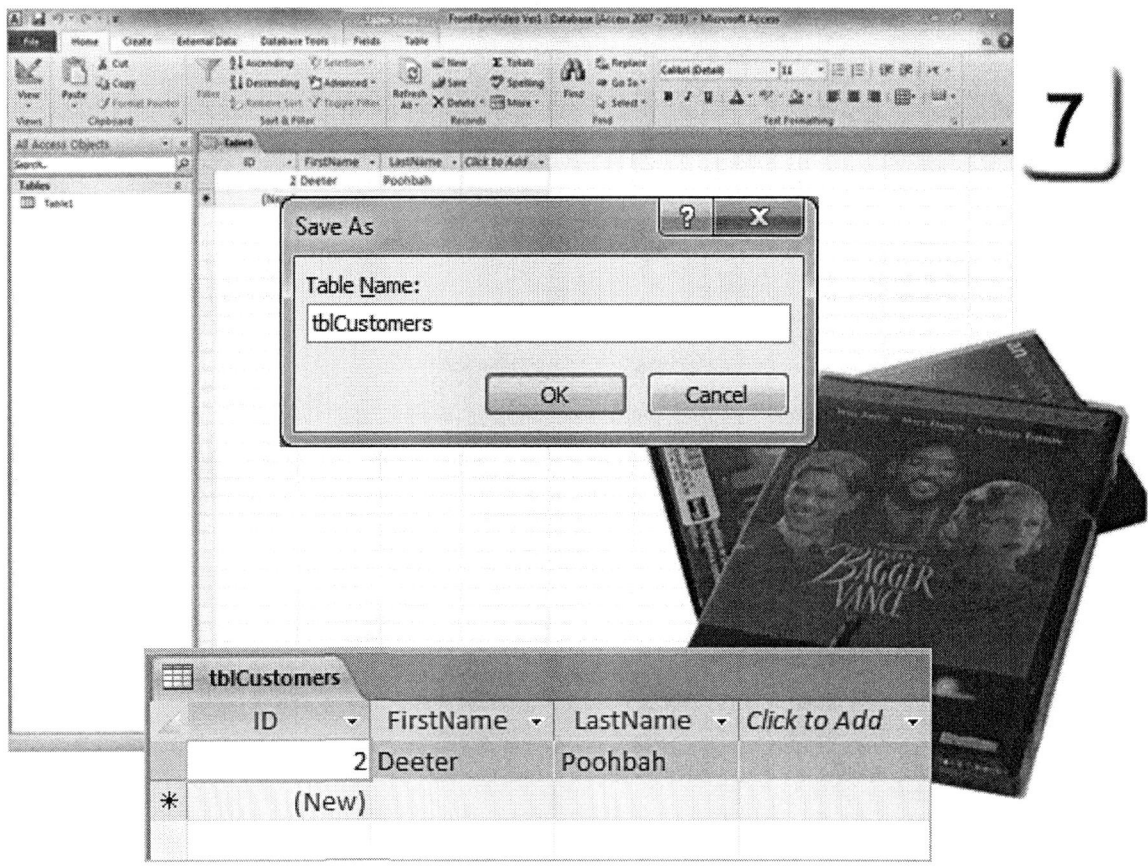

Exam 77-885: Microsoft Access 2010
2. Building Tables
2.1. Create tables: Save a Table

Edit the Table

This Table will be designed for customer information. The demographic data will include name, address and phone number.

1. Try it: Add More Text Fields
Go to **Table Tools ->Fields->Add & Delete**
Click on **Text**.
Edit the Name: Address1.

Please add the following Text fields:
City
State
Zip

Keep going...

Table Tools ->Fields->Add & Delete->Text

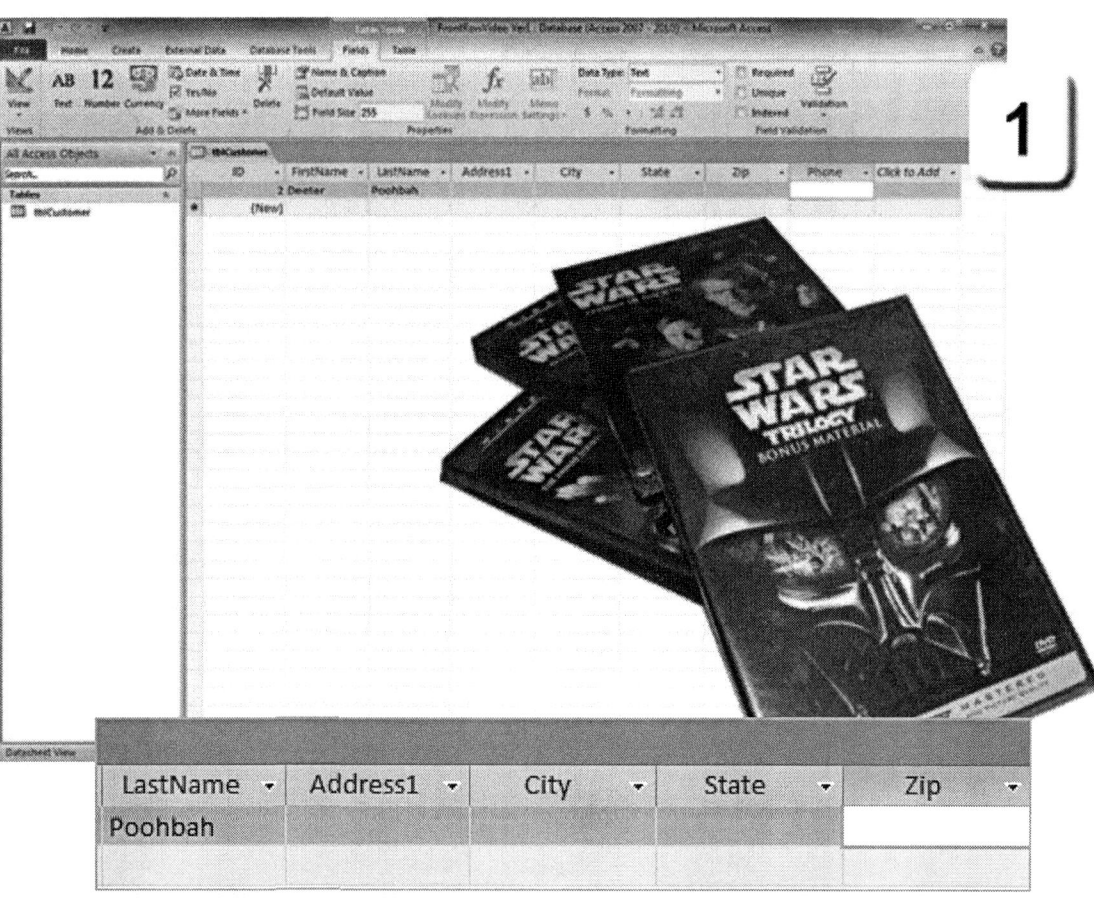

Exam 77-885: Microsoft Access 2010
2. Building Tables
2.2. Create and Modify Fields: Add a Text Field

Fields: Number or Text?

When you add a Field for the customer's phone number you may be tempted to add a Number Field. Indeed, there are many Number Formats (Currency, Percent, Decimals). But, a phone number is really a Text Field: it uses punctuation to separate the Area Code from the number. For example: (810) 555-1212, where (810) is the Area Code. Can a Text Field be formatted for phone numbers?

2. Try it: Find More Fields
Go to **Table Tools ->Fields->Add & Delete**.
Go to **More Fields**.

What Do You See? The list includes:
Basic Types
Number
Date and Time
Yes/No
Quick Start

Try This, Too: Add the Phone Fields
Go to **Table Tools ->Fields->Add & Delete**.
Go to **More Fields-->Quick Start-> Phone**.
Keep going.

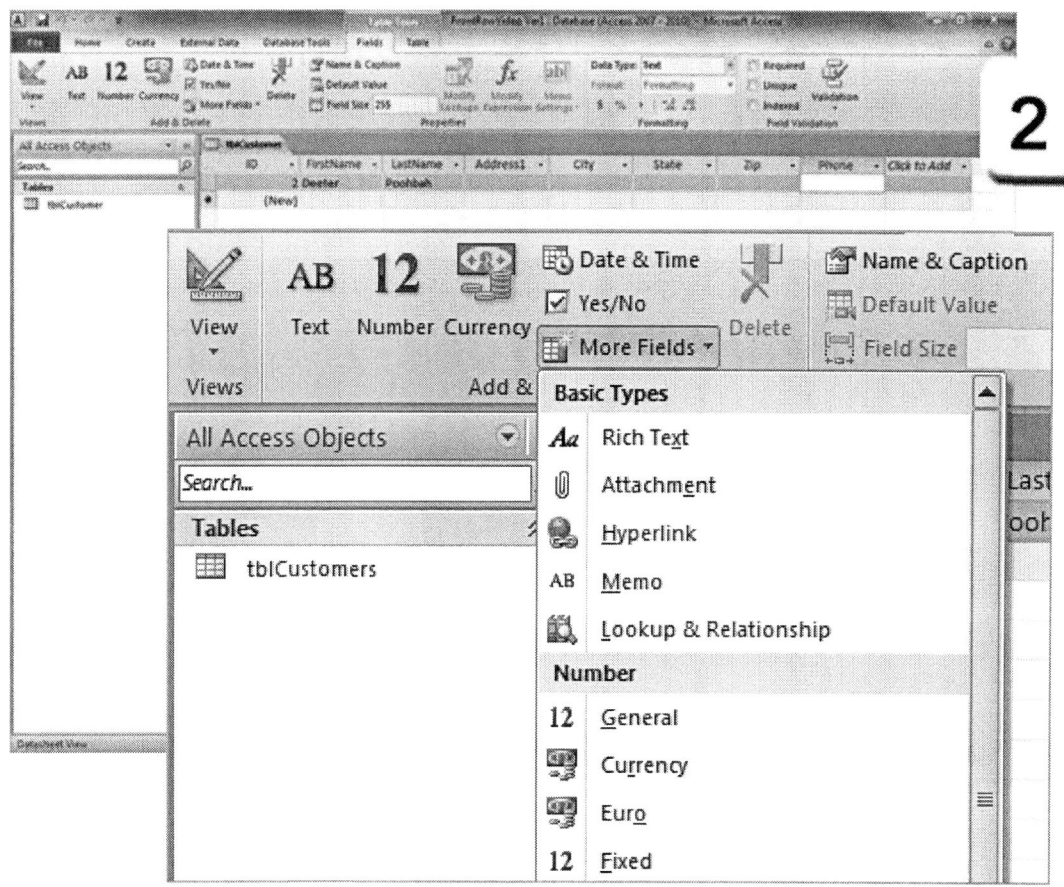

Exam 77-885: Microsoft Access 2010
2. Building Tables
2.2. Create and Modify Fields: Add a Phone Field

More Fields: Phone Numbers

3. What Do You See? The Quick Start added four new Fields for the customer's phone:
Business Phone
Home Phone
Mobile Phone
Fax Number

Design Consideration: What is the purpose of collecting this data? In our Front Row Video store, a clerk can use the phone number to look up a customer. How many phone numbers are needed? And, how many numbers are your customers willing to share?

Keep going...

Table Tools ->Fields->Add & Delete->More Fields->Quick Start->Phone

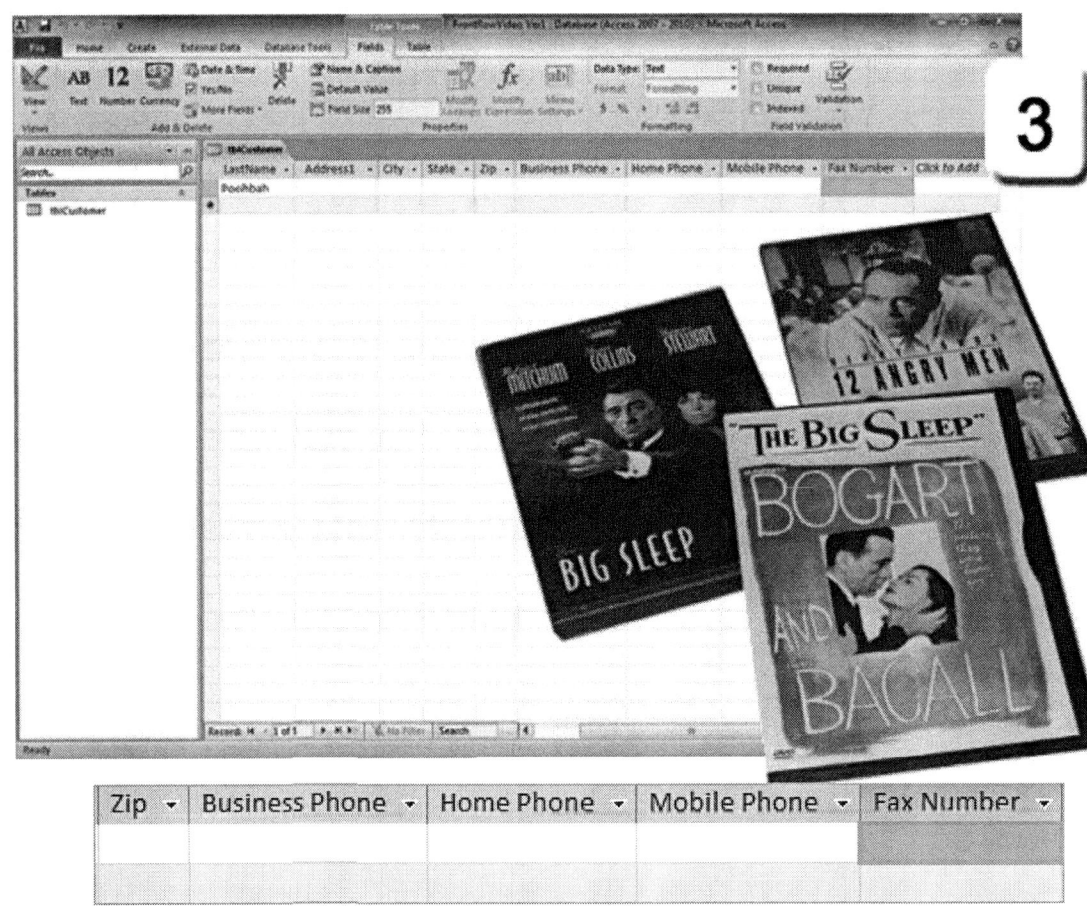

Zip ▾	Business Phone ▾	Home Phone ▾	Mobile Phone ▾	Fax Number ▾

Exam 77-885: Microsoft Access 2010
2. Building Tables
2.2. Create and Modify Fields: Add a Phone Field

Fields: Delete a Field

A database has only one job: keep the data. Microsoft Access is very emphatic when you delete something. So, you will see some in-your-face screens when you delete a Field.

4. Try it: Delete A Field
Select a Field: Fax Number.
Go to **Table Tools ->Fields->Add & Delete.**
Click on **Delete.**

What Do You See? Access will prompt you that deleting a Field is permanent: no Undo.

Click **Yes** to delete the Field.

Try This, Too: Delete Another Field
Select a Field: Business Phone
Go to **Table Tools ->Fields->Add & Delete.**
Click on **Delete.**
Click **Yes** to delete the Field.

Keep going...

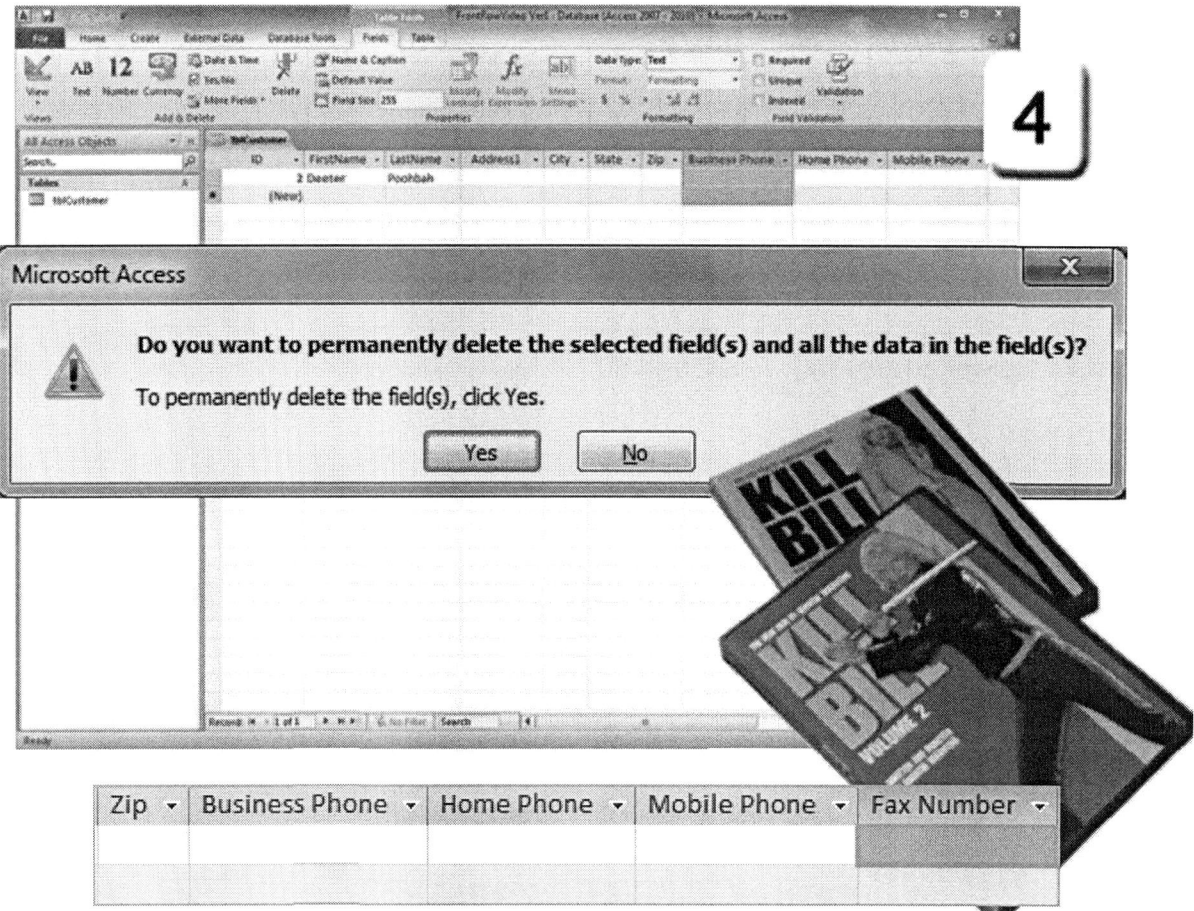

Exam 77-885: Microsoft Access 2010
2. Building Tables
2.2. Create and Modify Fields: Delete a Field

Field Properties: Required

Validation means the the right data is in the right place. In Front Row Video, the customer's phone number is essential to our business. You can use the Table Tools to make a Field **Required**.

5. Try it: Review the Data Validation
Go to **Table Tools ->Fields** and review the **Field Validation.** The options include:
Required
Unique
Indexed
Validation

Try This: Make a Field Required
Select a Field: Home Phone
Go to **Table Tools ->Fields.**
Go to **Field Validation->Required.**

What Do You See? Selecting **Required** changes the Field Property. Microsoft Access will prompt you to confirm, again.

Please click on **Yes**. Keep going...

Exam 77-885: Microsoft Access 2010
2. Building Tables
2.2. Create and Modify Fields: Data Validation

Test the Field Validation

Adding Fields and changing the Table Field Properties changes everything in a database.

So, does it work? The only way you can tell if it worked is to try it. Pretend you are a User, not the Programmer, and add some data.

6. Try it: Test the Field Validation

tblCustomers is still open.
Select an ID: 2
Enter Address1: 123 Main Street
Enter the City: Brighton
Enter the State: MI
Enter the Zip: 48116
Enter the Home Phone: 8105551212.
So far, so good.

Keep going...

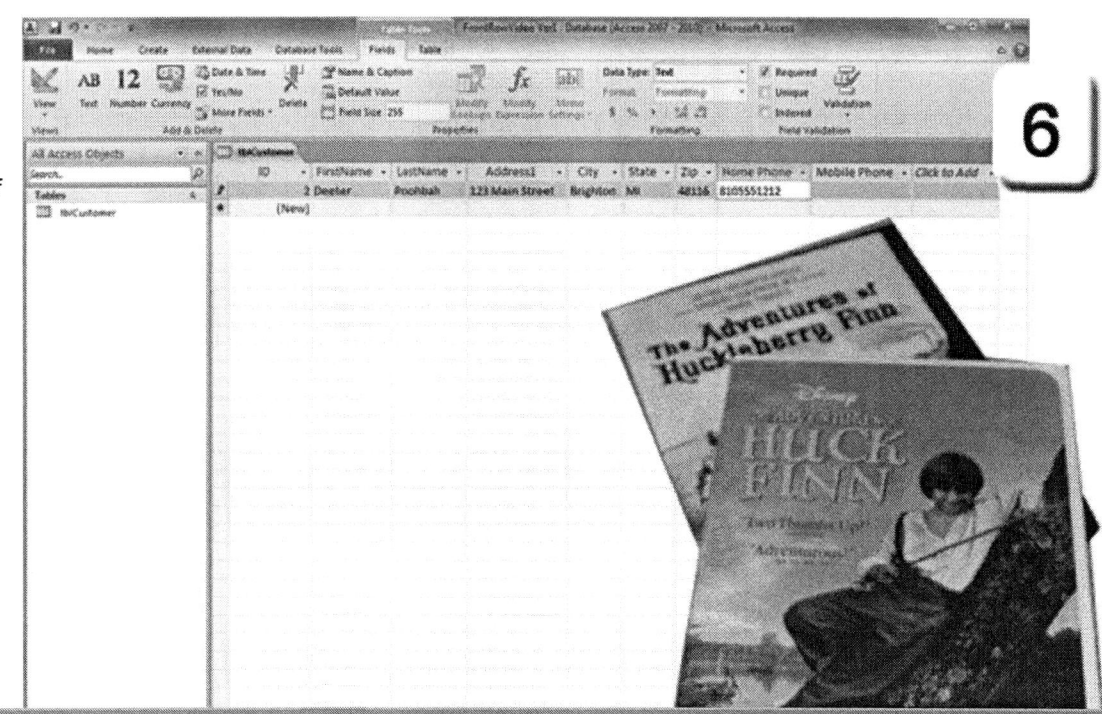

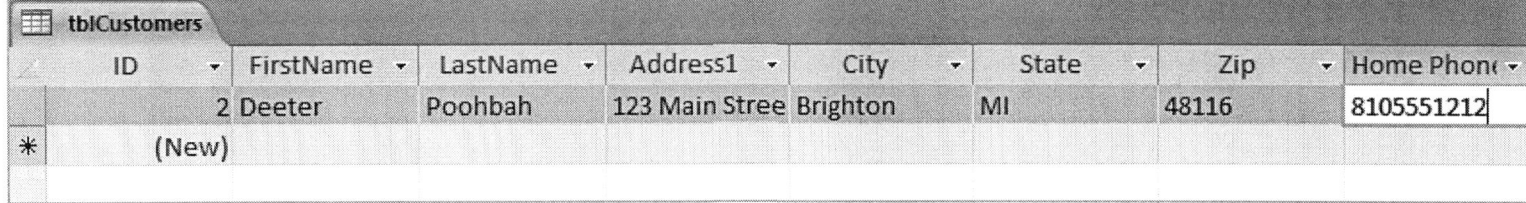

ID	FirstName	LastName	Address1	City	State	Zip	Home Phone
2 Deeter	Poohbah	123 Main Stree	Brighton	MI	48116	8105551212	
* (New)							

Exam 77-885: Microsoft Access 2010
2. Building Tables
2.2. Create and Modify Fields: Data Validation

Table Tools ->Fields->Field Validation->Validation

Test the Validation

7. Try This: Add an Incomplete Record.
This will be a test of what happens when a User does NOT add a phone number.

Create a new record. Click on **(New)**.
Enter the First Name: Mary.
Enter the Last Name: Contrary.
Enter Address1: 24 Elm Street.
Enter the City: Pinckney
Enter the State: MI
Enter the Zip: 48169
Do NOT enter the Home Phone.

Click the pencil on the Record Selector to **Save** the new customer information.

What Do You See? Microsoft Access will prompt you to enter a value in the HomePhone Field, the one that is Required.

Click **OK**.
Enter the Hone Phone: 7345551212.
Save the record.
That's good enough.

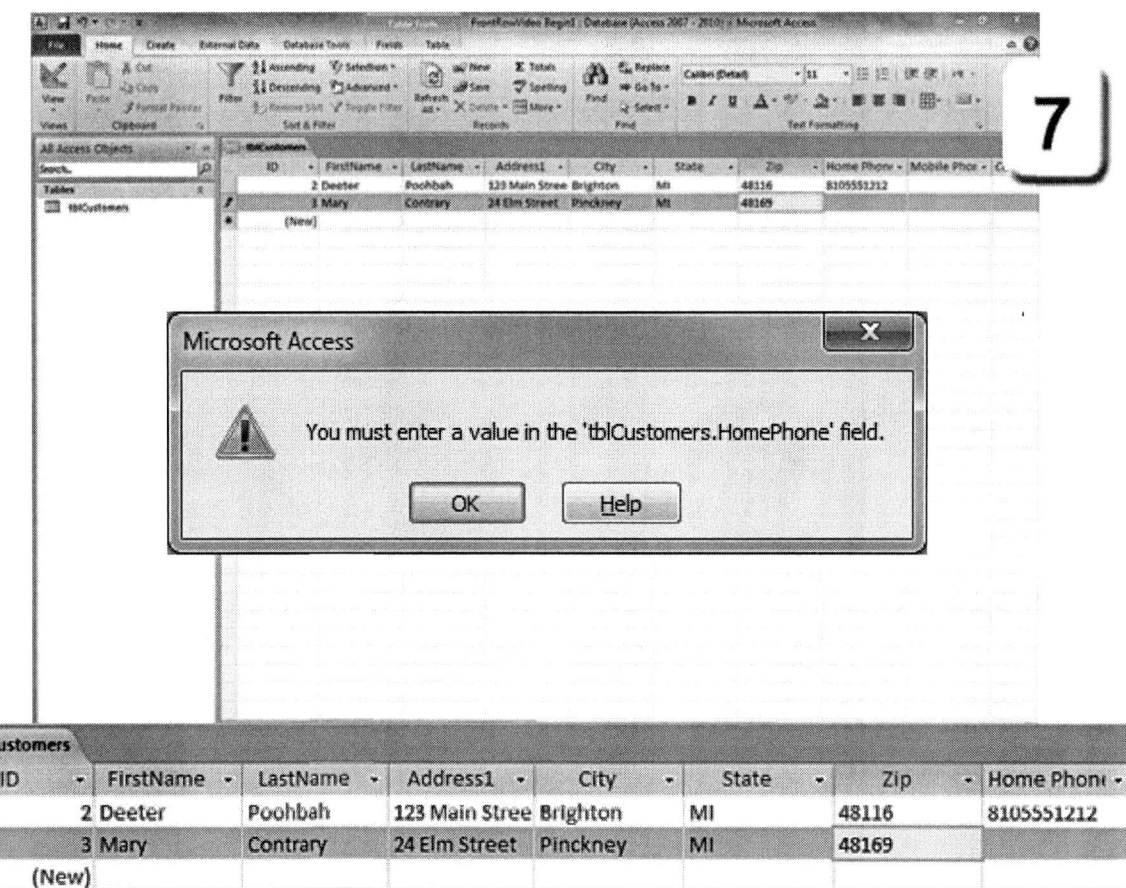

Microsoft Access

⚠ You must enter a value in the 'tblCustomers.HomePhone' field.

| OK | Help |

ID	FirstName	LastName	Address1	City	State	Zip	Home Phone
2 Deeter	Poohbah	123 Main Stree	Brighton	MI	48116	8105551212
3 Mary	Contrary	24 Elm Street	Pinckney	MI	48169	
(New)						

Exam 77-885: Microsoft Access 2010
2. Building Tables
2.2. Create and Modify Fields: Data Validation

Data, Data, Data

The purpose of a database is to keep the data. The database has only one job: the data, the data, the data.

If you delete any record, the database will ask you to confirm. If you change or modify a Table Field, you will be prompted to save your changes.

Data Validation is one method worth considering when you design Tables.

This is a good start to understanding Tables. But, it is just the beginning.

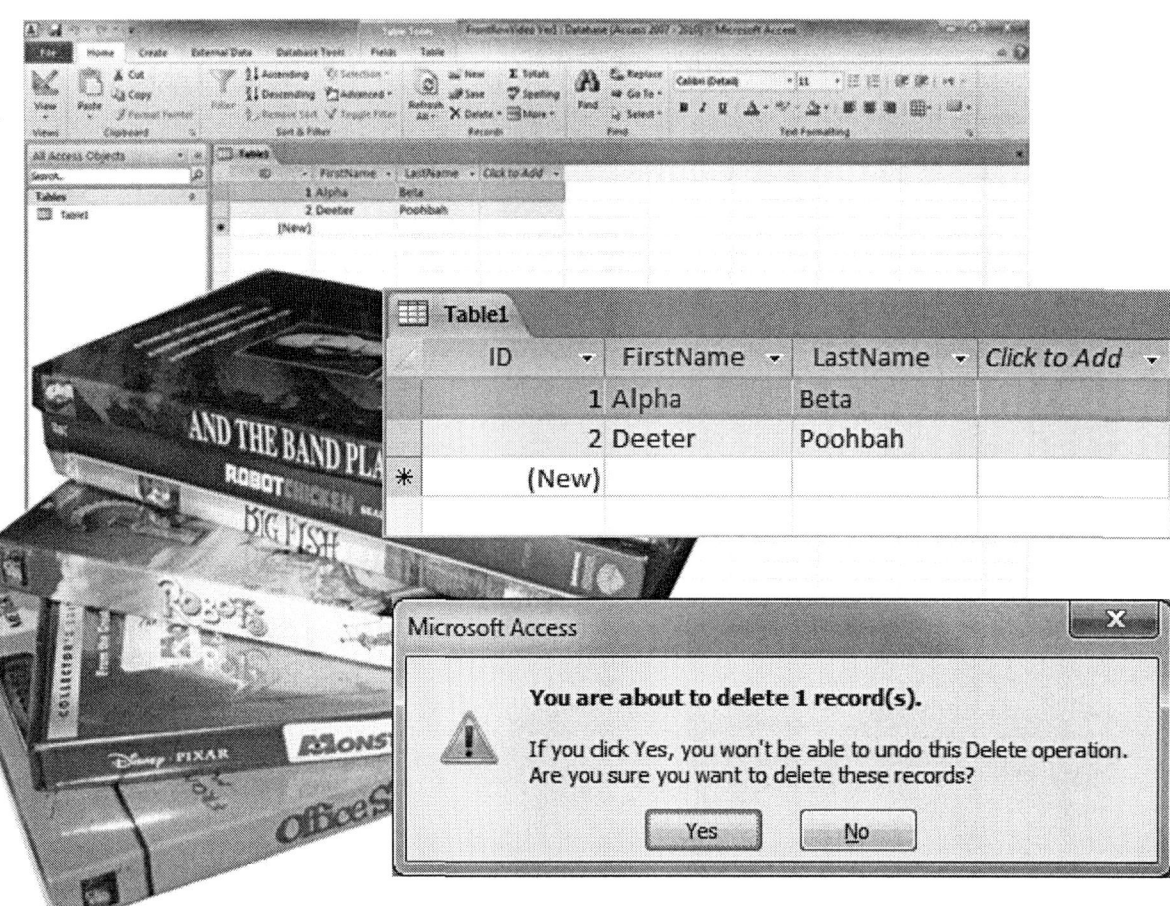

Exam 77-885: Microsoft Access 2010
2. Building Tables
2.2. Create and Modify Fields: Data Validation

Summary

This lesson focused on creating and modifying a simple customer table, tblCustomers. In the next two lessons we will look at options for managing data.

Well, you done good.
You can get two cookies if you wish!

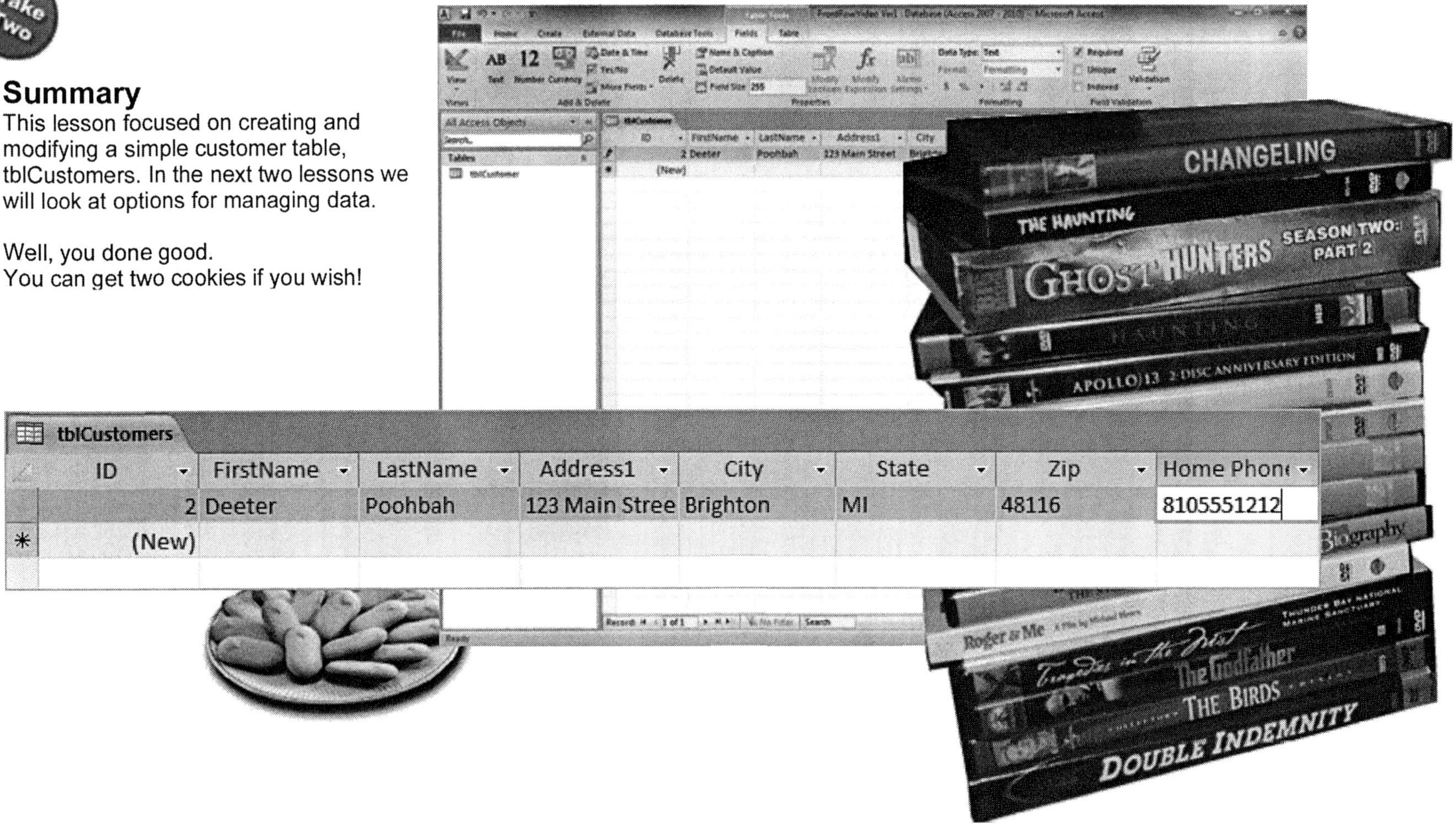

ID	FirstName	LastName	Address1	City	State	Zip	Home Phone
2	Deeter	Poohbah	123 Main Stree	Brighton	MI	48116	8105551212
* (New)							

Practice Activities

Lesson 2: Hello, Microsoft Access

Try This: Do the following steps

1. Open a new blank database. Name the database Brown Bag Lunch EAN database, where EAN is your initials.

2. Add the following Text Fields. Do NOT include spaces.

Company
FirstName
LastName
Address
City
State
Zip
Phone

3. Add a new Record with the following information:
Computer Zone, Jennifer Whittly, 987 Pontiac Trail, Wixom, MI, 48939, 248-555-9854

4. Add these additional records:

Company	FirstName	LastName	Address	City	State	Zip	Phone
Bright Futures Academy	Consuelo	Justice	123 Grand River Ave	Novi	MI	48734	248-555-3913
Rhino Paper Printing	Dwain	Coffey	5575 Michigan Ave	Novi	MI	48734	313-555-6589
Travel Pal	Stefan	Alonzo	1237 Main Street	Milford	MI	48380	810-555-9172
Pixel Butter Web Design	Valerie	Carter	3211 Eight Mile Road	Novi	MI	48734	248-555-6878

5. Use Data Validation to mark the Phone Number field as Required
6. Add the following record to test the Data Validation: Pest People, Andrew, June, 1258 Grand River Ave, Milford, MI, 48380
7. Add the following phone number for Pest People: 248-555-6882
8. Delete the Record for Travel Pal.
9. Save the Table as tblCustomers. Close the Brown Bag Lunch EAN database, where EAN is your initials.

Test Yourself

1. Which of the following is true about Access databases? (Give all correct answers.)
A. Access databases save the information in Tables
B. Data entry Forms, Queries, and Reports all use the information stored in Tables
C. Databases record a one-to-many relationship
Tip: Beginning Access, page 29, 34

2. Which are Field options?
(Give all correct answers.)
A. Text
B. Numbers
C. Date/ Time
D. Yes/ No
Tip: Beginning Access, page 29

3. Which of the following are Access database Objects?
(Give all correct answers.)
A. Spreadsheet
B. Table
C. Reports
D. Queries
E. Forms
Tip: Beginning Access, page 29

4. Which of the following is true about Queries? (Give all correct answers.)
A. Select Queries show records that match the criteria
B. Action Queries show records that match the criteria
C. Select Queries change or update data
D. Action Queries change or update data
E. None of the above
Tip: Beginning Access, page 30

5. Each Table may have a Form for data entry.
A. True
B. False
Tip: Beginning Access, page 31

6. What is displayed in the Navigation Pane?
(Give all correct answers.)
A. All Access Objects
B. The last Access Objects created
C. Objects formatted with a particular Theme
D. Text formatted with a Heading Styles
Tip: Beginning Access, page 36

7. Which is true about Field Names?
A. It is not possible to have a space in a Field Name
B. Access with change spaces to an underscore (such as First_Name)
C. Access will remove any spaces (changing First Name to FirstName) automatically
D. Access allows spaces and doesn't change them
Tip: Beginning Access, page 38

8. Which type of Field is a Phone Number Field?
A. Numerical field just for phone numbers, allows only numbers and provides the dashes
B. A Text field that includes text (numbers) and punctuation
C. A generic field with no special meaning
Tip: Beginning Access, page 43

Access 2010: Working with Data

Table Design

Beginning Access Objectives
In this lesson, you will learn how to:

1. Use the Table Design View to edit Field Properties.

2. Edit the Field Properties and add a Default Value.

3. Add an Input Mask to a Text Field: format the Phone Number to include placeholders.

4. Review the purpose of the Primary Key.

5. Rename the Primary Key.

© 2012 Comma Productions, LLC

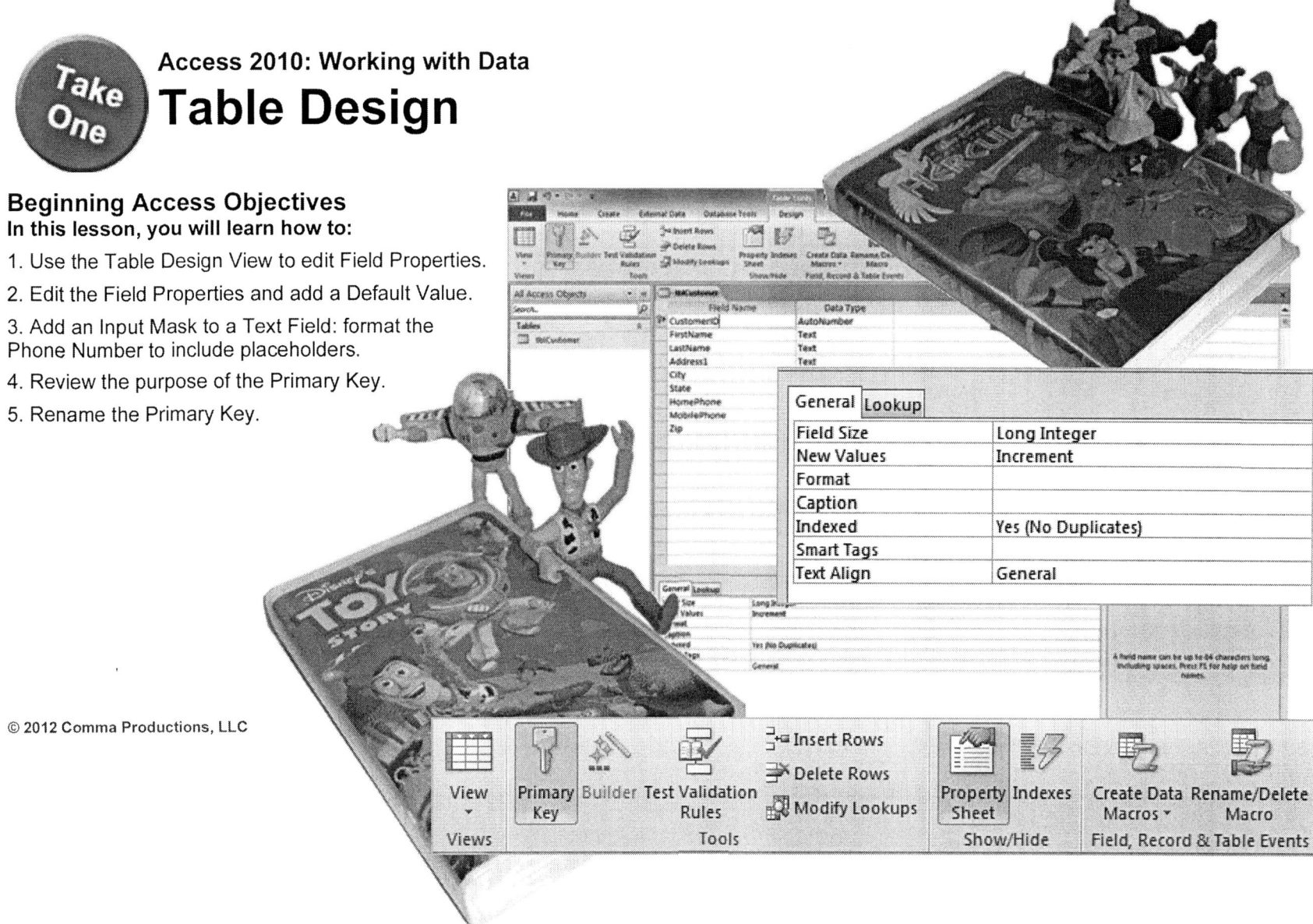

Lesson 3 : Table Design

1. Readings
Read Lesson 3 in the Beginning Access guide, page 53-72.

Project
Create and modify the Customer Table by adding new Fields in Design View.

Downloads
tblMovies.xlsx
FrontRowVideo Begin3.accdb
Brown Bag Lunch ver3.accdb
Lunch1.gif
Lunch2.gif
Lunch3.gif
Lunch4.gif

2. Practice
Complete the Practice Activity on page 73.

3. Assessment
Review the Test questions on page 74.

Table Tools-> Fields

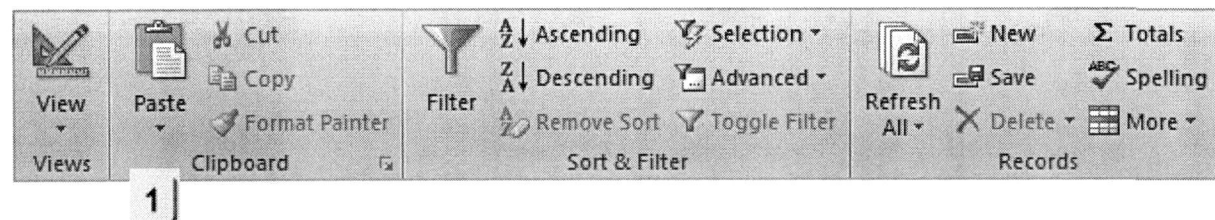

Table Tools-> Design

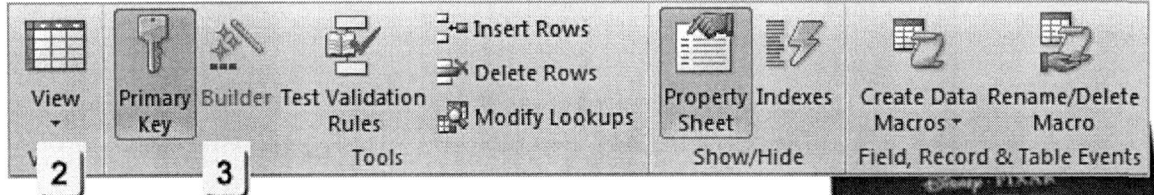

Menu Maps
From the **Home Ribbon**.
1. Home ->Views->View->Design View, page 57

From the **Table Tools-> Design Ribbon**.
2. Table Tools->Design, page 59
3. Design->Tools->Primary Key, page 68

Tables and Table Design

Everything in Microsoft Access has several Views. Each object (Table, Form, or Report) has a View that displays the object as a User would see it. For Tables, this is the Datasheet View. For Forms, it is the Form View, and for Reports, it is Print Preview.

In the first lesson, we created a simple customer table in Datasheet View. We used the **Table Tools** to add **Fields** to the Table. So far, so good. All objects in Access also have a **Design View**. The Design View is how a programmer sees the objects. For Tables, Design View lets the programmer define what data will be saved in a Table and how the information will be formatted.

Microsoft Access 2010: Example of a Table

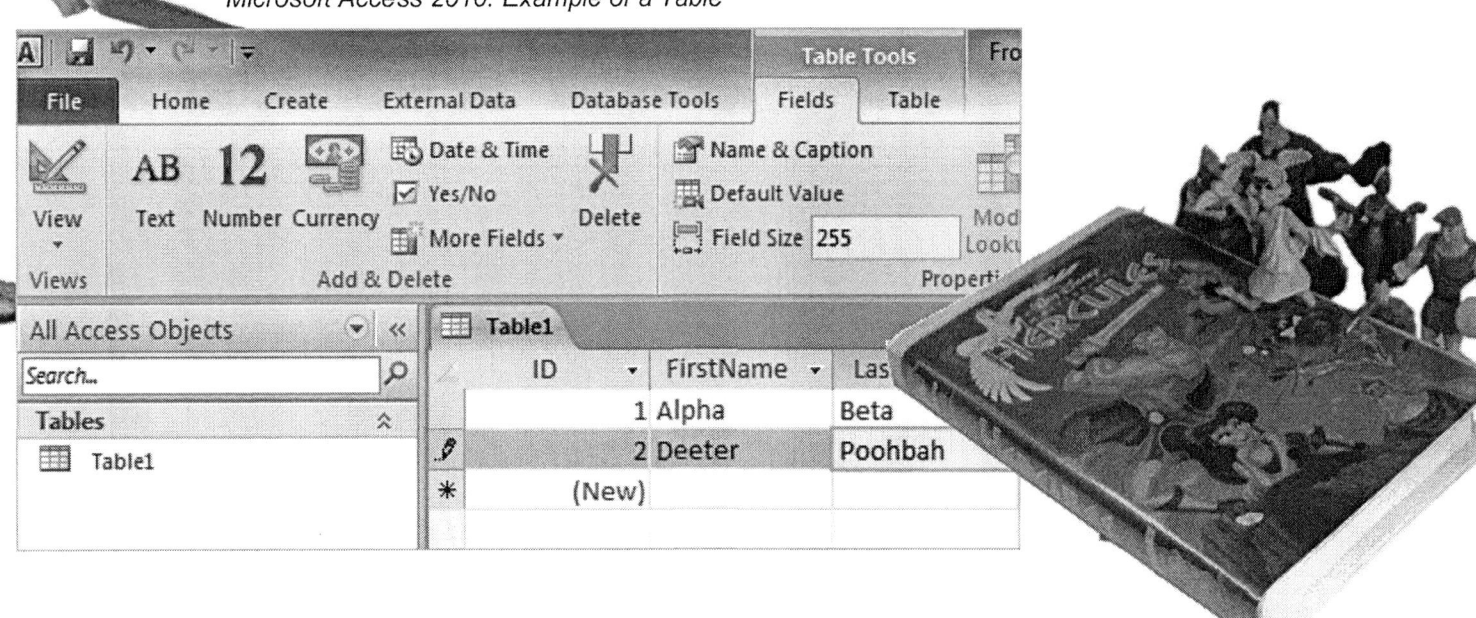

Start -> All Programs ->Microsoft Office-> Microsoft Office Access 2010

Before You Begin

This lesson uses the database that was created in the previous lesson, **FrontRowVideo Ver1.accdb**. You can continue with the database that you saved or download the sample database at the beginning of this lesson if you wish.

Before You Begin: Open the Sample Database
Go to **Start -> All Programs ->Microsoft Office**.
Click on **Microsoft Office Access 2010**.
Access will prompt you to **open** a database.

If you have been following with these lessons you can continue with the database you have been programming. Otherwise, please open the sample: **FrontRowVideo Begin3.accdb**.

What Do You See? This database has one Table, tblCustomers.

Double-click tblCustomers. The Table will open in **Datasheet View**. There should be two records.

Keep going...

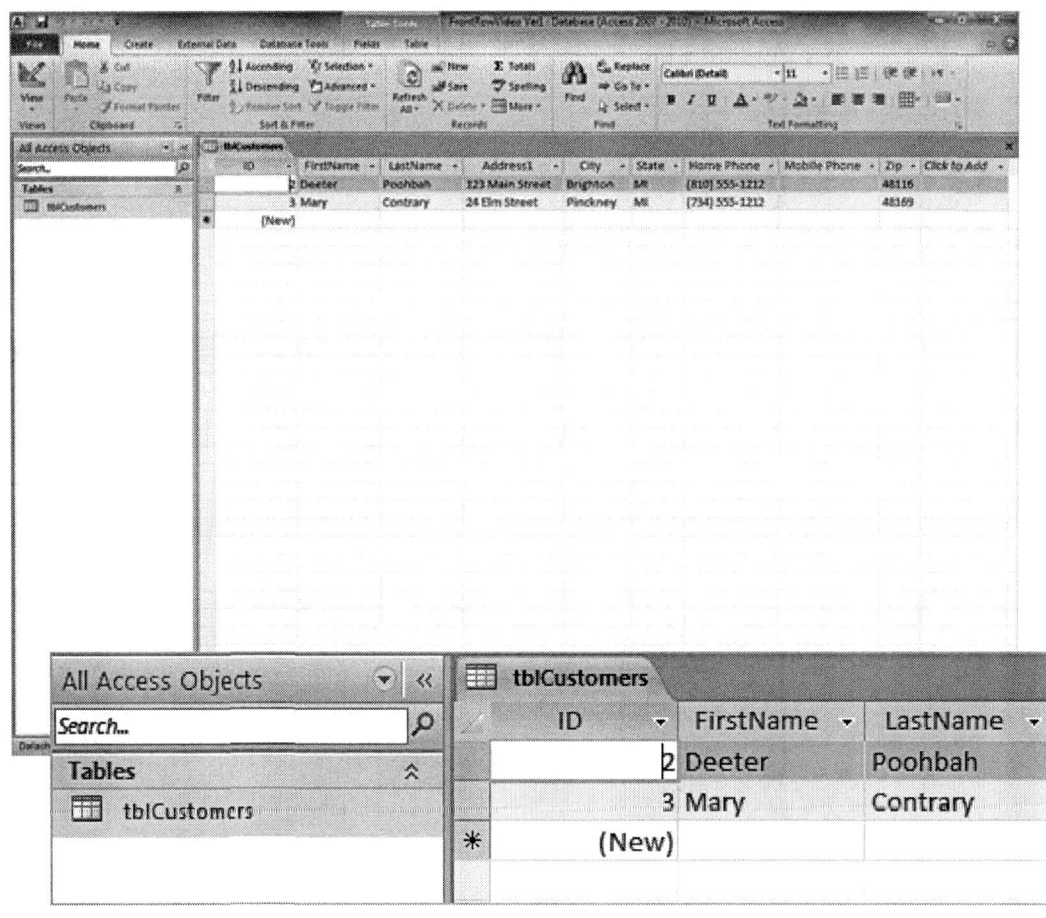

Exam 77-885: Microsoft Access 2010
1. Managing the Access Environment
1.1. Create and manage a database: Use Open

Table: Datasheet View

So far, we have been working with the Table in **Datasheet View**. The Datasheet View looks like a spreadsheet. Many of the Table options are similar to the ones in Microsoft Excel.

There are two **Table Tools** in the Datasheet View: Fields and Table. There is another Table Tool Ribbon in the **Design View**.

1. Try it: Change the View
Go to **Home ->Views->View**.
Select a View: **Design View**.

Keep going...

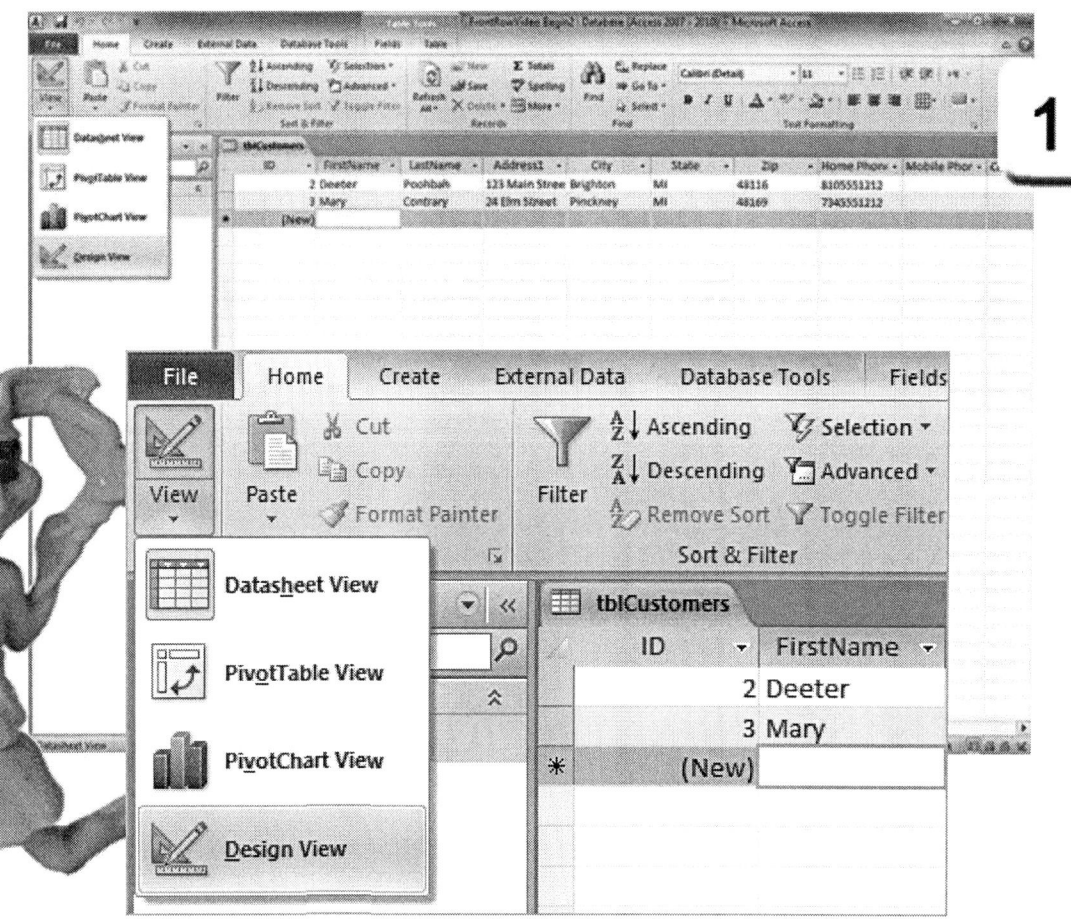

Exam 77-885: Microsoft Access 2010
2. Building Tables
2.1.1. Create tables in Design View

Hello, Design View!
2. Try it: Review the Design Ribbon
The **Design View** displays the Table Fields as a List. The list includes the Field Name, Data Type, and Description.

There are eleven **Data Types** including: Text, Memo, Date/Time, Currency, AutoNumber, Yes/No, OLE Object, Hyperlink, Attachment, Calculated and the Lookup Wizard.

The **Design Tools** are:
Views
Tools
Show/Hide
Field, Records & Table Events
Relationships

What Else Do You See?
When you select a Field Name from the list on the top, Access will show the General Field Properties on the bottom in the little reference pane.

Keep going...

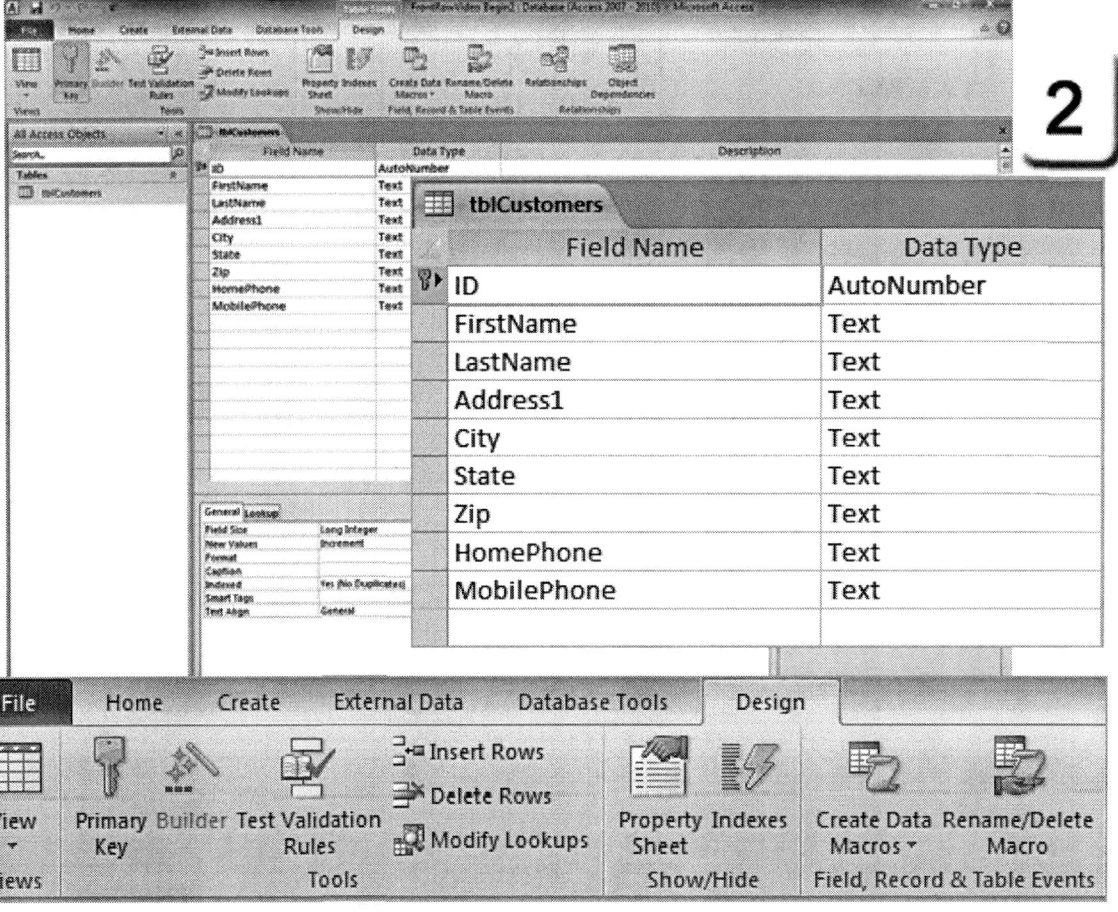

Exam 77-885: Microsoft Access 2010
2. Building Tables
2.1.1. Create tables in Design View: Modify the Data Types

Field Properties

3. Try it: Review the Field Properties

Select a Field: HomePhone.
Look at the General Field Properties listed on the bottom of the Table.

What Do You See? The Design View has a robust set of **Field Properties**:
Field Size
Format
Input Mask
Caption
Default Value
Validation Rule
Validation Text
Required
Allow Zero Length
Indexed
Unicode Compression
IME Mode
IME Sentence Mode
Smart Tags
Text Align

What Else Else You See? The HomePhone is a Text Field. It is Required. Go on...

Table Tools->Design

General	Lookup	
Field Size	255
Format	
Input Mask	
Caption	Home Phone
Default Value	
Validation Rule	
Validation Text	
Required	Yes
Allow Zero Length	No
Indexed	No
Unicode Compression	Yes
IME Mode	No Control
IME Sentence Mode	Phrase Predict
Smart Tags	

Exam 77-885: Microsoft Access 2010
2. Building Tables
2.1.1. Create tables in Design View

Take One

Edit the Field Properties

Many of the Field Properties are simple... and they make sense. Say the Front Row Video store was located in Michigan. How many customers are going to drive in from Texas or California?

You can edit the Field Properties for the State Field so that it automatically fills in "MI" by default. There are only two letters in the abbreviation for the State. You can make the Field Size smaller as well.

4. Try it: Edit the Field Properties
Select a Field: State

Edit the following Field Properties:
Field Size: 2
Default Value: MI

What Do You See? Microsoft Access will add the quote marks ("MI") as needed.

Keep going...

Table Tools->Design

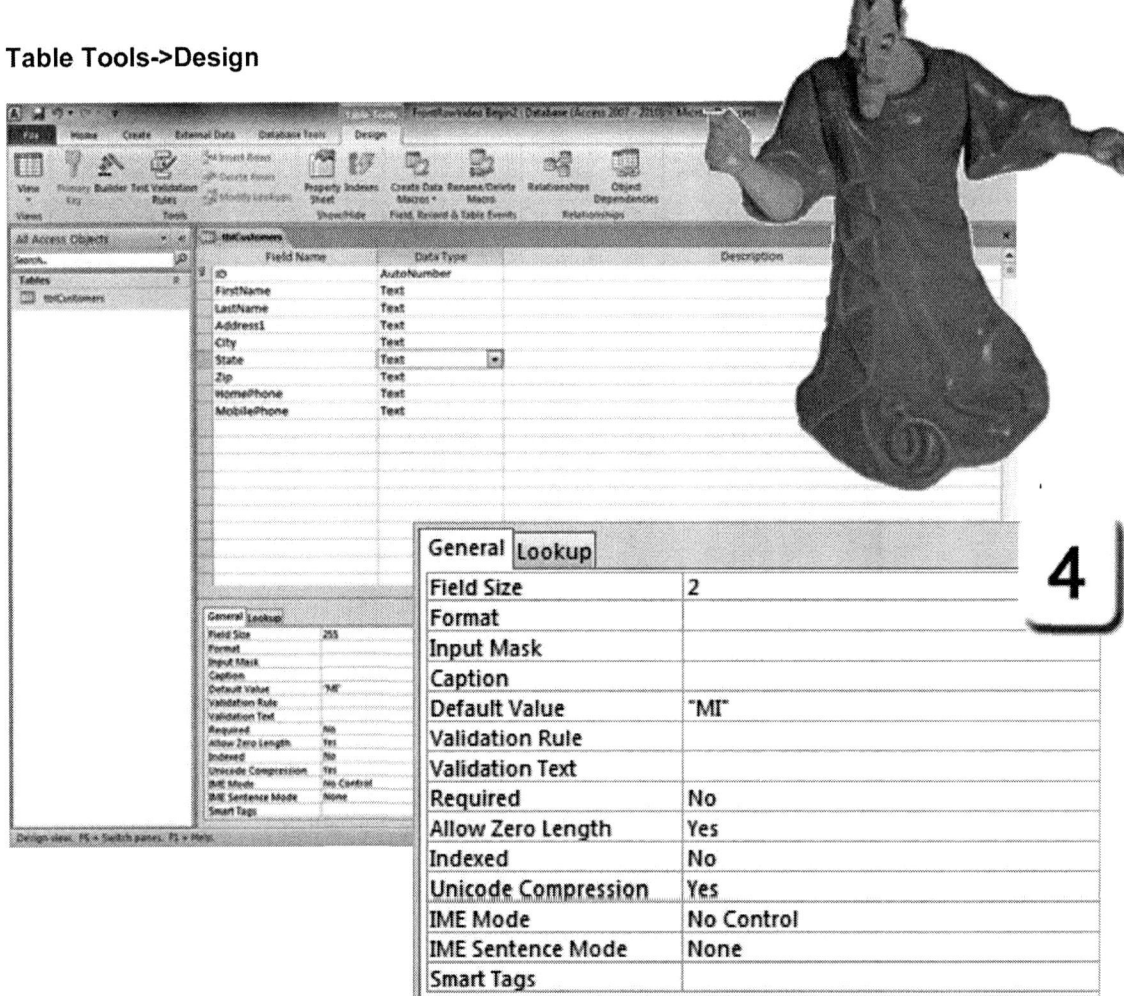

General	Lookup	
Field Size	2	
Format		
Input Mask		
Caption		
Default Value	"MI"	
Validation Rule		
Validation Text		
Required	No	
Allow Zero Length	Yes	
Indexed	No	
Unicode Compression	Yes	
IME Mode	No Control	
IME Sentence Mode	None	
Smart Tags		

Exam 77-885: Microsoft Access 2010
2. Building Tables
2.1.1. Create tables in Design View: Modify the Field Properties

Field Properties: Input Mask

An Input Mask helps Users fill in the right numbers. For example, you can use an **Input Mask** to show the places for the Area Code and phone number. There is an **Input Mask Wizard** that walks through the steps to select a format and write the code.

5. Try it: Find the Input Mask Wizard
The HomePhone Field is selected.
Select a Property: Input Mask.
Click on the **three-dot Builder** that is now available on the right side. This will launch the Wizard.

What Do You See? The Wizard has several templates including Phone Number, Social Security Number, Zip Code. Extension, Password, Time and Dates.

Try This, Too: Add an Input Mask
Select an Input Mask: Phone Number.
Click **Next**. Keep going...

Table Tools->Design->Tools->Builder->Input Mask Wizard

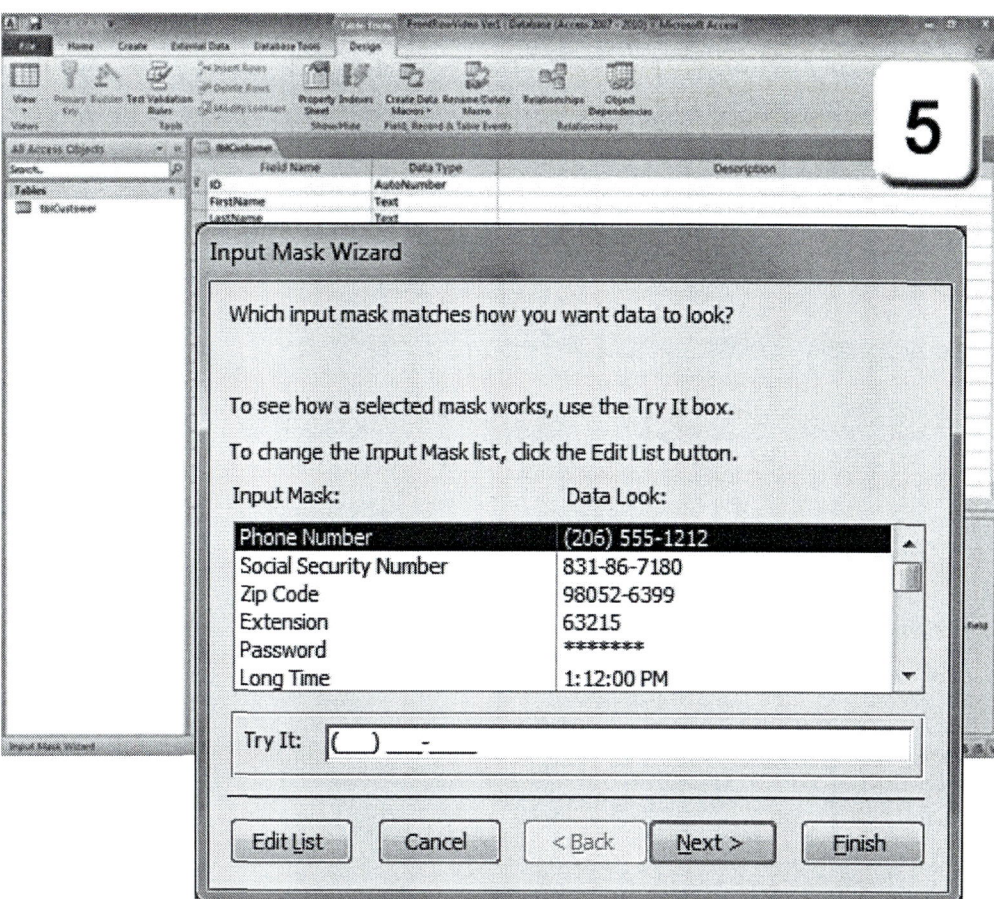

Exam 77-885: Microsoft Access 2010
2. Building Tables
2.1.1. Create tables in Design View: Modify the Field Properties

Take One

Table Tools->Design->Tools->Builder->Input Mask Wizard

Input Mask: Placeholders

The Input Mask Wizard will prompt you to select a Placeholder. Placeholders help Users by offering something visual that reminds them how many characters they need to enter. The default Placeholder is a dash. You can choose an asterisk or an underline if you wish.

6. Try it: Select a Placeholder
Select a Placeholder: Underscore.
Click **Next**. Keep going...

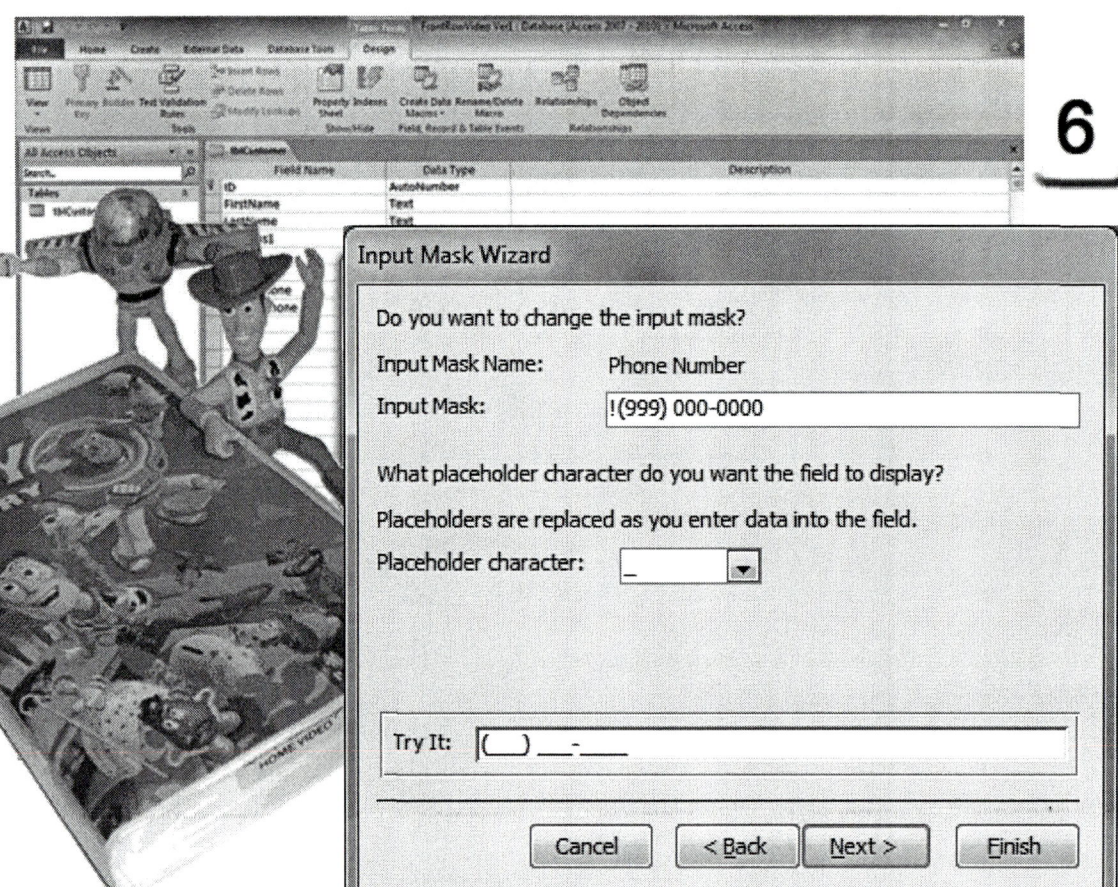

6

Input Mask Wizard

Do you want to change the input mask?

Input Mask Name: Phone Number

Input Mask: !(999) 000-0000

What placeholder character do you want the field to display?

Placeholders are replaced as you enter data into the field.

Placeholder character: _

Try It: (___) ___-____

Cancel   < Back   Next >   Finish

Exam 77-885: Microsoft Access 2010
2. Building Tables
2.1.1. Create tables in Design View: Modify the Field Properties

Input Mask: Store the Data

Now, the Wizard will ask if you would like to save (store) the data in tblCustomers with or without the symbols in the mask.

This is a challenging question that the Computer Mama has struggled with in many database designs. Saving the symbols makes the data look like phone numbers in tblCustomers.

However, symbols make it difficult to look up a phone number because you have to type it exactly, with the parentheses and all that.

The default programming is to store the data without the symbols.

7. Try it: Store the Data
Select the Default Option: Without the symbols.
Click **Next**. Keep going...

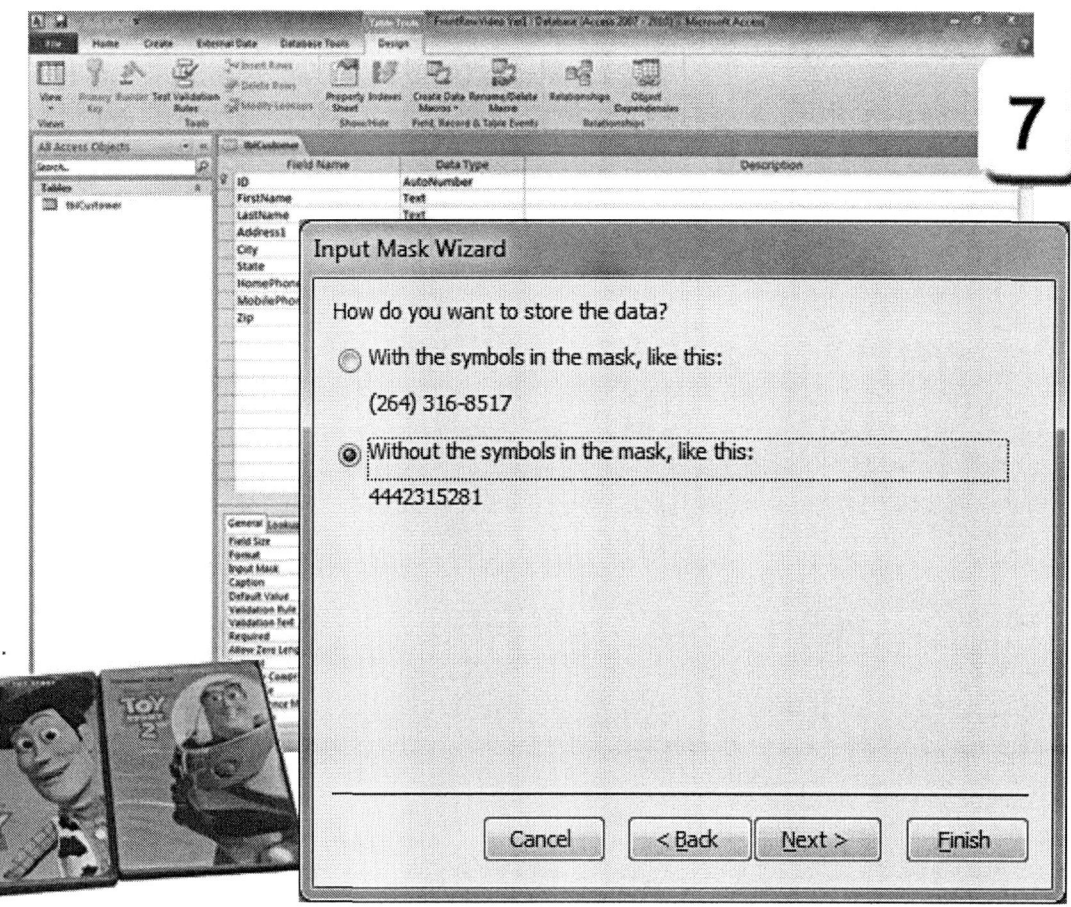

Exam 77-885: Microsoft Access 2010
2. Building Tables
2.1.1. Create tables in Design View: Modify the Field Properties

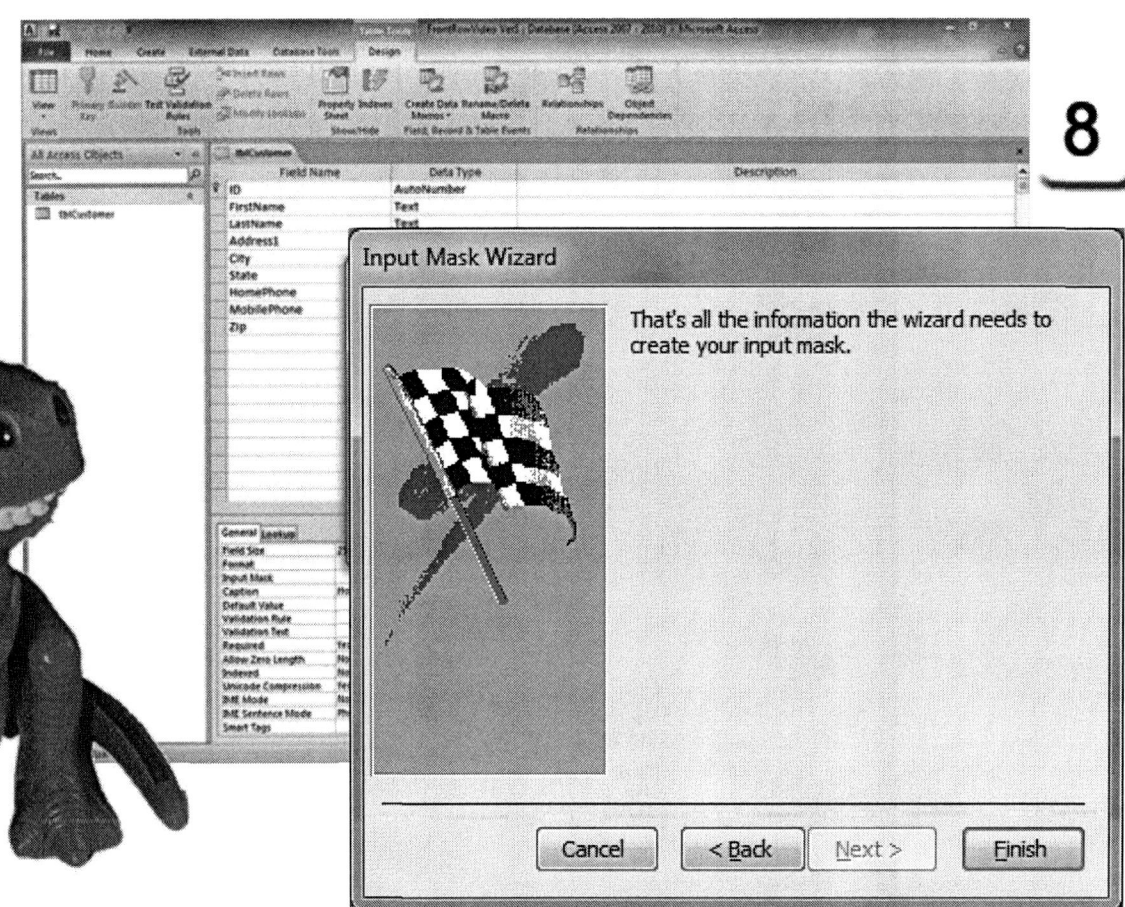

Table Tools->Design->Tools->Builder->Input Mask Wizard

Input Mask Wizard: Finish

8. Try it: Finish the Input Mask Wizard
The Input Mask Wizard displays a checkered flag on the final step.

Click **Finish**. The Wizard will close.
Please turn the page to review the results.

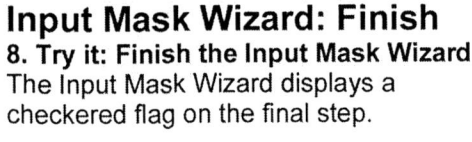

Exam 77-885: Microsoft Access 2010
2. Building Tables
2.1.1. Create tables in Design View: Modify the Field Properties

Review the Input Mask Code
The Wizard created the Input Mask code:
!\(999") "000\-000;;

Save the Table
All programming needs to be tested. Right now, the Customer Table is in **Design View**. This is how a programmer sees the Table Properties. When you are ready to test the Table, you will need to Save your changes and return to the **Datasheet View**.

Before You Leave: Save the Table
Go to **File->Save**.

9. Try it: Return to the Datasheet View
Go to **Home ->Views->View.**
Click on **Datasheet View.**

Keep going, there is one more step...

Home ->Views->View->Datasheet View

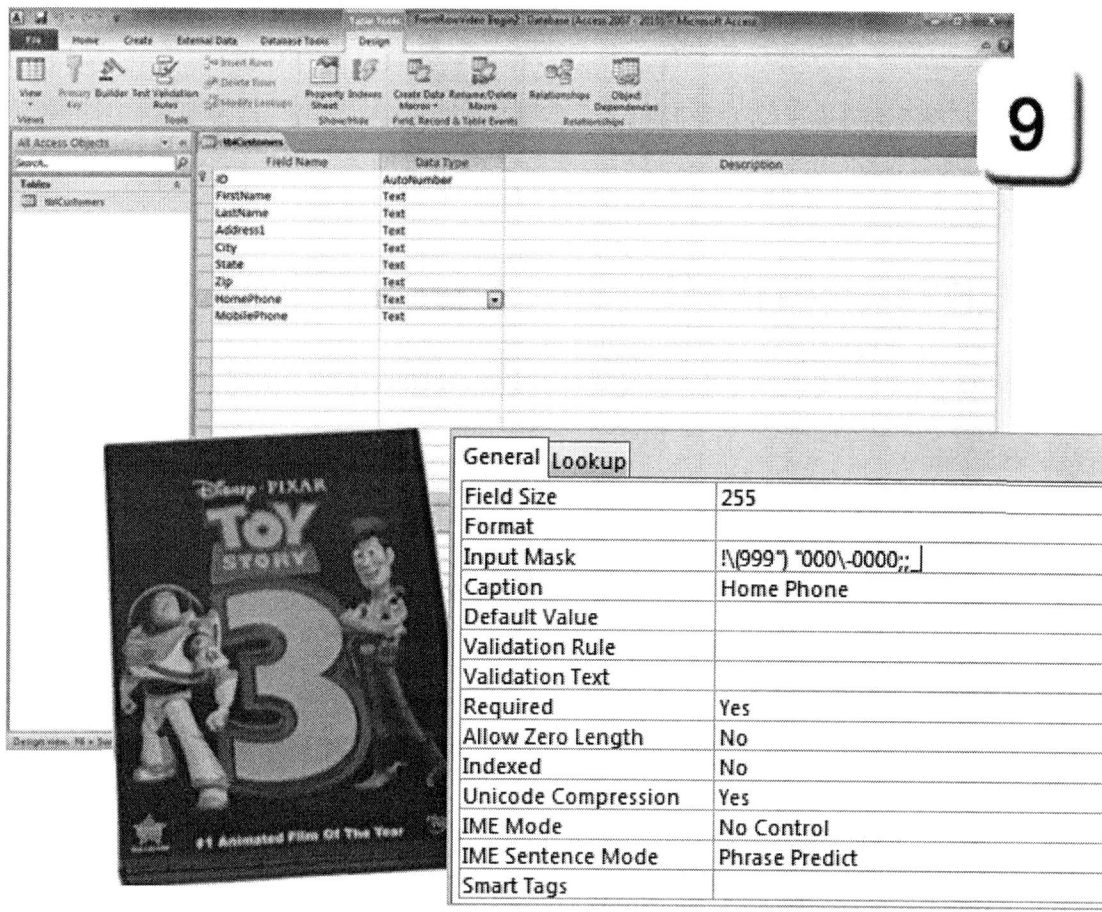

Exam 77-885: Microsoft Access 2010
2. Building Tables
2.1.1. Create tables in Design View: Save the Table

Test the Input Mask

Try it: Test the Input Mask
Create a new record. Click on **(New)**.
Enter the First Name: Timothy.
Enter the Last Name: Allen.
Enter Address1: 789 Second Street.
Enter the City: Ann Arbor
Enter the State: MI
Enter the Zip: 48103
Enter the Home Phone: 3135551212

Click the pencil on the Record Selector to
Save the new customer information.

What Do You See? The Home Phone
Field displayed the Placeholders as the
numbers were typed.

That worked.

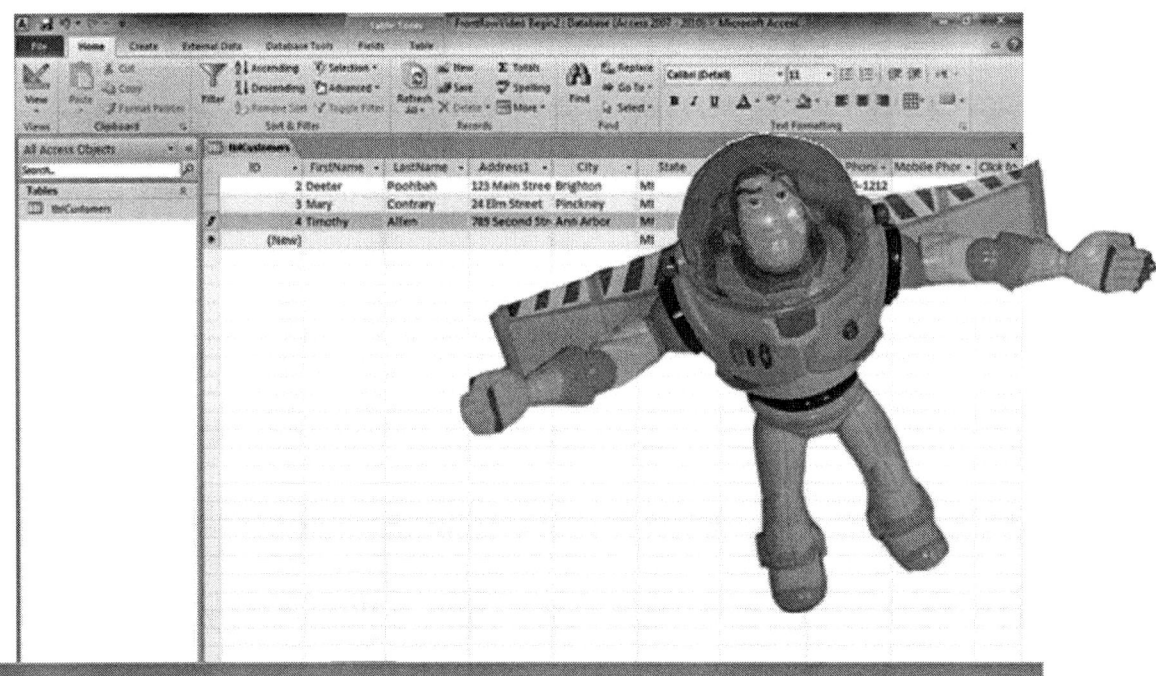

tblCustomers

ID	FirstName	LastName	Address1	City	State	Zip	Home Phone
2	Deeter	Poohbah	123 Main Stree	Brighton	MI	48116	(810) 555-1212
3	Mary	Contrary	24 Elm Street	Pinckney	MI	48169	(734) 555-1212
4	Timothy	Allen	789 Second Str	Ann Arbor	MI	48103	(313) 555-1212
* (New)					MI		

Wanted: Unique Records

In the previous lesson we created a new customer named Alpha Beta. This customer had ID number 1. During our practice, we deleted the customer named Alpha Beta. O.o

1. Try it: Enter the Customer, Again

tblCustomers is open in **Datasheet View**.
Create a new record. Click on **(New).**
Enter the First Name: Alpha.
Enter the Last Name: Beta.
Enter Address1: 123 Practice Street.
Enter the City: MyTown
Enter the State: MI
Enter the Zip: 48103
Enter the Home Phone: 8102313211

What Do You See? The new record has ID 5. It did not get ID 1, again.

Why?

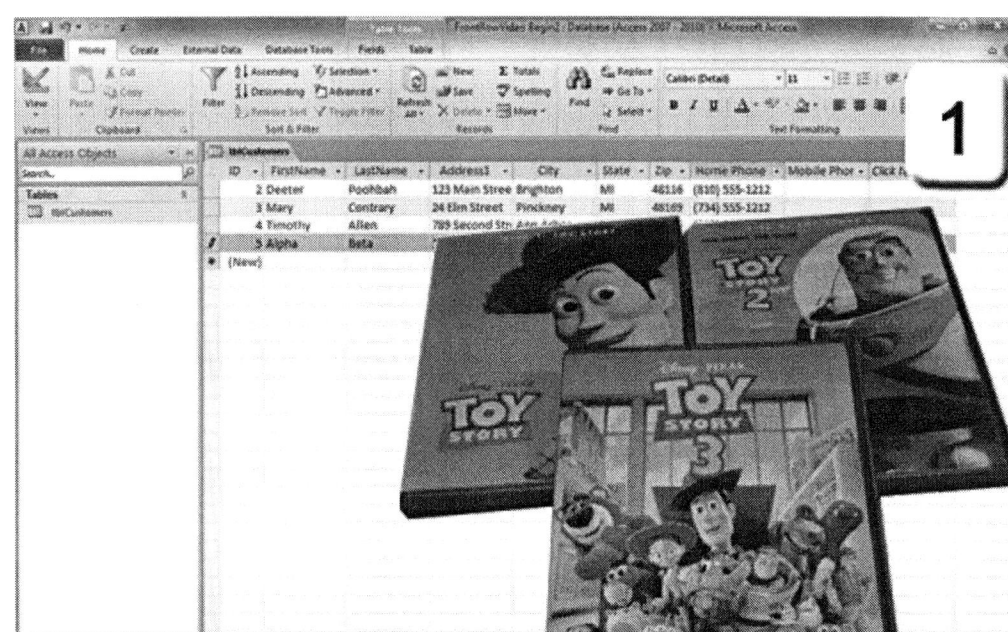

tblCustomers

Cust •	FirstName •	LastName •	Address1 •	City •	State •	Zip •	Home Phone •
2	Deeter	Poohbah	123 Main Stree	Brighton	MI	48116	(810) 555-1212
3	Mary	Contrary	24 Elm Street	Pinckney	MI	48169	(734) 555-1212
4	Timothy	Allen	789 Second Str	Ann Arbor	MI	48103	(313) 555-1212
5	Alpha	Beta	123 Practice Str	MyTown	MI	48103	(810) 231-3211
* (New)					MI		

Look For Clues in the Design

2. Try it: Return to the Design View
Go to **Home ->Views->View**.
Select a View: **Design View**.

Try This, Too: Find the Primary Key
Select a Field: ID

What Do You See? The ID Field is different from the Text Fields we have been editing.

This is the **Primary Key**. The Primary Key uniquely identifies each record. It is an Integer, a Whole Number.

A Primary Key cannot be empty, or null. The value entered for the Primary Key cannot be duplicated.

Home ->Views->View->Design View

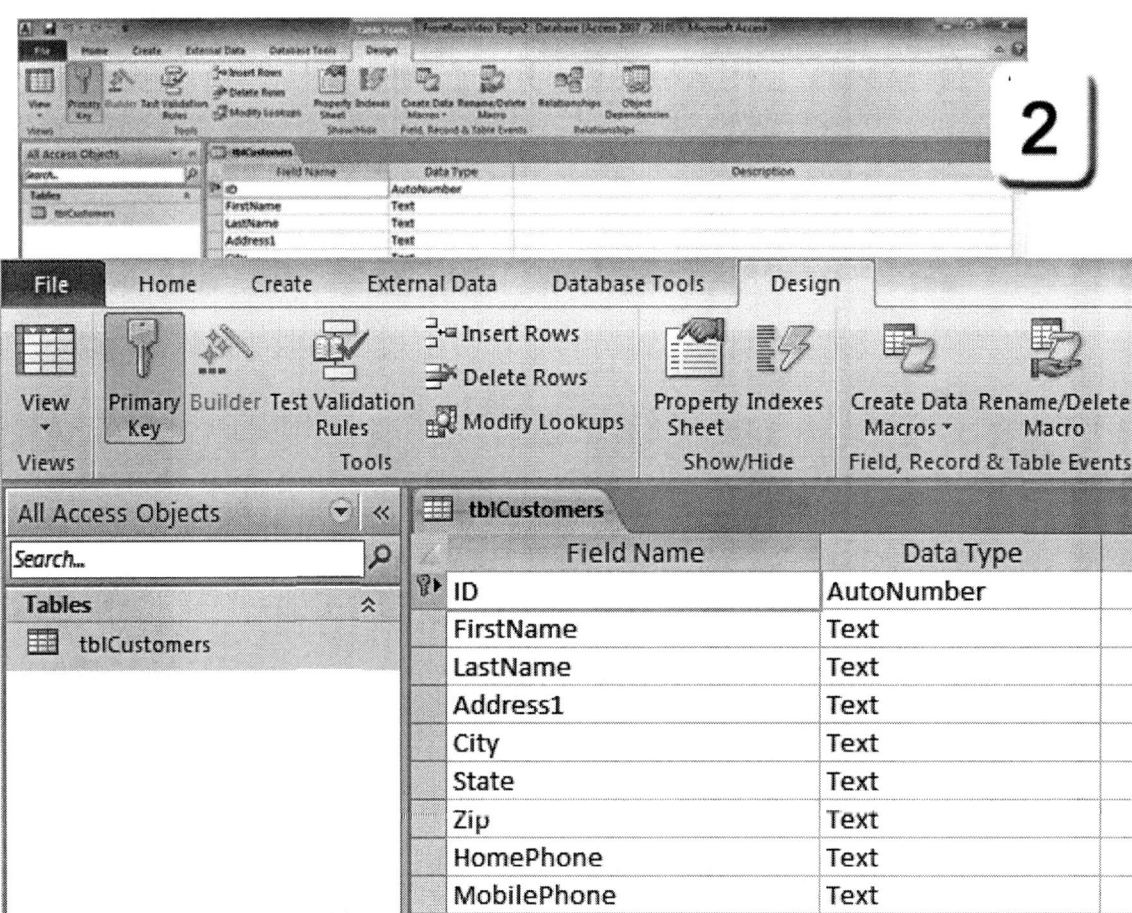

Exam 77-885: Microsoft Access 2010
2. Building Tables
2.1.1. Create tables in Design View

The Primary Key

Some organizations use a special numbering system. For example, many medical databases use the Social Security number to identify their patients. Each of us has our own unique, social security number. However, there are identity and security concerns about using SS numbers.

In Microsoft Access the **Primary Key** should be an AutoNumber. As you add new records, Access will use the next number automatically.

Databases crunch numbers quickly. If the Primary Key is text, such as a social security number, then each character must be evaluated by the database one at a time. This process is slow.

3. Try it: Review the Field Properties
tblCustomers is still open in **Design View**.
The **Table Tools** are available.
Select the first Field: ID

What Do You See? The ID Field is indentified with a Key. It is Indexed (No duplicates.) It is also an AutoNumber. Keep going, please.

Table Tools->Design->Tools->Primary Key

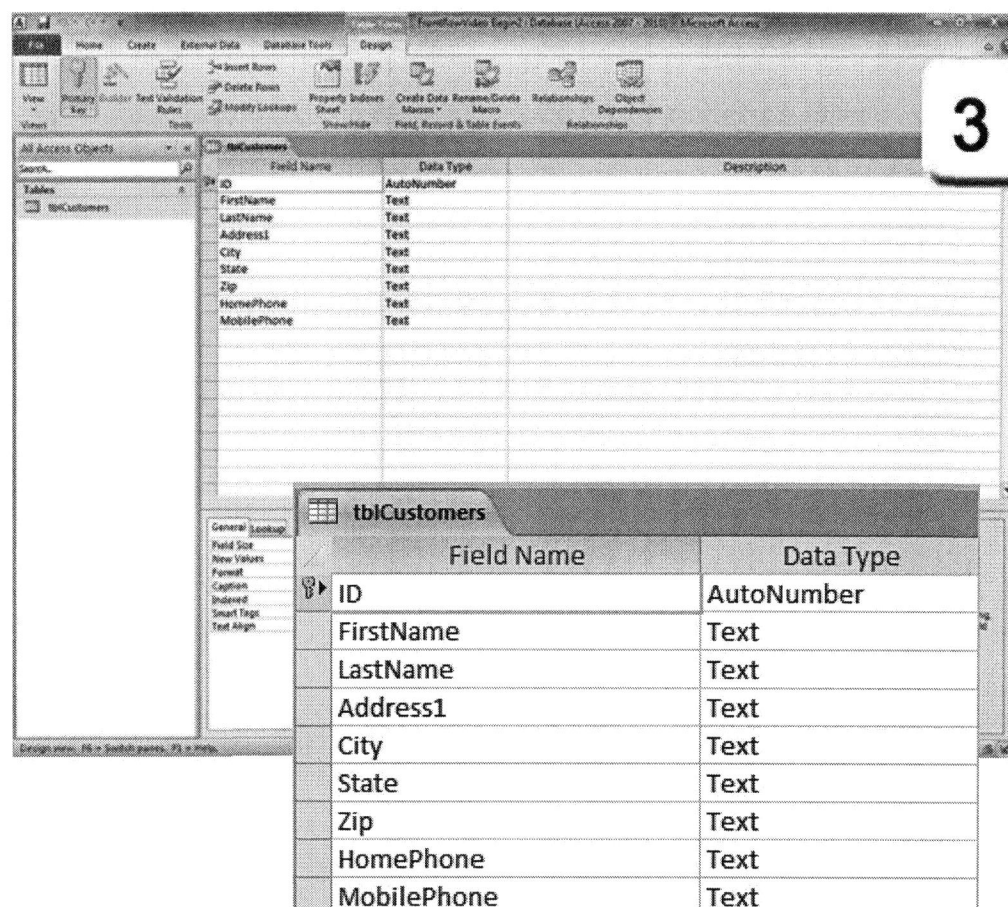

Field Name	Data Type
ID	AutoNumber
FirstName	Text
LastName	Text
Address1	Text
City	Text
State	Text
Zip	Text
HomePhone	Text
MobilePhone	Text

Exam 77-885: Microsoft Access 2010
2. Building Tables
2.4.1. Set Relationships: Define Primary Keys

Primary Key Properties

The definition of a Primary Key can be seen in the Field Properties at the bottom of the Table Design window.

4. Try it: Review the Field Properties

Field Size: Long Integer, a whole number* for counting.
New Values: Increment
Index: Yes (No Duplicates)

So, when a record is deleted from the Table, it is deleted permanently by design and by default in an Access database. The ID number is deleted as well. It cannot be reassigned to another customer or product.

Keep going...

* The Computer Mama sez: Last time we looked, we only had whole customers, although some may be half crazy. Others may be totally crazy.

Table Tools->Design->Tools->Primary Key

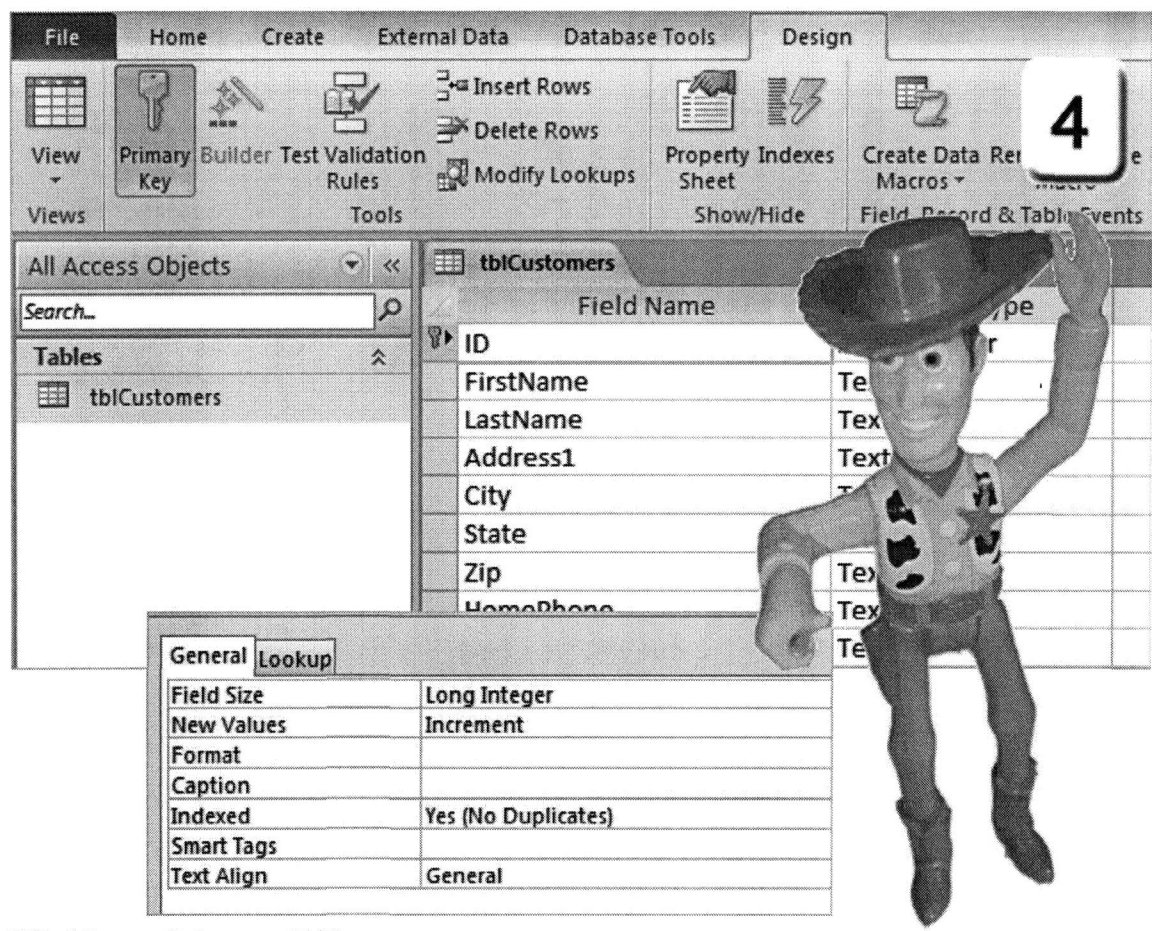

Exam 77-885: Microsoft Access 2010
2. Building Tables
2.4.1. Set Relationships: Define Primary Keys

Rename the Primary Key

The Primary Key creates unique numbers that are indexed (no duplicates). The Primary Key should have a unique name. By default, Microsoft Access just enters "ID" for the Field Name. We can do better.

5. Try it: Rename the Primary Key
Select the Field: ID
Edit the Field Name: CustomerID

Try this, Too: Save the Table
Go to **File->Save**.

Done and done. Keep going...

Memo to Self: Naming should conform to rules. The Primary Key Field Name should match the type of content the little Table stores. For example, CustomerID is the Primary Key for the customer Table, tblCustomers.

5

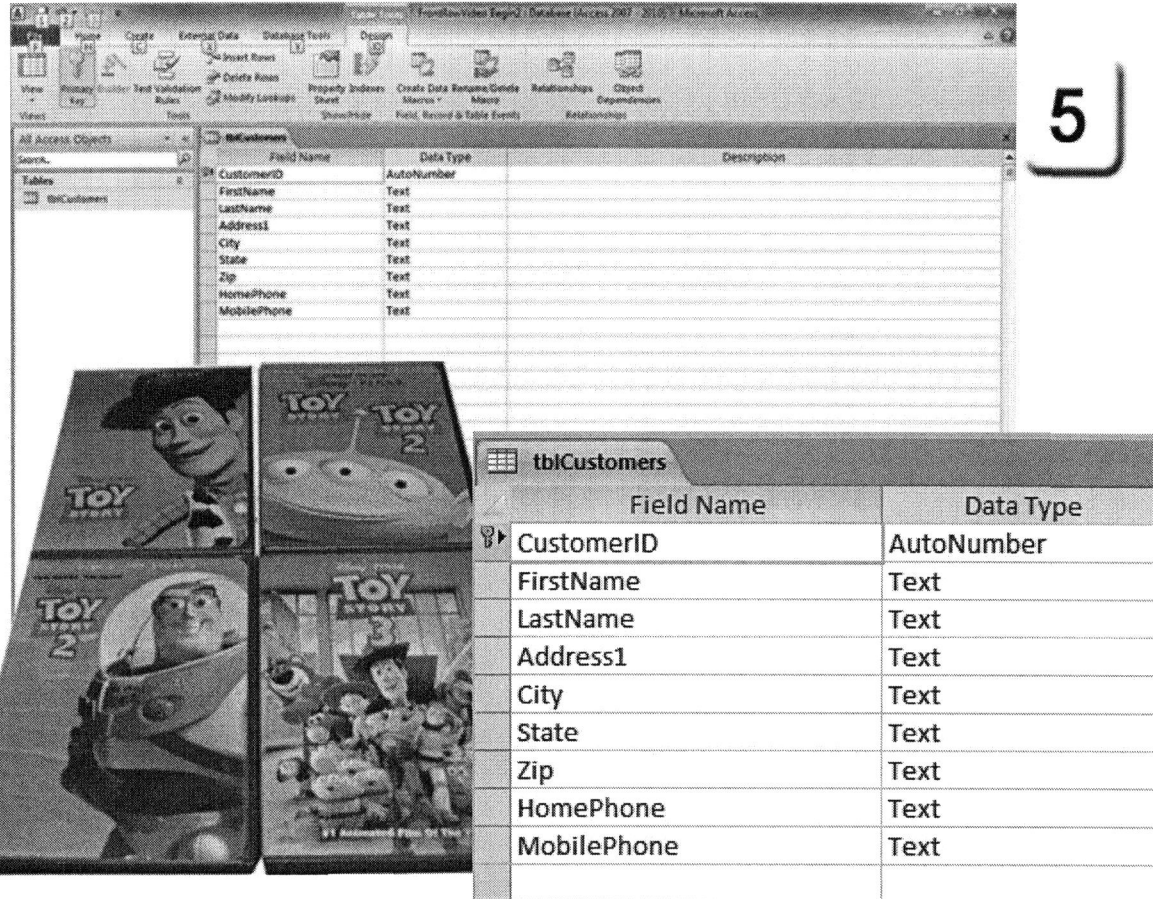

Field Name	Data Type
CustomerID	AutoNumber
FirstName	Text
LastName	Text
Address1	Text
City	Text
State	Text
Zip	Text
HomePhone	Text
MobilePhone	Text

Exam 77-885: Microsoft Access 2010
2. Building Tables
2.4.1. Set Relationships: Define Primary Keys

Summary: Table Design

This discussion introduced the Table Design View. We modified the Field Properties to fit the data and the user's needs. The Default Value for the State simplifies data entry and the Input Mask for the Phone field fills in the punctuation.

The introduction of the **Primary Key** is the most important concept in this lesson. All databases use the Primary Key to keep track of unique values.

Allez Allez in free. You done good. You get the cookie.

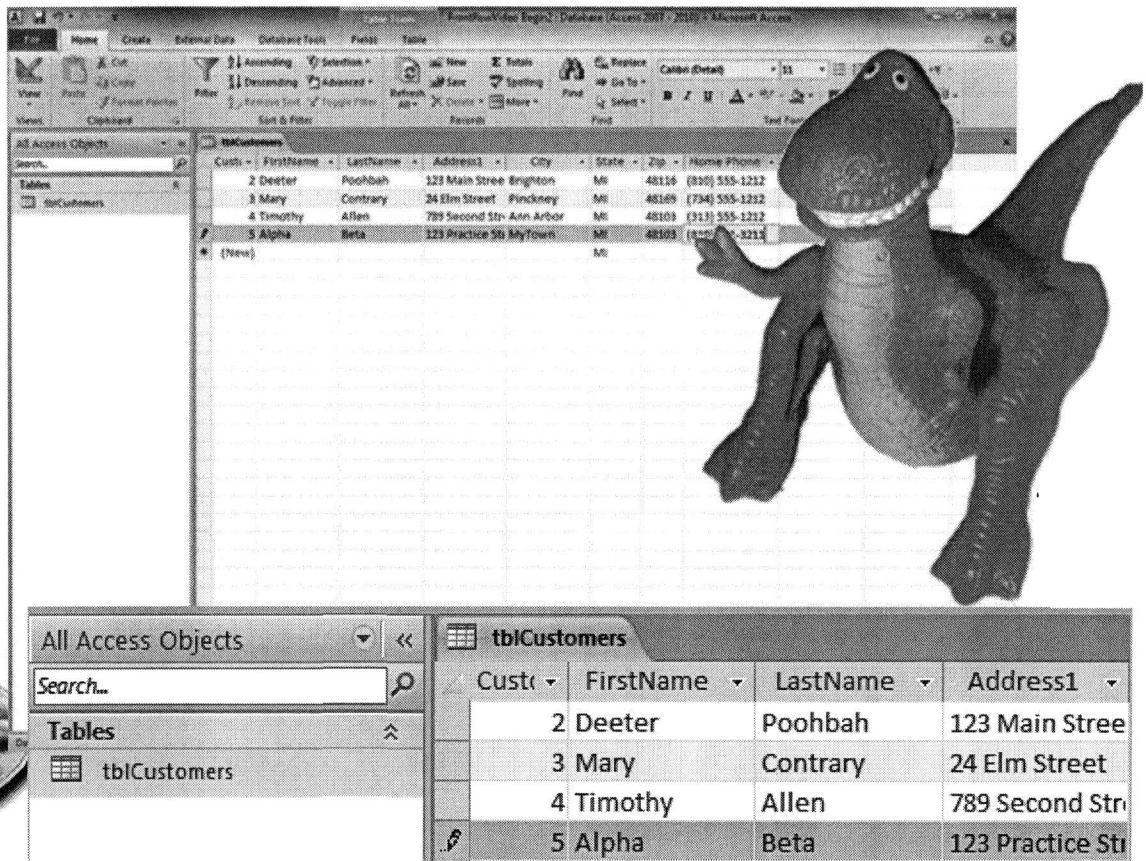

Cust⌄	FirstName ⌄	LastName ⌄	Address1 ⌄
2	Deeter	Poohbah	123 Main Stree
3	Mary	Contrary	24 Elm Street
4	Timothy	Allen	789 Second Str
5	Alpha	Beta	123 Practice St
* (New)			

All Access Objects

Search...

Tables

tblCustomers

Practice Activities

Lesson 3: Table Design

Try This: Do the following steps

1. Open the Brown Bag Lunch database you have been programming.
Or you may download the sample database **Brown Bag Lunch ver3.accdb** online.

1. Go to **All Access Objects->Tables**.

2. Open tblCustomers in Design View.

3. Apply an Input Mask to the Phone Field.

Use the phone number input mask, with asterisks (*) for the placeholder. Also store the data without symbols.

4. Set a default value for the State column. Enter MI for the default value.

5. Rename the Primary Key as CustomerID.

6. Save tblCustomers.

7. Return to the Datasheet View and add the following customer data to the Table.

Check that the Input Mask and Default Value work.

Company	FirstName	LastName	Address	City	State	Zip	Phone
Buzz Luv Marketing	Daryl	McGuire	4456 Wixom Road	Wixom	MI	48393	810-555-4793
Wire Spin Network Solutions	Selena	Sullivan	5575 Novi Road	Novi	MI	48374	517-555-5486
Moon Labs Gaming	Chester	Morrison	8945 W. Twelve Mile Road	Novi	MI	48374	248-555-7511

8. Close the Brown Bag Lunch database.

Test Yourself

1. Which are Table Views?
(Give all correct answers)
A. PivotTable View
B. Datasheet View
C. Design View
D. Normal View
Tip: Beginning Access, page 58

2. Which are available Input Masks?
(Give all correct answers.)
A. Phone
B. Social Security Number
C. Zip Code
D. Extension
E. Password
F. Time
G. Dates
Tip: Beginning Access, page 61

3. What does clicking the pencil icon on a Record do?
A. Opens the Record for editing
B. Saves the Record
C. Selects the Record
Tip: Beginning Access, page 66

4. Which is true about the Primary Key?
(Give all correct answers.)
A. Uniquely identifies each record
B. It is an Integer, a whole number
C. It cannot be empty or null
D. The value entered for the Primary Key cannot be duplicated
Tip: Beginning Access, page 68

5. When a Record is deleted from Access, the ID number is also permanently deleted and can never be reassigned.
A. True
B. False
Tip: Beginning Access, page 70

Access 2010: Working with Data

More Data, More Tables

Beginning Access Objectives
In this lesson, you will learn how to:

1. Import a Microsoft Excel spreadsheet into a new Table in an Access database.

2. Use the Design View to edit the Field Properties.

3. Sort and Filter Records in Access.

© 2012 Comma Productions, LLC

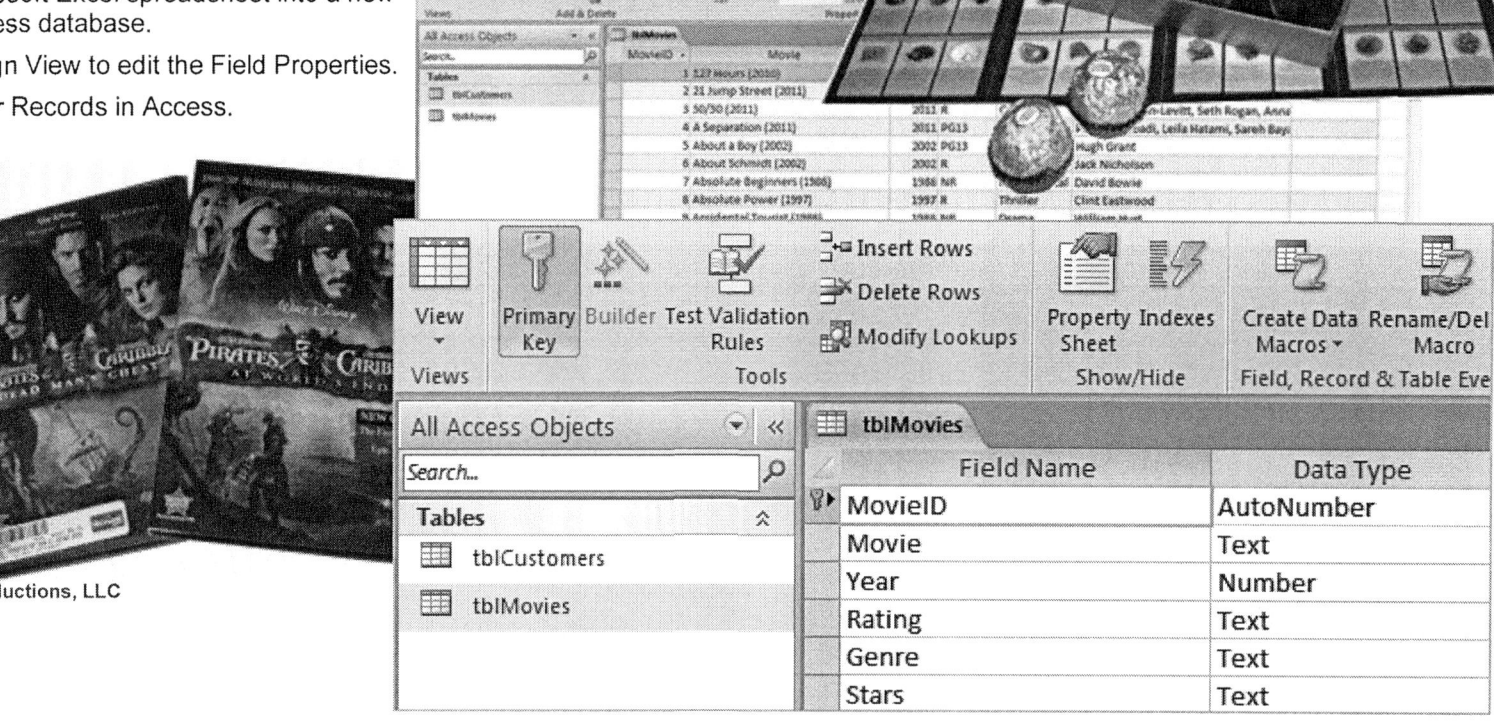

Lesson 4 : More Data, More Tables

1. Readings
Read Lesson 4 in the Beginning Access guide, page 75-99.

Project
Import an Excel spreadsheet into Microsoft Access. Create and modify a product table.

Downloads
FrontRowVideo Begin4.accdb.
tblMovies.xlsx.
Brown Bag Lunch ver4.accdb
Brown Bag Products.xlsx

2. Practice
Complete Practice Activity on page 100.

3. Assessment
Review the Test questions on page 100.

The External Data Ribbon

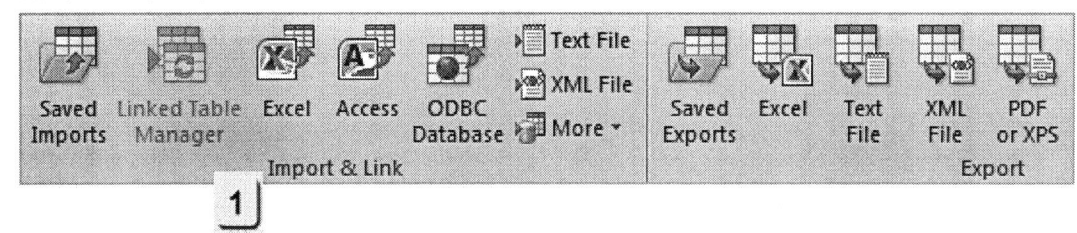

The Home Ribbon (continued)

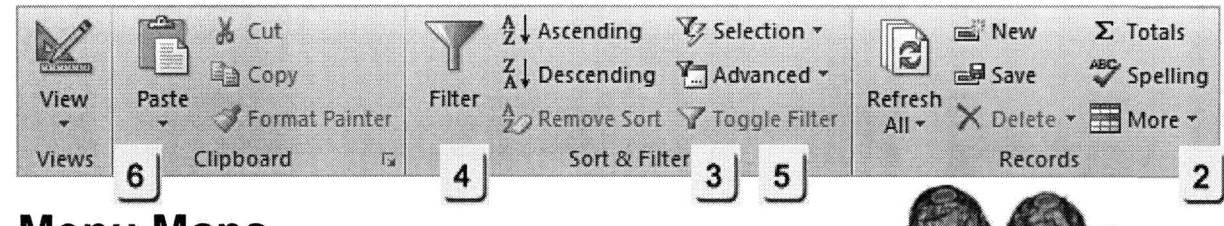

Menu Maps
From the **External Data Ribbon**.
1. External Data ->Import & Link->Excel, page 85

From the **Home Ribbon**.
2. Home ->Find ->Find, page 93
3. Home ->Sort & Filter-> Descending, page 94
4. Home ->Sort & Filter-> Filter, page 95
5. Home ->Sort & Filter-> Selection, page 96
6. Home ->Views->View->Design View, page 97

More Data, More Tables

The information that we need for the Front Row Video database is in Microsoft Excel. It is a spreadsheet with hundreds of movie titles. The information includes the name of the movie, the year the movie was released, and even the rating. Question: how do we get the data from here to there? The answer is rather easy: there is a Wizard that will guide you through the process of selecting and importing the spreadsheet data into a new Microsoft Access table.

Top: Microsoft Excel, Bottom: Microsoft Access

	A	B	C	D	
1	Movie	Year	Rating	Genre	Stars
2	127 Hours (2010)	2010	R	Drama	James Franco, A
3	21 Jump Street (2011)	2012	R	Action	Jonah Hill, Char
4	50/50 (2011)	2011	R	Comedy	Joseph Gordon-
5	A Separation (2011)	2011	PG13	Drama	Peyman Moadi,
6	About a Boy (2002)	2002	PG13	Comedy	Hugh Grant
					Jack Nicholson
					David

All Access Objects

Search...

Tables

- tblCustomers
- tblMovies

tblMovies

MovieID	Movie	Year
1	127 Hours (2010)	2010
2	21 Jump Street (2011)	2012
3	50/50 (2011)	2011
4	A Separation (2011)	2011
5	About a Boy (2002)	2002
6	About Schmidt (2002)	2002
7	Absolute Beginners (1986)	1986

Before You Begin

We will begin by reviewing the information in the Microsoft Excel spreadsheet. It is useful to see the original data so that you can compare it with the data after it is imported into a Microsoft Access table.

1. Try it: Download the Sample File
Go online to this course.
Go to the Downloads.
Find the sample file: **tblMovies.xlsx**.

Right click the sample spreadsheet.
Select: **Save** (not Open!)

Browse to your Documents Folder
Save, Save, **Save**!

Keep going...

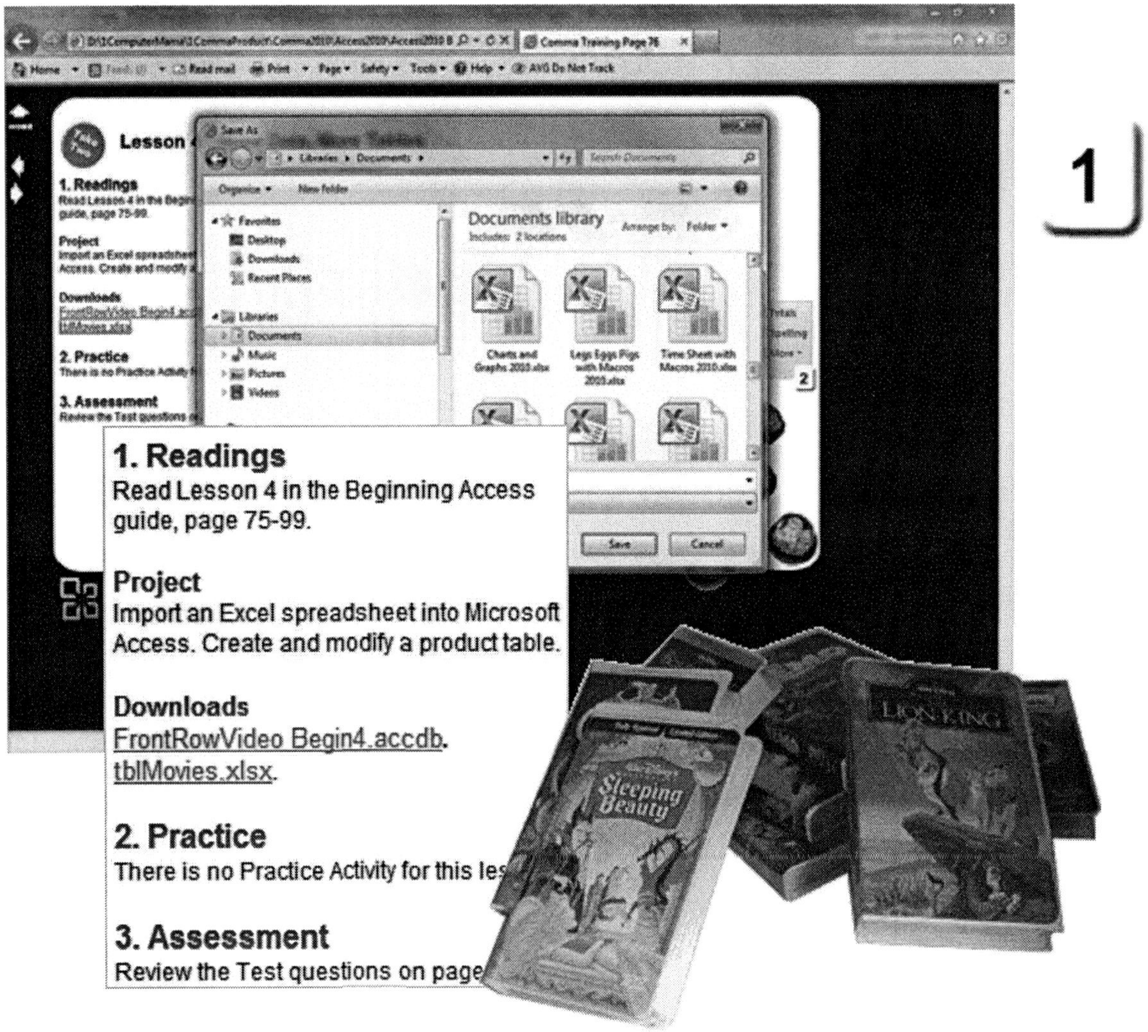

1. Readings
Read Lesson 4 in the Beginning Access guide, page 75-99.

Project
Import an Excel spreadsheet into Microsoft Access. Create and modify a product table.

Downloads
FrontRowVideo Begin4.accdb.
tblMovies.xlsx.

2. Practice
There is no Practice Activity for this les

3. Assessment
Review the Test questions on page

Review the Product Data

2. Try it: Review the Product Data
Go to the Documents folder.
Open the spreadsheet: **tblMovies.xlsx**.

What Do You See? This spreadsheet has the product data. It is a list of movies that is sorted alphabetically on Column A, the name of the movie. The first Row is the Header Row. The labels are Bold and each one has a Filter.

Keep going...

Microsoft Excel 2010

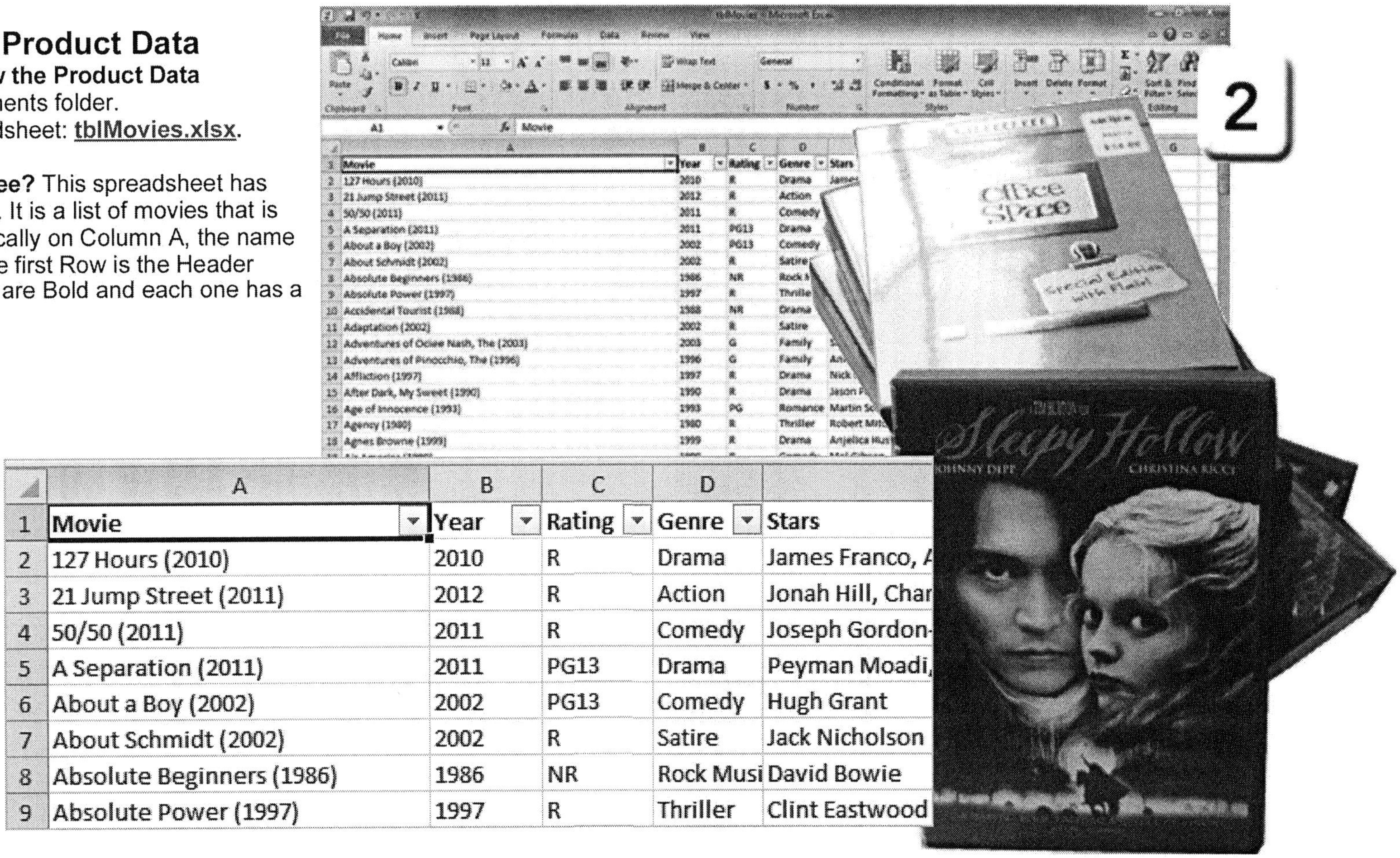

	A	B	C	D	
1	Movie	Year	Rating	Genre	Stars
2	127 Hours (2010)	2010	R	Drama	James Franco, A
3	21 Jump Street (2011)	2012	R	Action	Jonah Hill, Char
4	50/50 (2011)	2011	R	Comedy	Joseph Gordon-
5	A Separation (2011)	2011	PG13	Drama	Peyman Moadi,
6	About a Boy (2002)	2002	PG13	Comedy	Hugh Grant
7	About Schmidt (2002)	2002	R	Satire	Jack Nicholson
8	Absolute Beginners (1986)	1986	NR	Rock Musi	David Bowie
9	Absolute Power (1997)	1997	R	Thriller	Clint Eastwood

Home ->Editing-> Find & Select->Find

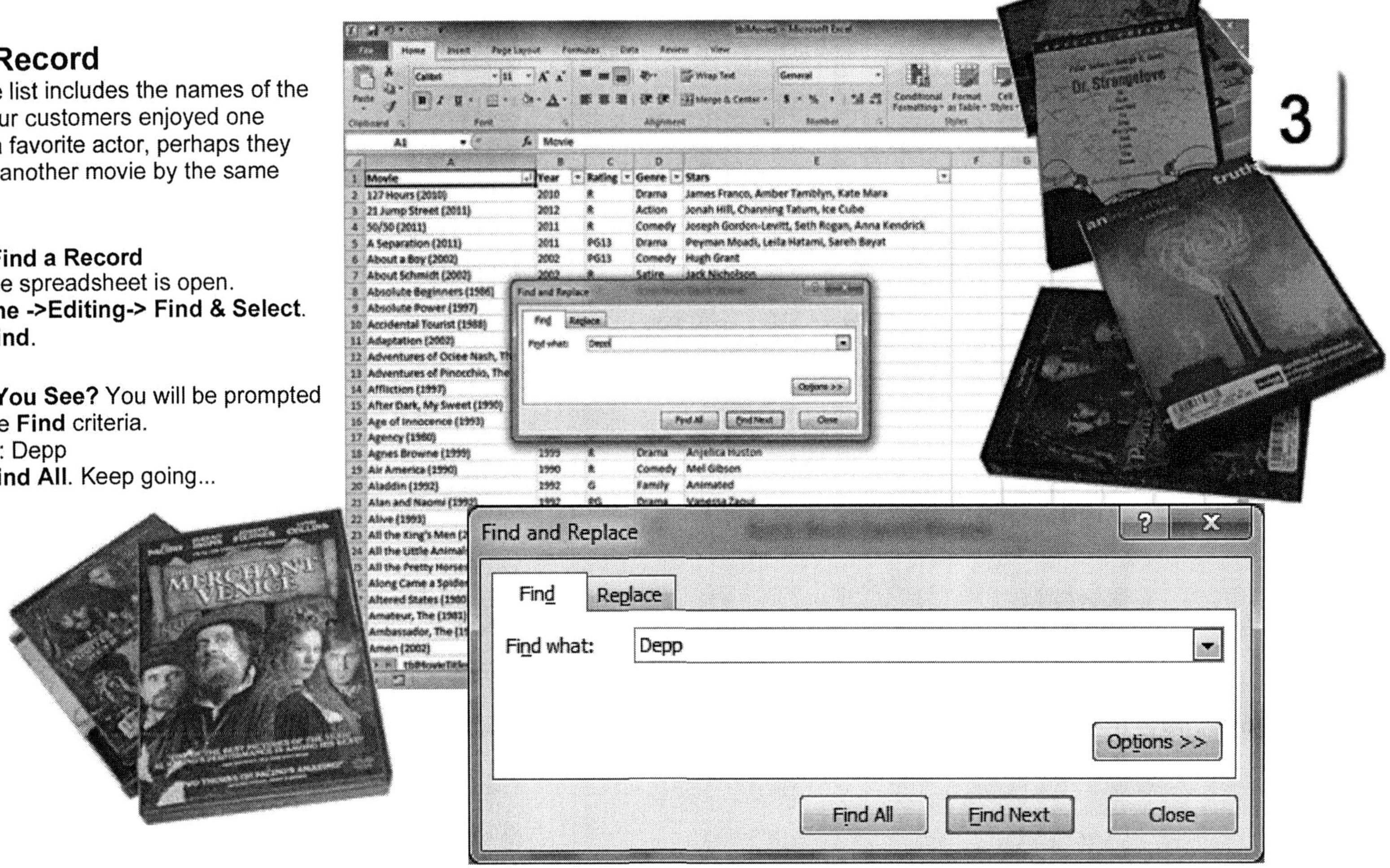

Find a Record

This movie list includes the names of the stars. If your customers enjoyed one movie by a favorite actor, perhaps they would like another movie by the same actor.

3. Try it: Find a Record
The sample spreadsheet is open.
Go to **Home ->Editing-> Find & Select**.
Click on **Find**.

What Do You See? You will be prompted to enter the **Find** criteria.
Find What: Depp
Click on **Find All**. Keep going...

Find and Replace

| Find | Replace |

Find what: Depp

Options >>

Find All   Find Next   Close

Find All, Find Next
This list has 10 movies that have Johnny Depp as one of the Stars.

4. Try it: Review the Results
Go to results and select one.
Microsoft Excel will highlight the Cell that includes "Depp" in the Value.

Keep going...

Home ->Editing-> Find & Select->Find

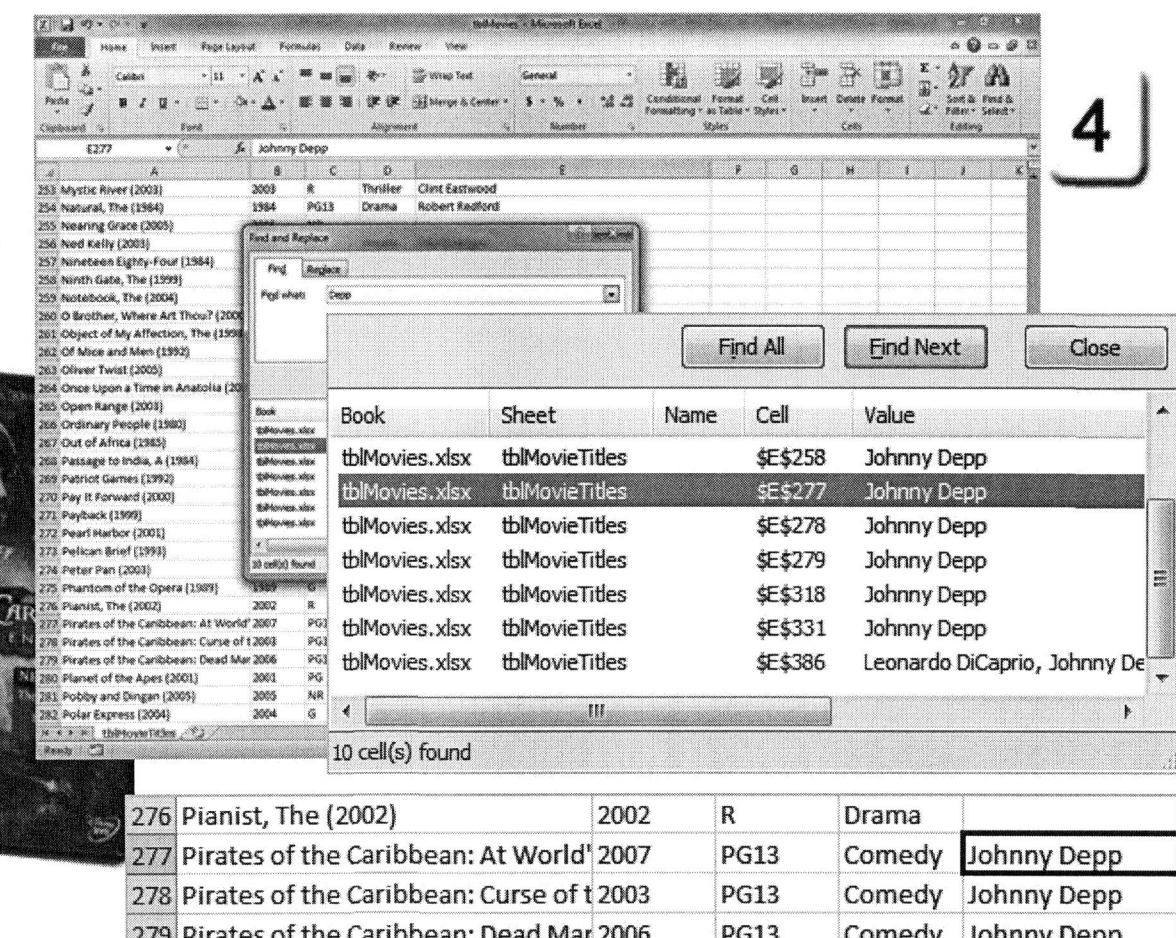

Book	Sheet	Name	Cell	Value
tblMovies.xlsx	tblMovieTitles		E258	Johnny Depp
tblMovies.xlsx	tblMovieTitles		E277	Johnny Depp
tblMovies.xlsx	tblMovieTitles		E278	Johnny Depp
tblMovies.xlsx	tblMovieTitles		E279	Johnny Depp
tblMovies.xlsx	tblMovieTitles		E318	Johnny Depp
tblMovies.xlsx	tblMovieTitles		E331	Johnny Depp
tblMovies.xlsx	tblMovieTitles		E386	Leonardo DiCaprio, Johnny De

10 cell(s) found

276	Pianist, The (2002)	2002	R	Drama	
277	Pirates of the Caribbean: At World'	2007	PG13	Comedy	Johnny Depp
278	Pirates of the Caribbean: Curse of t	2003	PG13	Comedy	Johnny Depp
279	Pirates of the Caribbean: Dead Mar	2006	PG13	Comedy	Johnny Depp

Sort the Data

Microsoft Excel has data tools to analyze data. What does our product inventory look like? How many movies are new?

5. Try it: Sort the Data
Select the entire spreadsheet.
Go to **Data ->Sort & Filter->Sort.**

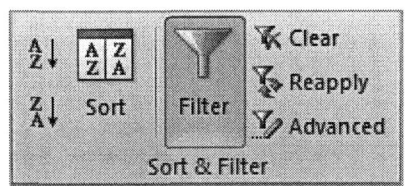

What Do You See? You will be prompted to select the **Sort** criteria.
Sort by: Year
Sort on: Values
Order: Largest to Smallest

Click **OK**. Keep going...

Data ->Sort & Filter->Sort

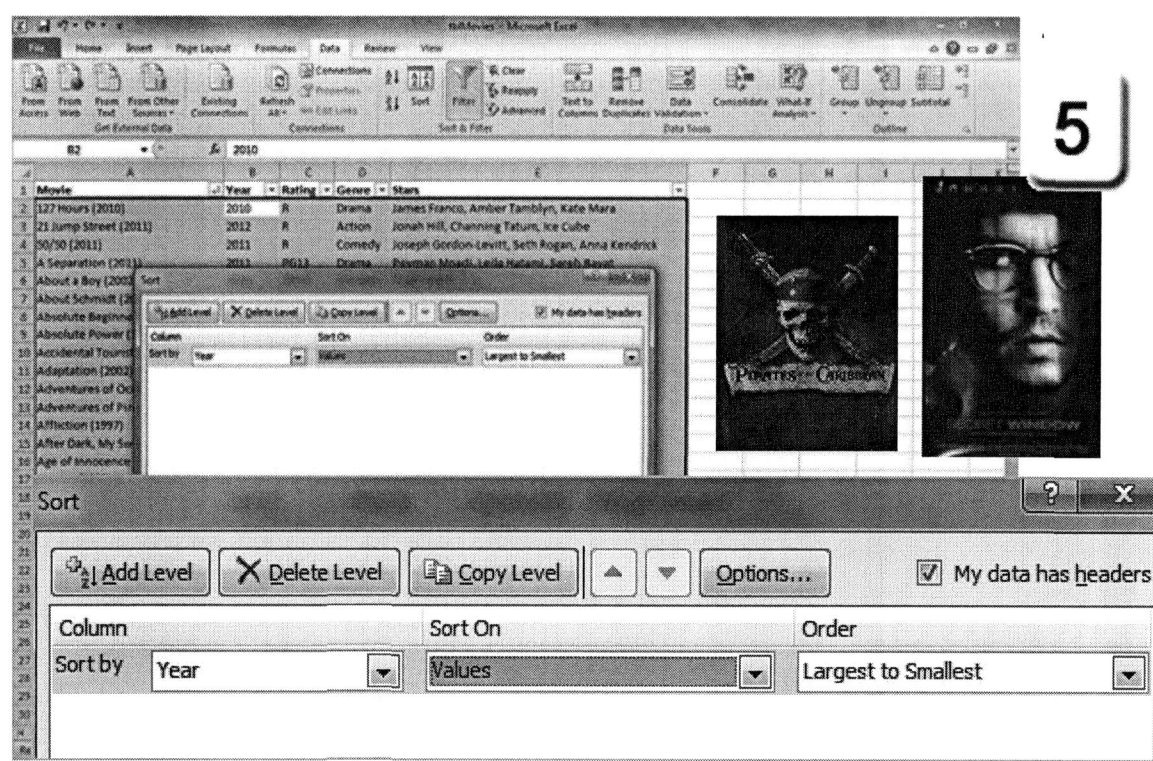

Exam 77-882: Microsoft Excel 2010 Core
8. Analyzing and Organizing Data
8.2. Sort data

Filter the Data

Each field in the Header Row has a Filter. You can use the filters to show the records that meet your criteria, say only the new movies released in 2012.

6. Try it: Filter the Data

The sample spreadsheet is open.
Go to Cell B1: Year.
Click on Filter.
Clear all of the check marks EXCEPT: 2012

What Do You See? There are three movies in this list that were released in 2012. The filter Hides the other movies that do not match the criteria for the year.

Try This, Too: Remove the Filters
Go to **Data ->Sort & Filter->Filter**
The Filters should be gone.

Do This: Save the Spreadsheet.
Go to **File->Save**.
Close Microsoft Excel, please.

Let's start our work with Microsoft Access.

Data ->Sort & Filter->Filter

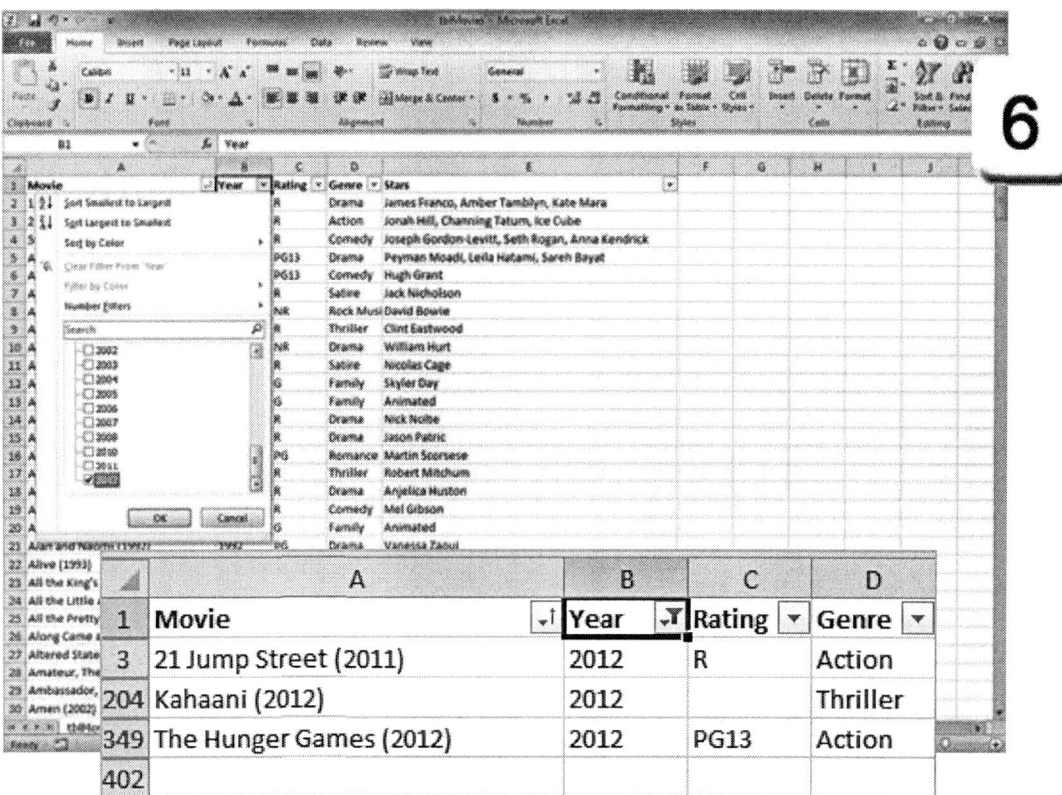

	A	B	C	D
1	Movie	Year	Rating	Genre
3	21 Jump Street (2011)	2012	R	Action
204	Kahaani (2012)	2012		Thriller
349	The Hunger Games (2012)	2012	PG13	Action
402				

Exam 77-882: Microsoft Excel 2010 Core
8. Analyzing and Organizing Data
8.2. Sort data

Take Two

Microsoft Access

Start Microsoft Access
This demonstration uses the Front Row Video database that was created in the previous lesson. You can open the mighty Access database that you programmed or download the sample database if you wish.

1. Try it: Open the Sample Database
Go to the Documents folder.
Open the sample database:
FrontRowVideo Begin4.accdb.

What Do You See? There is one Table.
Go to **All Access Objects->Tables.**
Double click to open tblCustomers.

What Do You See Now: tblCustomers has four Records.

Click the small "X" to the far right of the tab that says tblCustomers to **Close** the Table.

Keep going...

ONE TASTE IS ALL IT TAKES

Chocolat

File	Home	Create	External Data	Database Tools	Fields

Views — View, Paste — Cut, Copy, Format Painter — Clipboard

Filter — Ascending, Descending, Remove Sort — Selection, Advanced, Toggle Filter — Sort & Filter

All Access Objects

Search...

Tables

tblCustomers

Cust	FirstName	LastName
2	Deeter	Poohbah
3	Mary	Contrary
4	Timothy	Allen
5	Alpha	Beta
* (New)		

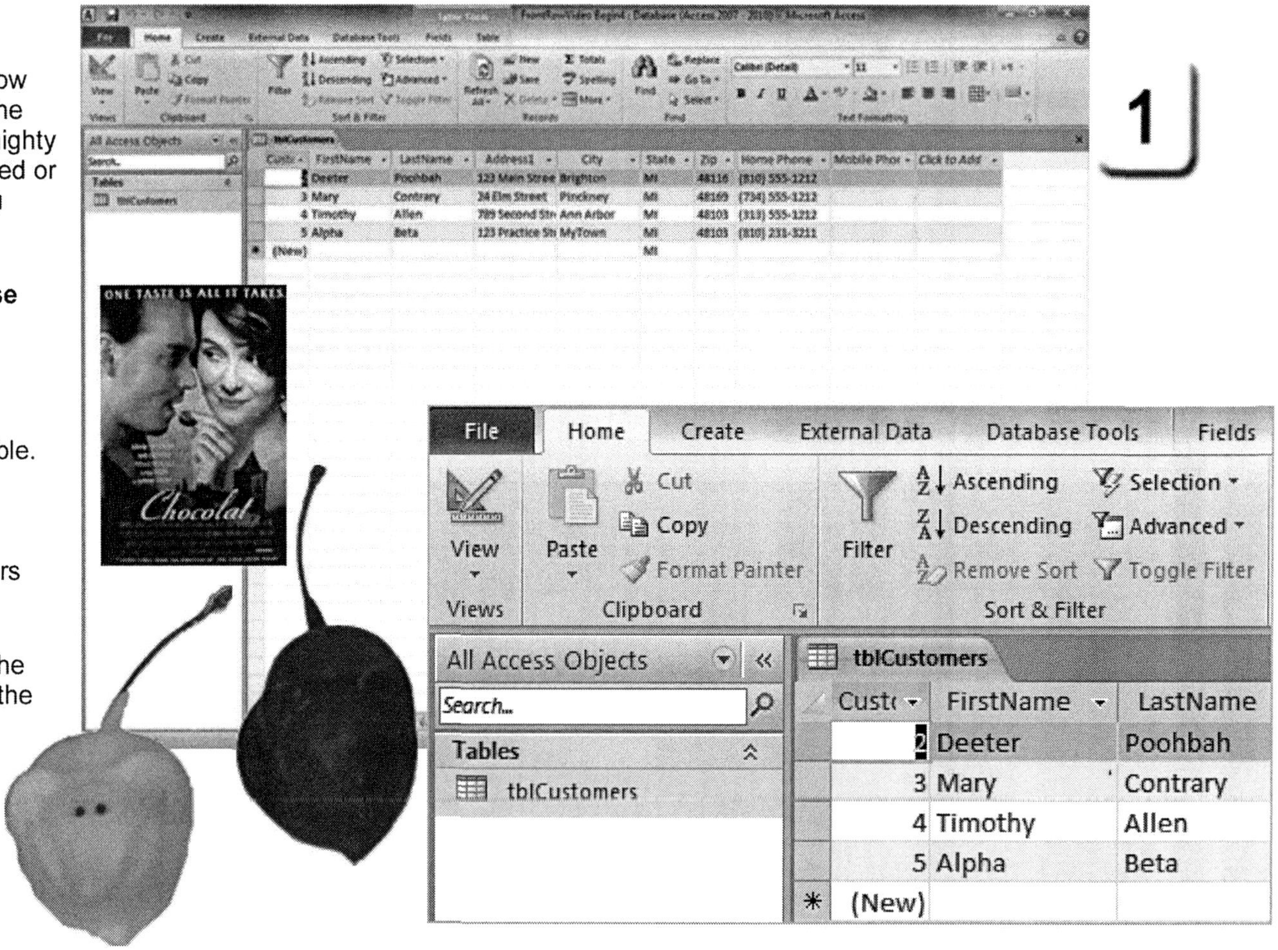

Get External Data

Microsoft Access can import records from almost any data source including big IBM mainframe systems and small QuickBooks financial records. Of course, Microsoft Access can import data from Excel.

2. Try it: Get External Data
The sample database is open.
Go to **External Data ->Import & Link.**
Click on **Excel.**

There is a wizard that walks you through the process. Keep going...

External Data ->Import & Link->Excel

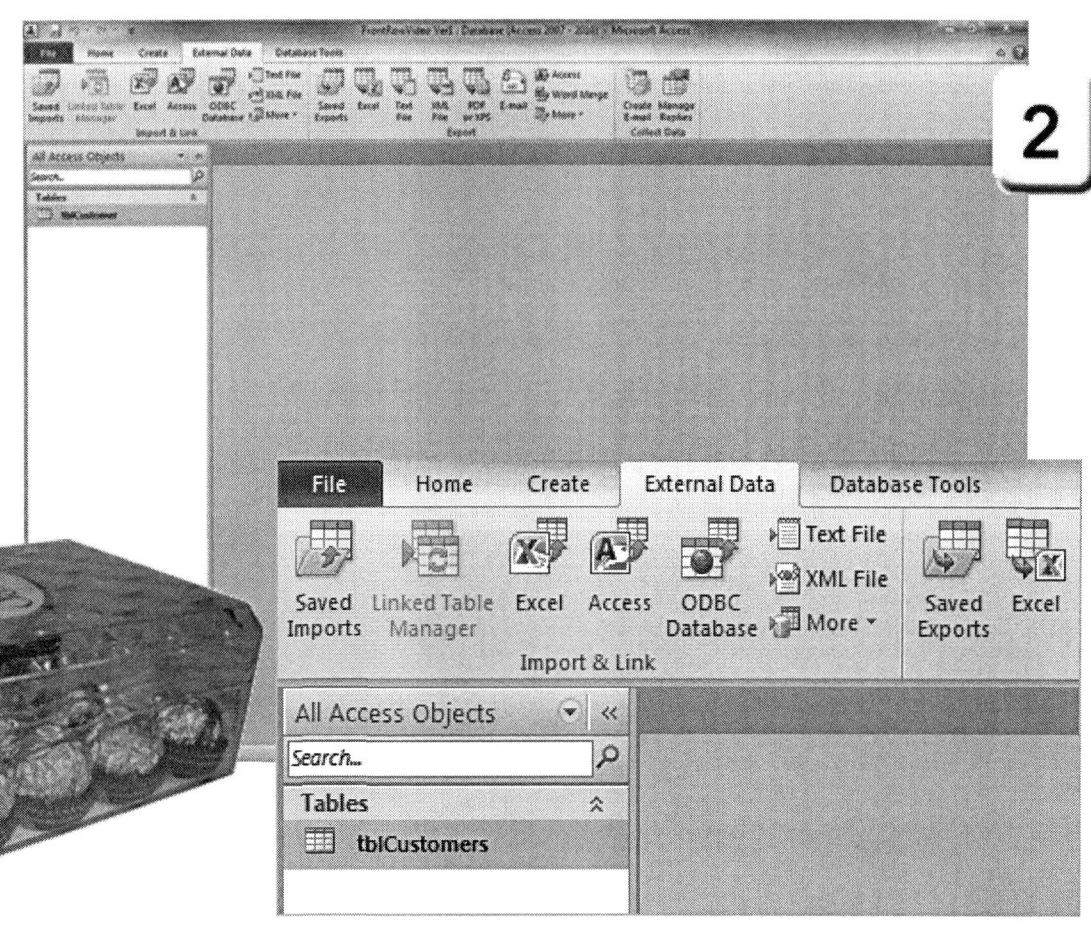

Exam 77-885: Microsoft Access 2010
2. Building Tables
2.5. Import data from a single data file: Import into a New Table

External Data ->Import & Link->Excel

External Data: Find the Source
The Import Wizard asks questions. The first step in the Wizard asks you to **find** the data that you wish to import. The Wizard also asks asks you where you would like to **store** the data in your current database.

3. Try it: Browse for the Data Source
The database is still open.
The Import Wizard is on step 1.
Place your cursor to the right of the File Name.
Browse to your Documents folder.
Select: tblMovies.xlsx

Try This, Too: Specify How to Store the Data
The three import options include:
Import into a new table
Append (add) records to a table
Link to an external table

Select: Import the source data into a new table.
Click **OK**. Keep going...

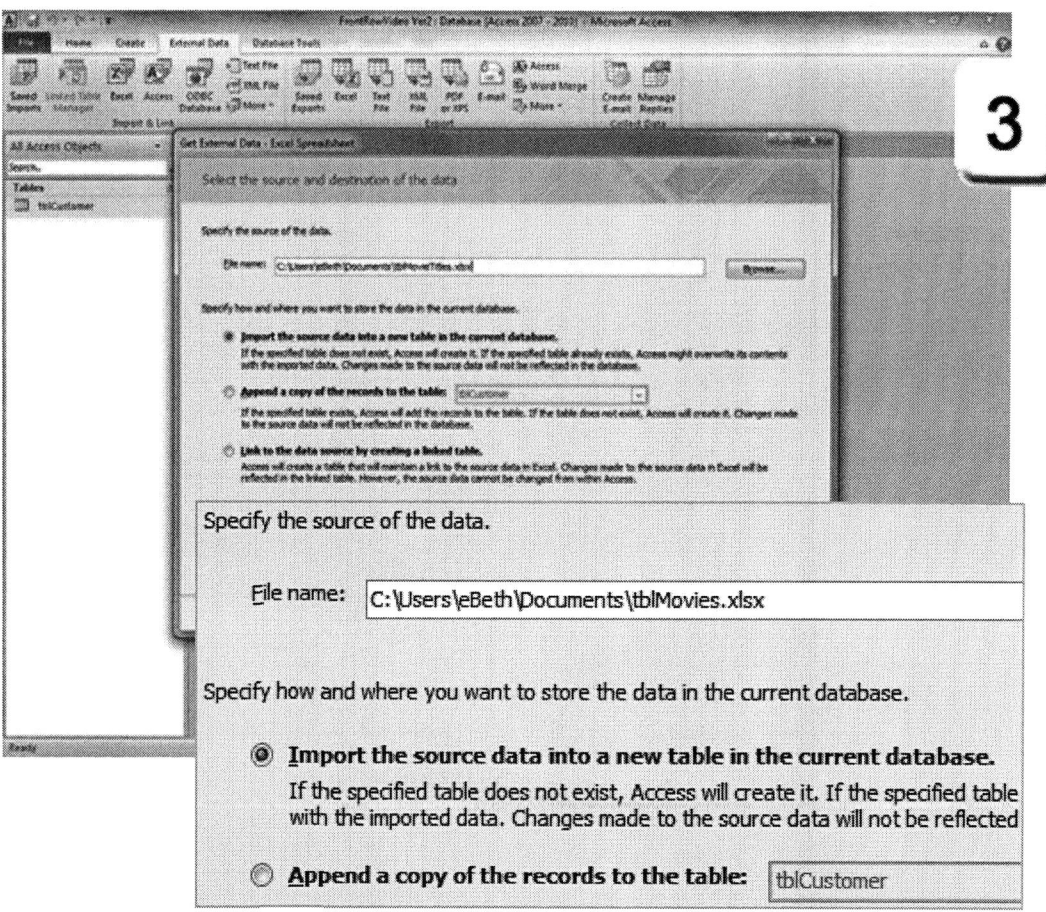

Exam 77-885: Microsoft Access 2010
2. Building Tables
2.5. Import data from a single data file: Import into a New Table

External Data: Show Worksheets

A spreadsheet may have many Worksheets or Named Ranges. The Wizard will ask you to select which **Worksheet** you wish to import.

4. Try it: Show the Worksheet
The database is still open.
The Import Wizard is on step 2.

There is one Worksheet and it is selected. The sample data is displayed below in the preview.

Click **Next**. Keep going...

External Data ->Import & Link->Excel

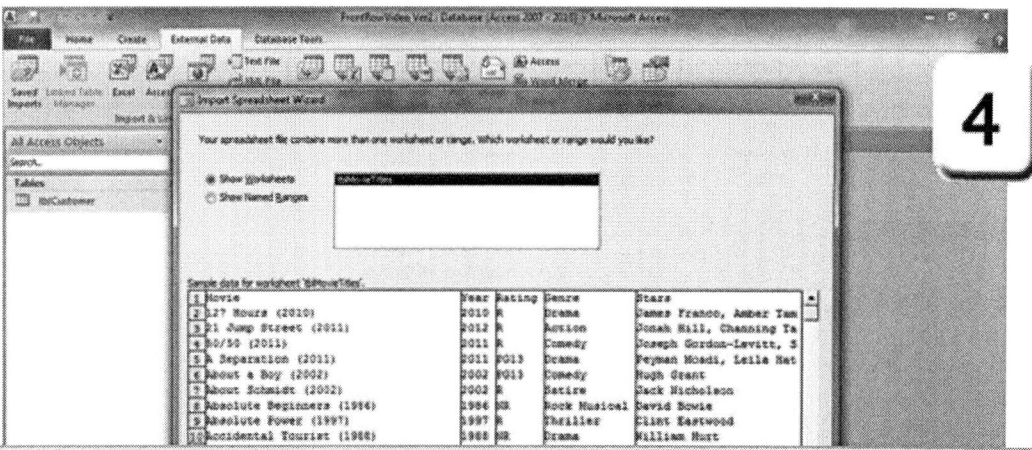

Your spreadsheet file contains more than one worksheet or range. Which worksheet or range would you like?

◉ Show <u>W</u>orksheets   tblMovieTitles
◯ Show Named <u>R</u>anges

Sample data for worksheet 'tblMovieTitles'.

1	Movie	Year	Rating	Genre	Stars
2	127 Hours (2010)	2010	R	Drama	James
3	21 Jump Street (2011)	2012	R	Action	Jonah

Exam 77-885: Microsoft Access 2010
2. Building Tables
2.5. Import data from a single data file: Import into a New Table

External Data ->Import & Link->Excel

External Data: Column Headings

This sample spreadsheet has a Header Row. The Header Row contains all of the data field names. This step lets you identify the **Column Headings**.

5. Try it: Use Column Headings for Field Names

The database is still open.
The Import Wizard is on step 3.
Select: First Row Contains Column Headings.

What Do You See? The first Row is now selected for the Field Names.

Click **Next**. Keep going...

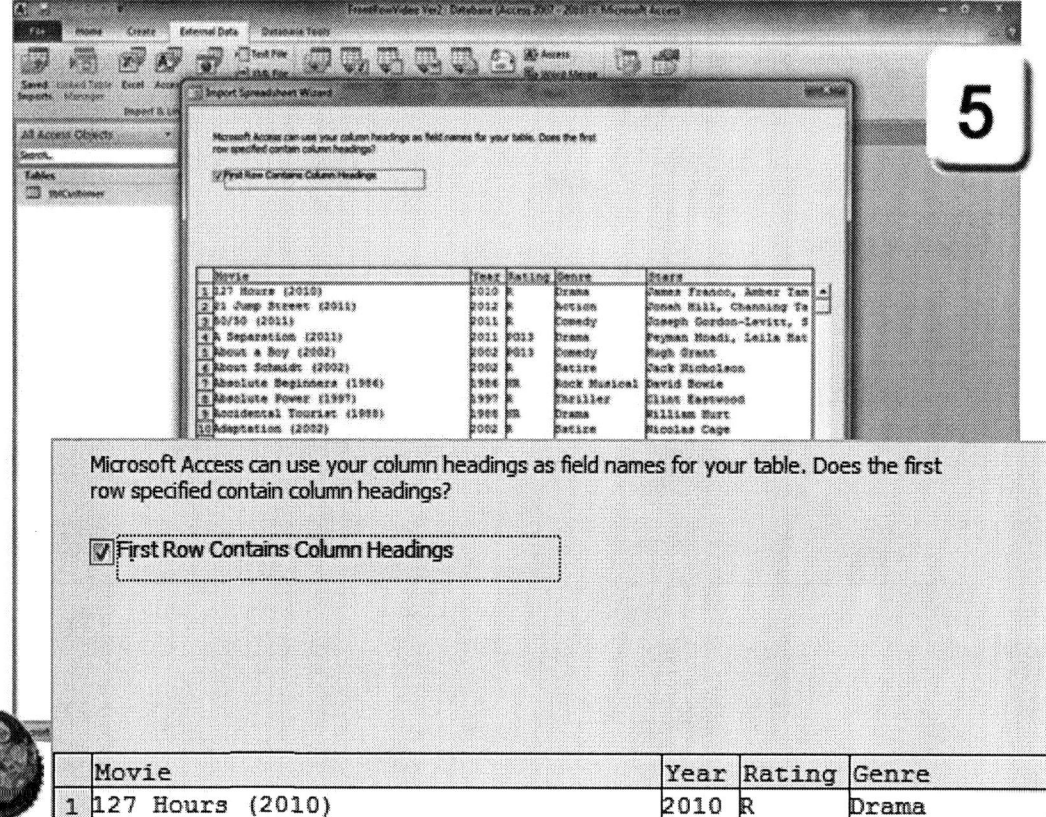

Microsoft Access can use your column headings as field names for your table. Does the first row specified contain column headings?

☑ First Row Contains Column Headings

	Movie	Year	Rating	Genre
1	127 Hours (2010)	2010	R	Drama
2	21 Jump Street (2011)	2012	R	Action
3	50/50 (2011)	2011	R	Comedy

Exam 77-885: Microsoft Access 2010
2. Building Tables
2.5. Import data from a single data file: Import into a New Table

External Data: Field Options

The Import Wizard will prompt you to review the **Field Options** for each Column in the spreadsheet.

6. Try it: Review the Field Options
The Import Wizard is on step 4.
The First Column, Movie, is selected.

What Do You See? The Field Options include:
File Name
Indexed: No (Duplicates are allowed)
Data Type: Text

Please accept the default answers for File Name, Indexed and Data Type.

Click **Next**. Keep going...

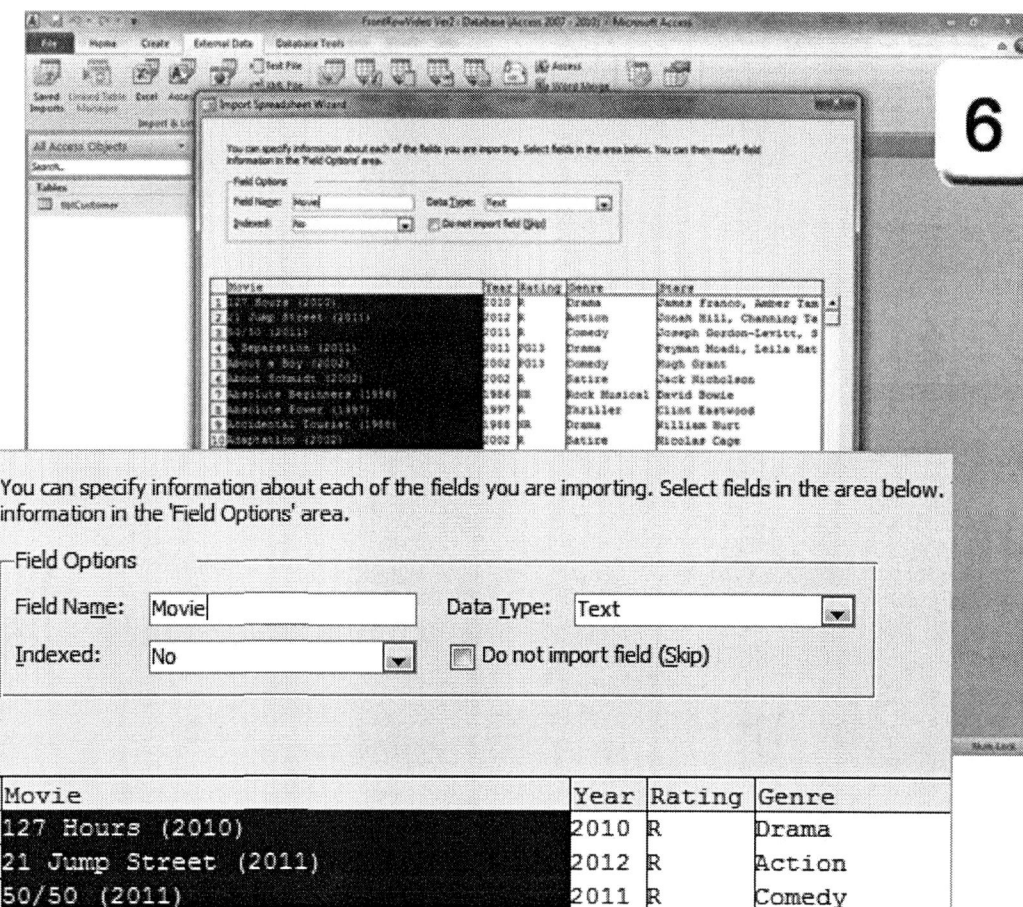

You can specify information about each of the fields you are importing. Select fields in the area below. information in the 'Field Options' area.

Field Options

| Field Name: | Movie | Data Type: | Text ▾ |
| Indexed: | No ▾ | ☐ Do not import field (Skip) |

	Movie	Year	Rating	Genre
1	127 Hours (2010)	2010	R	Drama
2	21 Jump Street (2011)	2012	R	Action
3	50/50 (2011)	2011	R	Comedy

Exam 77-885: Microsoft Access 2010
2. Building Tables
2.5. Import data from a single data file: Import into a New Table

External Data: Primary Key

The original data in the Excel spreadsheet did not have a unique number for each record. It is not indexed, yet. This step creates a **Primary Key**.

7. Try it: Create a Primary Key
The Import Wizard is on step 5.
There is a new First Column, ID.

What Do You See? The Import Wizard offers three choices for the Primary Key:
Let Access add primary key
Choose my own primary key
No primary key.

Select an option: **Let Access add primary key**

Click **Next**. Keep going...

External Data ->Import & Link->Excel

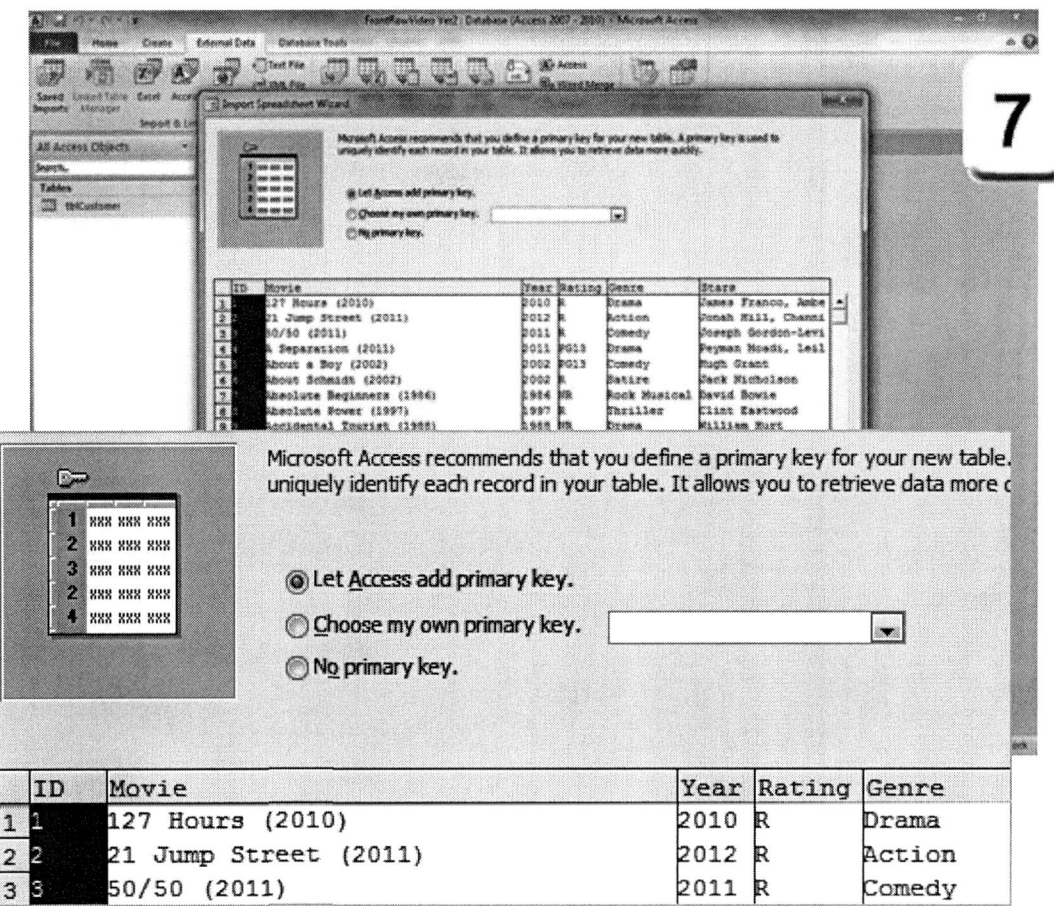

Microsoft Access recommends that you define a primary key for your new table. uniquely identify each record in your table. It allows you to retrieve data more c

⦿ Let Access add primary key.
○ Choose my own primary key.
○ No primary key.

ID	Movie	Year	Rating	Genre
1 1	127 Hours (2010)	2010	R	Drama
2 2	21 Jump Street (2011)	2012	R	Action
3 3	50/50 (2011)	2011	R	Comedy

Exam 77-885: Microsoft Access 2010
2. Building Tables
2.5. Import data from a single data file: Import into a New Table

External Data: Name the Table

The little checkered flag is a good clue that we have come to the finish line. The last step in the Import Wizard asks you to name the new table.

8. Try it: Name the Table

The Import Wizard is on step 6.
Import to Table: tblMovies.

Click **Finish** to complete the Import Wizard. You will be prompted to **Save** the choices that you made as you answered the Wizard's questions. You do not have to save these steps.

Click **Done**. Keep going...

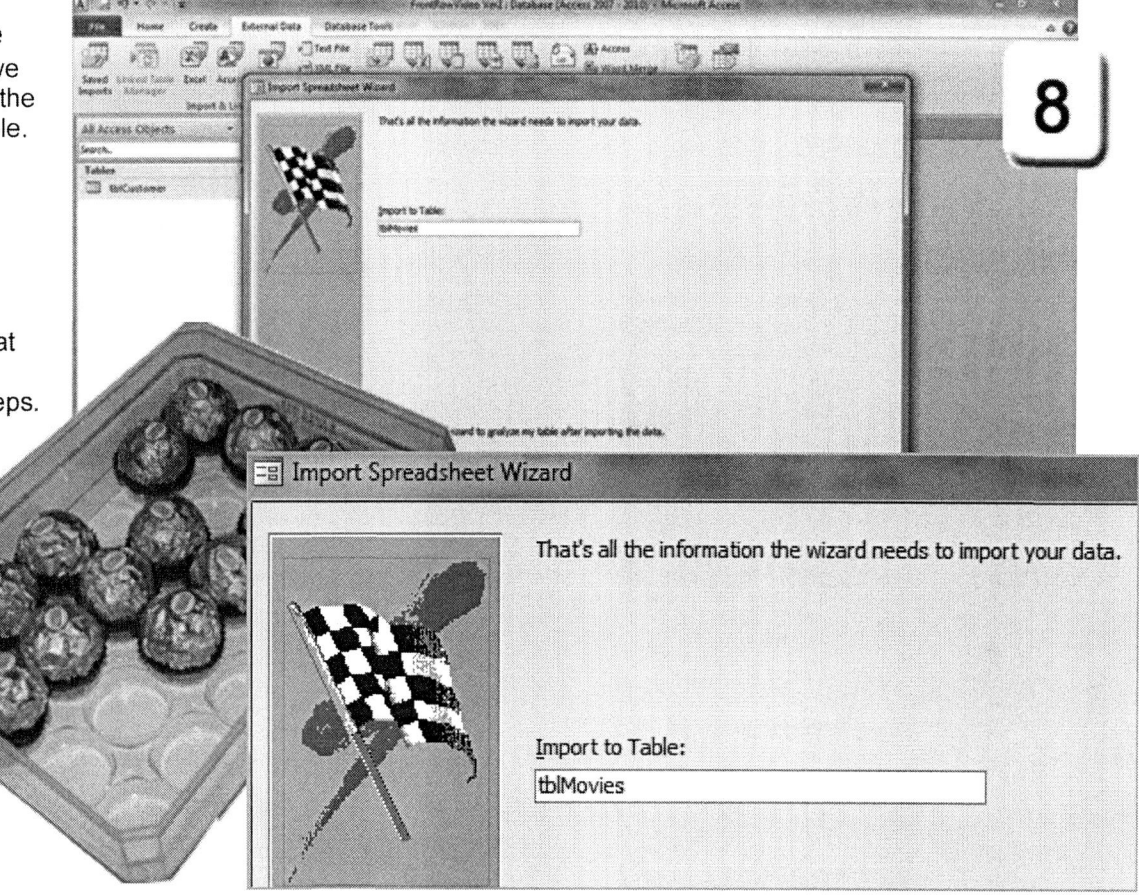

Exam 77-885: Microsoft Access 2010
2. Building Tables
2.5. Import data from a single data file: Import into a New Table

Hello, Movie Table

There are now two Tables in the Navigation Pane on the left side of the database: tblCustomers and tblMovies.

1. Try it: Open the Movie Table

Double-click tblMovies.
The Table should open in Datasheet View.

What Do You See? The Field Names in the Table match the Header Fields in the Microsoft Excel spreadsheet. This Table has the following Fields: Movie, Year, Rating, Genre and Stars. There is a unique ID number for each record.

What Else Do You See? (Look at the Bottom of the Table) There are 400 records in tblMovies.

So far, so good...

Microsoft Access: All Access Objects

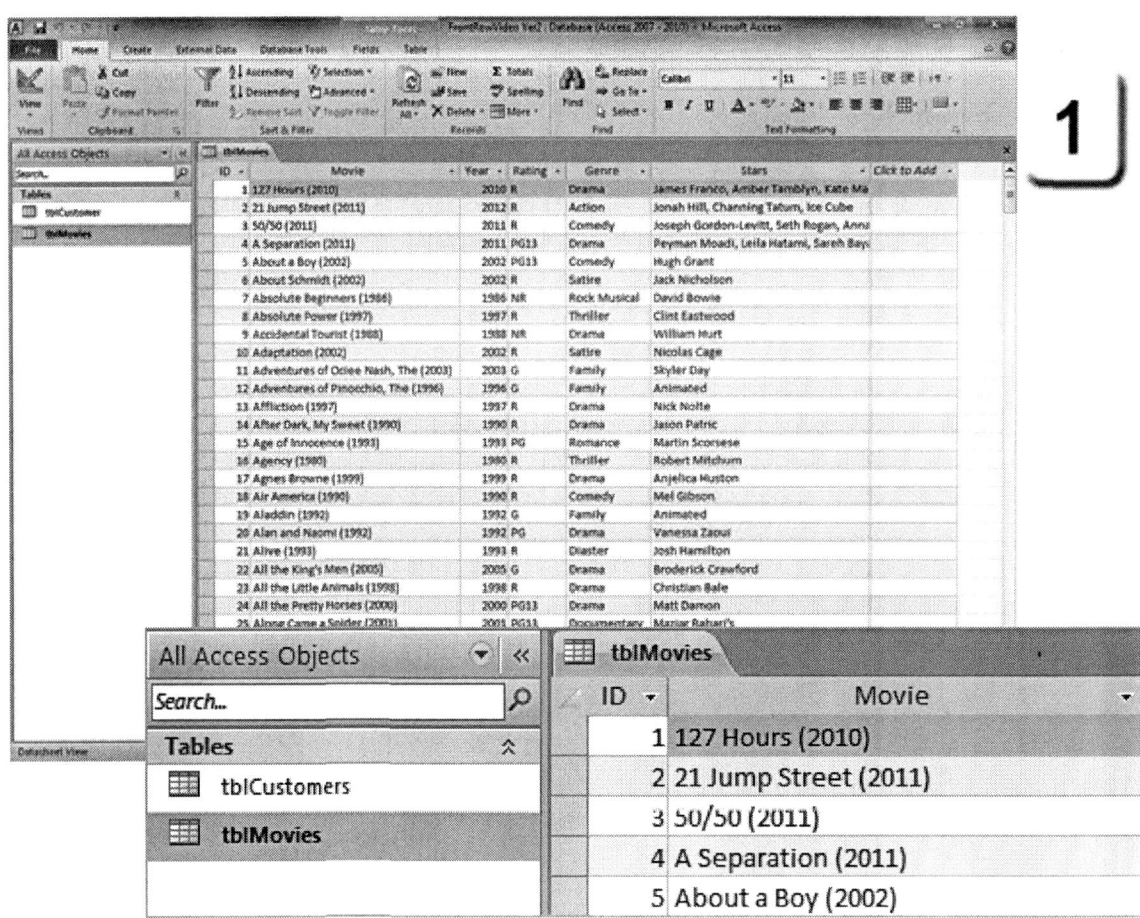

Review the Data: Find

Let's **Find** the same records that we did in Excel. The steps are similar.

2. Try it: Find a Record
tblMovies is open in Datasheet View.
Select a Field: Stars.
Go to **Home ->Find ->Find**.
Find What: Depp.
Look In: Current field.
Match: Any Part of Field.
Click **Find Next**.

What Do You See? Microsoft Access will highlight each Field that contains "Depp."

Close the Find and Replace window.
Keep going, please.

Memo to Self: The default selection in Microsoft Access is to Match the Whole Field. When you select **Match Any Part of the Field**, Access will look for anything the matches the criteria in the Find box.

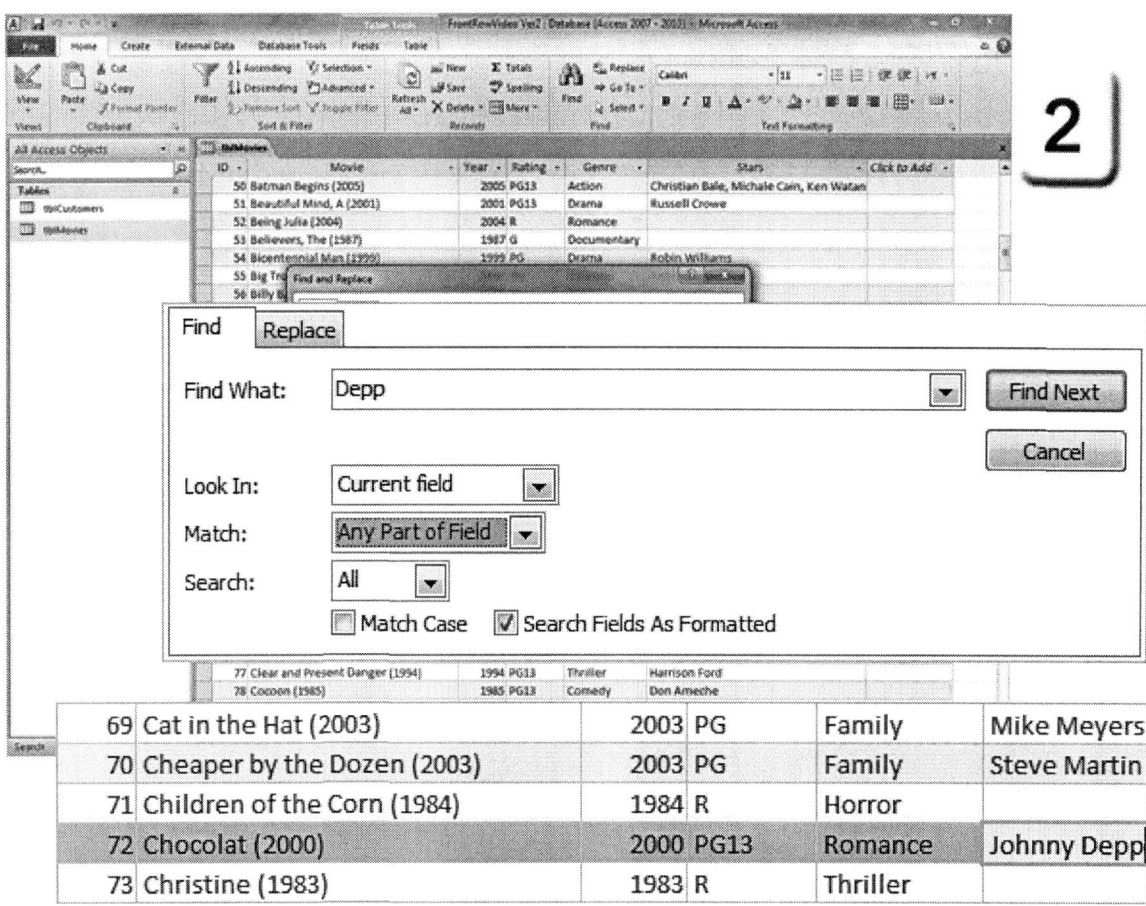

Exam 77-885: Microsoft Access 2010
2. Building Tables
2.3. Sort and filter records: Find a Record

Review the Data: Sort

Access can **Sort** the records as well.

3. Try it: Sort the Records
Select a Field: Year.
Go to **Home ->Sort & Filter.**
Click on **Descending**.

What Do You See? The Movies are sorted by Year from the newest (2012) to the oldest (1953).

One more comparison to the Microsoft Excel spreadsheet....

Home ->Sort & Filter-> Descending

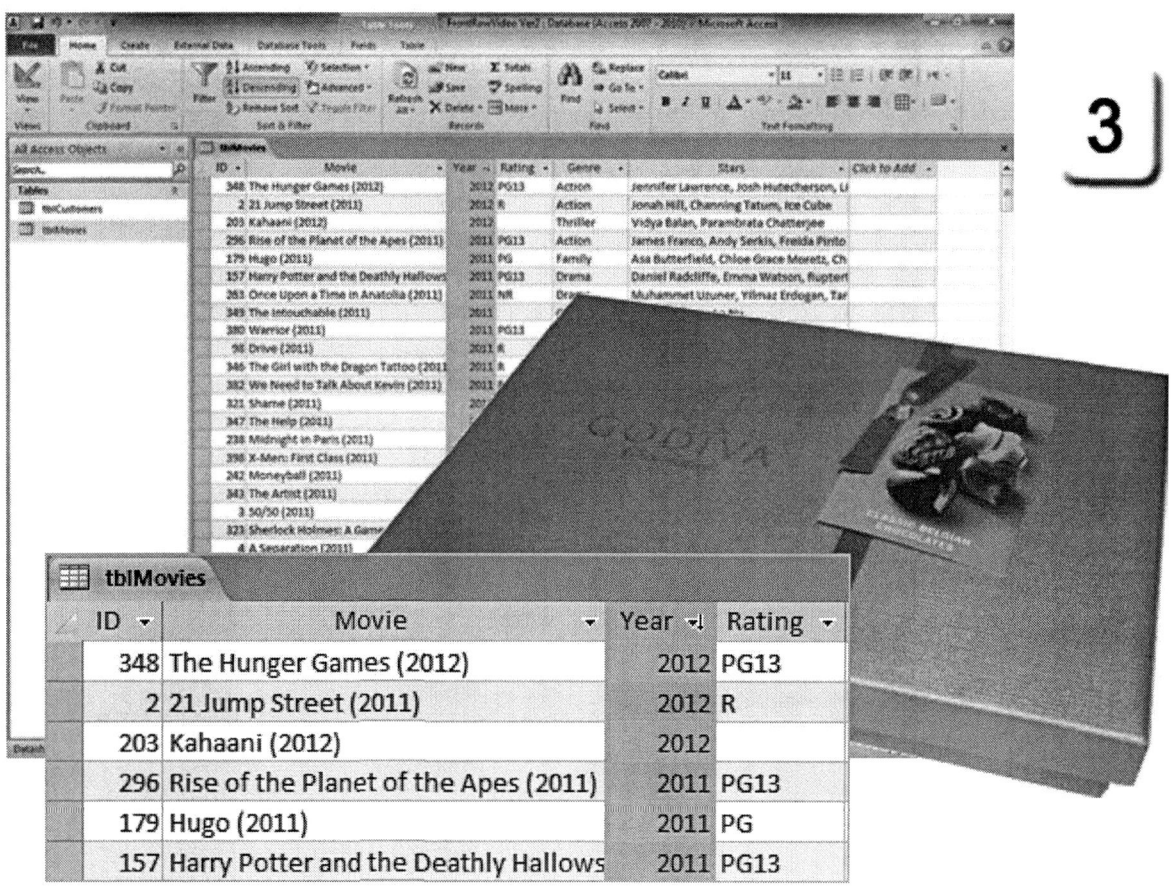

3

ID ▾	Movie ▾	Year ▾	Rating ▾
348	The Hunger Games (2012)	2012	PG13
2	21 Jump Street (2011)	2012	R
203	Kahaani (2012)	2012	
296	Rise of the Planet of the Apes (2011)	2011	PG13
179	Hugo (2011)	2011	PG
157	Harry Potter and the Deathly Hallows	2011	PG13

Exam 77-885: Microsoft Access 2010
2. Building Tables
2.3. Sort and filter records: Sort the Records

Review the Data: Filter

This Table has Filters in the Column Headings. The Filters can Sort and Select. The default option is Select All.

4. Try it: Filter the Records

Go to the Column Heading: Year
Select a Number Filter: 2012

What Do You See? There are 3 movies that were released in 2012 in this Table.

What Else Do You See? The Navigation Buttons at the bottom of tblMovies sez there are 1 out of 3. The other 397 records are still in the Table. Those Rows are just hidden, as they were in Excel.

Try This, Too: Remove the Filter

Go to the Column Heading: Year
Select a Number Filter: Select All

Keep going...

4

Exam 77-885: Microsoft Access 2010
2. Building Tables
2.3. Sort and filter records: Filter the Records

Filter Selection

There are several options for Filtering the records. The **Selection** tool offers:

Equal
Does Not Equal
Less Than or Equal To
Greater Than or Equal To
Between

5. Try it: Use the Filter Selection
Go to the Column Heading: Year
Select an example in the records: 2011
Go to **Home ->Sort & Filter.**
Make a **Selection**: Less Than or Equal to 2001

What Do You See? There are 397 movies that match the criteria.

Try This, Too: Toggle (Turn Off) the Filter
Go to **Home ->Sort & Filter-> Toggle Filter**

What Do You See, Now? There are 400 movies in tblMovies.

Keep going...

Home ->Sort & Filter-> Selection

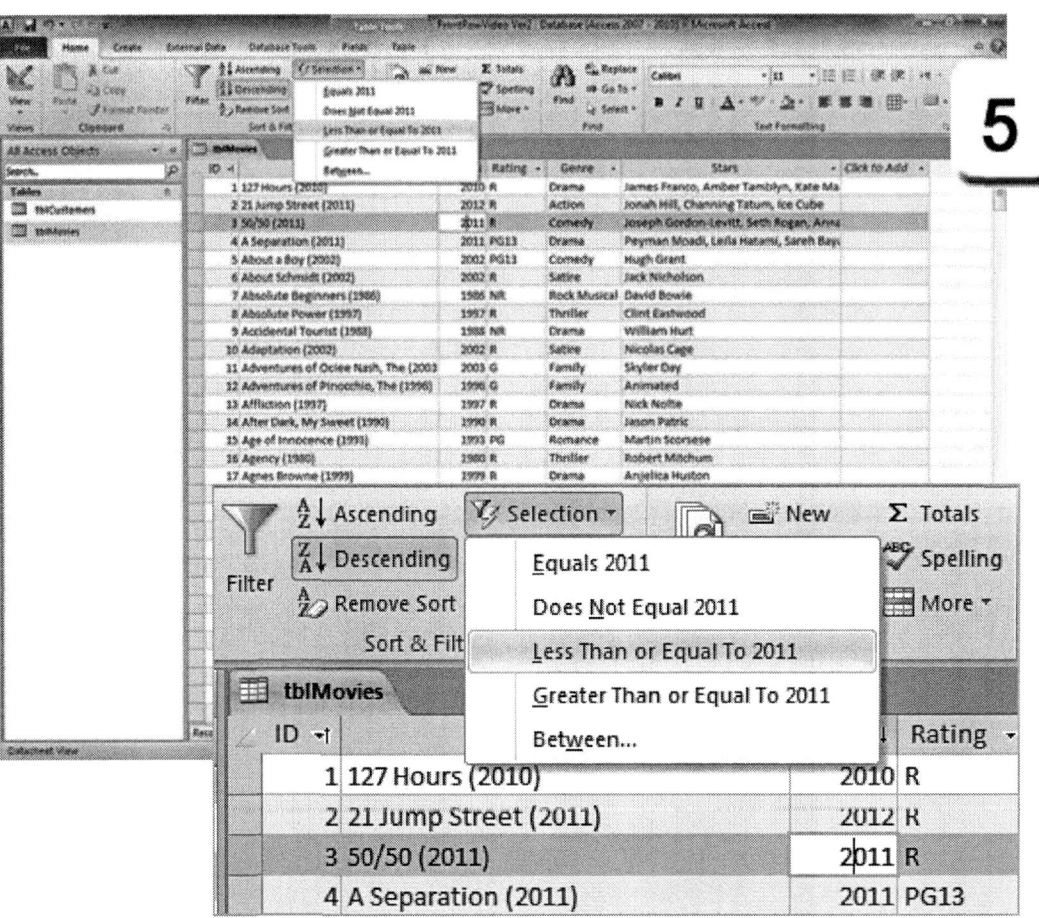

Exam 77-885: Microsoft Access 2010
2. Building Tables
2.3. Sort and filter records: Filter Selection

Last But Not Least...

Each of the simple steps in the previous pages confirmed that the Microsoft Excel spreadsheet was successfully imported into a new Table in Microsoft Access.

There is one more task to complete. This is the Movies Table. The Movies Table should have a MovieID that matches.

6. Try it: Change the Table View
tblMovies is open in Datasheet View.
Go to **Home ->Views->View.**
Select: **Design View.**

Keep going...

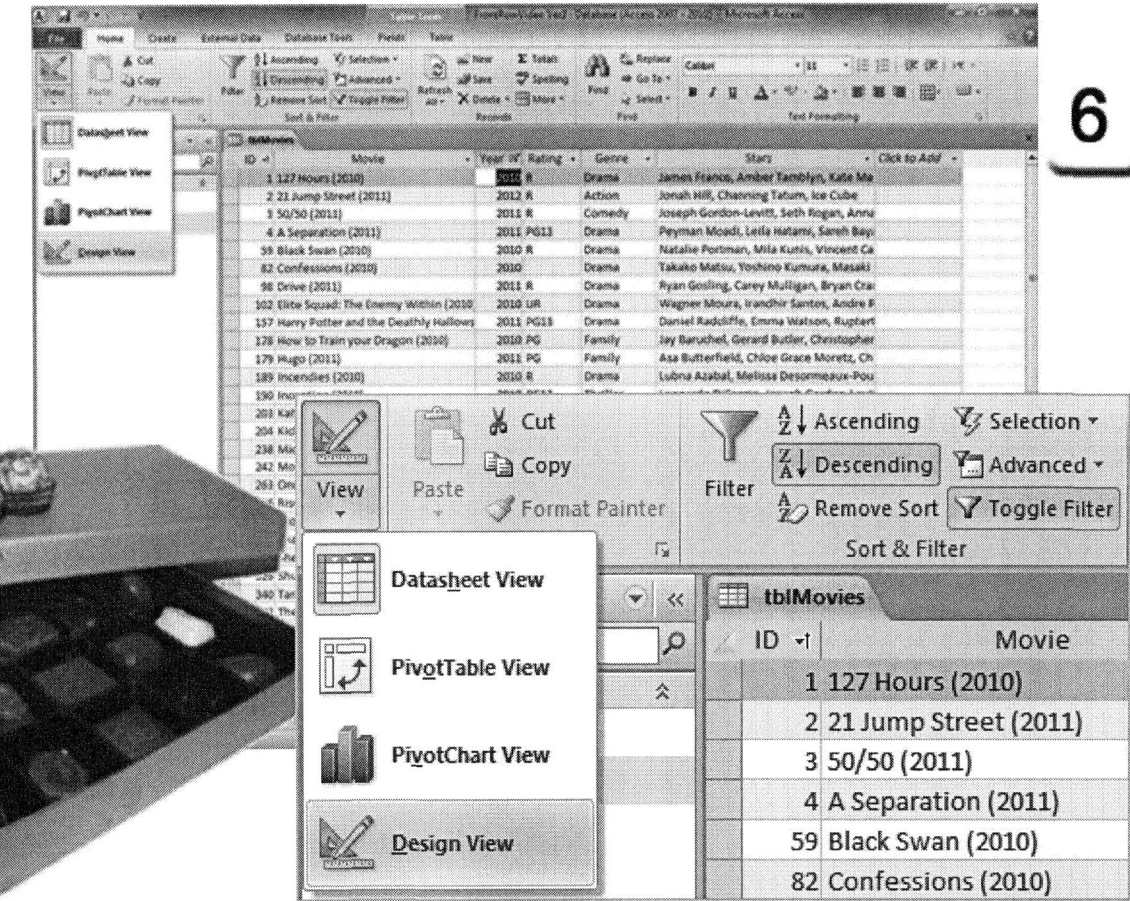

Exam 77-885: Microsoft Access 2010
2. Building Tables
2.1.1. Create tables in Design View

HOME

Table Tools ->Design

Edit the Field Name

The first Field in tblMovies is the Primary Key. The Data Type for the Primary Key is AutoNumber, which means that it is an Integer (a Whole Number) and that it increments automatically. It is indexed so that there are no duplicate numbers.

7. Try it: Rename the ID Field
Select the Field: ID
Type a New Name: MovieID

Do This: Save the Table
Go to **File->Save**.

And Do This: Change the View
Go to **Table Tools-> Design->Views**.
Select a View: **Datasheet View**.

Done and done.

Exam 77-885: Microsoft Access 2010
2. Building Tables
2.2. Create and Modify Fields: Rename a Field

Summary

This lesson demonstrated a common business task: importing data into Microsoft Access. We looked at the options available in the Import Wizard.

It was also interesting to compare how Access and Excel work with data.

OK, you done good. You get two cookies.

All Access Objects	⊙	«

Search...

Tables ⊗

tblCustomers

tblMovies

MovieID ▾	Movie ▾	Year ▾
1	127 Hours (2010)	2010
2	21 Jump Street (2011)	2012
3	50/50 (2011)	2011
4	A Separation (2011)	2011
5	About a Boy (2002)	2002
6	About Schmidt (2002)	2002
7	Absolute Beginners (1986)	1986

Practice Activities

Lesson 4: More Data, More Tables

Try This: Do the following steps

1. Open the Excel Spreadsheet: **Brown Bag Products.xlsx**

2. Use the Filter function to show only the records with the Specialty Gluten Free. How many Records do you see? Remove the Filter and close Excel.

3. Open the Brown Bag Lunch database you have been programming. Or you may download the sample database online:

Brown Bag Lunch ver4.accdb

4. Import External Data from Excel. Select the spreadsheet Brown Bag Lunch Products.xlsx.

5. Import the data into a new Table in the Current Database.

6. Select the Worksheet named Products.

7. Select that the first Row contains Column Headings.

8. Accept default settings for Field Options.

9. Name the table tblProducts. Finish the Wizard.

10. Use the Find command to find the Records with Ham.

11. Use the Filter to show only the items with the Specialty Gluten Free. How many Records do you see?

12. Remove the Filter.

13. Rename the ID field to. ProductID

14. Save the changes to tblProducts.

Test Yourself

1. Which types of files can Access import? (Give all correct answers.)
A. IBM Mainframe system files
B. QuickBooks financial records
C. Microsoft Excel files
Tip: Beginning Access, page 85

2. Which are options for imported data? (Give all correct answers.)
A. Import into a new Table
B. Append (add) records to an existing Table
C. Link to an external table
Tip: Beginning Access, page 86

3. Which are options for adding a Primary Key to imported data? (Give all correct answers.)
A. Choose my own Primary Key
B. Let Access add the Primary Key
C. No Primary Key
Tip: Beginning Access, page 90

4. Access column headings have Filters by default.
A. True
B. False
Tip: Beginning Access, page 95

5. Which functions does an Access Table share with a spreadsheet? (Give all correct answers.)
A. Find
B. Sort
C. Filter
Tip: Beginning Access, page 94, 95

Access 2010: Presenting Data Visually

Forms and Form Design

Beginning Access Objectives
In this lesson, you will learn how to:

1. Create a Form with the Form Wizard.

2. Modify the Forms in Layout View with the Form Design Tools.

3. Apply a Theme to a Form.

4. View the Property Sheet and use the Properties to resize and position a picture.

5. Use the Design Ribbon to Format the Header.

© 2012 Comma Productions, LLC

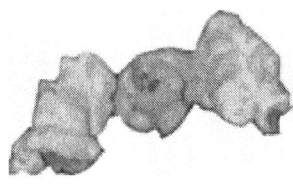

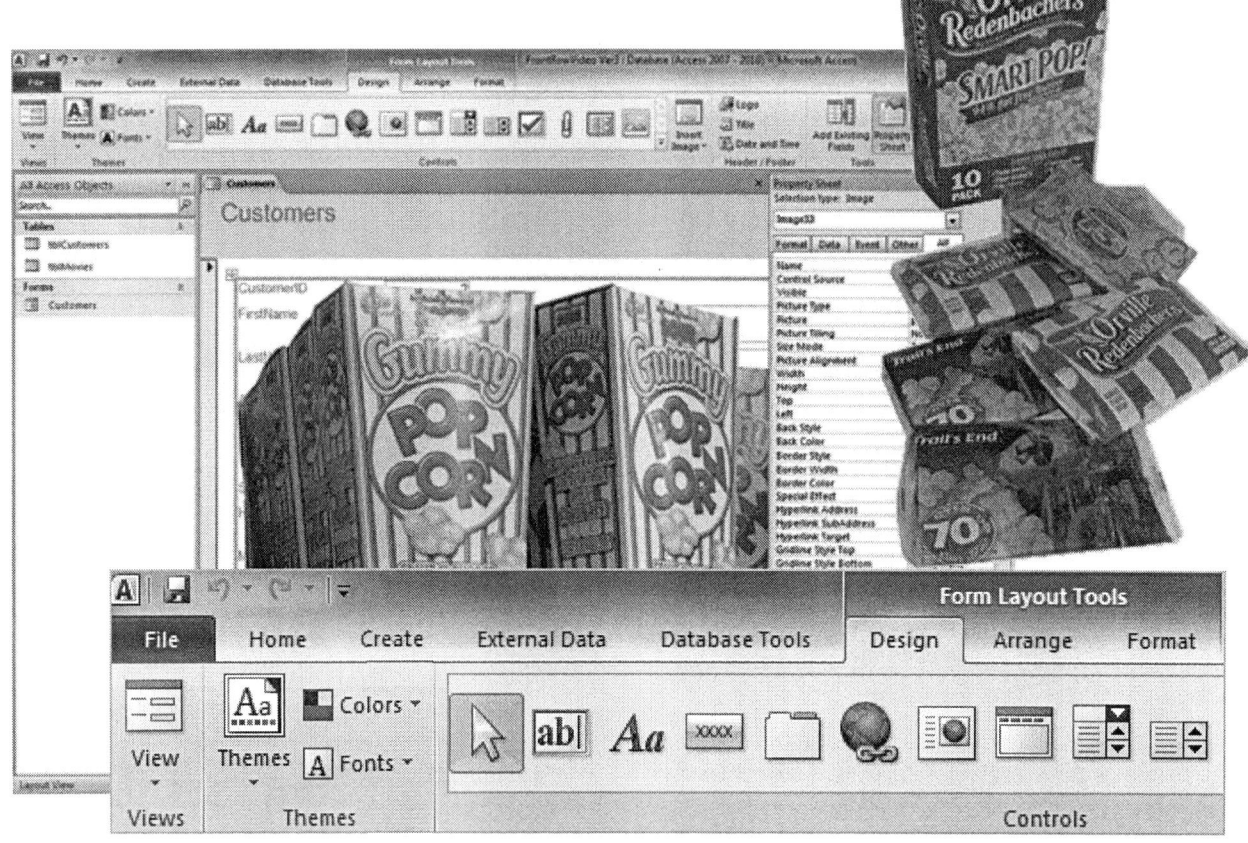

Lesson 5 : Forms and Form Design

1. Readings

Read Lesson 5 in the Beginning Access guide, page 101-126.

Project

Create two Forms with the Form Wizard.

Downloads

FrontRowVideo Begin5.accdb
popcorn1.gif, popcorn2.gif,
popcorn3.gif,
popcorn4.gif

Brown Bag Lunch ver5.accdb
BB Customers Logo.jpg
Brown Bag Logo.jpg
Lunch1.gif, Lunch2.gif, Lunch3.gif,
Lunch4.gif

2. Practice

Complete the Practice Activity on page 127.

3. Assessment

Review the Test questions on page 128.

Form Design Tools: Arrange

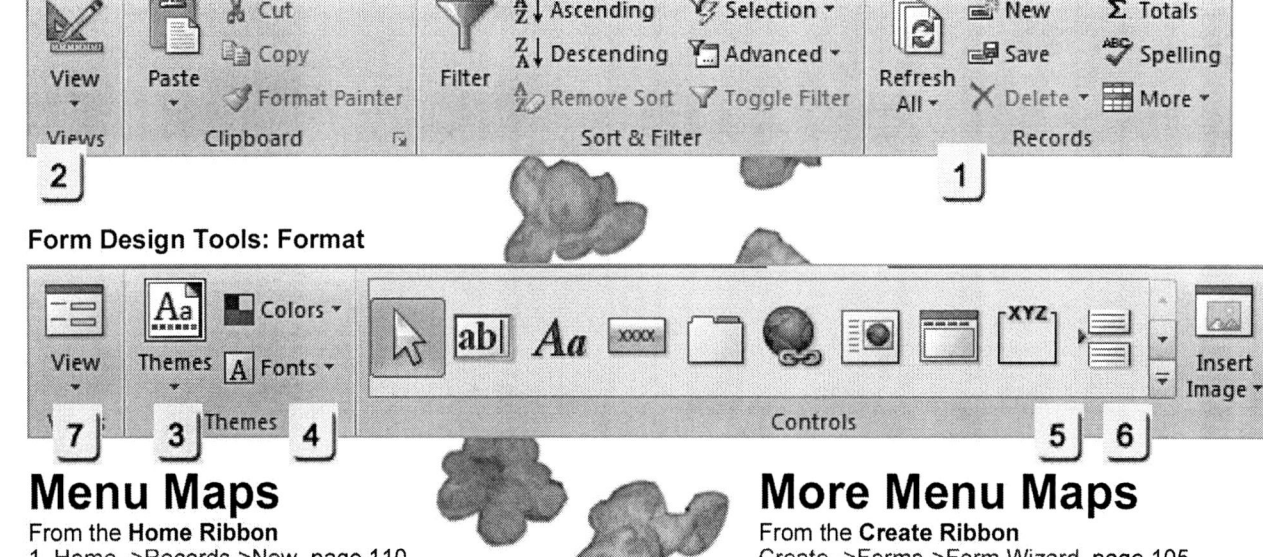

Form Design Tools: Format

Menu Maps

From the **Home Ribbon**
1. Home ->Records->New, page 110
2. Home ->View-> Layout View, page 112

From the **Form Design Tools: Design**.
3. Form Design Tools, page 113
4. Form Design Tools ->Design->Themes, page 114
5. Form Design Tools ->Design->Controls, page 115
6. Form Design Tools ->Design-> Tools->Property Sheet, page 116
7. Form Design Tools ->Design->Views, page 125

More Menu Maps

From the **Create Ribbon**
Create ->Forms->Form Wizard, page 105

Forms and Form Design

The first time I tried to create a form in Microsoft Access was the longest week I ever wasted. I cussed and ranted for 40 hours straight. I couldn't figure out how to put the "blanks" on the form so people could enter and review their data. I was not aware that a Form is just a pretty face on a Table. You need to have Tables, first. Then, the Form can help users fill in the blanks.

Forms can be simple: showing one record at a time. Forms can be complex as well: filtering records and updating data automatically every time it is opened. In general, forms are built from Tables or Queries. The Table, or Record Source, presents the data. The Table also provides the Form Fields. The Front Row Video database has two tables: tblCustomers and tblMovies. This lesson will create a Form using the Form Wizard.

Sample Microsoft Office Access 2010 Form

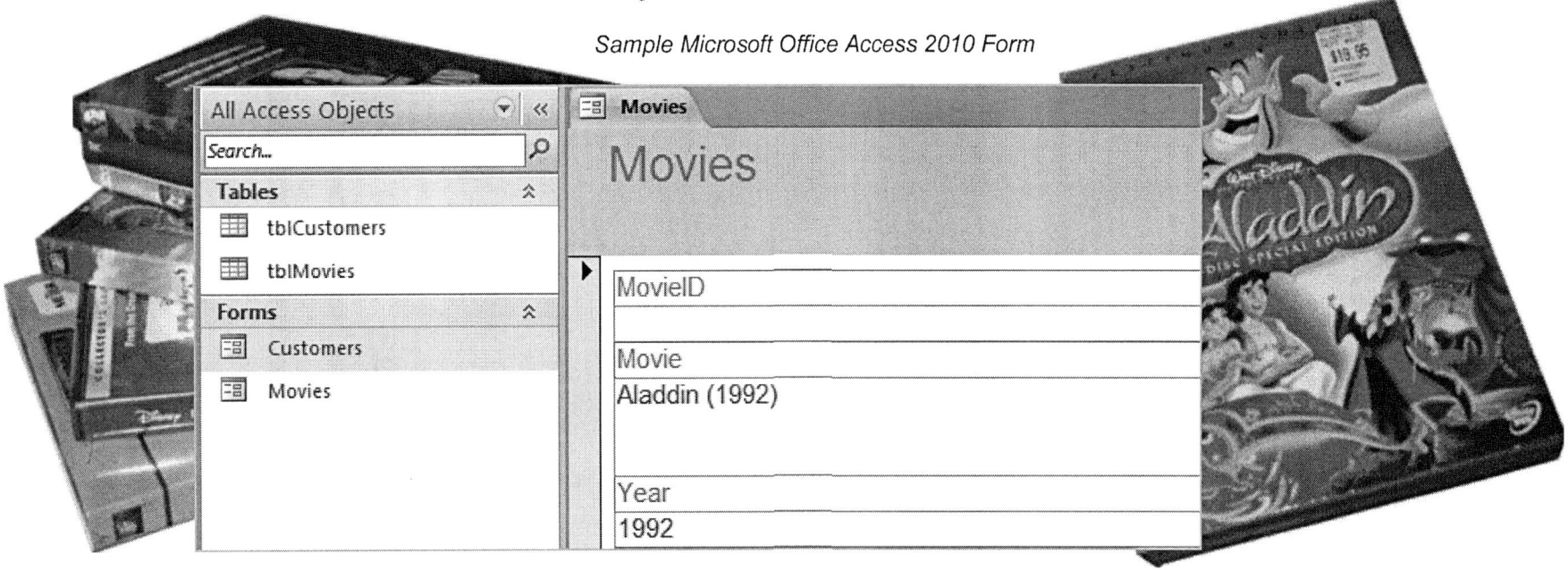

Before You Begin

This demonstration uses the Front Row Video database that we programmed in the previous lessons. You can continue with the database you have been working on. You can also download the sample Access database at the beginning of this lesson.

1. Try it: Open the Sample Database
Go to the Documents folder.
Open the sample database.
FrontRowVideo Begin5.accdb

What Do You See? There are two tables in the mighty Access database:
tblCustomers
tblMovies

What Else Do You See? This database has a Security Warning. In order to edit the objects and save your work, you need to click on **Enable Content**.

2. Do This, Now: Enable Content
Click on **Enable Content**.
Keep going...

Microsoft Access 2010

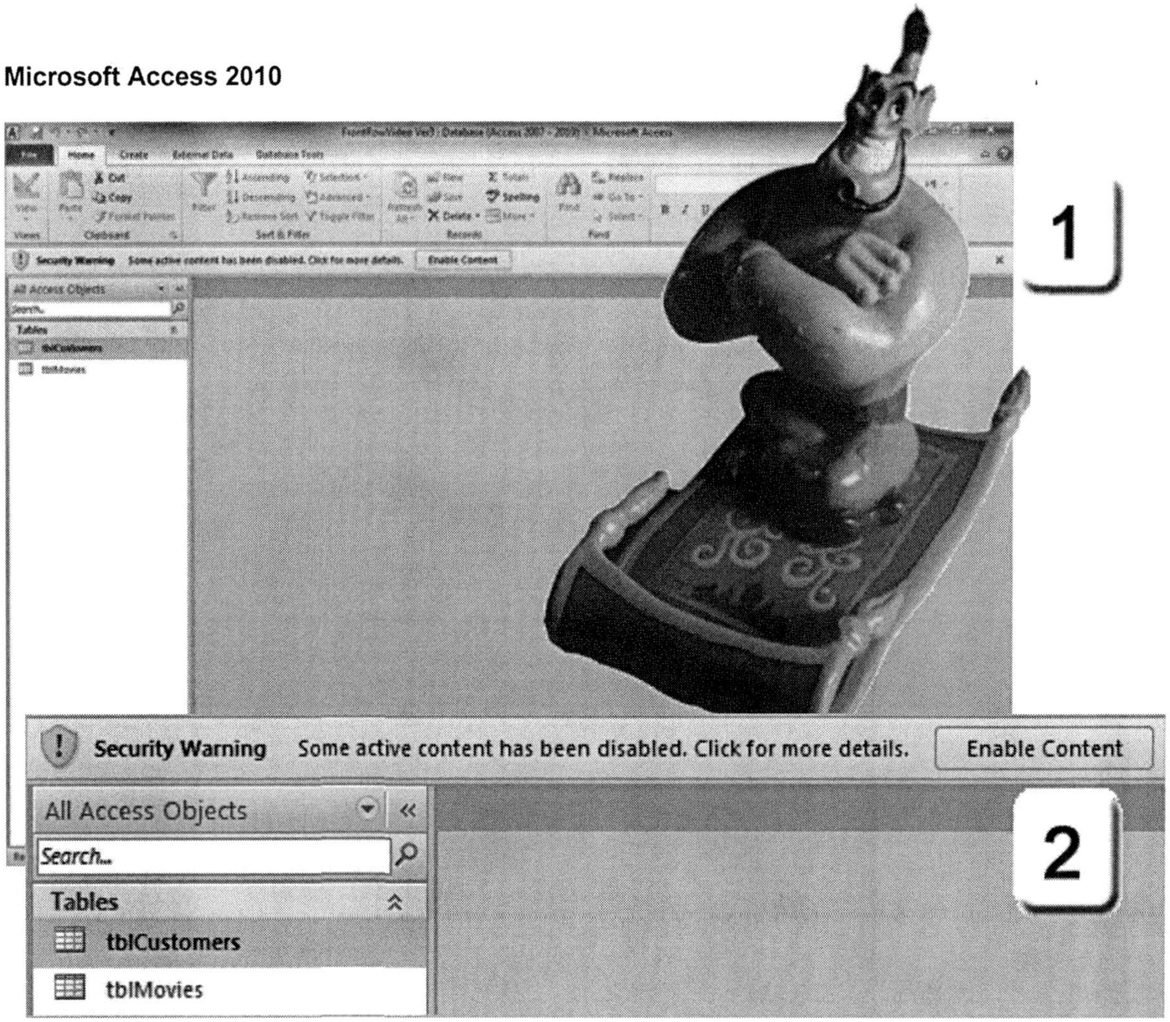

Create a Customer Form

There are three ways to create a Form in Microsoft Access: templates, design from scratch (begin with a blank form) and the Form Wizard. This lesson will walk through creating a Form with the **Form Wizard**.

In the next lesson, we will create another Form using **Form Design**.

1. Try it: Create a Form with the Wizard
The sample database is open and enabled.
Select a Table: tblCustomers
Go to **Create ->Forms->Form Wizard**.

What Do You See? The Form Wizard will open and guide you through the process.

Click **Next**. Keep going...

Create ->Forms->Form Wizard

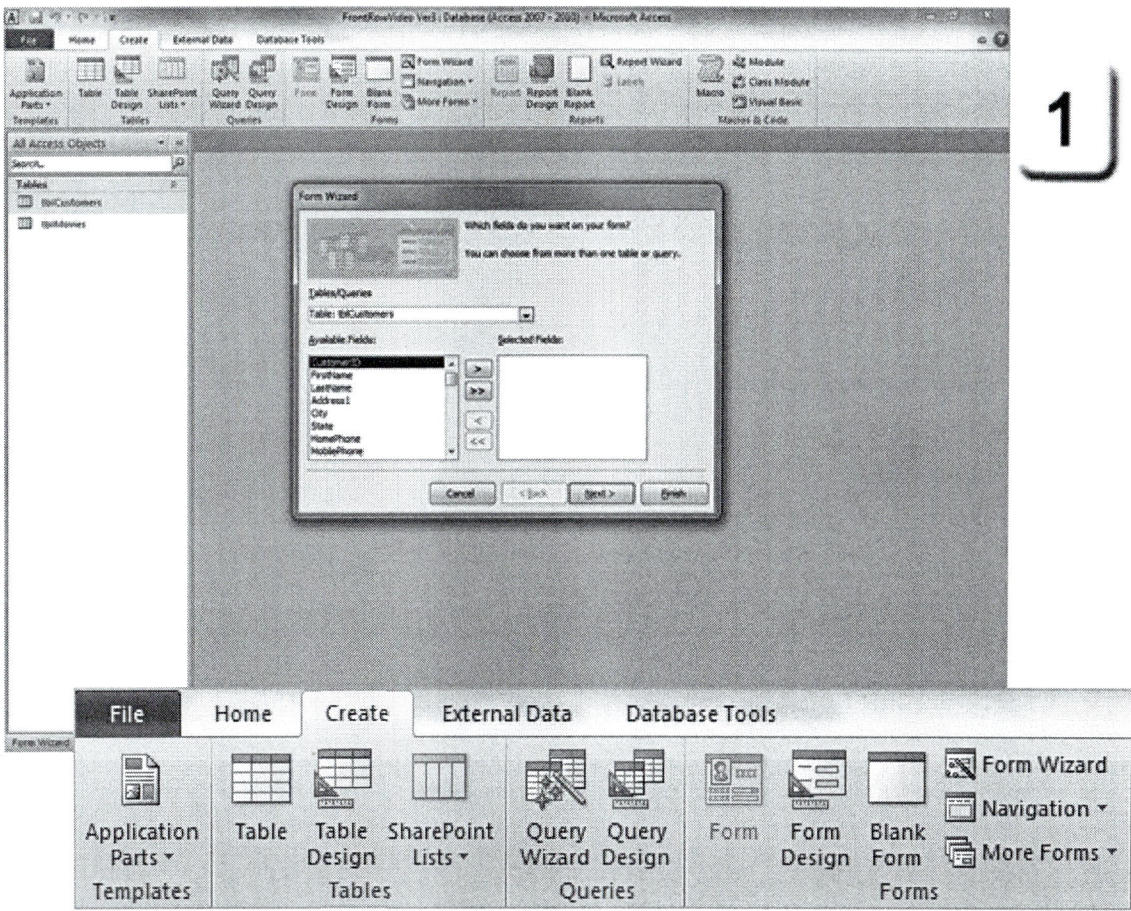

Exam 77-885: Microsoft Access 2010
3. Building Forms
3.1. Create forms: Use the Form Wizard

Form Wizard Design:
Select the Record Source

The Form is just a pretty face on a Table or Query. The Form Wizard asks which Table or Query you wish to use for this Form.

2. Try it: Select a Record Source
Select a Table/Query: tblCustomers

What Do You See? When you select a Record Source, you should see all of the Fields that are available in that Table or Query on the left side of the screen.

Try This, Too: Choose the Fields
Use the Right Double Arrow to move all of the **Available Fields** to the **Selected Fields** on the right side of the screen.

Click **Next**. Keep going...

Create ->Forms->Form Wizard

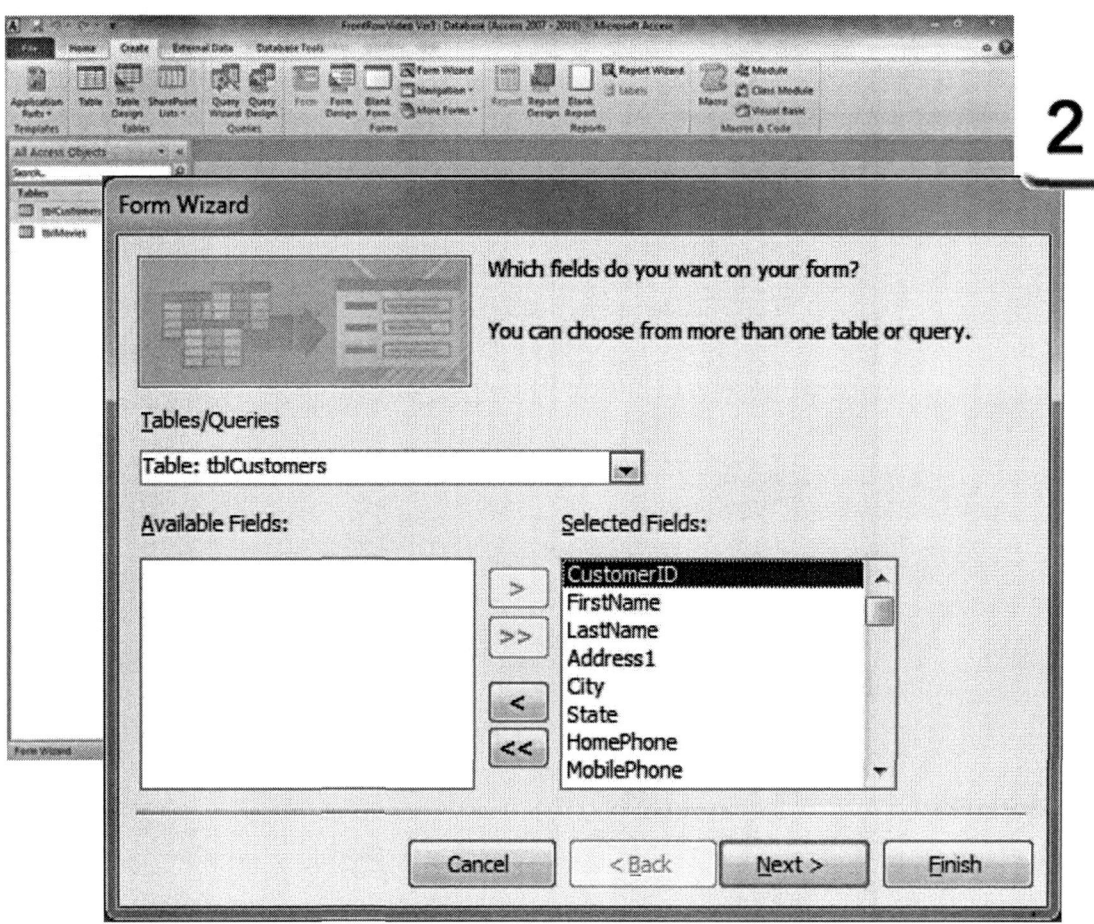

Exam 77-885: Microsoft Access 2010
3. Building Forms
3.1. Create forms: Use the Form Wizard

Create ->Forms->Form Wizard

Form Wizard Design:
Select a Form Layout

There are four different Form Layouts in this little Wizard. The options are:

Columnar: organizes the Fields in columns. This option is good for data entry.

Tabular: organize the Fields in a Table.

Datasheet: creates a Form with Rows and Record Selectors like an Excel spreadsheet. This layout is good for forms that show a list of the products or customer names.

Justified: organizes the Fields evenly across the Form.

3. Try it: Select a Form Layout
Select a Layout: Columnar

Click **Next**. Keep going...

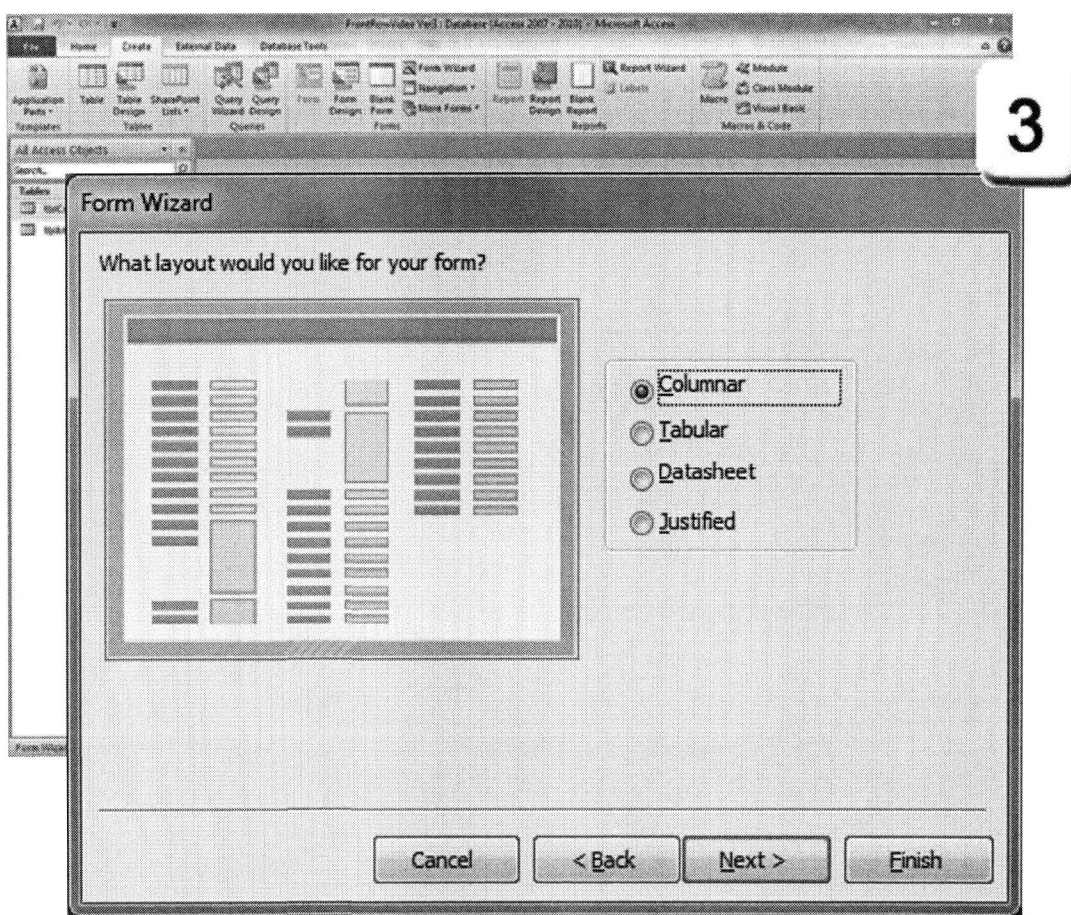

Exam 77-885: Microsoft Access 2010
3. Building Forms
3.1. Create forms: Use the Form Wizard

Form Wizard Design:
Edit the Form Title

The Form Title is the label that Users will see when they open the Form. Labels help Users navigate to the right place. If you open the Customer Form, it should say Customers.

The default text is simply the name of the Record Source. In this example, that would be tblCustomers. We can do better.

4. Try it: Edit the Form Title
Edit the Title: Customers.

What Else Do You See? There are two options when you complete the Wizard:
Open the form to view or enter information
Modify the form's design.

Let's **Open the Form** as a User would and see how it works.

Click **Finish**. Keep going...

Create ->Forms->Form Wizard

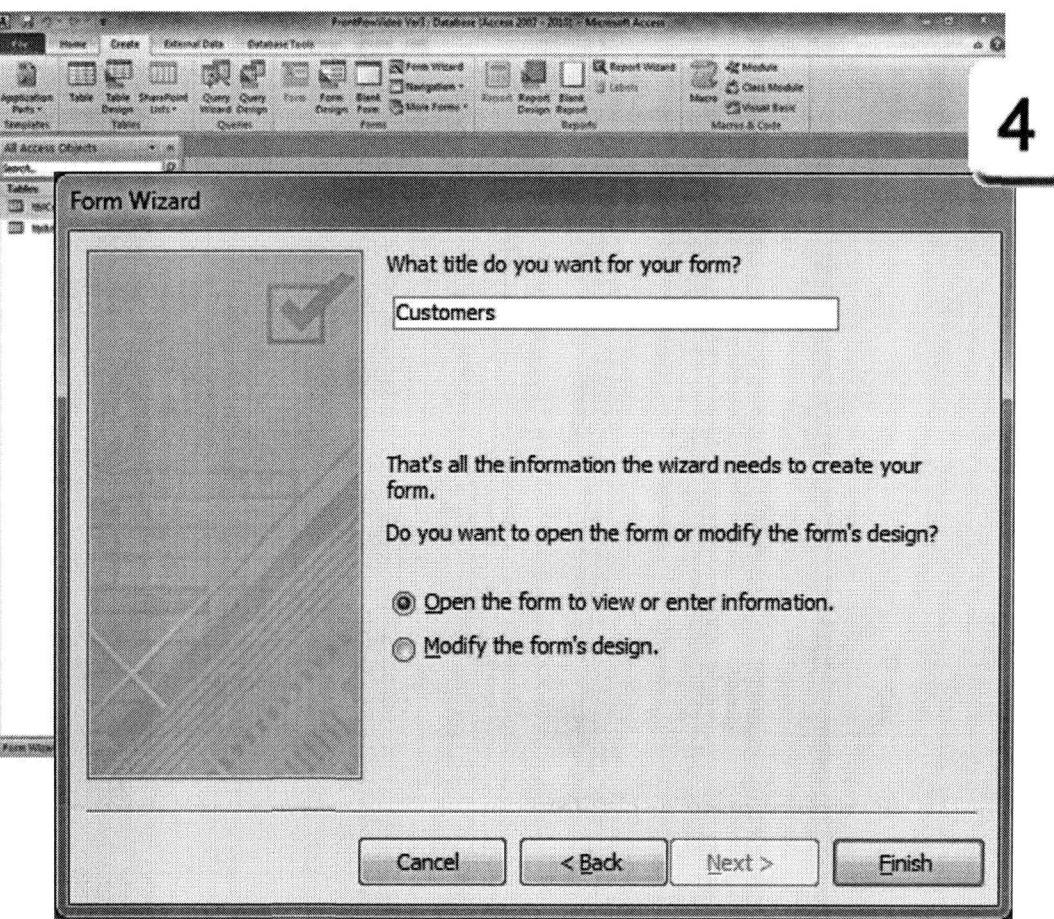

Exam 77-885: Microsoft Access 2010
3. Building Forms
3.1. Create forms: Use the Form Wizard

Hello, Customer Form

5. Try it: Review the New Form

When you finish the Form Wizard, you will see a new Form. The Customers Form is shown in the Navigation Pane on the left side of the database.

The Form tab includes the Title we entered on the previous page. The label at the top of the Form has the same Title as well.

What Else Do You See? Look at the bottom of the Form at the Records. There are four Records in tblCustomer, the Record Source for this Form.

Keep going...

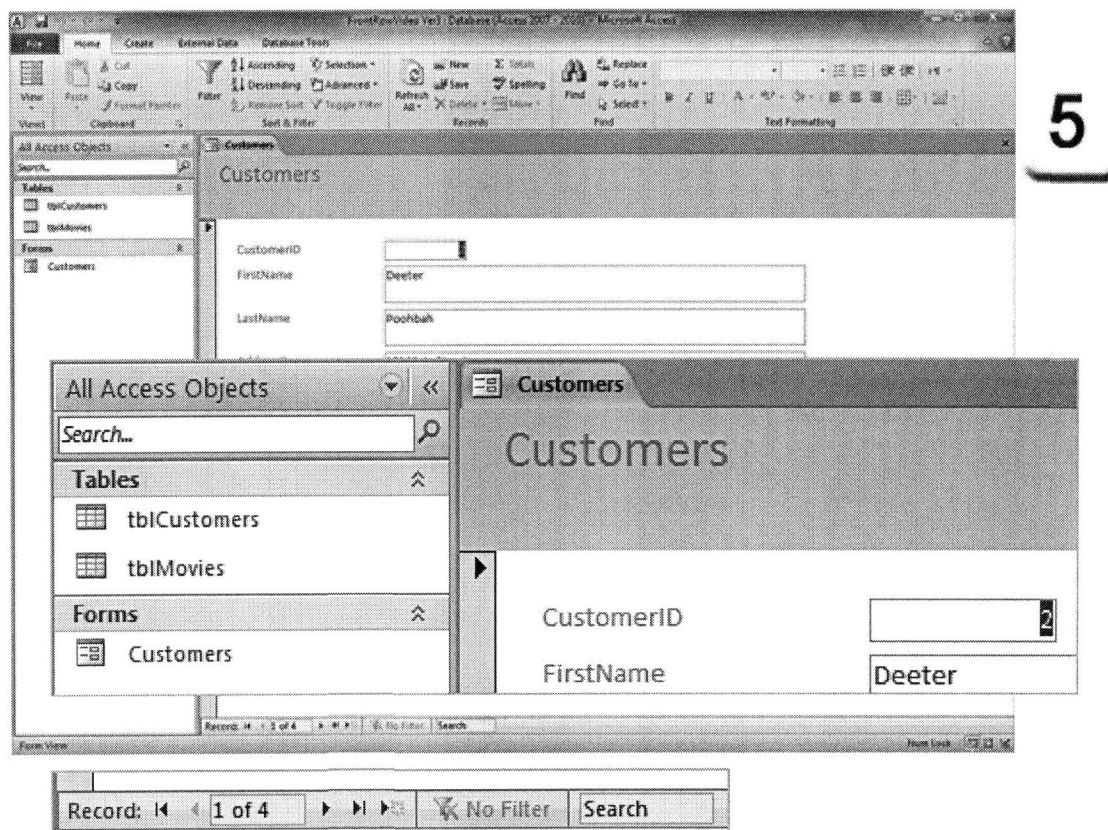

Exam 77-885: Microsoft Access 2010
3. Building Forms
3.1. Create forms: Use the Form Wizard

Test the Customer Form
The best way to learn how the new Form works is to enter some data.

6. Try it: Add a New Record
The Customer Form is open.
Go to **Home ->Records->New.**

A new, blank record will open.

Try This, Too: Edit the New Record
Enter the following information:
FirstName: Sage
LastName: Young
Address1: 123 Brighton Road
CIty: Brighton
State: MI
Zip: 48116
Home Phone: (810) 231-1111
Keep going...

Home ->Records->New

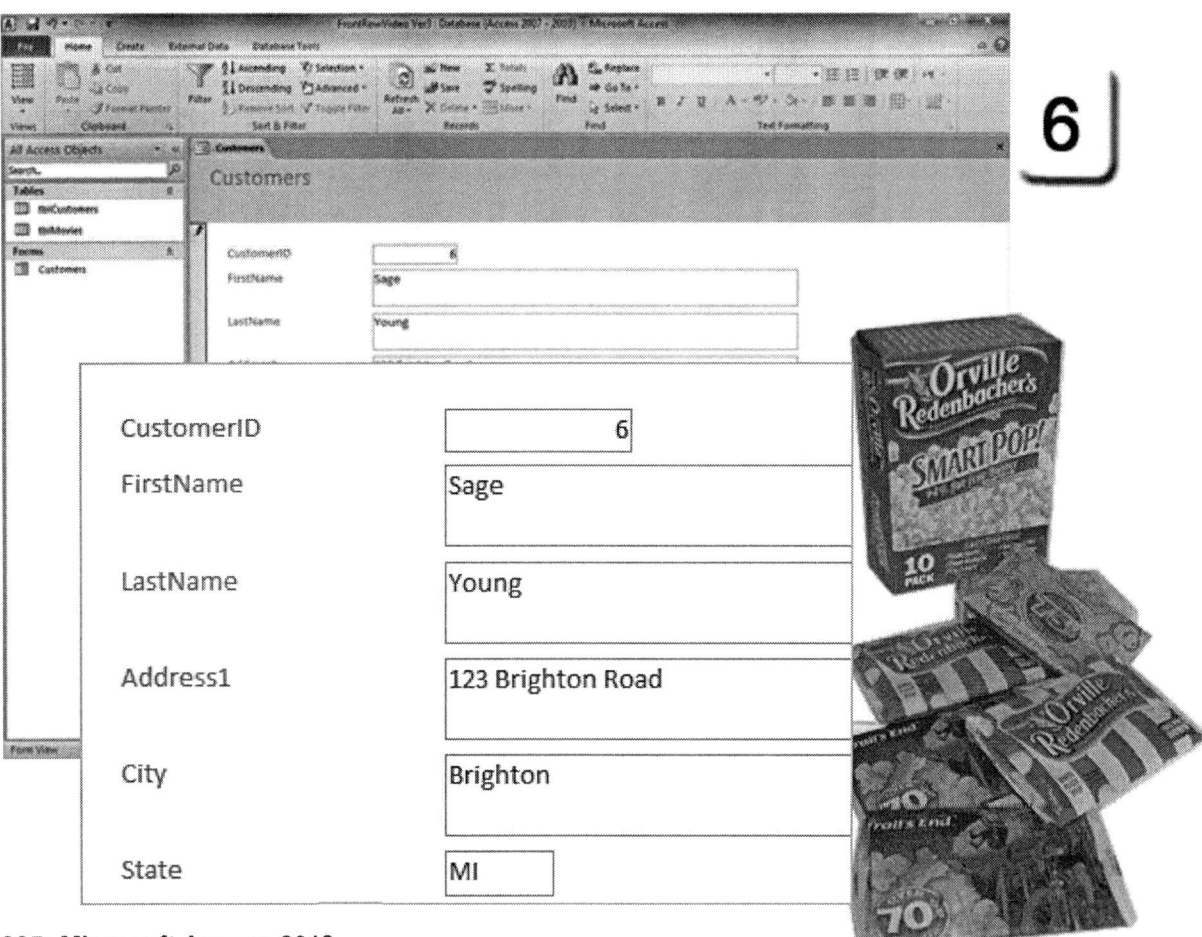

Exam 77-885: Microsoft Access 2010
3. Building Forms
3.1. Create forms: Use the Form Wizard

Design Considerations

7. Design Considerations

What should you look for when you test a Form? Here are some thoughts you might consider: Most people TAB to the next Form Field as they type in the information. Did your Form automatically TAB to the next logical Field, or did it bounce around the Form like a ping pong ball?

People like similar objects to be grouped together. Are all of the Form Fields for the Address in the same area? In the example on this page, the Zip Field is not located near the rest of the Address Fields.

Did the Home Phone Field use the Input Mask that you added in tblCustomer?

The Form Wizard is a good start, but it is just a start. The next pages introduce the wonderful programming options that are available in a different View.

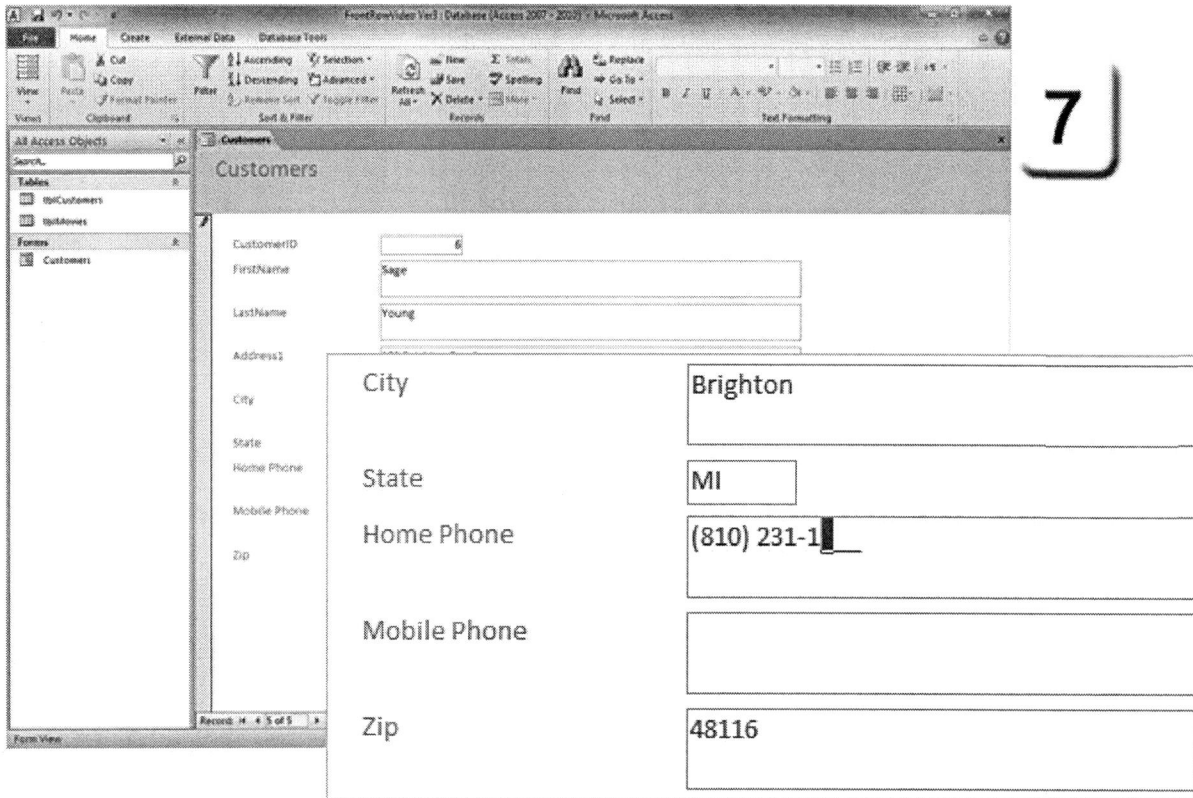

Exam 77-885: Microsoft Access 2010
3. Building Forms
3.1. Create forms: Use the Form Wizard

Home->Views->View-> Layout View

Form Views: Layout

Each object in Access has several Views.
The Form View is the one we have been
using to test the functionality. There are
two more Views that can be used to edit
the Form: Layout View and Design View.

Layout View is a simple editor.
Design View is a more detailed editor.

1. Try it: Go to the Layout View
Go to **Home ->Views->View.**
Select a View: Layout View.

Keep going...

Exam 77-885: Microsoft Access 2010
3. Building Forms
3.1. Create forms: Use Form Design Tools

Hello, Form Layout Tools

2. Try it: Review the Form Layout Tools
There are three Form Layout Ribbons:
Design, Arrange and Format.

The Design Ribbon includes:
Views
Themes
Controls
Header/Footer
Tools

The Arrange Ribbon includes:
Table
Rows & Columns
Merge/Spilt
Move
Position

The Format Ribbon includes:
Selection
Font
Number
Background
Control Formatting
So far, so good. Keep going, please...

Form Layout Tools

Exam 77-885: Microsoft Access 2010
3. Building Forms
3.1. Create forms: Use Form Design Tools

Choose a Theme

Color and Fonts are important in Form Design. You can use the Form Layout Tools to apply a **Theme** to this Form.

3. Try it: Select Theme
The Customer Form is open.
It is still in Layout View.
Go to **Form Layout Tools ->Design->Themes.**
Click on **Themes.**
Select a **Theme**: Essential

What Do You See? As you run your mouse over the Theme Library, you should see a Live Preview of the formatting. The Theme specifies the formatting for the Colors and Fonts.

Keep going...

Form Layout Tools ->Design->Themes->Themes

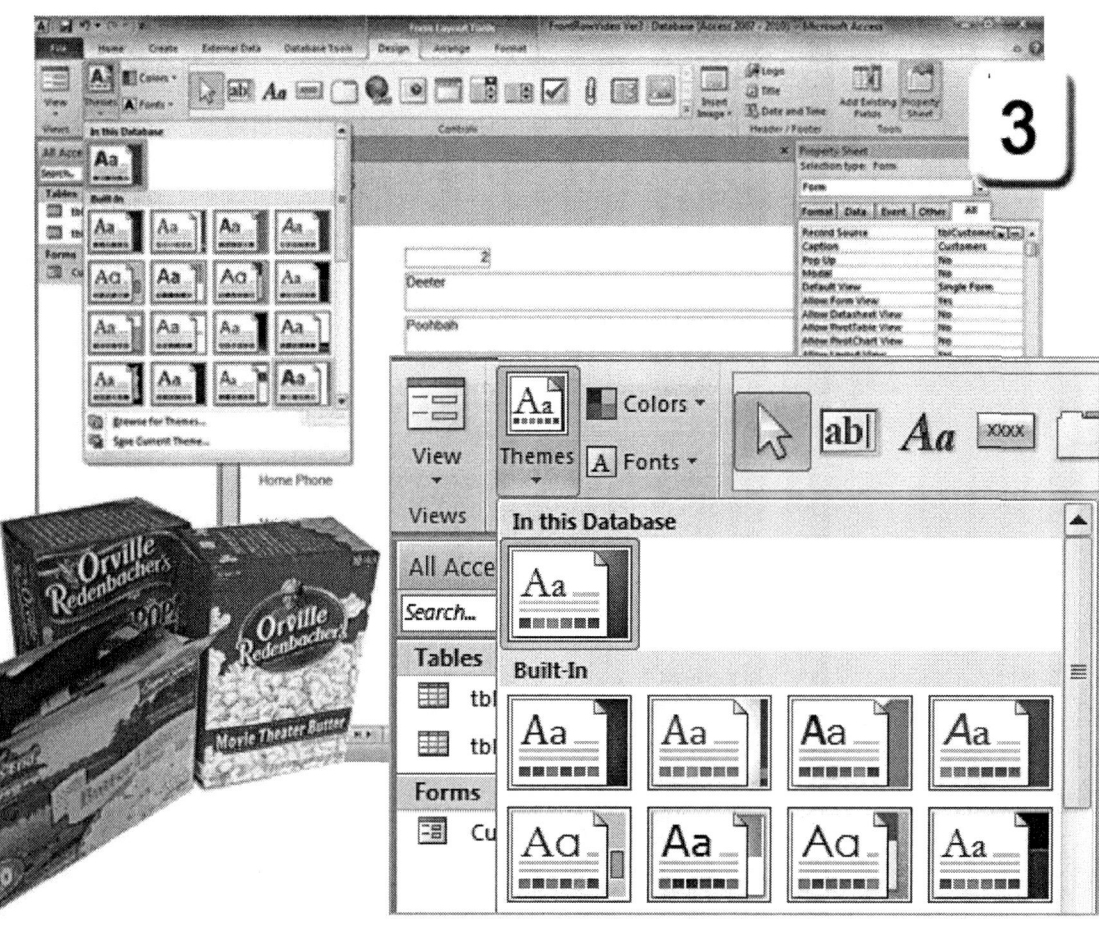

Exam 77-885: Microsoft Access 2010
3. Building Forms
3.2. Apply Form Design options: Apply a Theme

#3

Add an Image to a Form
People use pictures to confirm that they are in the right place. The following pages will show how to add an image **Control**. We will also use the **Property Sheet** to edit the size and position.

4. Try it: Add an Image
The Customers Form is open in Layout View.
Go to **Form Layout Tools ->Design->Controls.**
Select a Control: **Image**

Browse to the Documents folder.
Select an Image: popcorn1.gif.
Click **OK**, Keep going...

Controls

Exam 77-885: Microsoft Access 2010
3. Building Forms
3.1. Create forms: Use Form Design Tools

Review the Image Properties

Every object in a database has **Properties**. The **Property Sheet** lists all of the options that can be edited. The numerous options are grouped by purpose: Format, Data, Event, etc.

We will use the Property Sheet to resize the Image and place it in a corner of the Form.

Before You Begin: Find the Properties
The Customers Form is open in Layout View.
Go to **Form Layout Tools ->Design->Tools.**
Click on **Property Sheet.**

What Do You See? The **Property Sheet** should be available on the right side.

5. Try it: Review the Image Properties
Click on the Image to see the Properties.
Go to the **All** tab.

The Property Sheet now shows all of the options for the Image, popcorn1.gif.

Keep going...

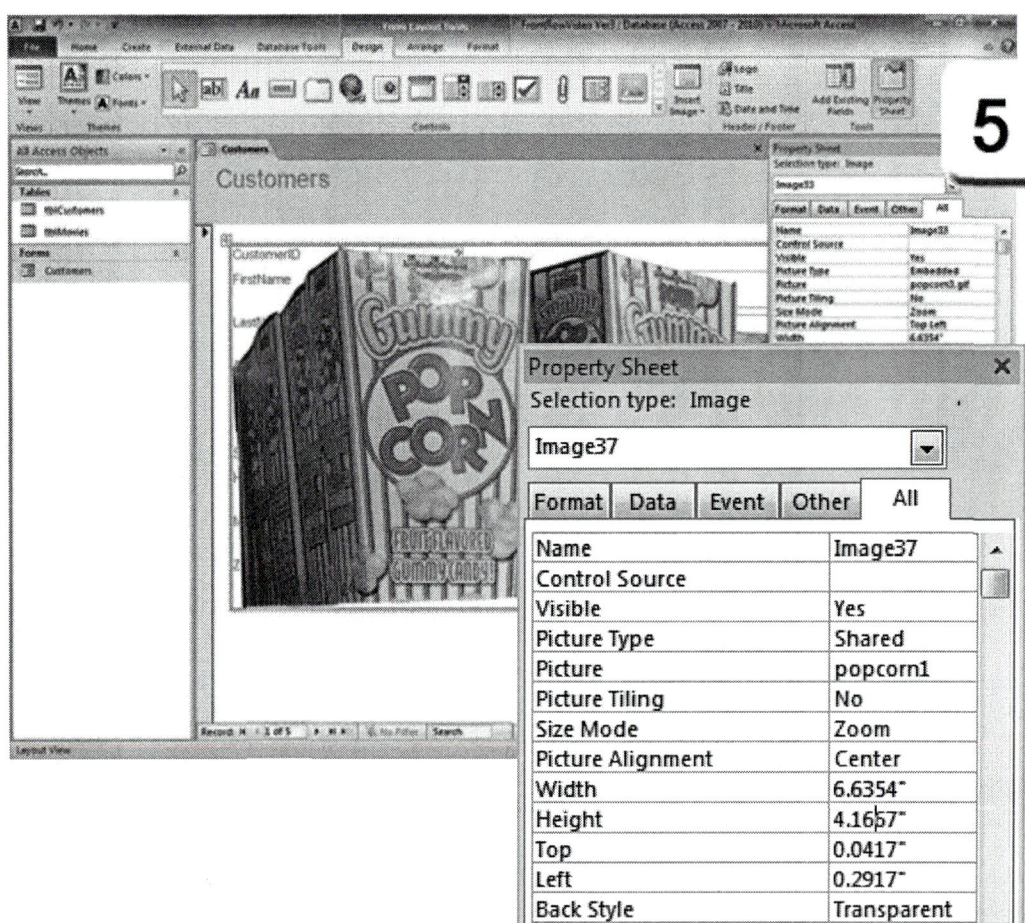

5

Property Sheet	
Selection type: Image	
Image37	
Name	Image37
Control Source	
Visible	Yes
Picture Type	Shared
Picture	popcorn1
Picture Tiling	No
Size Mode	Zoom
Picture Alignment	Center
Width	6.6354"
Height	4.1657"
Top	0.0417"
Left	0.2917"
Back Style	Transparent

Exam 77-885: Microsoft Access 2010
3. Building Forms
3.2. Apply Form Design options: View the Property Sheet

Resize the Image

6. Try it: Edit the Image Properties
Name: popcorn1
Width: 2"
Height: 1.25"
Top: 4.3 (Access may align the image to the grid, hence the odd number)
Left: 0.5"

Try This, Too: Save Your Form
Go to **File-> Save**.
Close the Customers Form.

Very well. We have a simple customer form. And it has a picture of popcorn.

Form Layout Tools ->Design-> Tools->Property Sheet

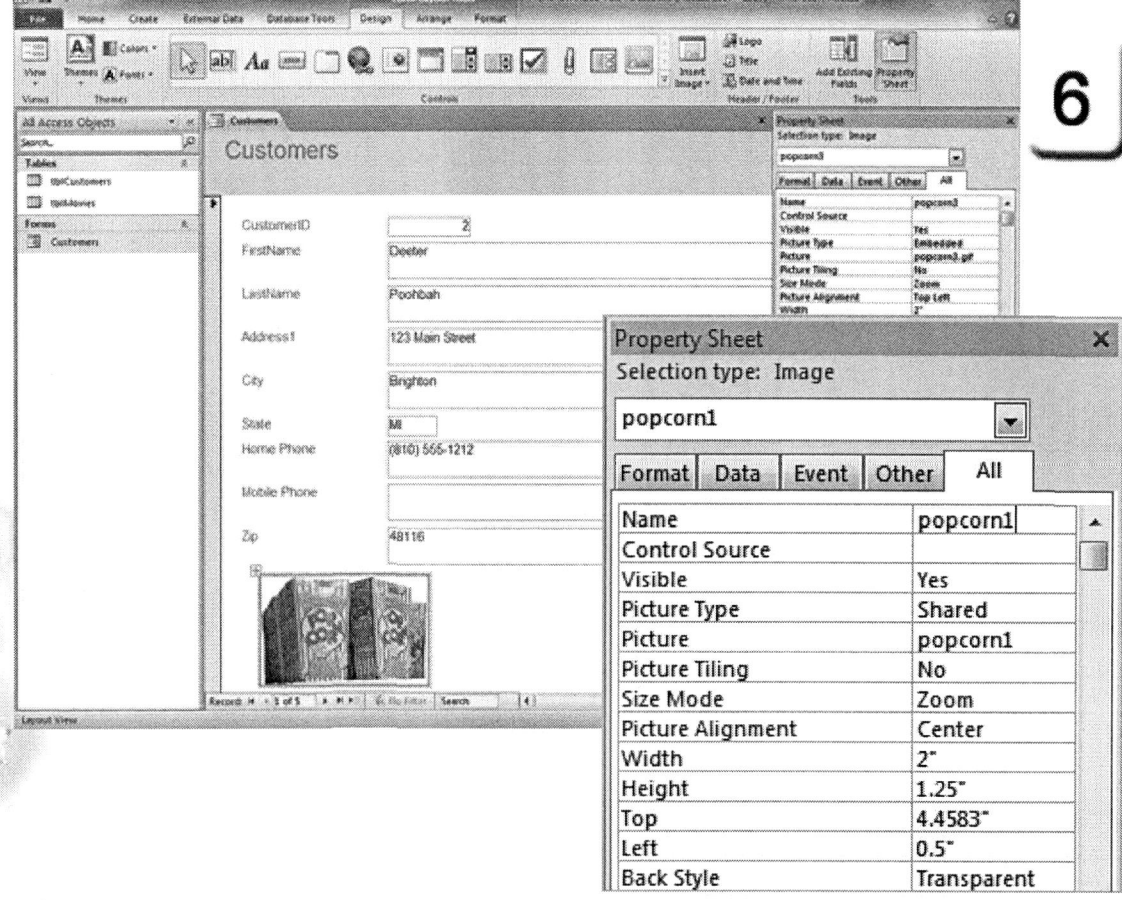

Exam 77-885: Microsoft Access 2010
3. Building Forms
3.3. Apply Form Arrange options: Reposition/Format Controls

HOME

Create ->Forms->Form Wizard

Create Another Form
Please use the Form Wizard to create a Form for the movie Table. Here are the steps.

1. Try it: Create a Form
Go to the Access Objects.
Select: tblMovies

Go to **Create ->Forms->Form Wizard.**
Select a Record Source: tblMoveis
Select All Available Fields.

Keep going...

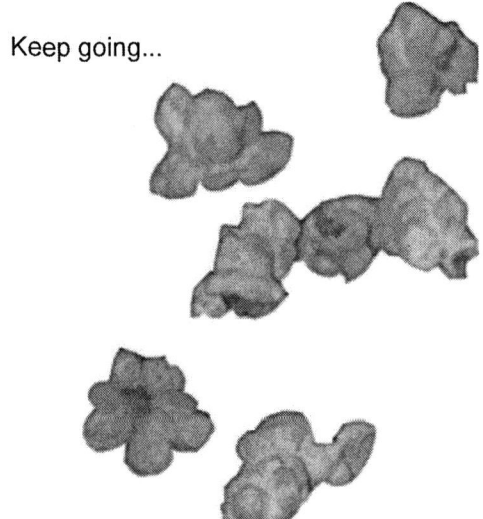

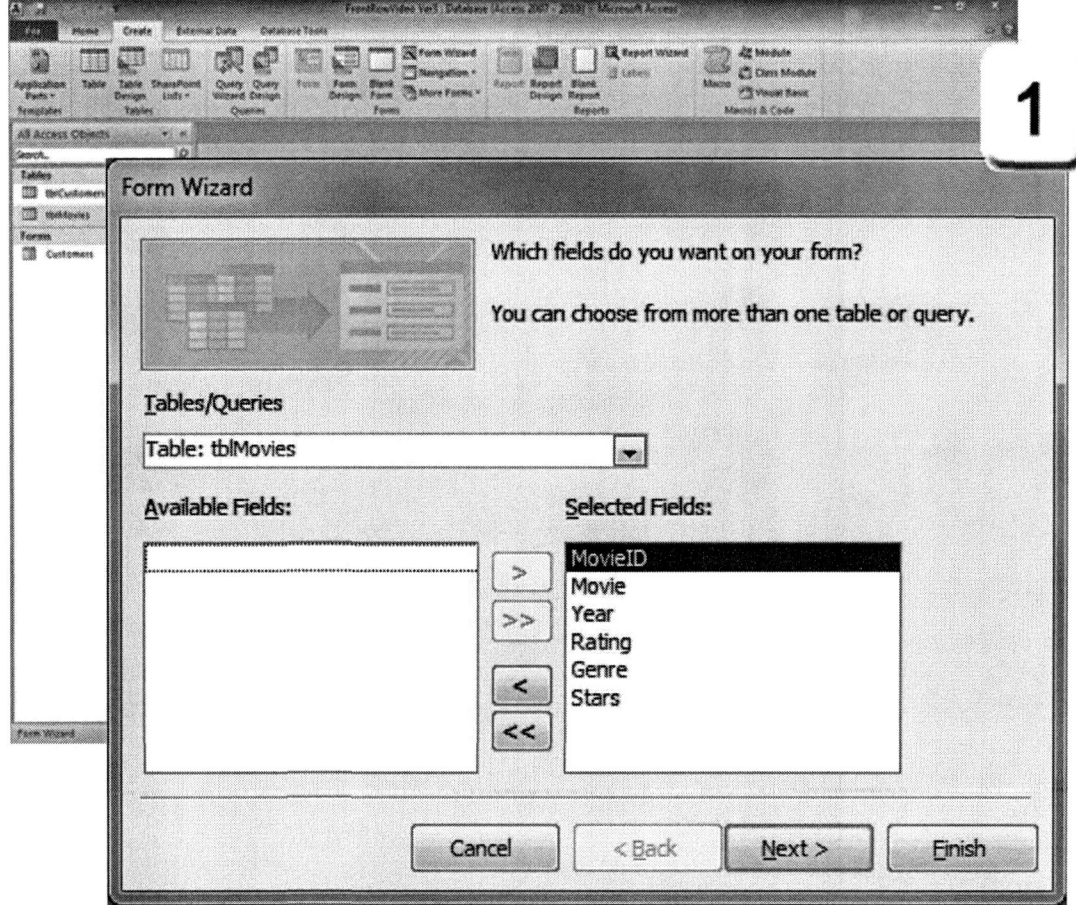

Exam 77-885: Microsoft Access 2010
3. Building Forms
3.1. Create forms: Use the Form Wizard

Form Wizard: Layout
2. Try it: Select a Form Layout
Select a **Layout**: Justified

So, what does the **Justified** Form Layout look like? Click **Next**. Keep going..

Create ->Forms->Form Wizard

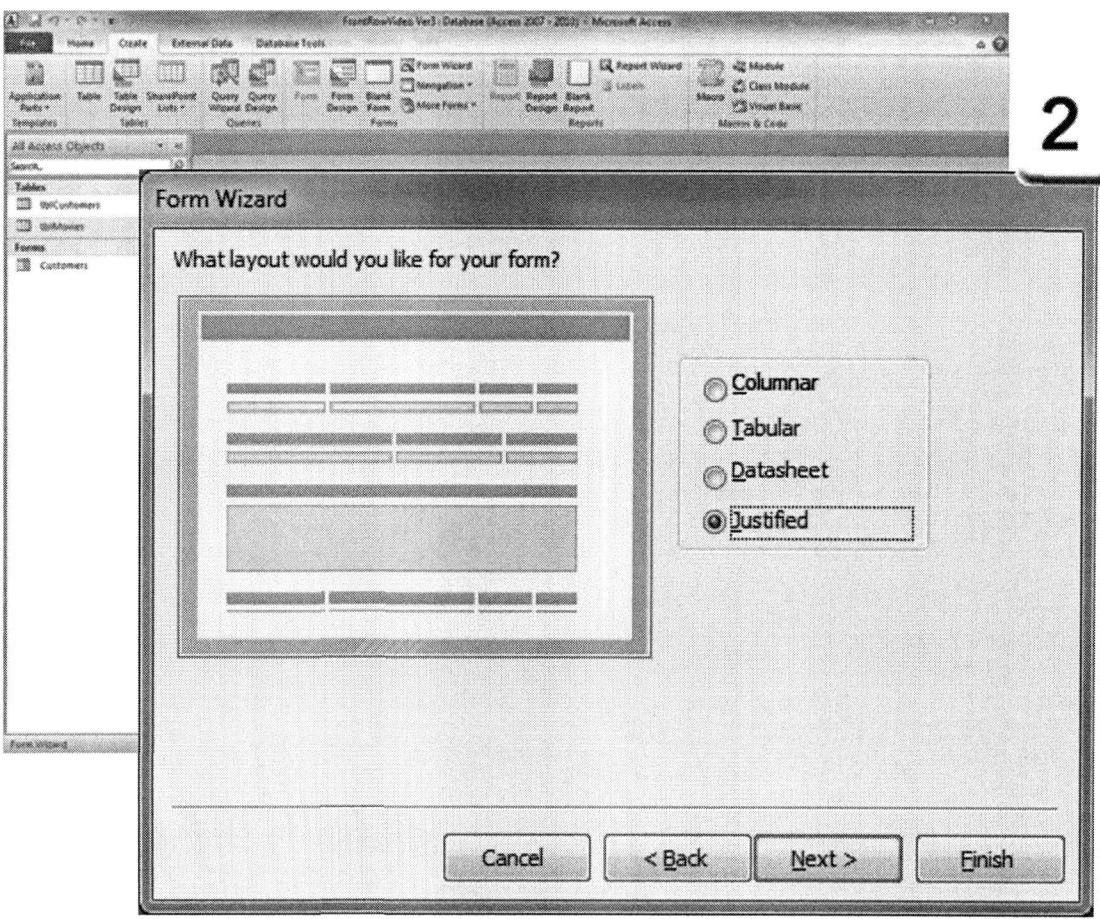

Exam 77-885: Microsoft Access 2010
3. Building Forms
3.1. Create forms: Use the Form Wizard

Finish the Form Wizard

3. Try it: Finish the Form Wizard

Enter the Title: Movies.
Select an option: Open the form to view or enter information.

Click **Finish**. Keep going, let's see it.

Create ->Forms->Form Wizard

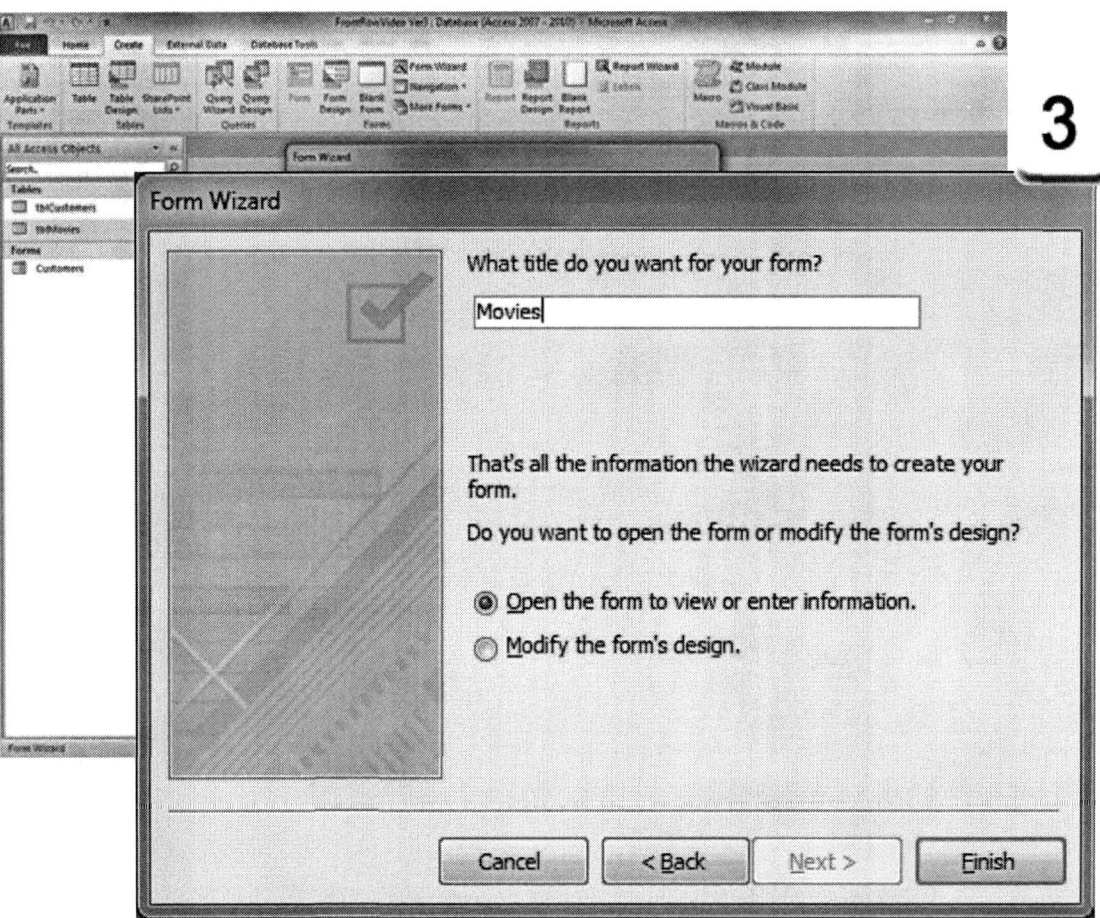

Exam 77-885: Microsoft Access 2010
3. Building Forms
3.1. Create forms: Use the Form Wizard

Hello, Movies

4. Try it: Review the Movies Form

The Movies Form is a **Single Form**: it shows one Movie per form. The Form Fields are Justified which means the Fields are all the same width. The Fields are formatted with an outline as well.

What Else Do You See? Look at the bottom of the Form at the Records. There are 400 Records in tblMovies, the Record Source for this Form.

Keep going...

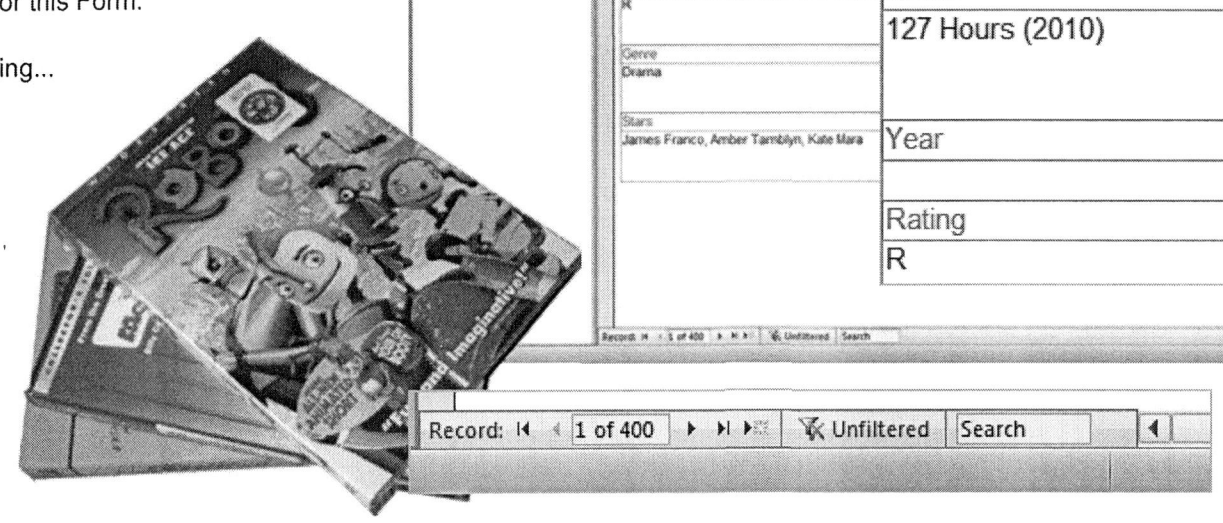

Record: I◄ ◄ 1 of 400 ► ►I ►⯈ 🗙 Unfiltered | Search

Exam 77-885: Microsoft Access 2010
3. Building Forms
3.1. Create forms

HOME

Change the View

The following pages will use the Layout View to format the Movie Form.

1. Try it: Change the View.
Go to **Home-> Views-> View.**
Select a View: **Layout View**.

Keep going...

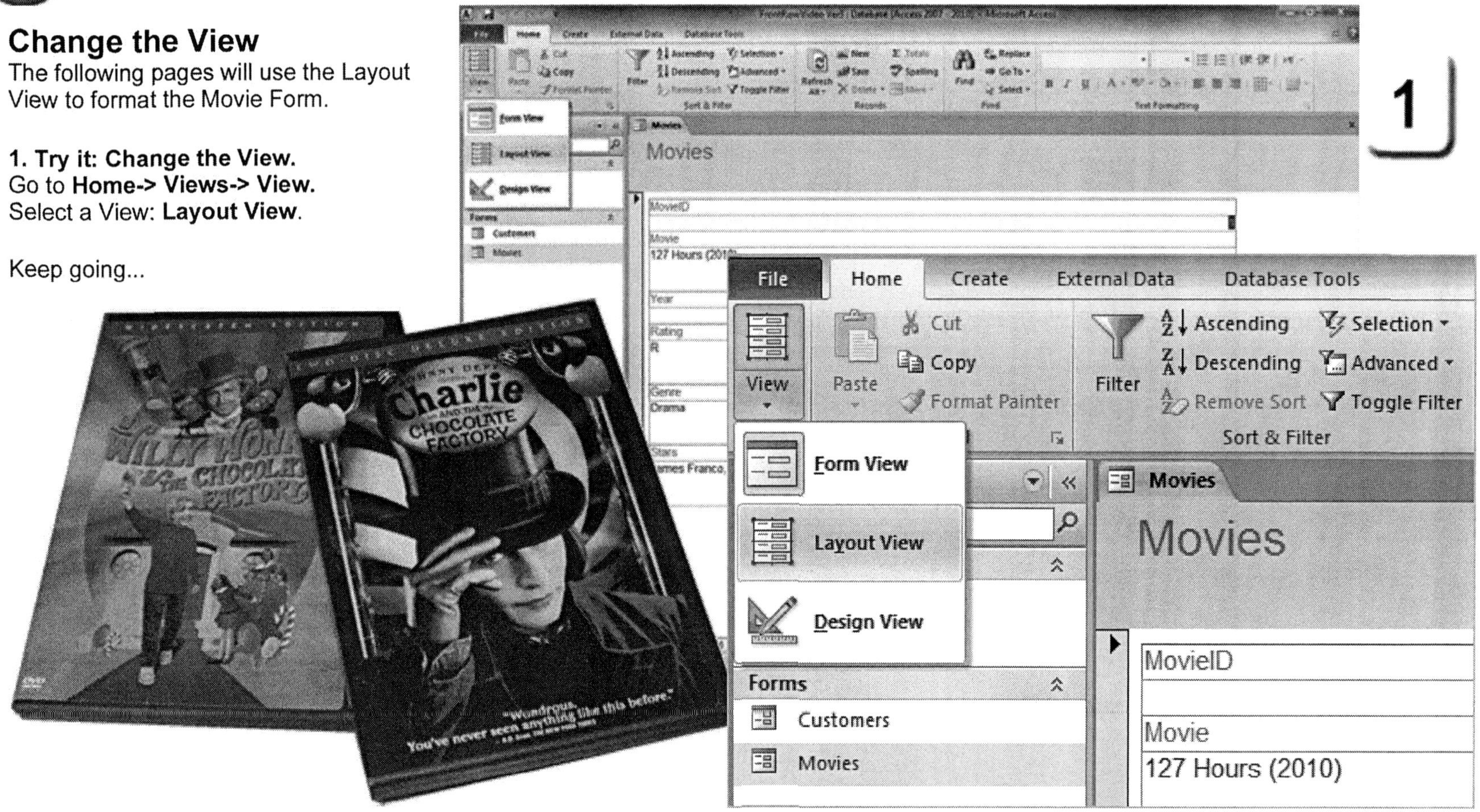

Exam 77-885: Microsoft Access 2010
3. Building Forms
3.1. Create forms: Use Form Design Tools

Format the Form Fields

Look again at the Movies Form. Some of the data is aligned to the right, which makes it difficult to read.

The **Form Design Tools** include a Format Ribbon that looks very similar to the one in Microsoft Word.

2. Try it: Format the Form Field
Select the Year Field.
Go to **Form Layout Tools ->Format->Font**
Select: Align Left

Keep going...

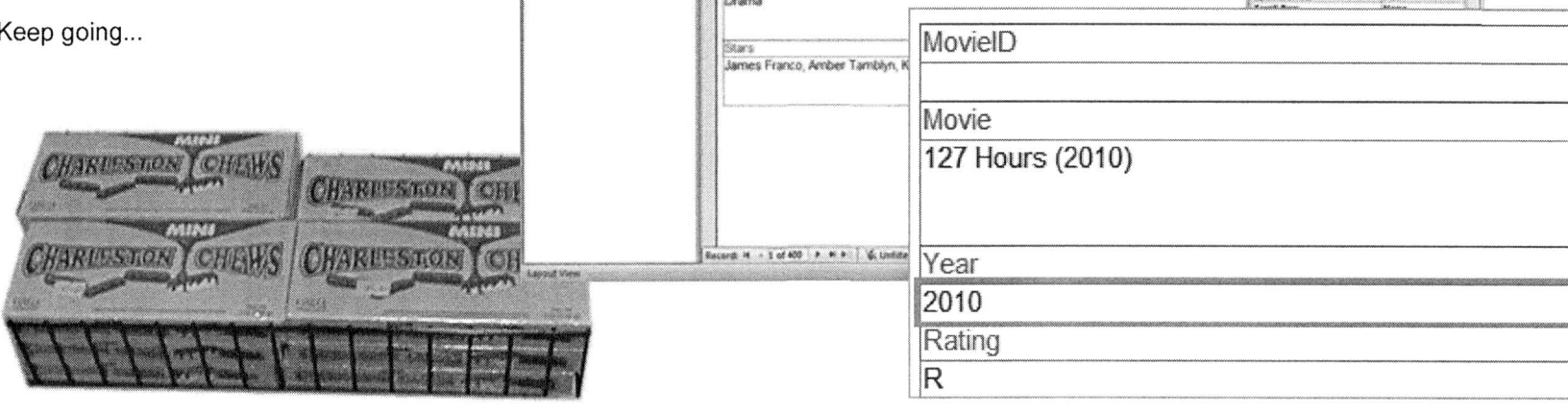

Exam 77-885: Microsoft Access 2010
3. Building Forms
3.4. Apply Form Format options: Reformat Font in a Form

Take One

Edit the Form Header

The **Header** is the banner at the top of the Form. The Header can include a Title, Logo and the Date and Time.

The **Form Header** has Properties, as well. The example will use the Property Sheet to change the Background Color.

3. Try it: Edit the Form Header

The Movies Form is open in Layout View.
Select the Header.
Go to **Form Layout Tools ->Design.**
Click on **Property Sheet**.
The Property Sheet should show the options for the FormHeader.

Try This, Too: Edit the Form Header

Go to the **Format** Tab.
Click on **Back Color**. The Three-dot Builder should be available.
Click on the Three-dot Builder.
Select a color: Gold, Accent 2. Lighter 40%.

Keep going...

Form Layout Tools ->Design->Property Sheet

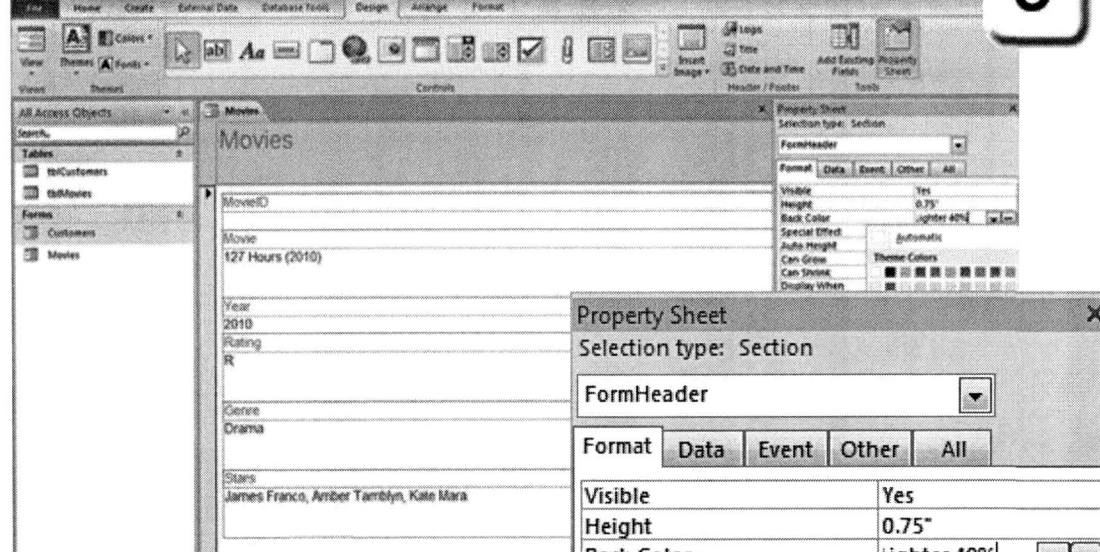

Exam 77-885: Microsoft Access 2010
3. Building Forms
3.2. Apply Form Design options: Edit the Form Header

Save and View

Even a simple Form should be tested as a User would see it.

Before You Begin: Save the Form
Go to **File->Save.**

Still Before You Begin: Change the View
Go to **Form Layout Tools ->Design->Views.**
Go to **View->Form View.**

4. Try it: Test the Movies Form
The Movies Form is open.
Go to **Home ->Records->New.**
A new, blank record will open.

Try This, Too: Edit the New Record
Enter the following information:
Movie: Titanic 3D
Year: 2012
Rating: PG13
Genre: Romance
Stars: Leonardo DiCaprio, Kate Winslet

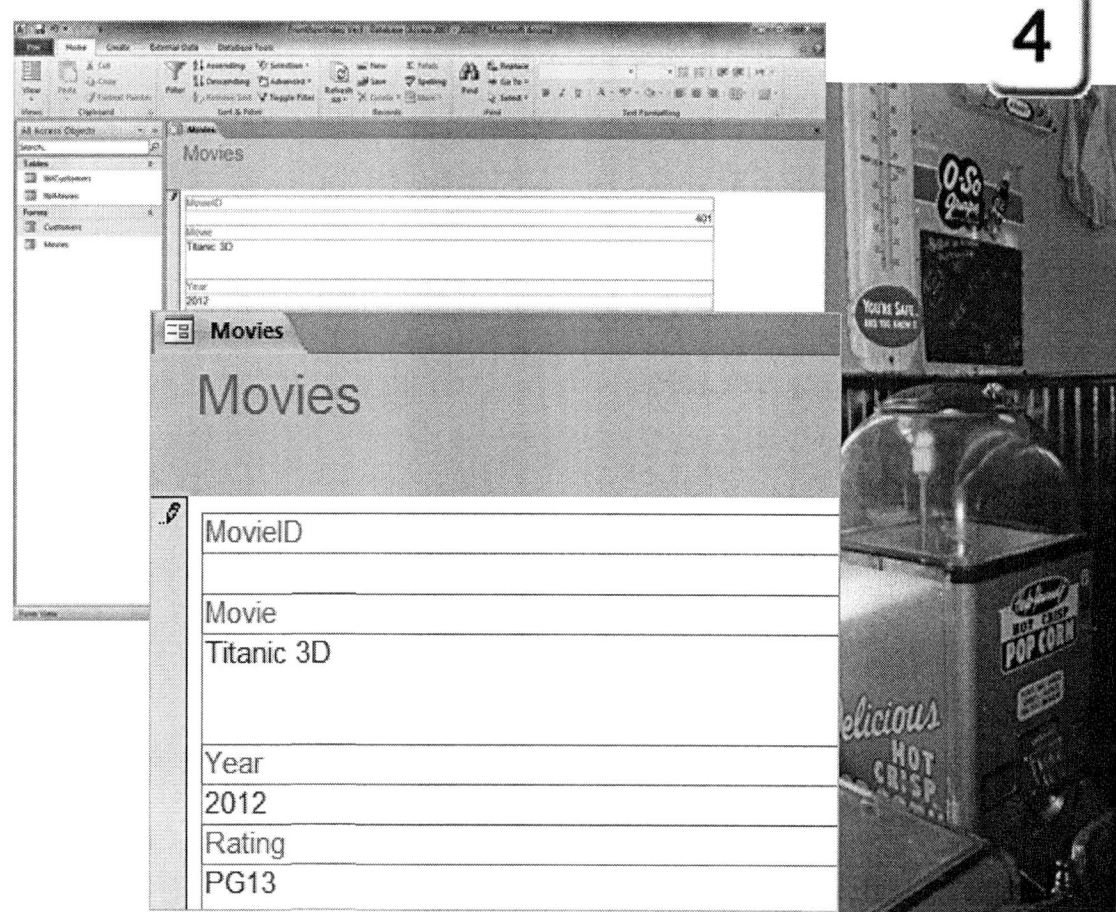

Exam 77-885: Microsoft Access 2010
3. Building Forms
3.1. Create forms

Summary
We created two new Forms with the Form Wizard: Customers and Movies. This lesson also introduced the Form Design Tools that are available in Layout View.

The next lesson looks at what you can do with Forms in Design View.

Allez Allez In Free. You done good.
You get the cookie...
or popcorn if you wish!

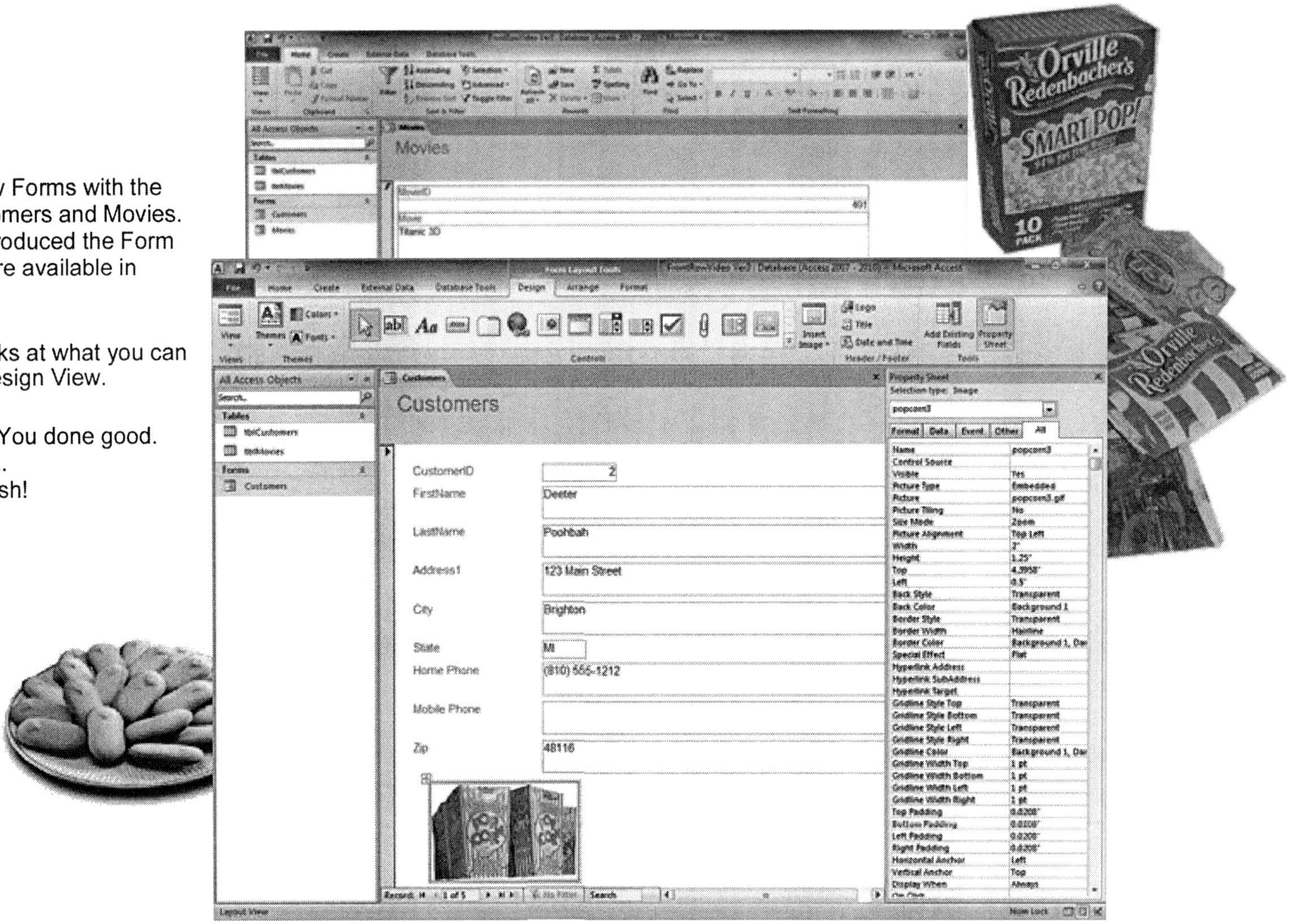

Practice Activities

Lesson 5: Form Design
Try This: Do the following steps

1. Open the Brown Bag Lunch database you have been programming. Or you may download the sample database **Brown Bag Lunch ver5.accdb** online.

2. Create a New Form with the Form Wizard. Use tblCustomers as the Record Source.

3. Select all available Fields for the Form.

4. Select the Columnar Layout.

5. Name the Title Customers. Select the option to open the Form to view or enter info. Finish the Wizard.

6. Add a new record to verify that the Form works.
Wordnation, Andrea Carter, 1275 Grand River Ave., Milford, MI, 48380, 248-555-6100

7. Go to Layout View. Select the Theme Hardcover.

8. Save the Form as Customers.

9. Create a second Form with the Form Wizard. Use tblProducts as the Record Source.

10. Select all available Fields. Select the Justified Layout.

11. Name the title Products. Select the option to open and enter information then finish the Wizard.

12. Add a new Record to test the Form.
Sandwich, Peanut Butter and Honey, Vegetarian, Peanut butter and Michigan honey on fresh bread.

13. Return to the Layout View. Select all of the Controls in the Detail Section and resize them so that the Width is 3".

Add the image **Lunch1.gif** Resize the image to 2" x 1.5" and place it in the lower right corner of the Form.

14. Save the Form as Products.

15. Close the Brown Bag database and get some cookies.

Test Yourself

1. Which are ways to create a Form in Access? (Give all correct answers.)
A. Templates
B. Design from Scratch
C. Form Wizard
D. Import from Word
Tip: Beginning Access, page 105

2. Which are Form Layouts available in the Form Wizard? (Give all correct answers.)
A. Columnar
B. Tabular
C. Data Sheet
D. Justified
Tip: Beginning Access, page 107

3. Which is are options for finishing the Form Wizard? (Give all correct answers.)
A. No action, which returns you to the Table
B. Modify the Form opens it for editing
C. Open the Form to show it as a user would see it
Tip: Beginning Access, page 108

4. The TAB key, when pressed, should advance the cursor to the next logical field.
A. True
B. False
Tip: Beginning Access, page 171

5. Which are Form Views available? (Give all correct answers.)
A. Form (to use and to enter data)
B. Layout (a simple editor)
C. Design (a detailed editor)
Tip: Beginning Access, page 112

6. Which are the Layout Tools Ribbons? (Give all correct answers.)
A. Layout
B. Design
C. Format
D. Arrange
E. Advanced
Tip: Beginning Access, page 113

7. The part at the top of Form that can include the title, logo, date and time, etc is called what?
A. Heading
B. Branding
C. Header
D. Title Space
Tip: Beginning Access, page 124

8. Any Form created should be tested as User would see it.
A. True
B. False
Tip: Beginning Access, page 125

9. The Form Wizard always arranges Fields ideally, making sure related fields stay together.
A. True
B. False
Tip: Beginning Access, page 111

Access 2010: Presenting Data Visually

Designing Forms for Real Users

Beginning Access Objectives
In this lesson, you will learn how to:

1. Go to the Design View and use the Form Design Tools to edit the Form Fields.

2. View the Property Sheet for the Form and the individual Form Controls.

3. Add a picture to the Form Header and use the Property Sheet to resize the picture.

4. Arrange the Form Fields and edit the Tab Order.

© 2012 Comma Productions, LLC

Lesson 6 : Designing Forms for Real Users

1. Readings
Read Lesson 6 in the Beginning Access guide, page 129-150.

Project
Edit the Form Controls with the Form Design Tools and the Property Sheet.

Downloads
FrontRowVideo Begin6.accdb
popcorn1.gif, popcorn2.gif,
popcorn3.gif, popcorn4.gif, movies1.gif.

Brown Bag Lunch ver6.accdb
BB Customers Logo.jpg
Brown Bag Logo.jpg
Lunch1.gif, Lunch2.gif, Lunch3.gif,
Lunch4.gif

2. Practice
Complete the Practice Activity on page 151.

3. Assessment
Review the Test questions on page 152.

Form Design Tools: Design

Form Design Tools: Design

Menu Maps
From the **Home Ribbon**.
Home ->Views->View->Design View, page 133

From the **Form Design Tools: Design Ribbon**.
1. Form Design Tools, page 134
2. Form Design Tools ->Design->Tools->Property Sheet, page 136
3. Form Design Tools ->Design->Header/Footer->Logo, page 138
4. Form Design Tools ->Format->Font, page 144
5. Form Design Tools ->Design->Tools->Tab Order, page 146

Forms: Designing for Real Users

A **Real User** is the person who has to use your database to get their job done. If your Forms are easy to enter information, then the data will get typed in. If not,...images of playing whack-a-programmer come to mind. Real Users get real frustrated if the Form does not behave as expected. Each time the Form is changed, we will test it to see if it still works.

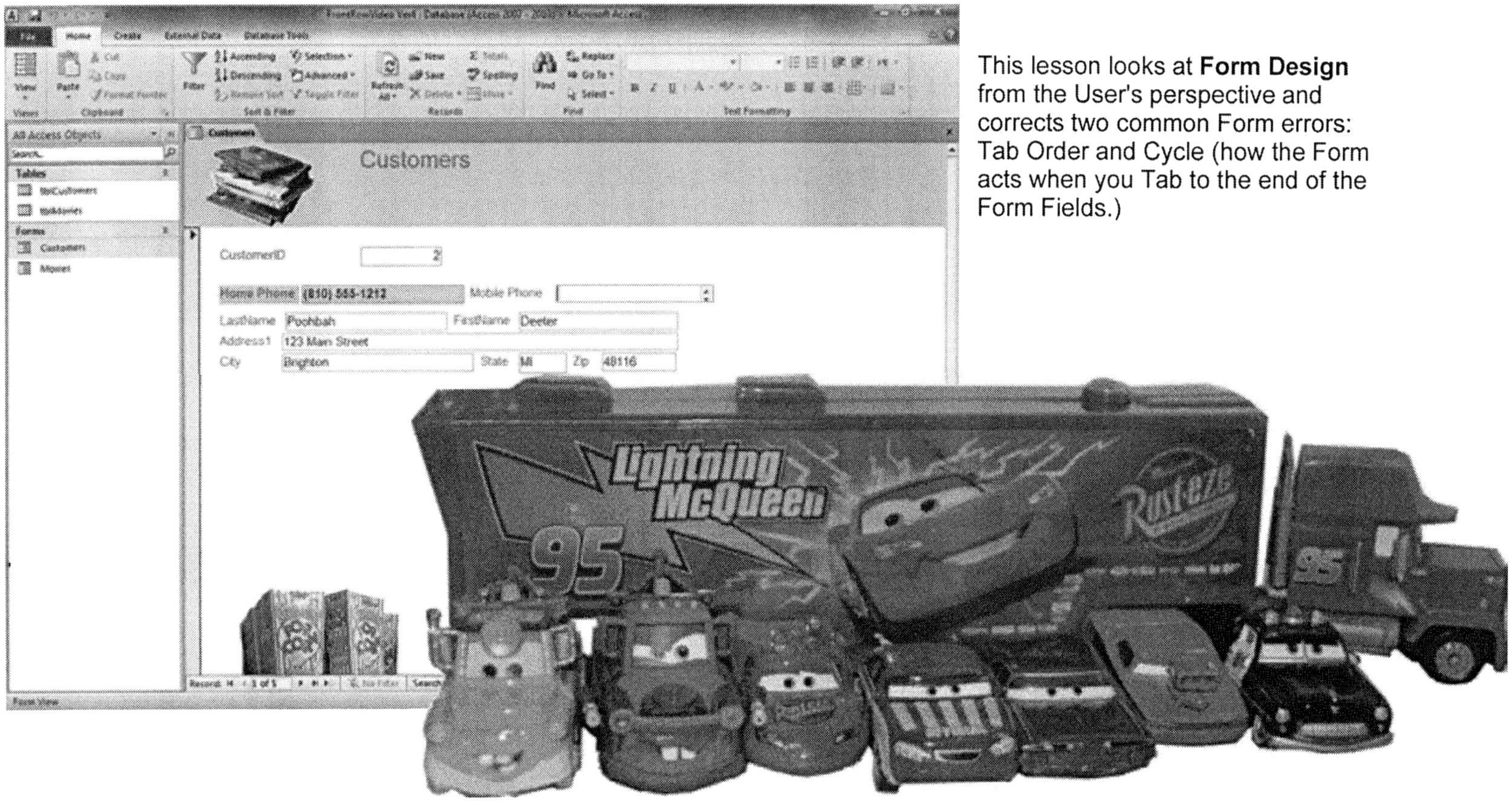

This lesson looks at **Form Design** from the User's perspective and corrects two common Form errors: Tab Order and Cycle (how the Form acts when you Tab to the end of the Form Fields.)

Before You Begin

This demonstration uses the Front Row Video database that we programmed in the previous lessons. You can continue with the database you have been working on. You can also download the sample Access database at the beginning of this lesson.

1. Try it: Open the Sample Database
Go to the Documents folder.
Open the sample database:
FrontRowVideo Begin6.accdb

What Do You See? There are two tables:
tblCustomers
tblMovies

There are two forms as well:
Customers
Movies

What Else Do You See? This database may have a Security Warning. In order to edit the objects and save your work, you need to click on **Enable Content**.

Microsoft Access 2010

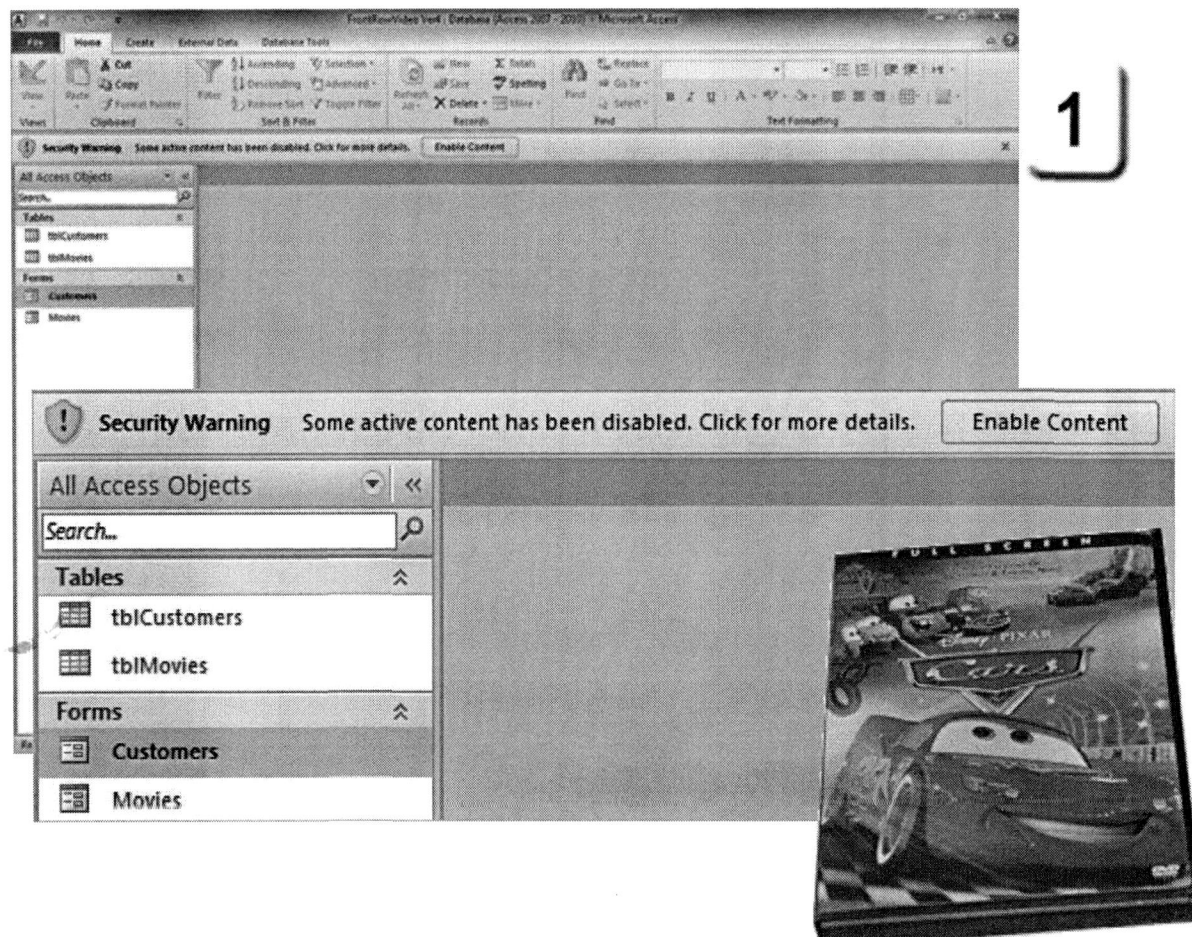

Change the View

The previous lesson considered the options available when a Form is in **Layout View**. This lesson uses the **Design View**.

2. Try it: Go to the Design View
Go to the Access Navigation Panel. Double-click the Customer Form to open it.

Go to **Home ->Views->View.**
Click on **Design View.**

Keep going, please...

Home ->Views->View->Design View

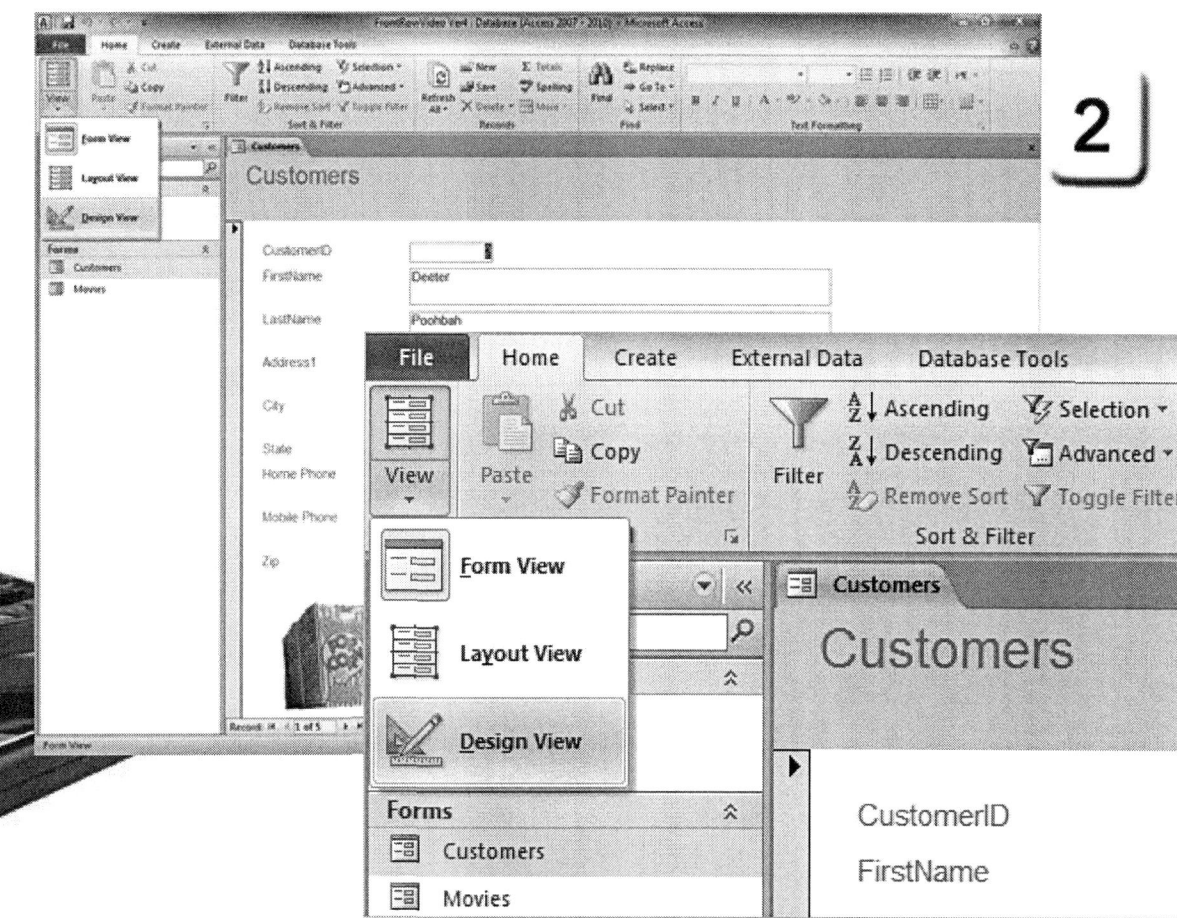

Exam 77-885: Microsoft Access 2010
3. Building Forms
3.1. Create forms: Use Form Design Tools

Hello, Design View
3. Try it: Review the Form Design Tools
There are three Form Design Ribbons:
Design, Arrange and Format.

The Design Ribbon includes:
Views
Themes
Controls
Header/Footer
Tools

The Arrange Ribbon includes:
Table
Rows & Columns
Merge/Spilt
Move
Sizing & Ordering

The Format Ribbon includes:
Selection
Font
Number
Background
Control Formatting

Keep going, please...

Form Design Tools

Exam 77-885: Microsoft Access 2010
3. Building Forms
3.1. Create forms: Use Form Design Tools

Form Headers and Detail

4. Try This: Find the Sections

A Microsoft Access Form may have many sections. Each section has a purpose. The **Form Header** is used for navigation and corporate logos. Users look for clues or signs that they are on the right page. Color and images are part of good form design.

The **Detail** section is used for the Form Fields. This is the data from the Customer Table, tblCustomer.

Here are the changes we will make to the Customer Form:
1. Edit the Label on the Form Header
2. Insert a picture
3. Change the Layout
4. Fix the Tab Order
5. Change the Form Properties

Form Design Tools

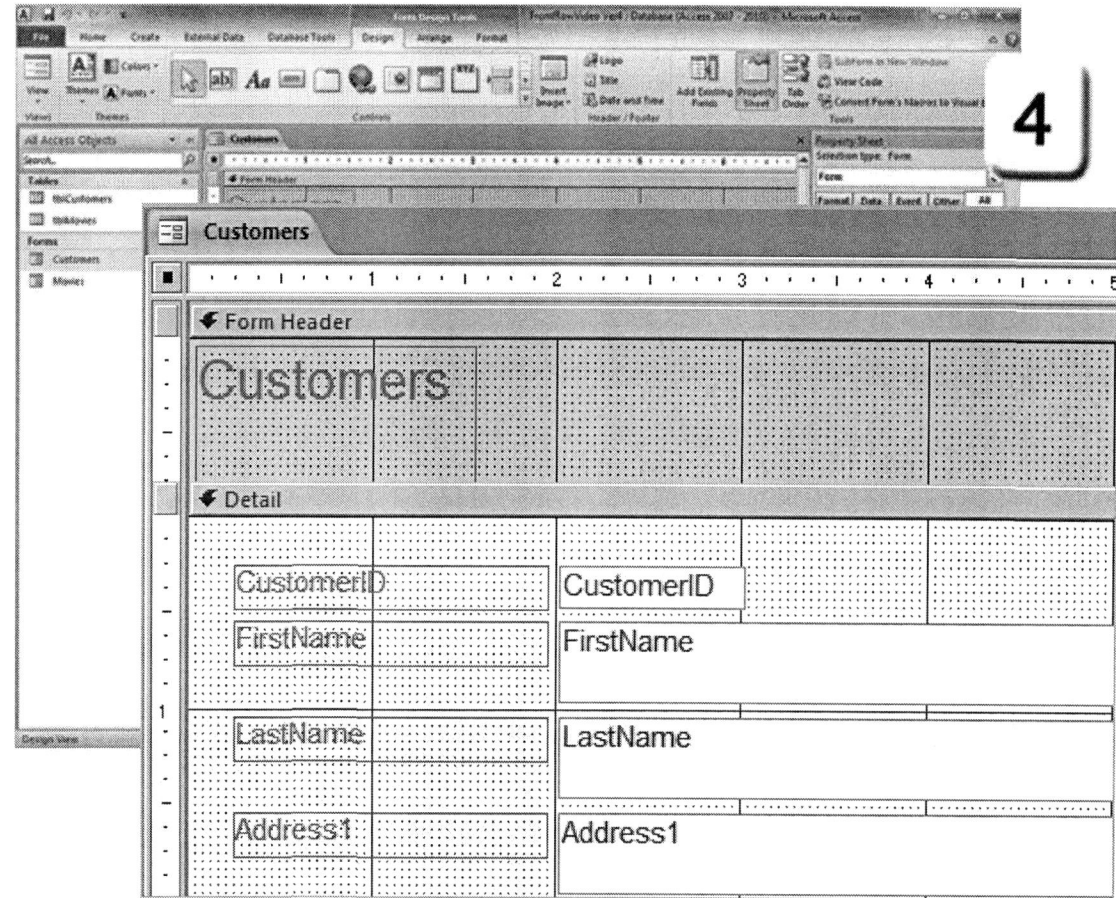

Exam 77-885: Microsoft Access 2010
3. Building Forms
3.1. Create forms: Use Form Design Tools

Form Controls: Labels

A **Label** is a simple box to display your descriptions. This step edits the Label in the Form Header by editing the Property Sheet.

5. Try it: Find the Property Sheet
The Customer Form is open in Design View.
Go to the Form Header.
Select a Label: Customers.
Go to **Form Design Tools ->Design->Tools.**
Click on **Property Sheet.**

What Do You See? The Property Sheet for the Label shows the following:
Name: Label18
Caption: Customers
Visible: Yes

And more...keep going.

Memo to Self: The name in your Property Sheet may or may not match the example on this page. That is OK.

Form Design Tools ->Design->Tools->Property Sheet

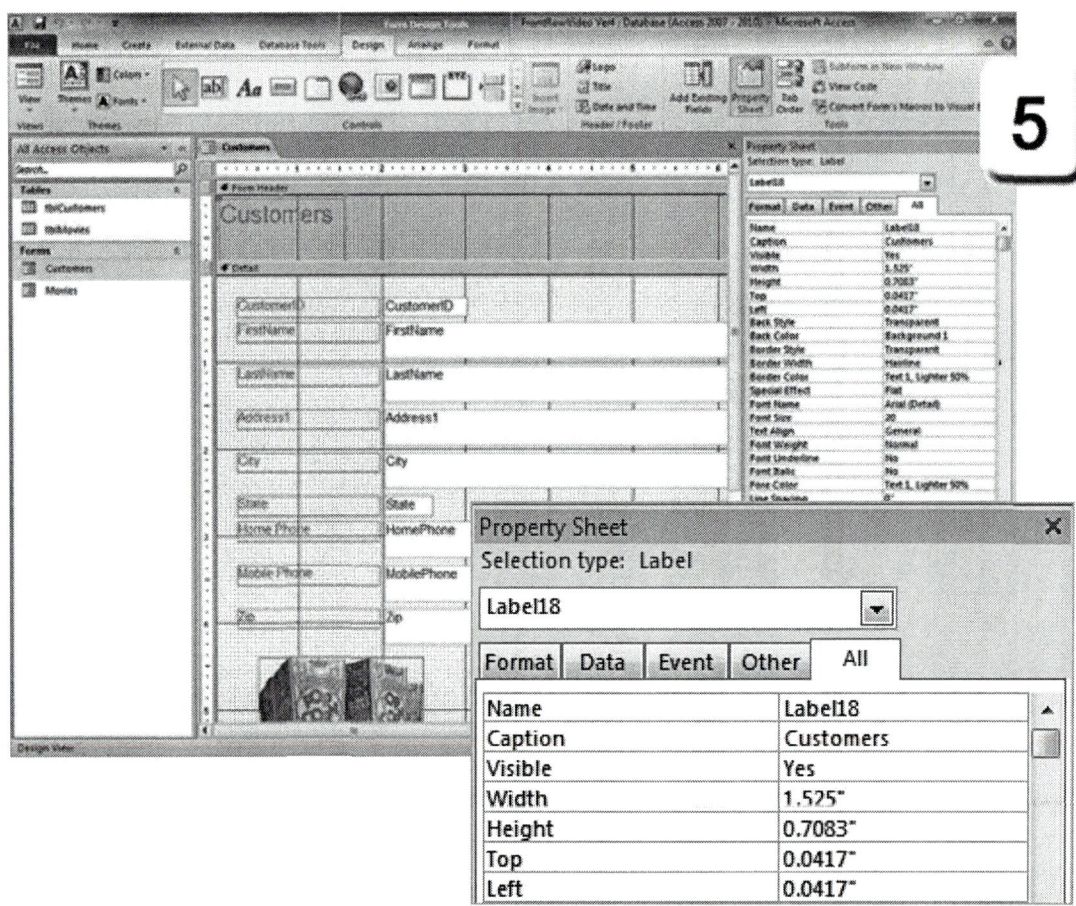

Exam 77-885: Microsoft Access 2010
3. Building Forms
3.2. Apply Form Design options: View Property Sheet

Edit the Label

6. Try it: Edit the Label
Click on the Label to select it.
Edit the following Properties:
Name: CustomerLabel
Left: 2

What Do You See? The Label is now placed 2" from the Left edge of the Form.

Keep going...

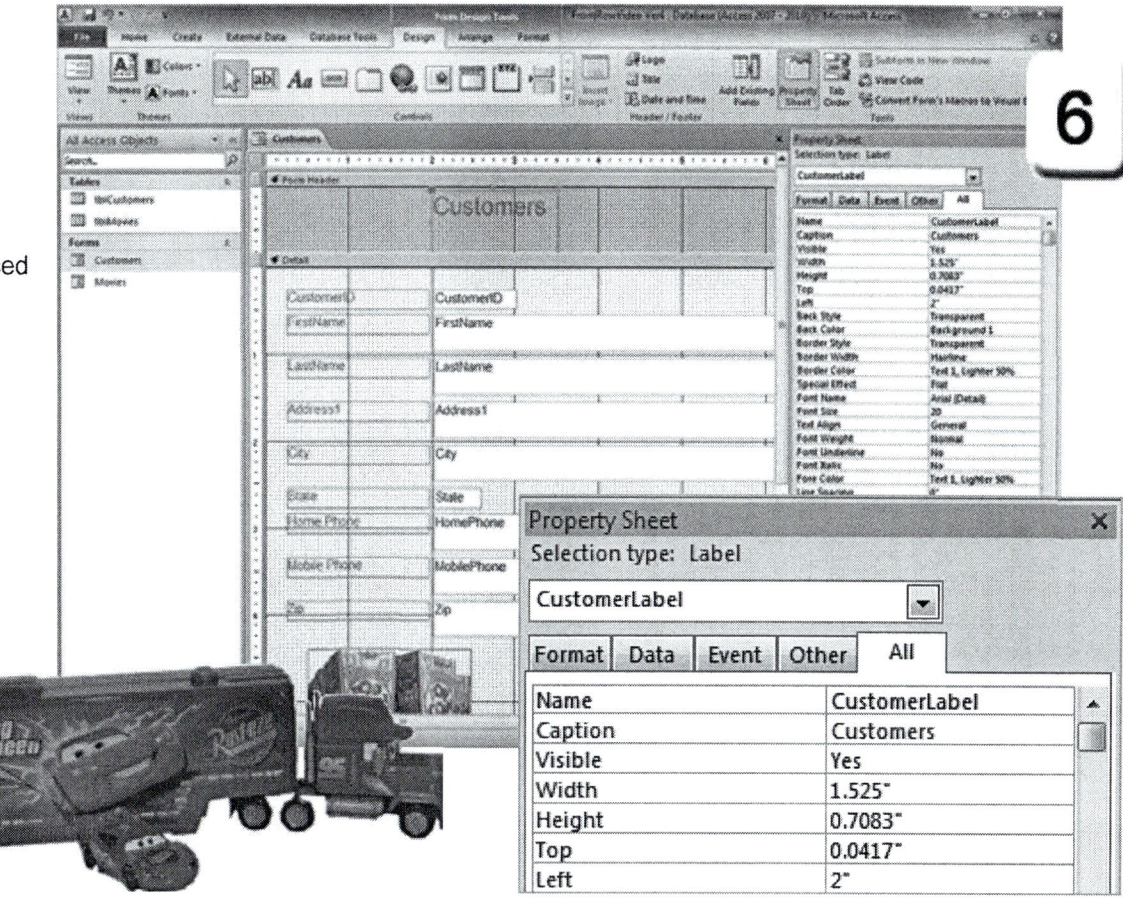

6

Property Sheet
Selection type: Label

CustomerLabel

Format	Data	Event	Other	All

Name	CustomerLabel
Caption	Customers
Visible	Yes
Width	1.525"
Height	0.7083"
Top	0.0417"
Left	2"

Exam 77-885: Microsoft Access 2010
3. Building Forms
3.2. Apply Form Design options: View Property Sheet

Form Design Tools ->Design->Header/Footer->Logo

Add a Logo
You can use the Form Design Tools to add a **Logo** to this Header. Here are the steps.

7. Try it: Add a Logo to the Header
The Customer Form is open in Design View.
Click on the Form Header to select it.
Go to **Form Design Tools ->Design.**
Go to **Header/Footer->Logo.**

What Do You See? You will be prompted to Browse for an image.
Go to the Documents folder.
Select an image: movies1.gif

Click **OK**. Keep going...

Memo to Self: It is not necessary to MATCH the images in this lesson. You can use your own picutres if you wish.

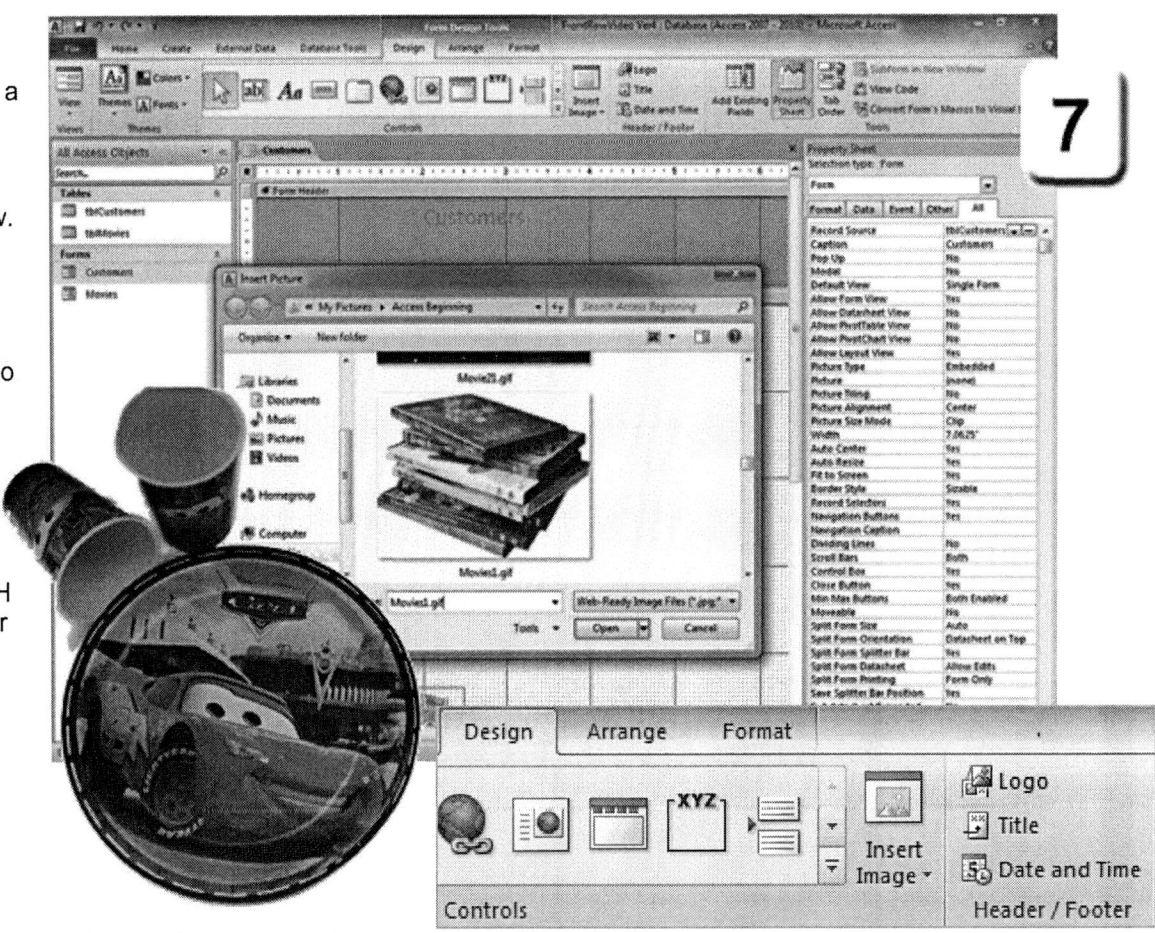

Exam 77-885: Microsoft Access 2010
3. Building Forms
3.2. Apply Form Design options: Format the Header/Footer

Resize the Logo

8. Try it: Edit the Logo

Click on the Logo to select it.
Edit the following Properties:
Name: FrontRowLogo
Size Mode: Zoom
Picture Alignment: Center
Width: 1.5"
Height: 1"
Top: 0.0417"
Left: 0.2"

What Do You See? The Logo is now resized to be 1.5" x 1".

What Else Do You See? The Page Header did NOT automatically resize when you changed the Logo. Please resize the Page Header.

Looking good. Keep going...

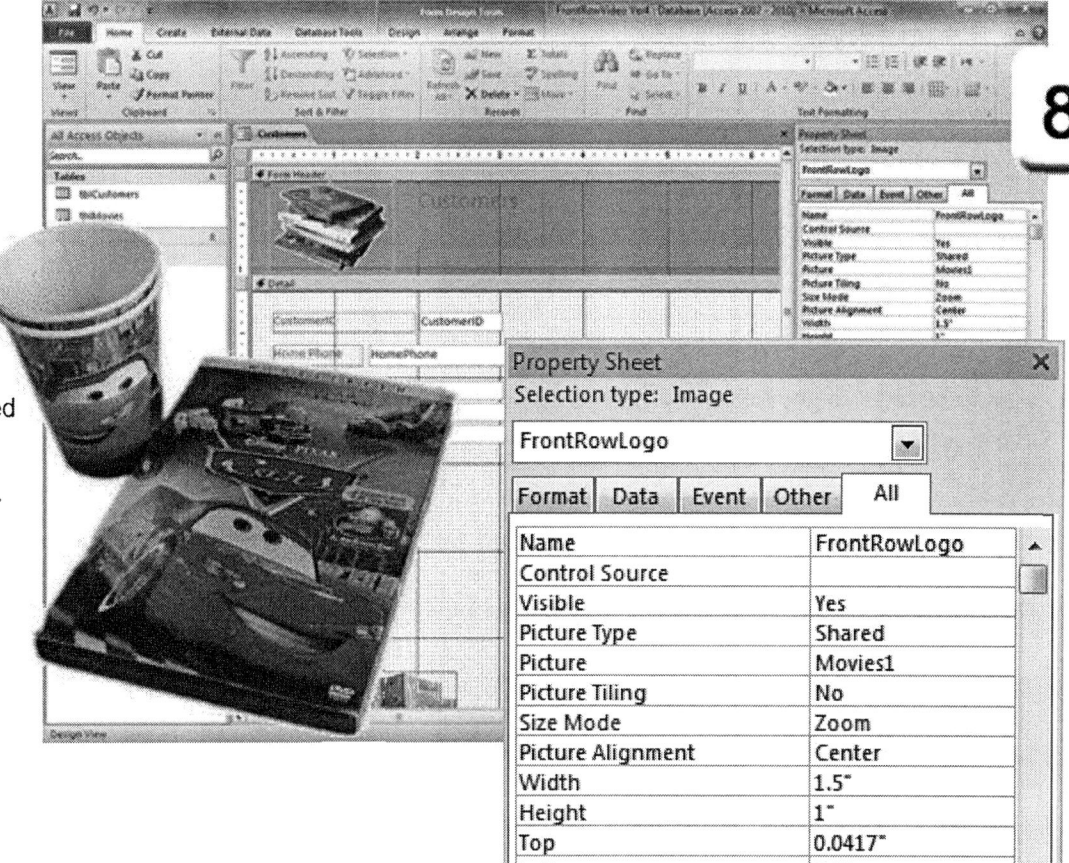

Exam 77-885: Microsoft Access 2010
3. Building Forms
3.2. Apply Form Design options: Format the Header/Footer

Format the Header

9. Try it: Format the Header
The **Form Header** is selected.
Go to **Property Sheet-> All**.
Click on **Back Color**.
Use the **three-dot builder** to select a
Theme Color: Light Grey 2.

So far, so good.

Form Design Tools ->Design->Tools->Property Sheet

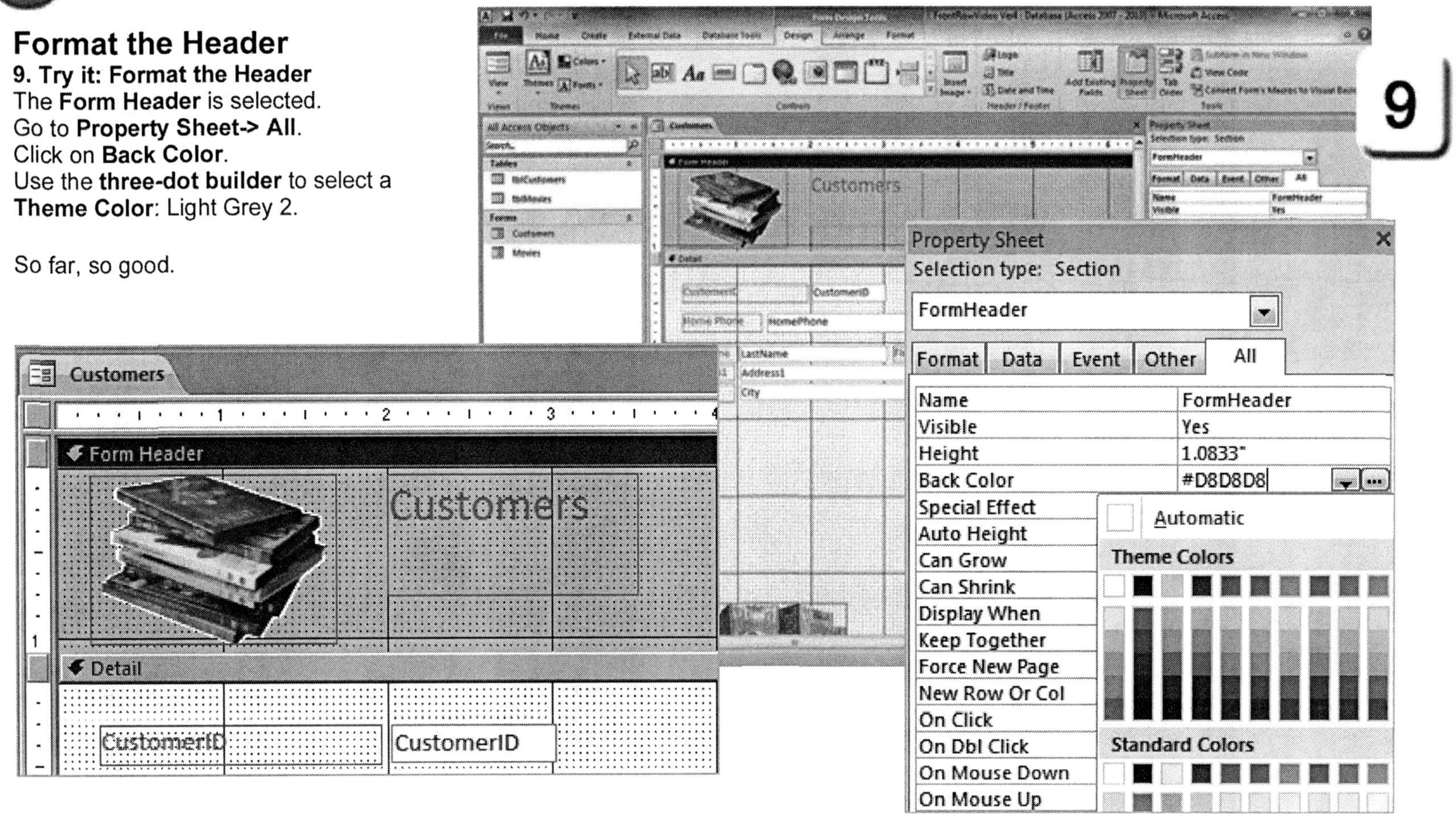

Property Sheet
Selection type: Section

FormHeader

Format	Data	Event	Other	All

Name	FormHeader
Visible	Yes
Height	1.0833"
Back Color	#D8D8D8
Special Effect	
Auto Height	Automatic
Can Grow	Theme Colors
Can Shrink	
Display When	
Keep Together	
Force New Page	
New Row Or Col	
On Click	
On Dbl Click	Standard Colors
On Mouse Down	
On Mouse Up	

Exam 77-885: Microsoft Access 2010
3. Building Forms
3.2. Apply Form Design options: Format the Header/Footer

Working with Form Controls

Each Form Field has two parts: Label and Control. The previous pages looked at the Label and the various Properties that can be edited to resize and position the Label.

The **Control** is where users enter and change data. The **Detail** Section of this Form has several Controls that we will edit and arrange.

1. Try it: Select the Control
Select the FirstName Control.

What Do You See? The FirstName Control is highlighted. There are small square **handles** in each corner and side that can be used to resize the Control.

The Label and the Control both have special handles in the upper left corner that can be used to move them independently.

Keep going...

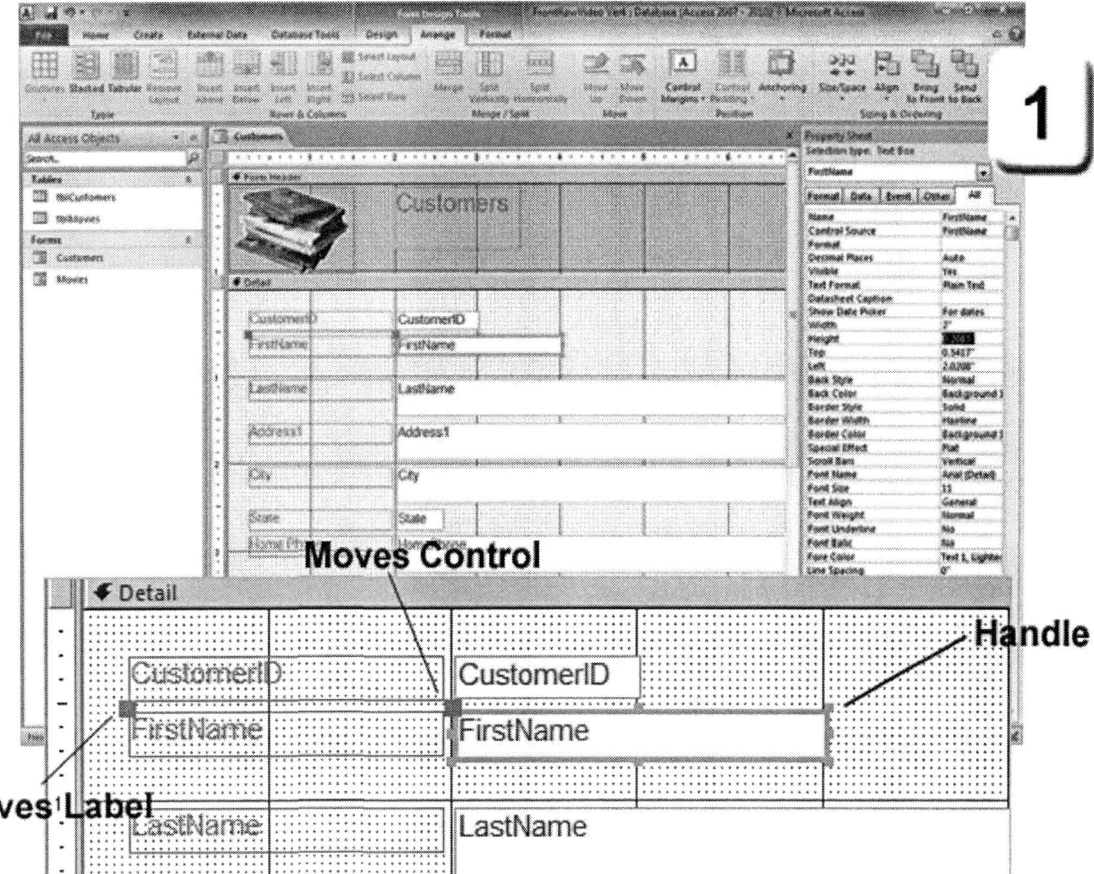

Exam 77-885: Microsoft Access 2010
3. Building Forms
3.3. Apply Form Arrange options: Reposition Controls

Take Two

Select Multiple Controls

Say there are a half dozen Controls that you would like to resize. You can select and edit them all at the same time.

2. Try it: Select Multiple Controls
Hold the Control (Ctrl) key on the keyboard as you select all of the Controls in the Detail Section of the Customers Form, EXCEPT the State Control.

Try This, Too: Resize Multiple Controls
Go to the Property Sheet.
Edit the Width: 2"
Edit the Height:0.2083"

Keep going...

Form Design Tools ->Design->Tools->Property Sheet

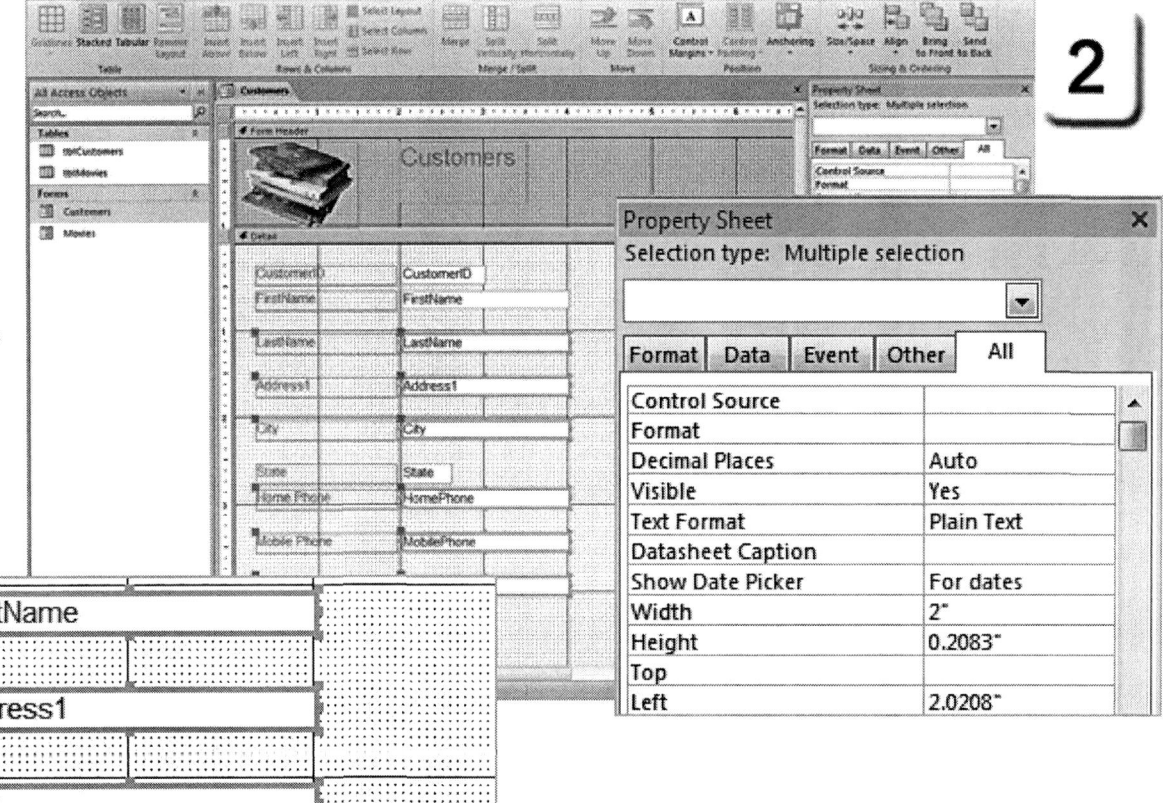

Exam 77-885: Microsoft Access 2010
3. Building Forms
3.3. Apply Form Arrange options: Reposition Controls

Reposition the Controls

The Customer Form collects information that can used for billing, reports and mail merges. This step arranges the Form Controls as they would look on an address label or sales receipt.

3. Try it: Move the Controls

Select the Controls one by one.
Resize and move them as shown on this page.

Keep going...!

Memo to Self: You can instantly resize a Label so that it fits the text.

Try this: Select the Label.
Place your cursor on the bottom right handle. When you see a double arrow, double click. Access will resize the Label precisely.

Don't Forget: You can move a Label and Control separately by using the grey handle in the upper left corner.

Form Design Tools

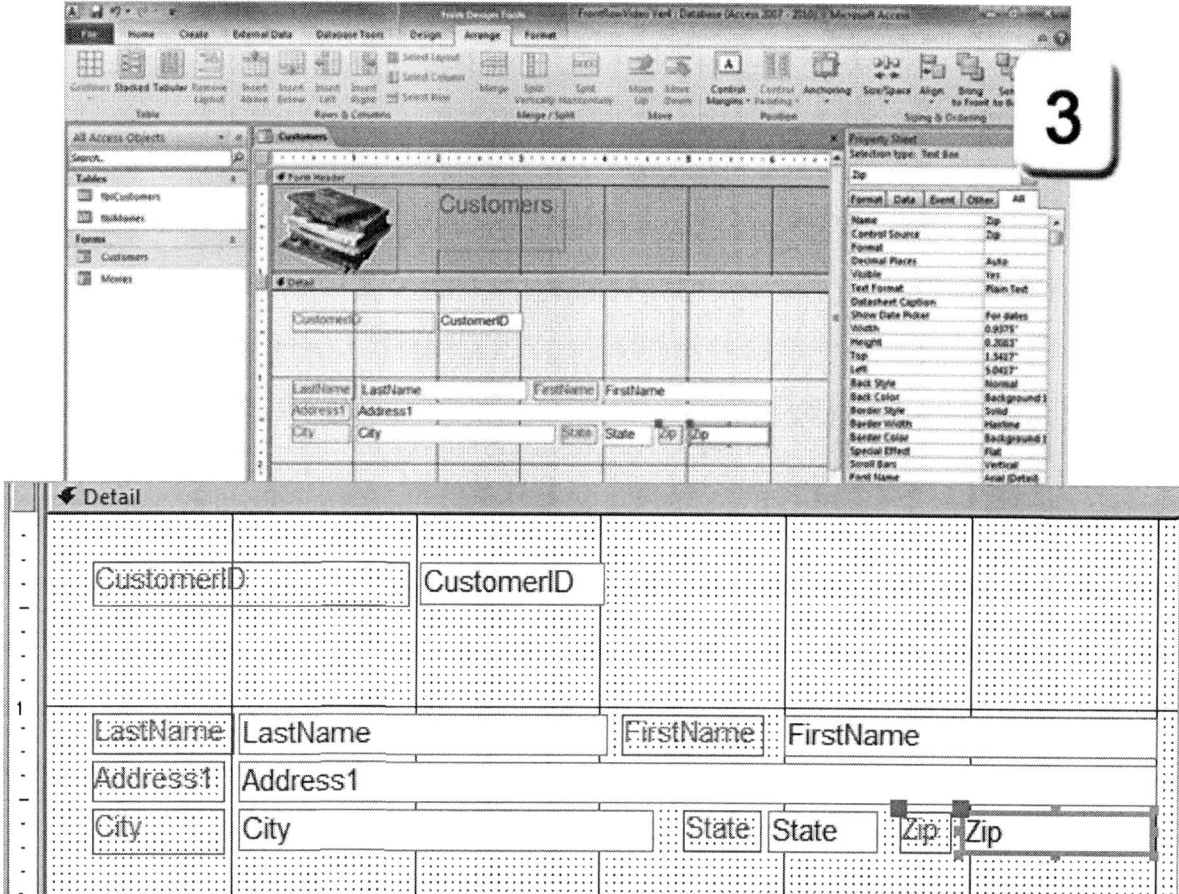

Exam 77-885: Microsoft Access 2010
3. Building Forms
3.3. Apply Form Arrange options: Reposition Controls

Format the Controls

In this business scenario, the Front Row Video employees look up customers by their phone numbers. So, the phone number is critical business data that users need to enter.

You can make the phone number very obvious by moving it to the top of the form and formatting the size and color.

4. Try it: Format the Controls
Place the HomePhone Control at the top of the Detail Section.
Both the Label and the Field are selected.
Go to **Form Design Tools ->Format**.
Go to the **Font** group and select:
Size: 12
Attribute: Bold
Fill: Gold, Accent 2, Lighter 60%.

Keep going...

Form Design Tools ->Format->Font

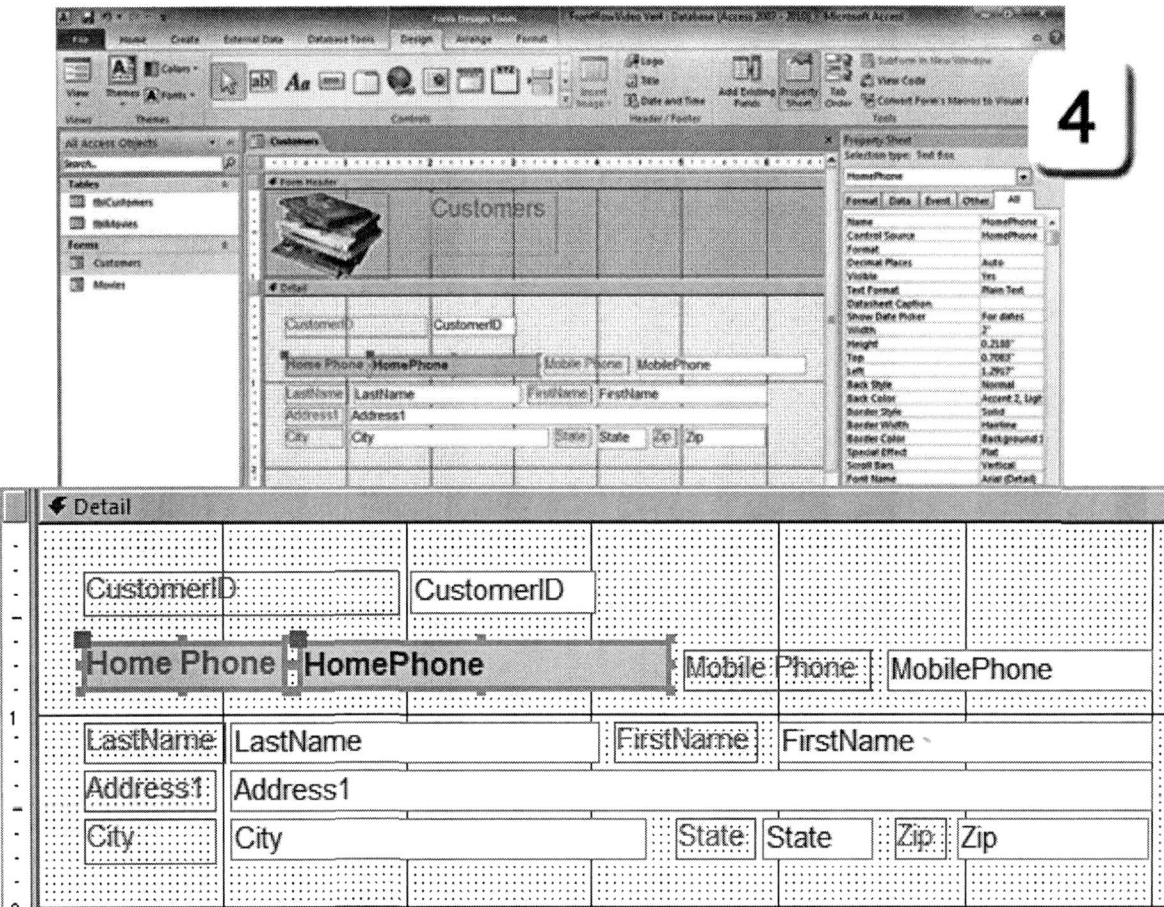

Exam 77-885: Microsoft Access 2010
3. Building Forms
3.4. Apply Form Format options: Reformat Font

Test the Form

Whenever you change a Form, it is a good idea to go back to Form View and test it.

Tab through your Form. Does it advance to the next Field as you expected?

5. Try it: Test in Form View
The Customer Form is open in Design View.
Go to **Form Design Tools ->Design->View**.
Select a View: **Form View**

Try This, Too: Test the Tab Order
Use the keyboard to **Tab** to each Field.

What Do You See? Does Tab begin at the top with the Home Phone, or First Name?

What happens after you Tab through all of the Fields. Does it return **(Cycle)** to the first Field on this Customer or go to the next Customer?

Good questions. Turn the page to see...

Form Design Tools ->Design->View->Form View

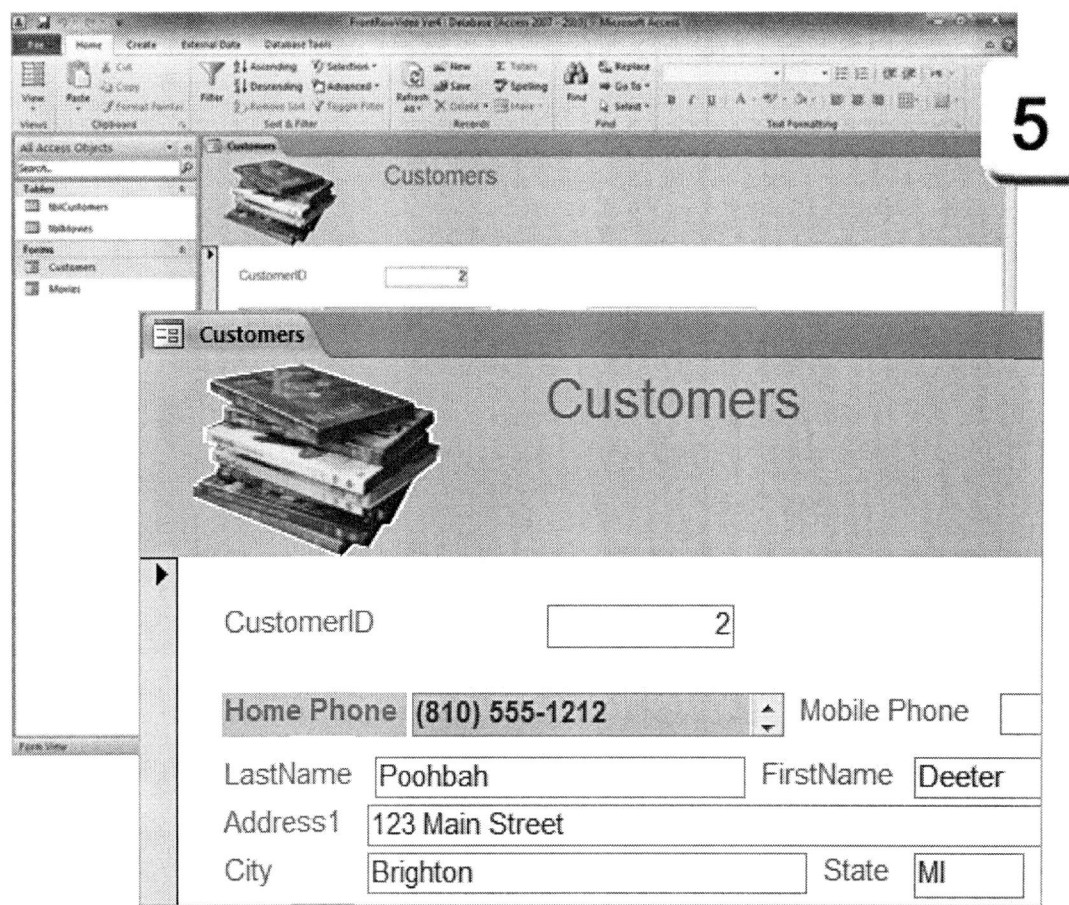

Form Design: Tab Order

Forms that Tab around like a ping pong ball can get old very fast. The **Tab Order** can be fixed with the Form Design Tools.

Before You Begin: Go to the Design View
The Customer Form is still open.
Go to **Form Design Tools ->Design->View**.
Select a View: **Design View**.

6. Try it: Edit the Tab Order
Go to **Form Design Tools ->Design->Tools**.
Click on **Tab Order**.

You will be prompted to edit the Tab Order:
Click on **Auto Order**.

What Do You See? The Fields in the Detail Section will be reordered as they appear, top to bottom, in the Customer Form.

What Else Do You See? You can drag the rows by hand if you wish.

Click **OK**. Keep going, please.

Form Design Tools ->Design->Tools->Tab Order

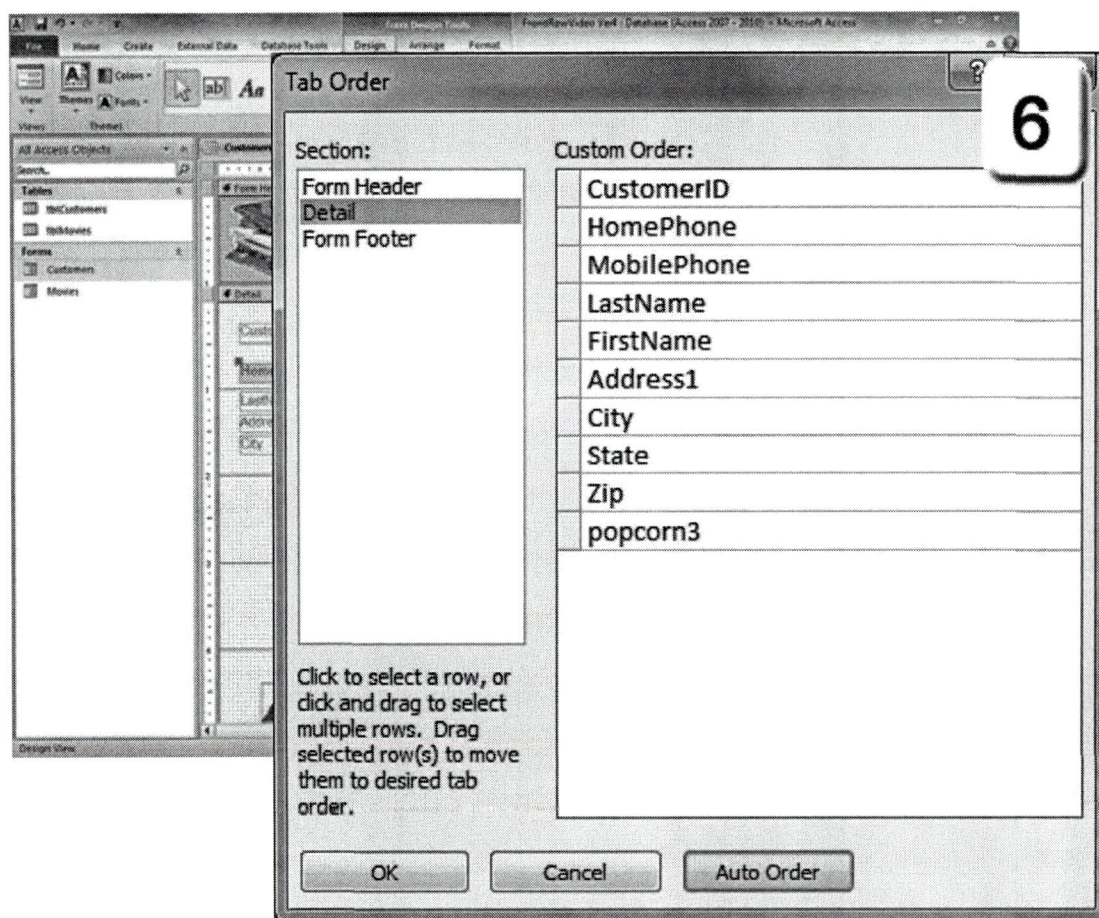

Exam 77-885: Microsoft Access 2010
3. Building Forms
3.3. Apply Form Arrange options: Format Controls Tab Order

Form Design: Cycle Records

Cycle is the term used to describe what happens after you Tab to the last Form Field. You can stay in the current record and Tab back to the top. You can also advance to the next record until you have tabbed through all of them. Cycle is in the Form Properties.

Before You Begin: Select the Form
Click on the **Form Selector**, the small square at top where the two rulers meet.

7. Try it: Edit the Cycle Property
The Customer Form is open in Design View. The Form is selected.
Go to **Form Design Tools ->Design->Tools.**
Click on **Property Sheet.**
Go to the **Other Tab.**
Click on **Cycle: All Records.**
Select: **Current Record.**

Keep going...

Form Design Tools ->Design->Tools->Property Sheet

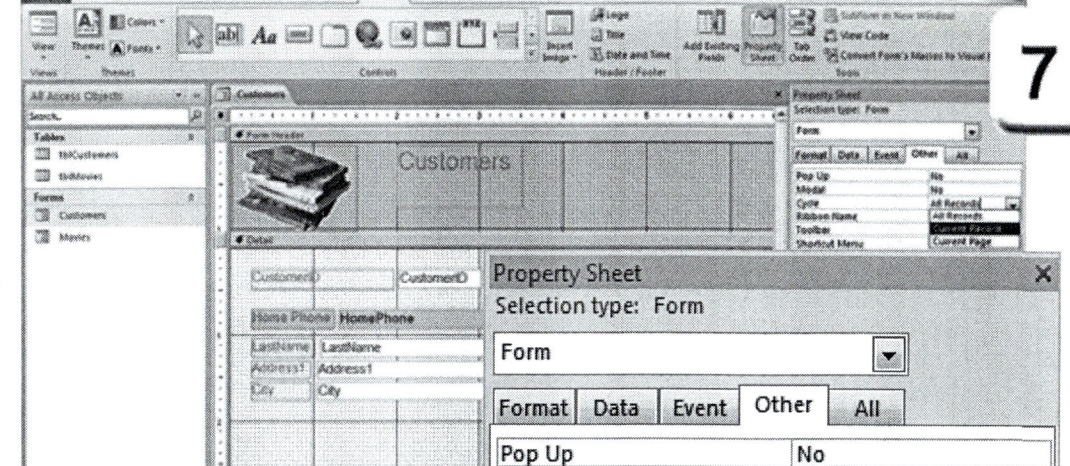

Pop Up	No
Modal	No
Cycle	All Records
Ribbon Name	All Records
Toolbar	Current Record
Shortcut Menu	Current Page
Menu Bar	
Shortcut Menu Bar	
Help File	
Help Context Id	0
Has Module	No
Use Default Paper Size	No
Fast Laser Printing	Yes
Tag	

Exam 77-885: Microsoft Access 2010
3. Building Forms
3.3. Apply Form Arrange options: Format Controls Tab Order

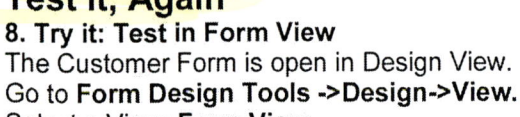

Test it, Again

8. Try it: Test in Form View
The Customer Form is open in Design View.
Go to **Form Design Tools ->Design->View.**
Select a View: **Form View**

Try This, Too: Test the Tab Order. Again
Use the keyboard to Tab to each Field.

What Do You See? Does Tab begin at the
top with the Home Phone and return to the
top after you Tab through each Field?

Good.

Form Design Tools ->Design->View->Form View

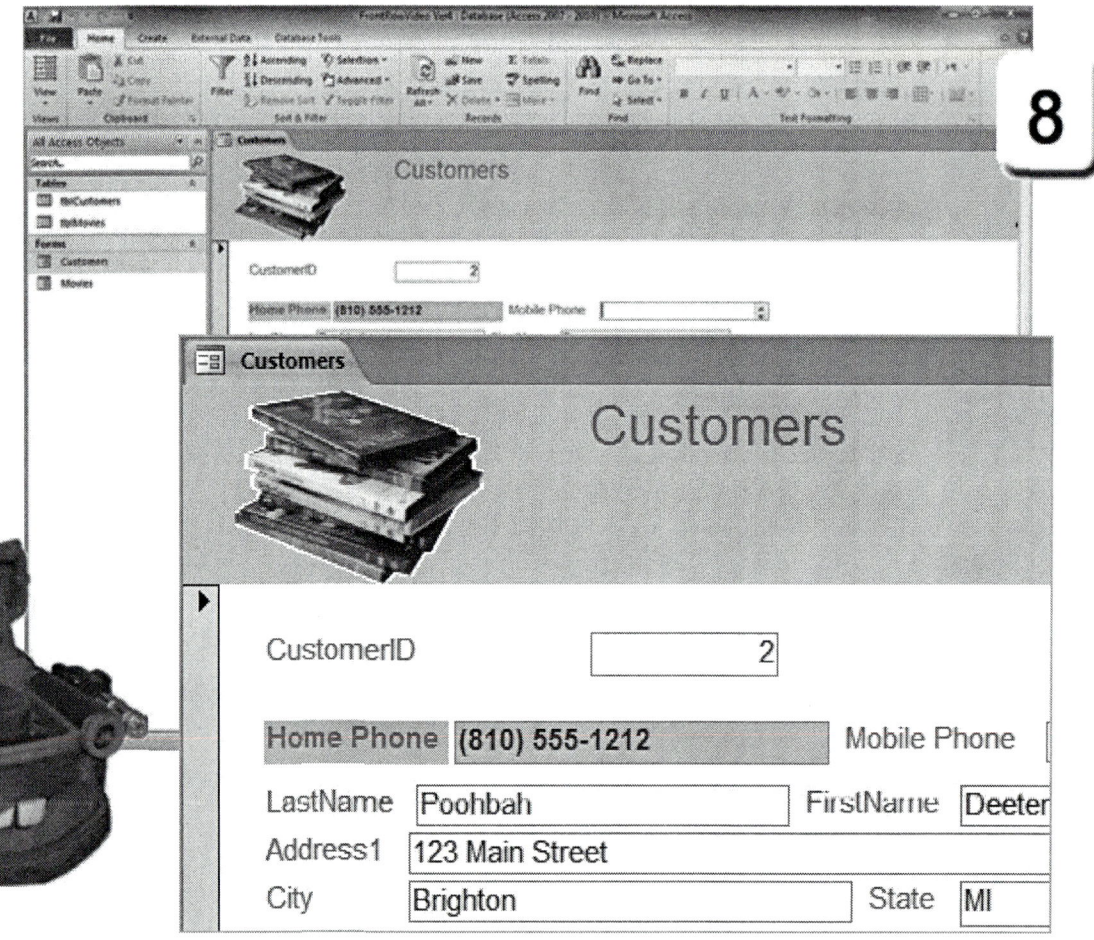

Save, Save, Save!

Now would be a good time to save your Form.
Especially if it works!

9. Try it: Save the Form

The Customer Form is still open.
Go to **File->Save**.

Done and done.

File ->Save

Summary

This discussion introduced the Form Design View and the Form Design Tools. We used the Tools to arrange and edit the Form Fields.

Keep in mind that you are designing for "Real Users." Users want to be fast and effective. Make it good enough even for you, the programmer.

OK, enough for now. Allez, Allez in Free. You get two cookies. Maybe three.

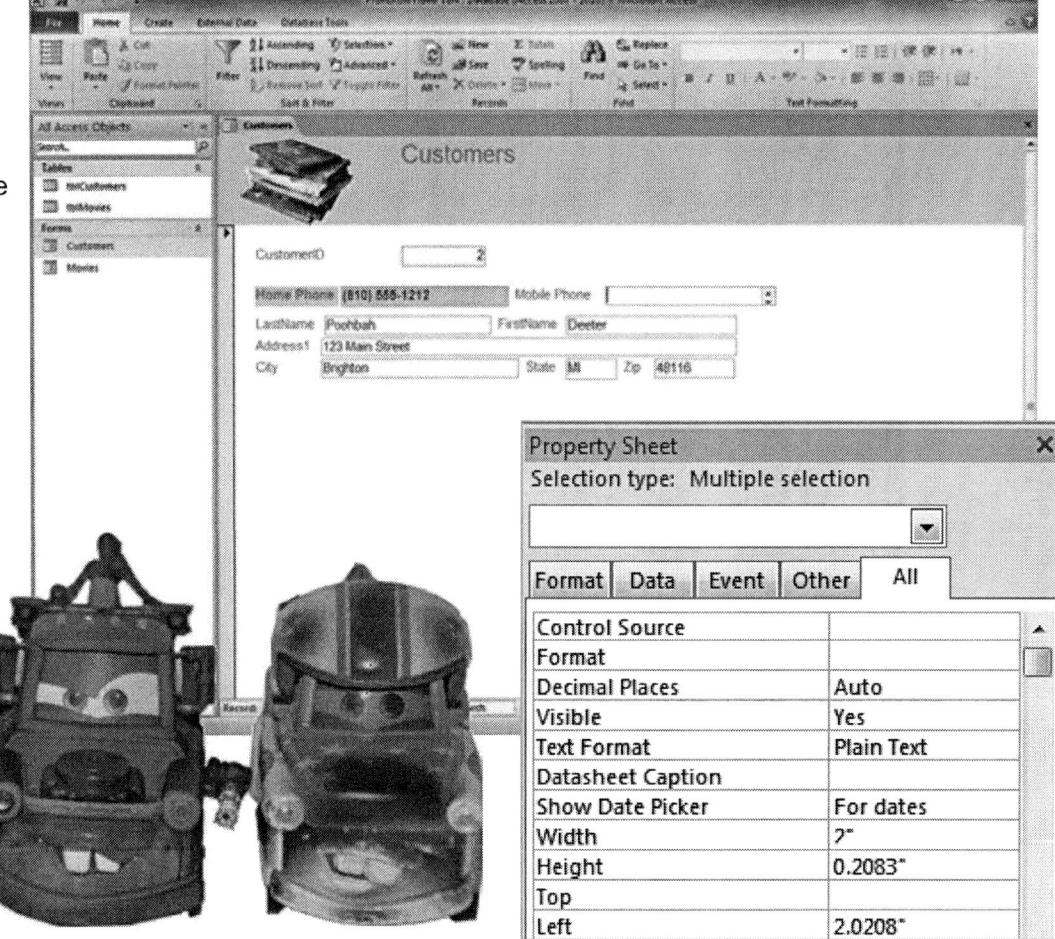

Practice Activities

Lesson 6: More Form Design
Try This: Do the following steps

1. Open the Brown Bag Lunch database you have been programming. Or you may download the sample database **Brown Bag Lunch ver6.accdb** online.

2. Open the Customers Form in Design View.

3. In the Form Header, change the name of the Customers Label to Customers. Using the Property Sheet, change the position of the Label to be left 1.25" and top .25"

4. Add the image **BB Customers Logo.JPG** to the Header. Resize the image to be width 1" and height 1".

5. Format the color of the Header with a Shape Fill to be Theme Color: Dark Blue 2.

6. Select ALL the Form Controls & Labels (except the Header Label). Change the width to 2.5" and the height to .25"

7. Resize each of the Labels so that they are just larger than the text. Move the fields so that they are next to the labels, with minimal space in between. Move the Controls and their Labels: Place Company below Last Name. Place Phone Number below Company.

8. Select the Form and change the Tab Order as follows:

Customer ID, First Name, Last Name, Company, Phone Number, City, State

9. Select the Form and set the Cycle Properties to Current Record.

10. Save the Customers Form.

Test Yourself

1. Which are the Form Design Ribbons?
(Give all correct answers.)
A. Design
B. Format
C. Layout
D. Arrange
E. Advanced
Tip: Beginning Access, page 134

2. Which is true about the sections of Form?
(Give all correct answers.)
A. Form Header contains the Form Fields
B. Form Header is for navigation and a logo
C. Detail contains the Form Fields
D. Detail is for navigation and a logo
Tip: Beginning Access, page 135

3. Which of the following is true about the Property Sheet? (Give all correct answers.)
A. The Label is edited with a Property Sheet
B. Resizing an image is done with the Property Sheet
C. Setting the distance from the edge of a Form is done with the Property Sheet
Tip: Beginning Access, page 136, 137, 139

4. What is the procedure for selecting multiple Fields at the same time?
A. Press the Shift Key before clicking each Field
B. Press and hold the CTRL (Control) key on the keyboard while clicking each Field
C. Press the Control command on the Home Ribbon while clicking each Field
Tip: Beginning Access, page 142

5. Which is true about the parts of a Field?
(Give all correct answers.)
A. The Label is the description of the Field
B. The Control is where users enter and change data
C. The Name is the description of the Field
D. The Cell is where users enter and change data
Tip: Beginning Access, page 142

6. Which of the following is true about Cycle?
(Give all correct answers.)
A. Describes what happens after a user tabs to the last Form Field
B. Can either stay on the current Record and return to the first Field
C. Can advanced to the next Record
Tip: Beginning Access, page 147

7. Double-clicking the bottom right handle of a Label does what?
A. Fills the Field with the selected Fill Color
B. Selects the Label
C. Resizes the Label to fit the text
Tip: Beginning Access, page 143

8. What are two common Form errors? (Give all correct answers.)
A. Tab Order
B. Font Size
C. Cycle
D. Layout
Tip: Beginning Access, page 131

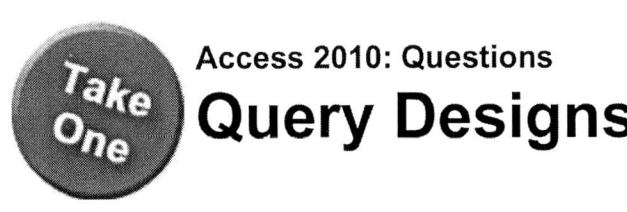

Access 2010: Questions
Query Designs

Beginning Access Objectives
In this lesson, you will learn how to:

1. Use the Query Wizard to select a Table as the Record Source and add Fields in a Select Query.

2. Sort the Query Results.

3. Edit the Query Criteria in Design View.

4. Add, Delete and Rearrange Fields in the QBE Grid.

5. Save the Select Query.

© 2012 Comma Productions, LLC

View   Run

Results

Field:	[MovieID]	[Movie]	[Year]	
Table:	tblMovies	tblMovies	tblMovies	
Sort:			Descending	
Show:	☑	☑	Ascending	☐
Criteria:			Descending	
or:			(not sorted)	

Lesson 7 : Query Designs

1. Readings
Read Lesson 7 in the Beginning Access guide, page 153-176.

Project
Create several Select Queries based on the Table tblMovies.

Downloads
FrontRowVideo Begin7.accdb
popcorn1.gif, popcorn2.gif,
popcorn3.gif, popcorn4.gif, movies1.gif.

Brown Bag Lunch ver7.accdb
BB Customers Logo.jpg
Brown Bag Logo.jpg
Lunch1.gif, Lunch2.gif, Lunch3.gif,
Lunch4.gif

2. Practice
Complete the Practice Activity on page 177.

3. Assessment
Review the Test questions on page 178.

Create Ribbon

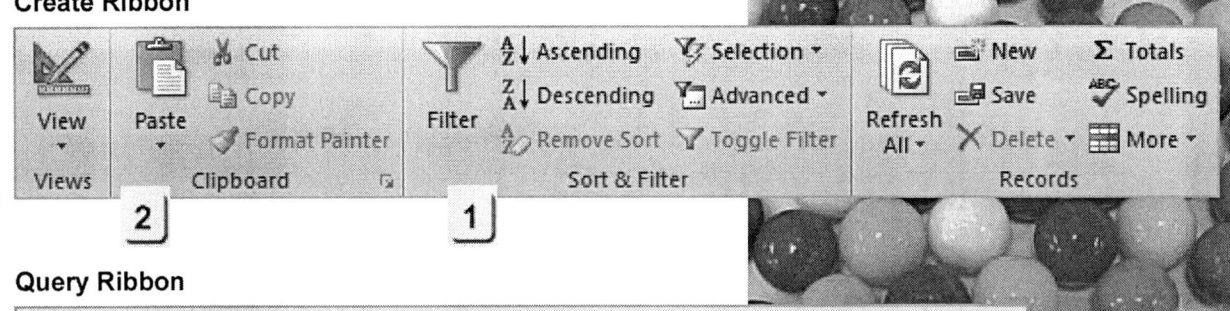

Query Ribbon

Menu Maps
From the **Create Ribbon**.
Create ->Queries-> Query Wizard, page 157

From the **Query Ribbon**.
1. Query Tools ->Design, page 164
2. Query Tools ->Design-> Results->Run, page 166
3. Query Tools ->Design->Query Setup, page 172

More Menu Maps
From the **Home Ribbon**
1. Home ->Sort & Filter->Descending, page 162
2. Home ->Views->View->Design View, page 163

Queries and Query Design

Queries ask questions. In a business database, the big question is: Who bought what? A query looks at all of the data in the Tables and pulls out a handful of records. Programmers sometimes describe it as getting the red jellybeans out of the jar. **Select Queries** look at the Tables and only return the Fields that you selected. There are **Action Queries** as well. An Action Query modifies the data in the Tables. Action Queries can Update, Append, Delete records. An Action Query can also Make a new Table.

This lesson will create a Select Query with the Query Wizard. We will edit the Query in Design View, too.

Microsoft Office Access 2010: Example of the QBE grid

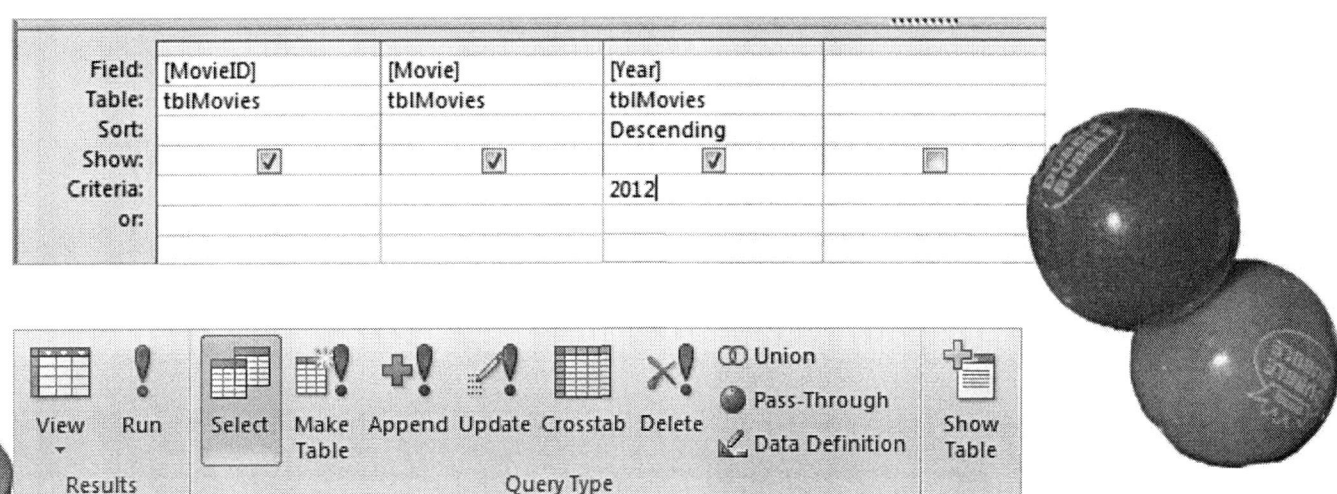

Before You Begin

This lesson uses the Front Row Video database that we have been developing.

You can continue with the database you have been programming if you wish. You can also download the sample Access database at the beginning of this lesson.

Try it: Open the Sample Database
Go to the Documents folder.
Open the sample database:
Brown Bag Lunch ver7.accdb

What Do You See? There are two Tables:
tblCustomers has 5 records.
tblMovies has 401 records.

There are two Forms as well:
Customers
Movies

What Else Do You See? This database may have a Security Warning. In order to edit the objects and save your work, you need to click on **Enable Content**.

Microsoft Access 2010

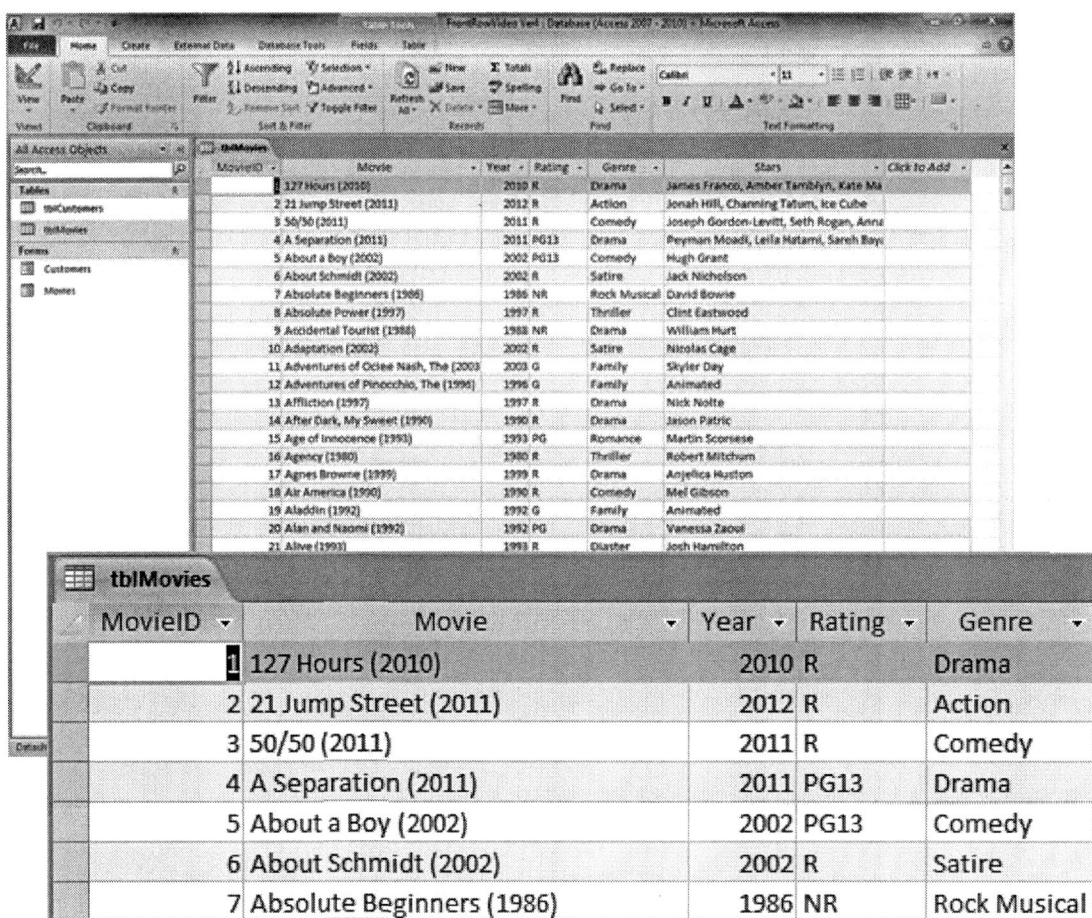

MovieID	Movie	Year	Rating	Genre
1	127 Hours (2010)	2010	R	Drama
2	21 Jump Street (2011)	2012	R	Action
3	50/50 (2011)	2011	R	Comedy
4	A Separation (2011)	2011	PG13	Drama
5	About a Boy (2002)	2002	PG13	Comedy
6	About Schmidt (2002)	2002	R	Satire
7	Absolute Beginners (1986)	1986	NR	Rock Musical

Create a Select Query

Microsoft Access has a **Query Wizard** that goes through the process of choosing a Record Source (a Table or another Query) and then selecting the Fields you want. This is a good way to get started.

1. Try it: Create a Select Query
Go to **Create ->Queries-> Query Wizard.**

What Do You See? The Query Wizard has four templates:
Simple Query Wizard
Crosstab Query Wizard
Find Duplicates Query Wizard
Find Unmatched Query Wizard

Select: Simple Query Wizard.
Click **OK**.Keep going...

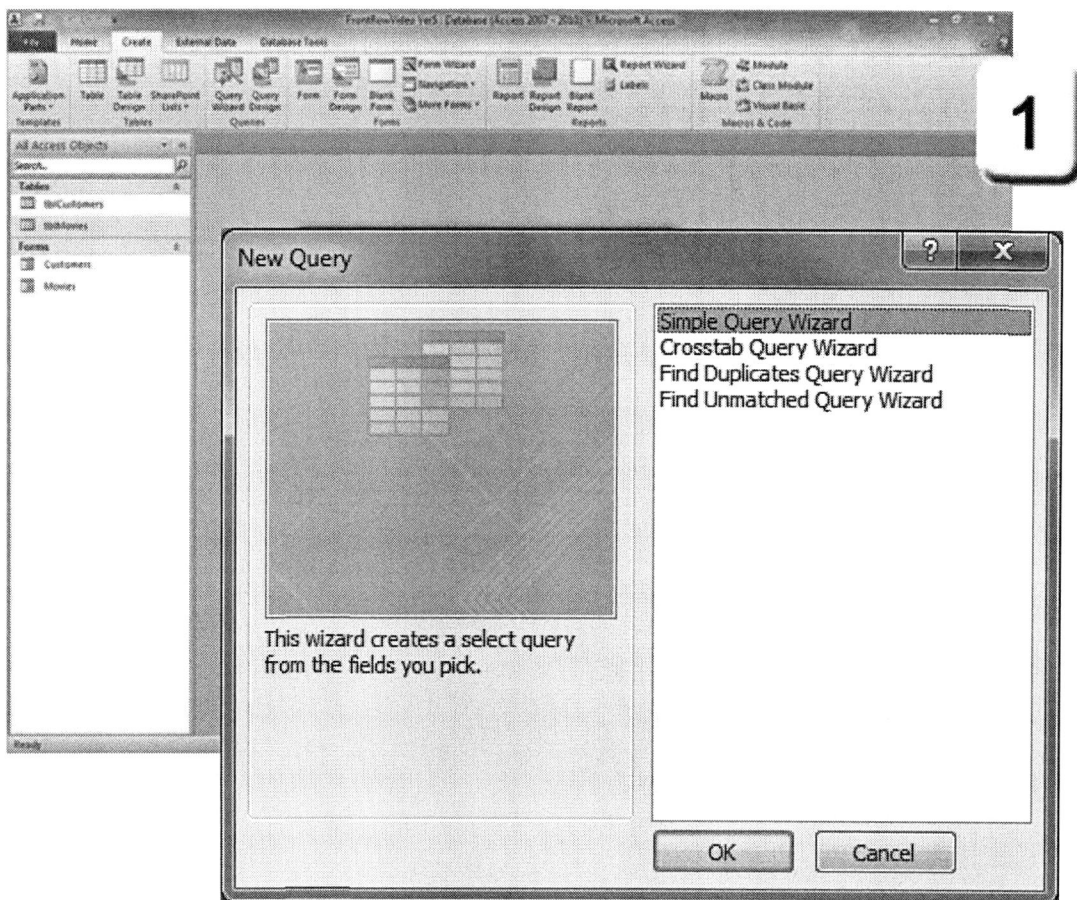

Exam 77-885: Microsoft Access 2010
4. Creating and Managing Queries
4.1. Construct queries: Create a Select Query

Query: Select a Record Source

2. Try it: Select a Record Source
Select a Table: tblMovies

What Do You See? There are six Fields
Available in tblMovies on the left side.

You can use the arrows pointing left or right to
move the Fields from the **Available Fields** on
the left to the **Selected Fields** on the right.

Select these Available Fields:
MovieID
Movie
Year

Click **Next**. Keep going...

Create ->Queries-> Query Wizard

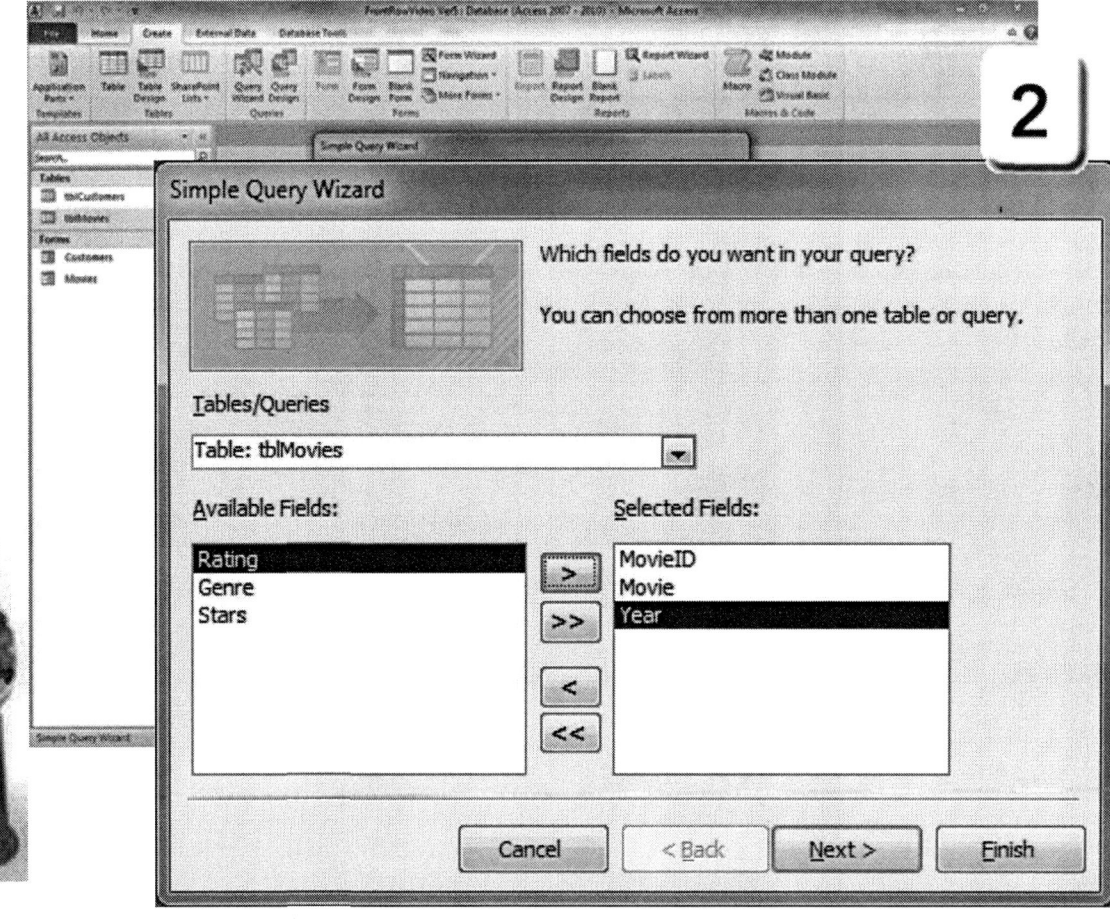

Exam 77-885: Microsoft Access 2010
4. Creating and Managing Queries
4.1. Construct queries: Create a Select Query

Query: Detail or Summary

3. Try it: Choose Detail

The Detail option will return all of the Movies in tblMovies. The Summary option will give you choices on how you want to Group the Movies.

Select: Detail
Click **Next**. Keep going...

Memo to Self: Sometimes the Query Wizard skips the option to select Detail or Summary: It depends on the data. The Movies Table has several Fields (Year, Rating, Genre) that can be Grouped and Sorted.

Create ->Queries-> Query Wizard

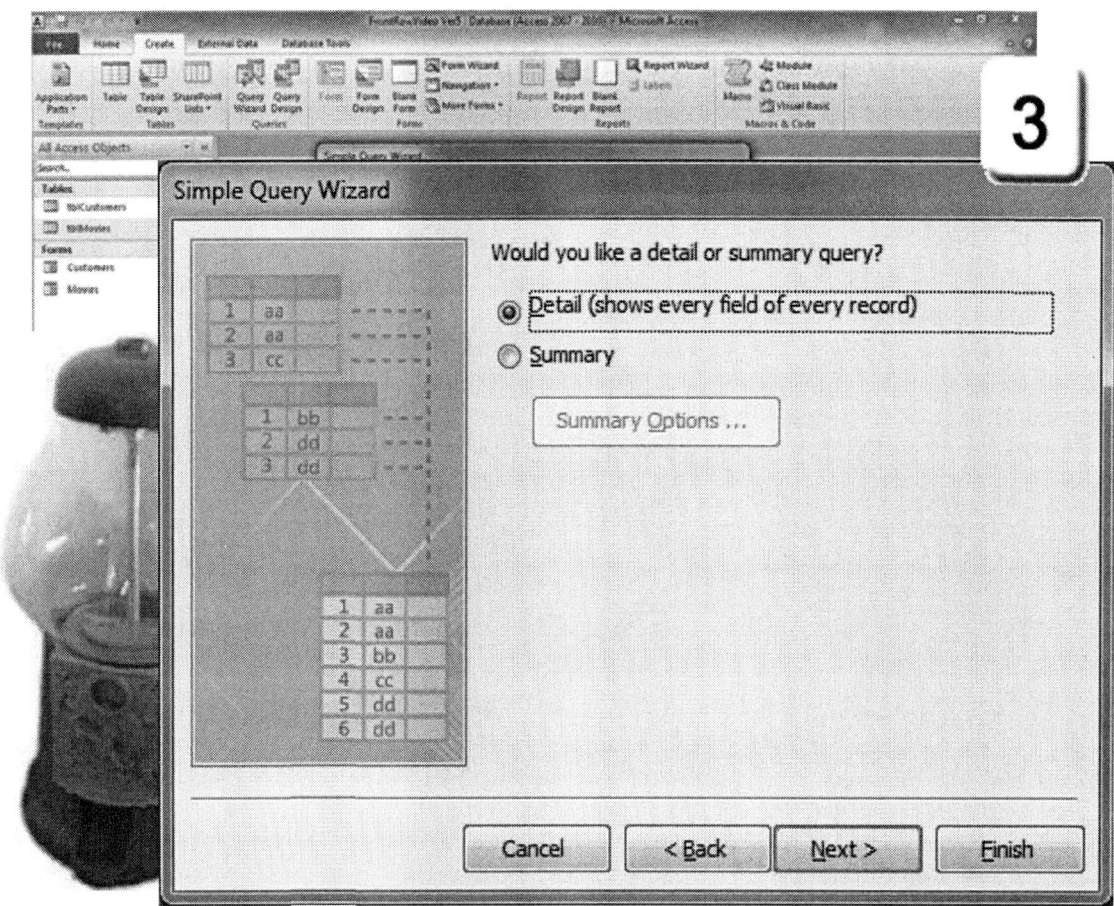

Exam 77-885: Microsoft Access 2010
4. Creating and Managing Queries
4.1. Construct queries: Create a Select Query

Save and Name the Query

4. Try it: Save and Name the Query
Enter the title: MovieSQ
Select: Open the query to view information.

Click **Finish**.

What Do You See? The Query Wizard will run your Movie Query. Please go to the next page to review the results.

Memo to Self: The names for Queries in this database are as follows:
(Name of my Record Source)SQ,

where SQ means this is a Select Query.

The names include upper and lower letters. There are no spaces in these names.

Create ->Queries-> Query Wizard

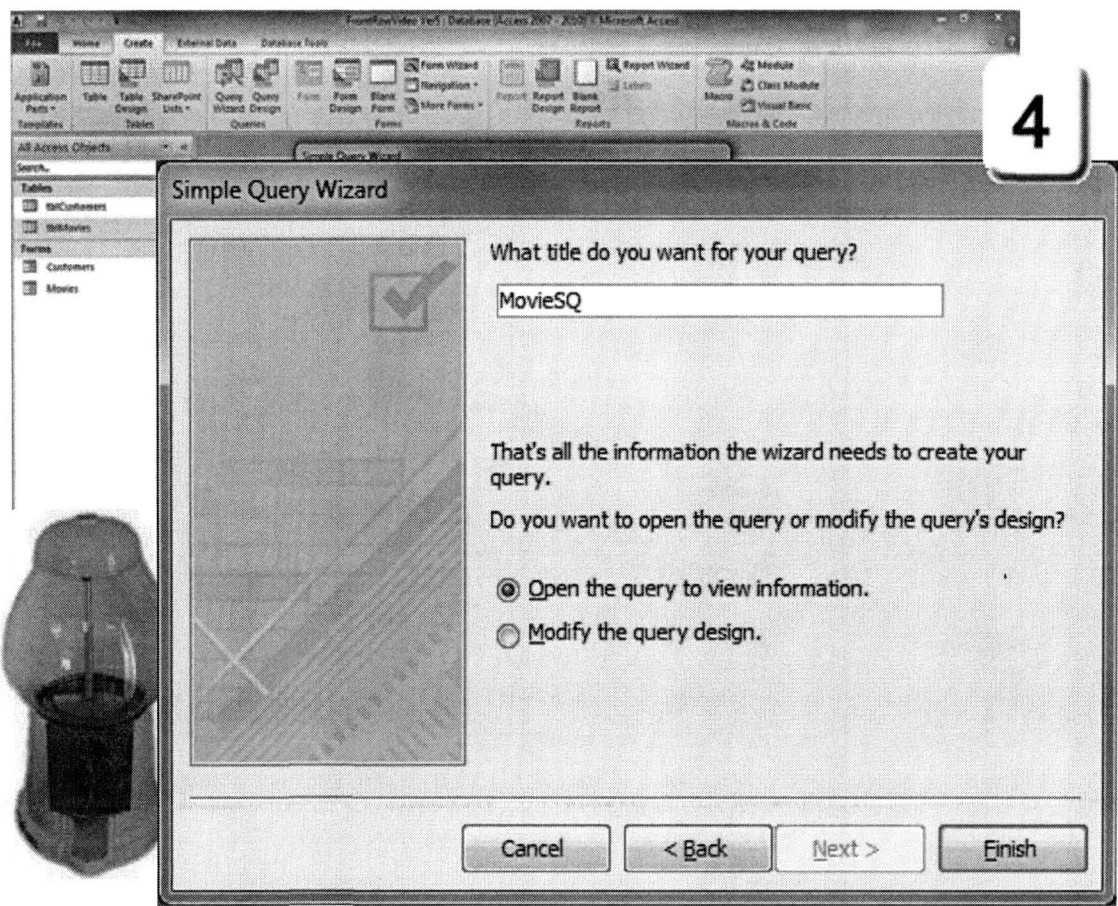

Exam 77-885: Microsoft Access 2010
4. Creating and Managing Queries
4.1. Construct queries: Create a Select Query

Query: Review the Results

5. Try it: Review the Query Results
The MovieSQ Query is in **Datasheet View**.

This is a Select Query: only the three Fields that were selected in the Query Wizard are displayed: MovieID, Movie and Year.

What Else Do You See? There is a new category for Queries in **All Access Objects**.

Keep going, please...

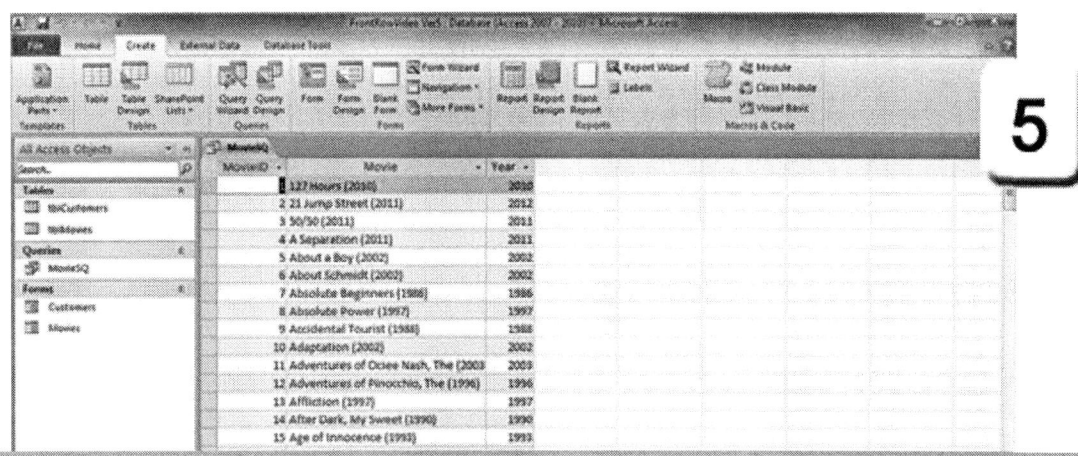

All Access Objects		MovieSQ		
Search...		MovieID	Movie	Year
Tables		1	127 Hours (2010)	2010
⊞ tblCustomers		2	21 Jump Street (2011)	2012
⊞ tblMovies		3	50/50 (2011)	2011
Queries		4	A Separation (2011)	2011
MovieSQ		5	About a Boy (2002)	2002
Forms		6	About Schmidt (2002)	2002
⊟ Customers		7	Absolute Beginners (1986)	1986
⊟ Movies		8	Absolute Power (1997)	1997
		9	Accidental Tourist (1988)	1988

Exam 77-885: Microsoft Access 2010
4. Creating and Managing Queries
4.1. Construct queries: Create a Select Query

Query: Sort

You can **Sort and Filter** a Query, just as you would a Table. Here are the steps.

6. Try it: Sort the Records

The MovieSQ results are still open in datasheet view.
Select a Field: Year
Go to **Home ->Sort & Filter.**
Click on **Descending**.

What Do You See? The Records should be sorted by Year: descending means the newest movies will be on top.

The Wizard is a good way to get started. Now, let's look at the Query Design.

Query: Design View

Every Access object has many Views.
Queries have the following Views:
Datasheet View
PivotTable View
PivotChart View
SQL View
Design View

1. Try it: Go to the Design View
The MovieSQ is open in Datasheet View.
Go to **Home ->Views->View.**
Select a View: **Design View.**

Please go to the next page to see...

Home ->Views->View->Design View

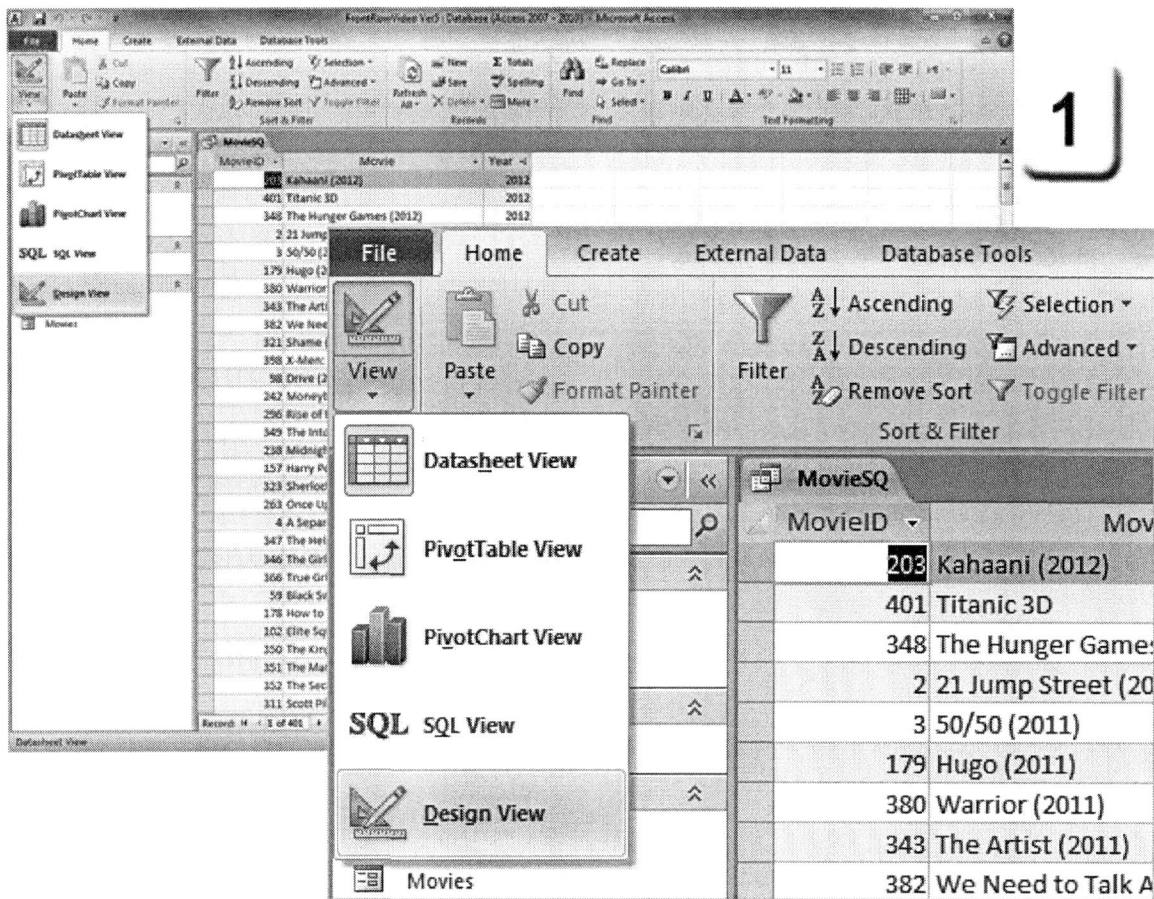

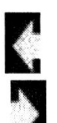

Hello, Query Design

2. Try it: Review the Query Design

The best feature in Microsoft Access is the Query Design. The **Query By Example (QBE)** is a visual format for programming.

At the top of the Query are the Record Sources. In this example, the Record Source is a Table: tblMovies.

The bottom of the Query is the QBE Grid. These are the three Fields that were selected in the Query Wizard:
MovieID
Movie
Year

What Else Do You See? The QBE Grid lists the name of the Table that each Field comes from.

Keep going...

Query Tools ->Design

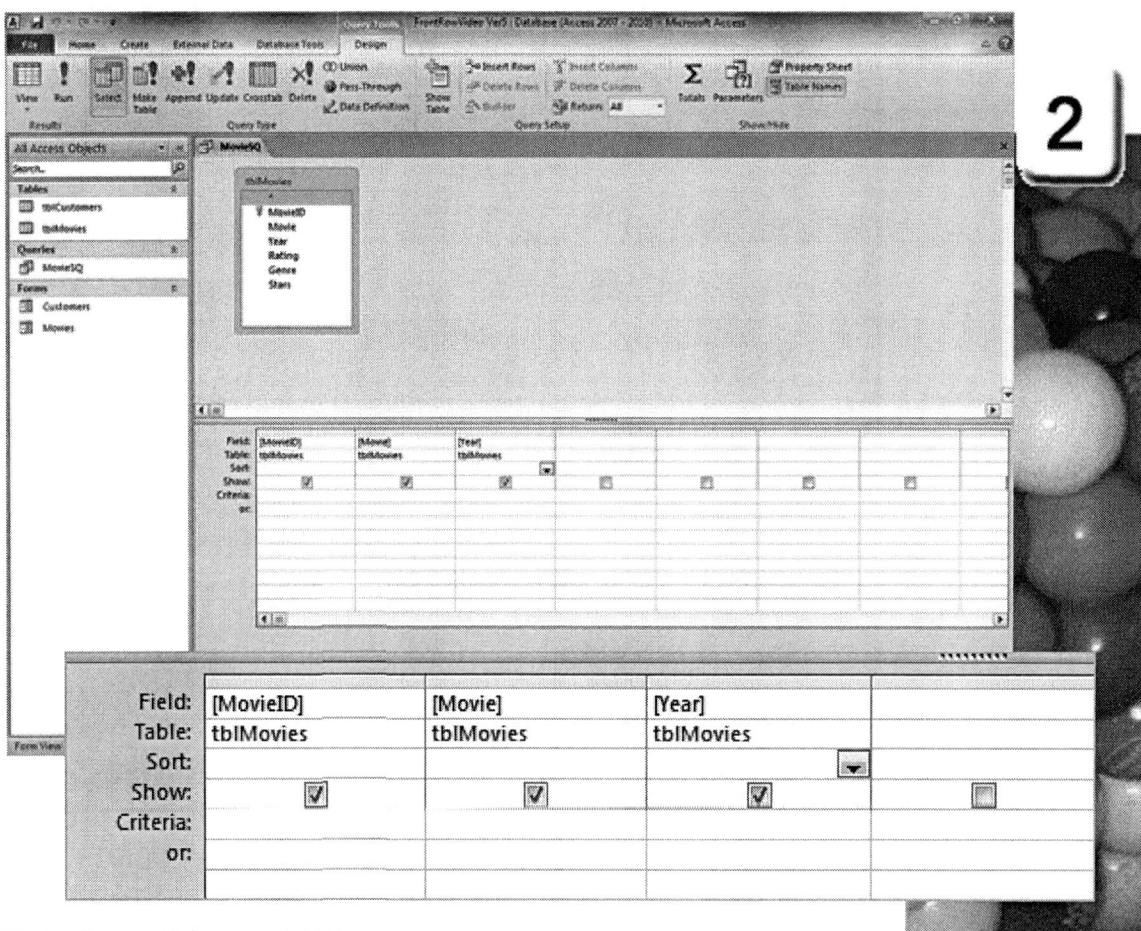

Field:	[MovieID]		[Movie]		[Year]		
Table:	tblMovies		tblMovies		tblMovies		
Sort:							
Show:		☑		☑		☑	☐
Criteria:							
or:							

Exam 77-885: Microsoft Access 2010
4. Creating and Managing Queries
4.1. Construct queries: Edit a Select Query in Design View

Query: The Query Tools

3. Try it: Review the Query Tools
The **Query Tools** include the following:
Results
Query Type
Query Setup
Show/Hide

There are several types of Queries.
Select and Cross Tab Queries **show** the data in the Tables.

Make Table, Append, Update and Delete are all **Action Queries** that **change** the data in the Tables.

We will create each Query Type in the Intermediate and Advanced lessons.

This lesson will look at the options in a simple Select Query that has only one Table. Keep going...

Query Tools ->Design

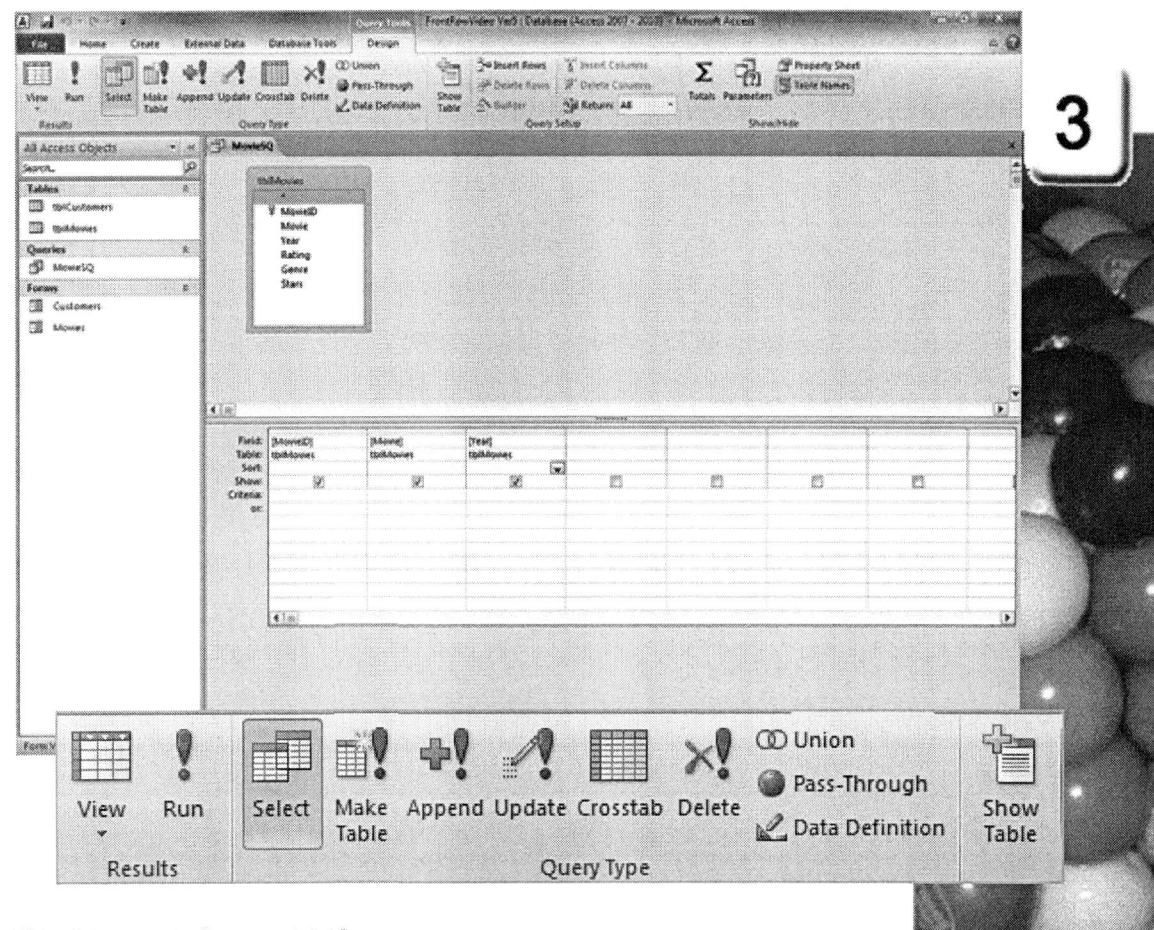

Exam 77-885: Microsoft Access 2010
4. Creating and Managing Queries
4.1. Construct queries: Edit a Select Query in Design View

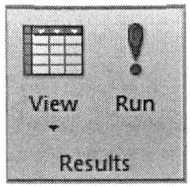

Query: Sort the Records

Look at the QBE Grid at the bottom. There are several Rows of options that you can program if you wish. Start with a simple function: Sort the Records.

4. Try it: Sort the Records
Go to a Field: Year
Click on the Sort Row under the Field.
Select a Sort Order: Descending.

Try This, Too: Run the Query
Go to **Query Tools ->Design-> Results**.
Click on **Run**.

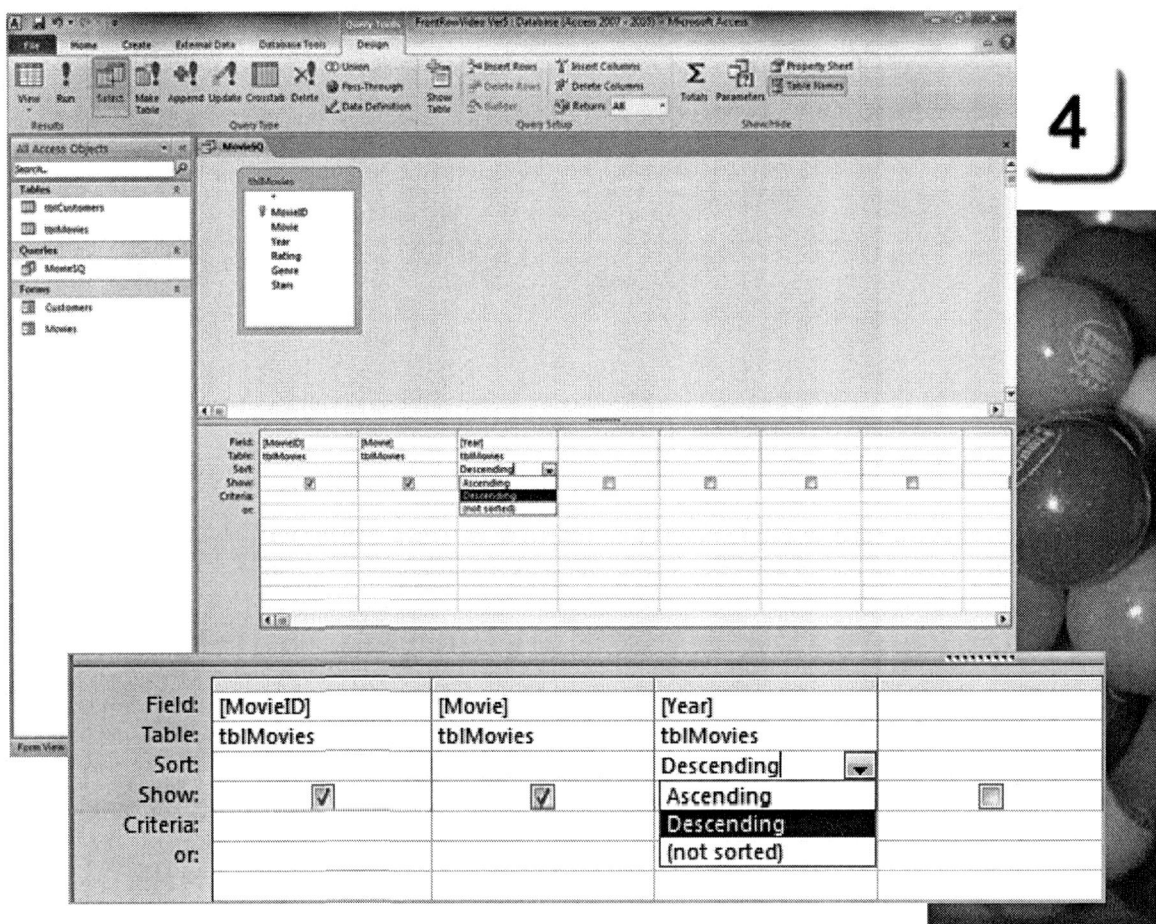

4

Field:	[MovieID]	[Movie]	[Year]	
Table:	tblMovies	tblMovies	tblMovies	
Sort:			Descending ▾	
Show:	☑	☑	Ascending	☐
Criteria:			**Descending**	
or:			(not sorted)	

View   Run

Results

Keep going...

Exam 77-885: Microsoft Access 2010
4. Creating and Managing Queries
4.3. Manipulate fields: Sort the Records

Query: Review the Results

5. Try it: Review the Query Results
The Query Results for MoviesSQ are:
Number of Records: 401
Sorted: By Year (descending).

Yes, this is correct.

Try This, Too: Go to the Design View
Go to **Home ->Views->View.**
Select a View: **Design View.**

Keep going...

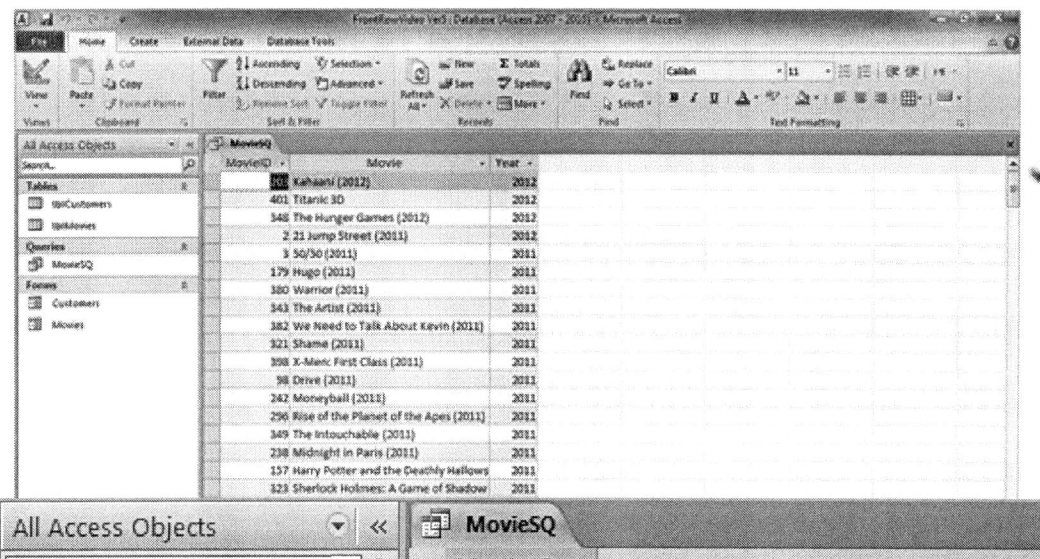

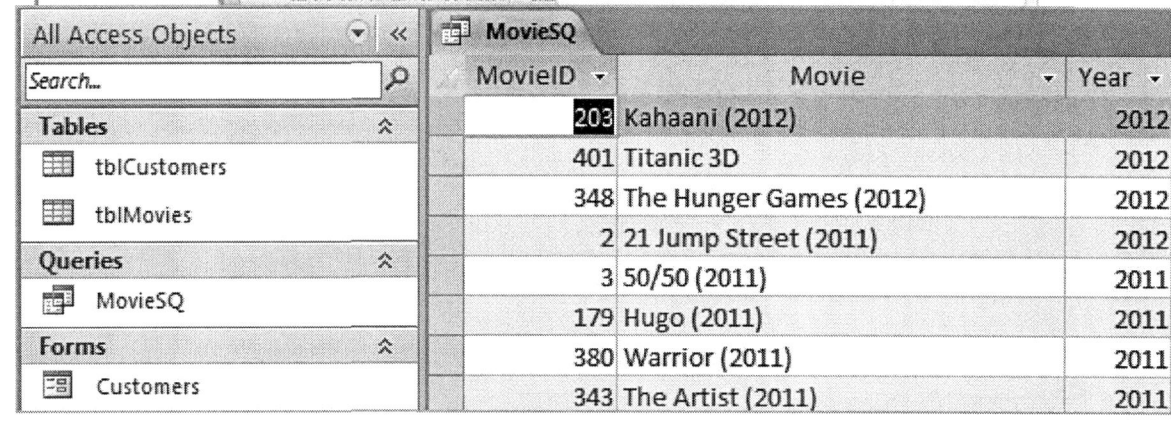

MovieID	Movie	Year
203	Kahaani (2012)	2012
401	Titanic 3D	2012
348	The Hunger Games (2012)	2012
2	21 Jump Street (2011)	2012
3	50/50 (2011)	2011
179	Hugo (2011)	2011
380	Warrior (2011)	2011
343	The Artist (2011)	2011

Exam 77-885: Microsoft Access 2010
4. Creating and Managing Queries
4.3. Manipulate fields: Sort the Records

Query: Criteria

Criteria can be used to Filter the Records.
Criteria can be words, phrases or numbers.
Say you wanted to find only the movies that
were released in 2012?

6. Try it: Edit the Criteria
Select a Field: Year
Enter a Criteria: 2012
Go to **Query Tools ->Design-> Results.**
Click on **Run.**

What Do You See? Your Query should find
four movies that have the year 2012.

Go to Home->Views->View->Design View
Enter a different Criteria: 2005.
Click on **Run.**

What Do You See, Now? Your Query should
find 25 movies that have the year 2005.

Try This, Too: Delete the Criteria
Go to the **Design View.**
Select a Field: Year
Delete the Criteria. Keep going...

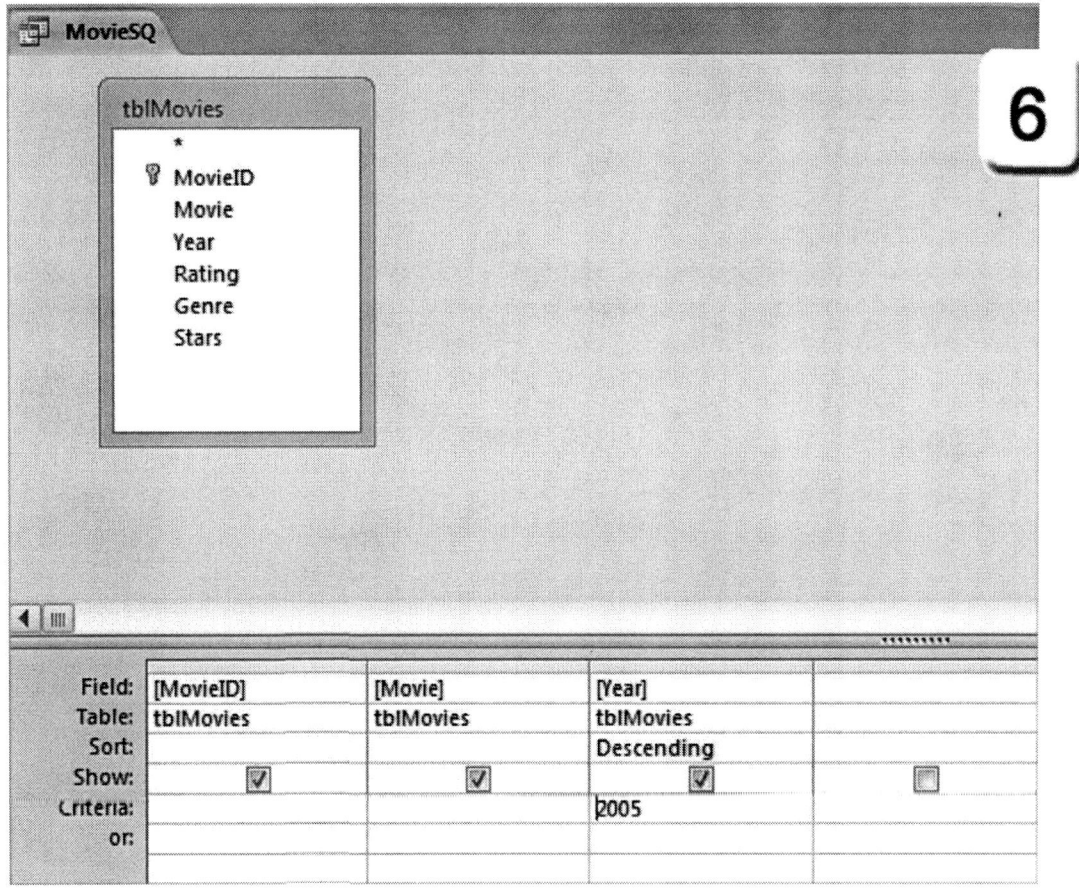

Exam 77-885: Microsoft Access 2010
4. Creating and Managing Queries
4.1. Construct queries: Create a Select Query

Rearrange the Fields

Queries read from Left to Right. You can move and rearrange the Fields. It is similar to moving a Column in Microsoft Excel.

7. Try it: Rearrange the Fields

Select the Year Field by clicking on the Field Header. The whole column should be highlighted (black).

Drag and Drop the Year Field between MovieID and Movie.

Try This, Too: Add Another Sort Order

Go to a Field: Movie
Click on the Sort Row under the Field.
Select a Sort Order: Ascending.

Keep going...

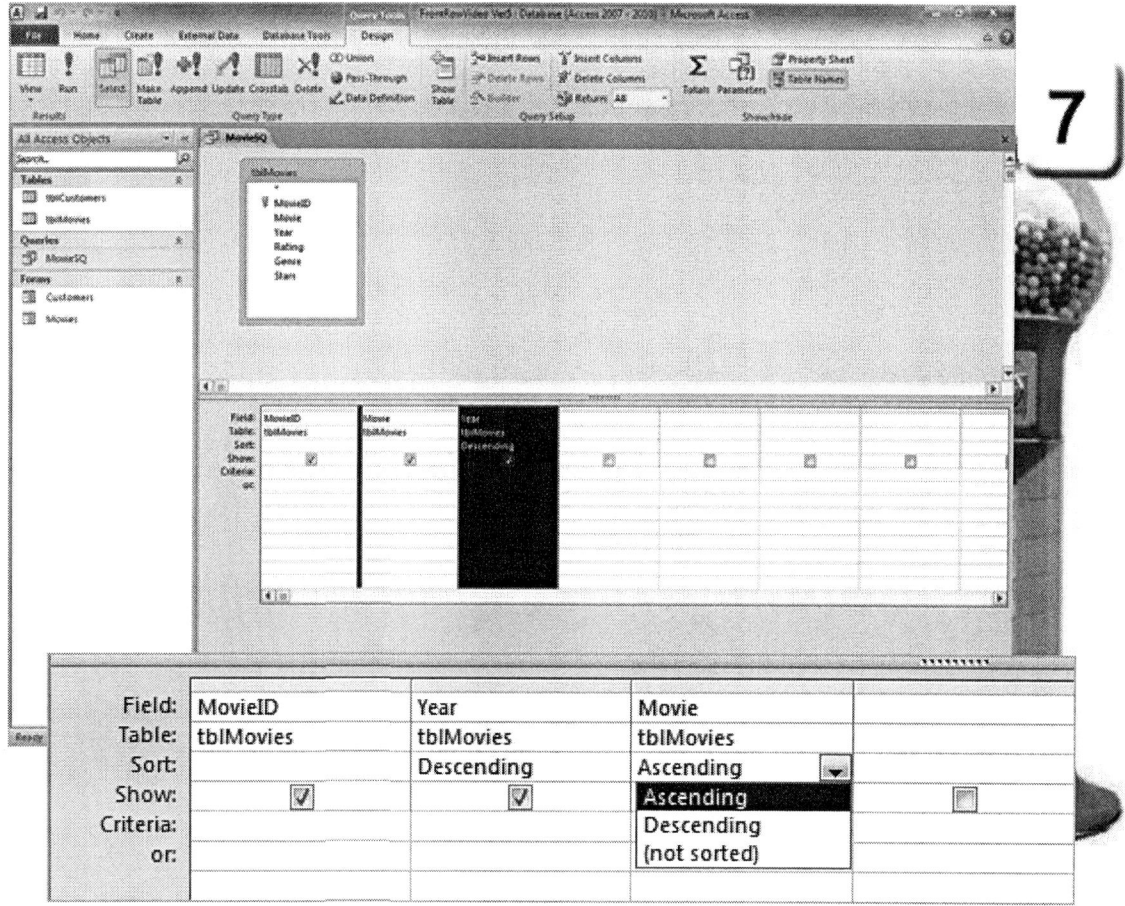

Field:	MovieID	Year	Movie	
Table:	tblMovies	tblMovies	tblMovies	
Sort:		Descending	Ascending ▾	
Show:	☑	☑	Ascending	☐
Criteria:			Descending	
or:			(not sorted)	

Exam 77-885: Microsoft Access 2010
4. Creating and Managing Queries
4.3. Manipulate fields: Rearrange the Fields

Run the Revised Query

This Query is supposed to Sort the movies by Year, then Sort them alphabetically. Does it? Please Run the Query and see.

8. Try it: Run the Revised Query
Go to **Query Tools ->Design->Results.**
Click on **Run.**

What Do You See? The MovieSQ should open in Datasheet View. The Year Field is first and is sorted descending (new movies first). The movies are sorted alphabetically by the movie title as well.

Do This: Save the Query
Go to **File->Save.**

And Do This: Return to the Design View
Go to **Home->Views->View.**
Select a View: **Design View.**

Keeeeep going...

Query Tools ->Design->Results->Run

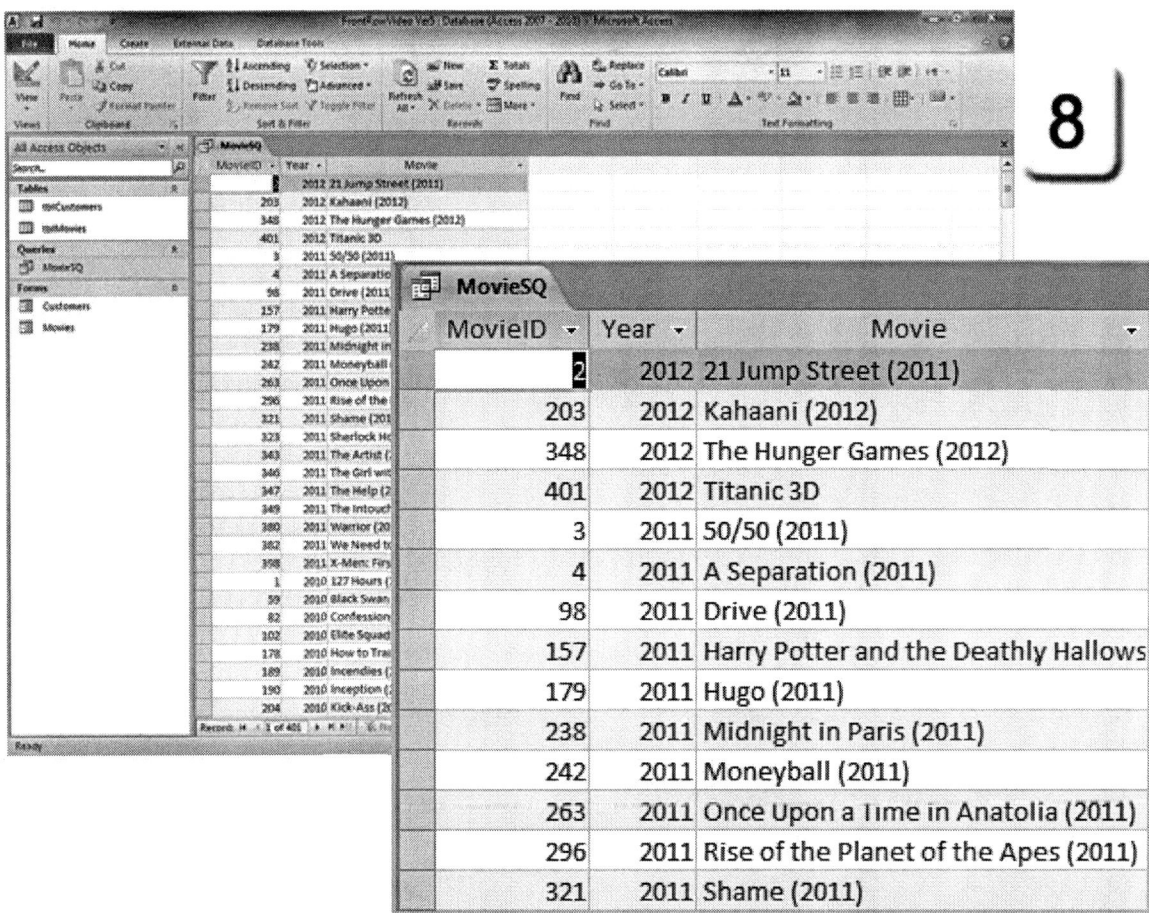

Exam 77-885: Microsoft Access 2010
4. Creating and Managing Queries
4.3. Manipulate fields: Rearrange the Fields

Add a Field

This Select Query shows three Fields from tblMovies: MovieID, Year and Movie. Say you wanted to **Add a Field**. Here are the steps to add the Rating Field.

1. Try it: Add a Field

MovieSQ is open in Design View.
Go to tblMovies.
Double-click a Field: Rating.

What Do You See? The Rating Field has been added to QBE Grid.

Keep going...

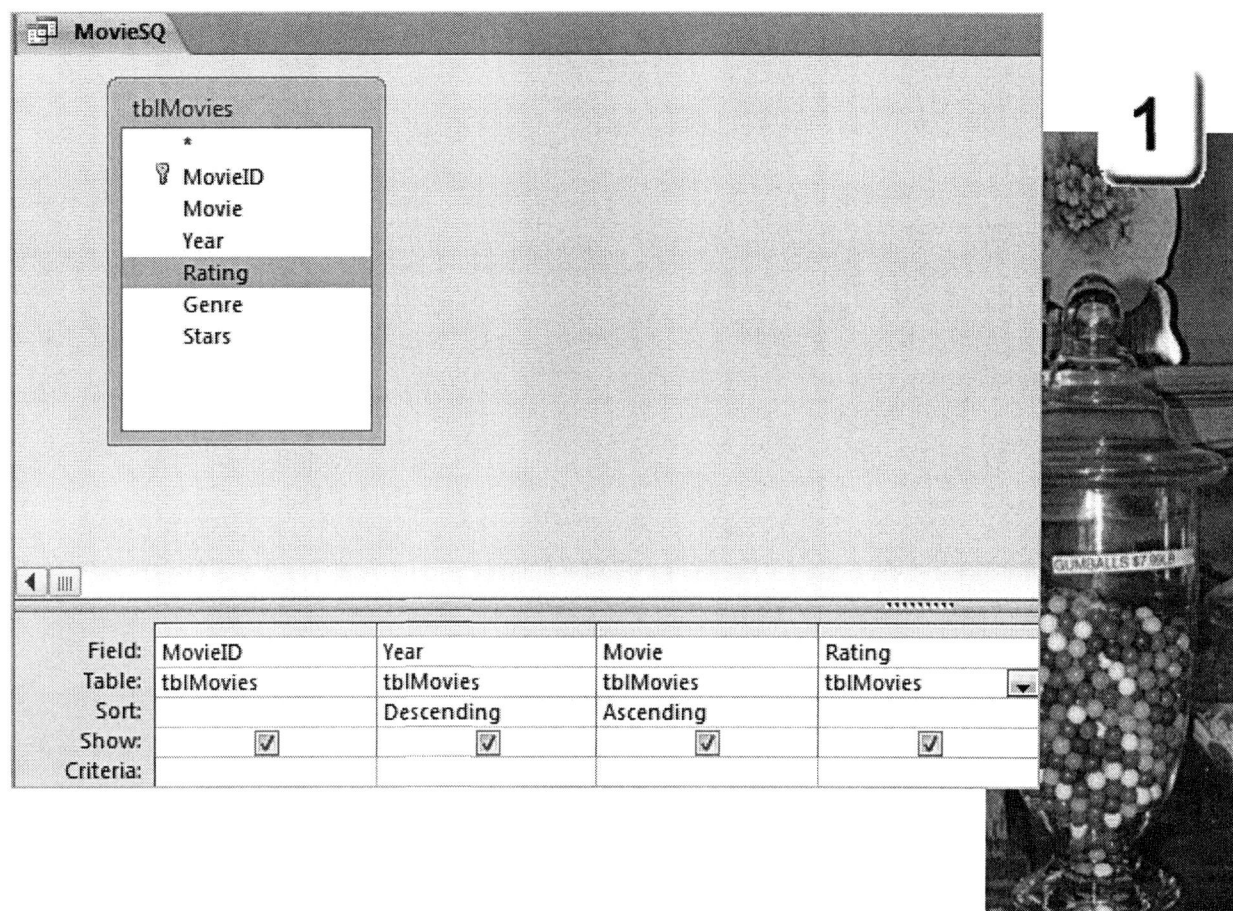

Field:	MovieID	Year	Movie	Rating	
Table:	tblMovies	tblMovies	tblMovies	tblMovies	▾
Sort:		Descending	Ascending		
Show:	☑	☑	☑	☑	
Criteria:					

Exam 77-885: Microsoft Access 2010
4. Creating and Managing Queries
4.3. Manipulate fields: Add Fields to a Query

Remove a Field

Say you added the Rating Field a couple of times as you were practicing. Here are the steps to **Remove a Field**.

Before You Begin: Add Another Field
MovieSQ is open in Design View.
Go to tblMovies.
Double-click a Field: Rating.

What Do You See? There should be two copies of the Rating Field in the QBE Grid.

2. Try it: Remove a Field
Select the second Rating Field by clicking on the Field Header. The whole column should be highlighted (black).

Delete the second Rating Field.
Go to **Query Tools ->Design->Query Setup**.
Click on **Delete Columns**.

What Do You See, Now? The second Rating Column should be removed.
Keep going, please...

Query Tools ->Design->Query Setup->Delete Columns

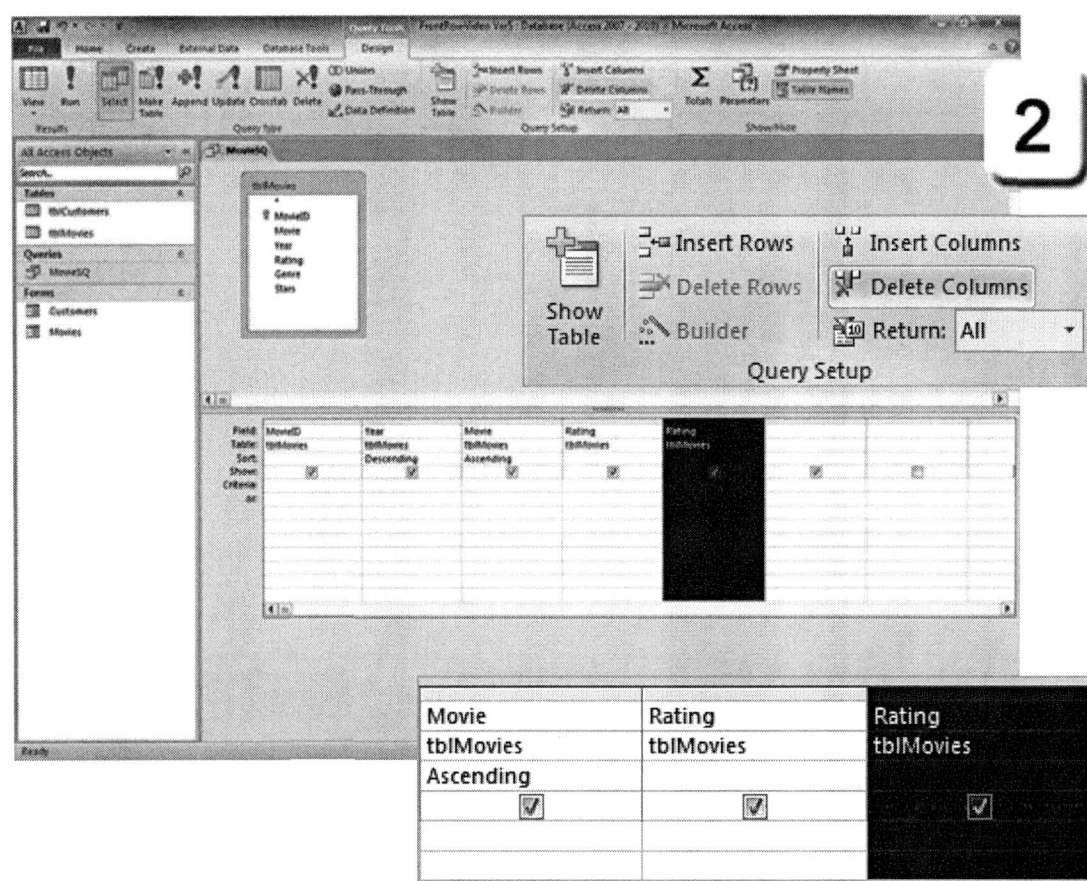

Movie	Rating	Rating
tblMovies	tblMovies	tblMovies
Ascending		
☑	☑	☑

Run the Query, Again

3. Try it: Run the Query, Again
Go to **Query Tools ->Design->Results.**
Click on **Run.**

What Do You See? The MovieSQ should open in Datasheet View. The Rating Field should be included in the results.

Please return to the **Design View.**

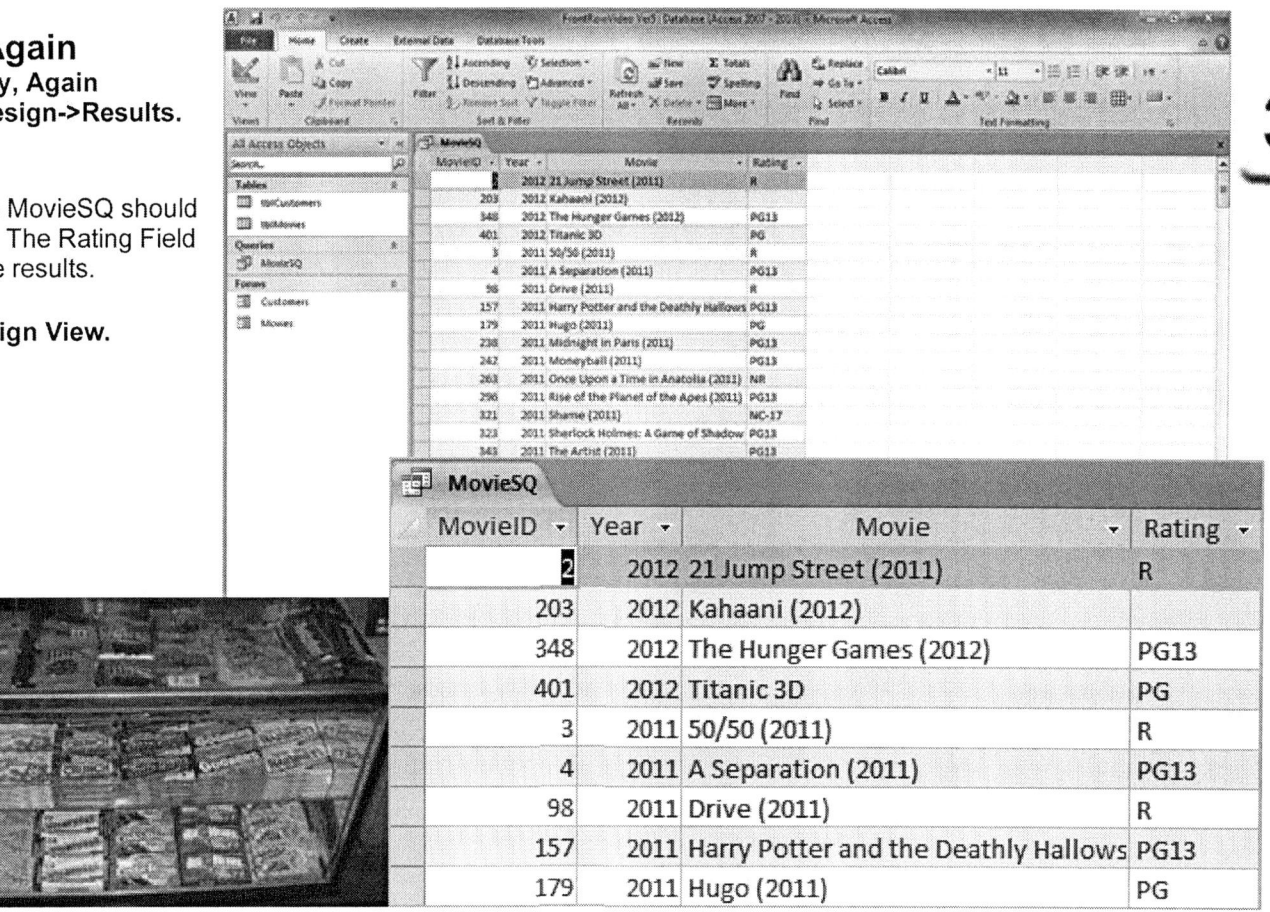

MovieID	Year	Movie	Rating
2	2012	21 Jump Street (2011)	R
203	2012	Kahaani (2012)	
348	2012	The Hunger Games (2012)	PG13
401	2012	Titanic 3D	PG
3	2011	50/50 (2011)	R
4	2011	A Separation (2011)	PG13
98	2011	Drive (2011)	R
157	2011	Harry Potter and the Deathly Hallows	PG13
179	2011	Hugo (2011)	PG

Exam 77-885: Microsoft Access 2010
4. Creating and Managing Queries
4.3. Manipulate fields: Add Fields to a Query

Add More Fields

4. Try it: Add Another Field

MovieSQ is in Design View.
Go to tblMovies.
Double-click a Field: Genre.

What Do You See? The Genre
Field should be added to the
QBE Grid.

Keep going...

Query Tools ->Design

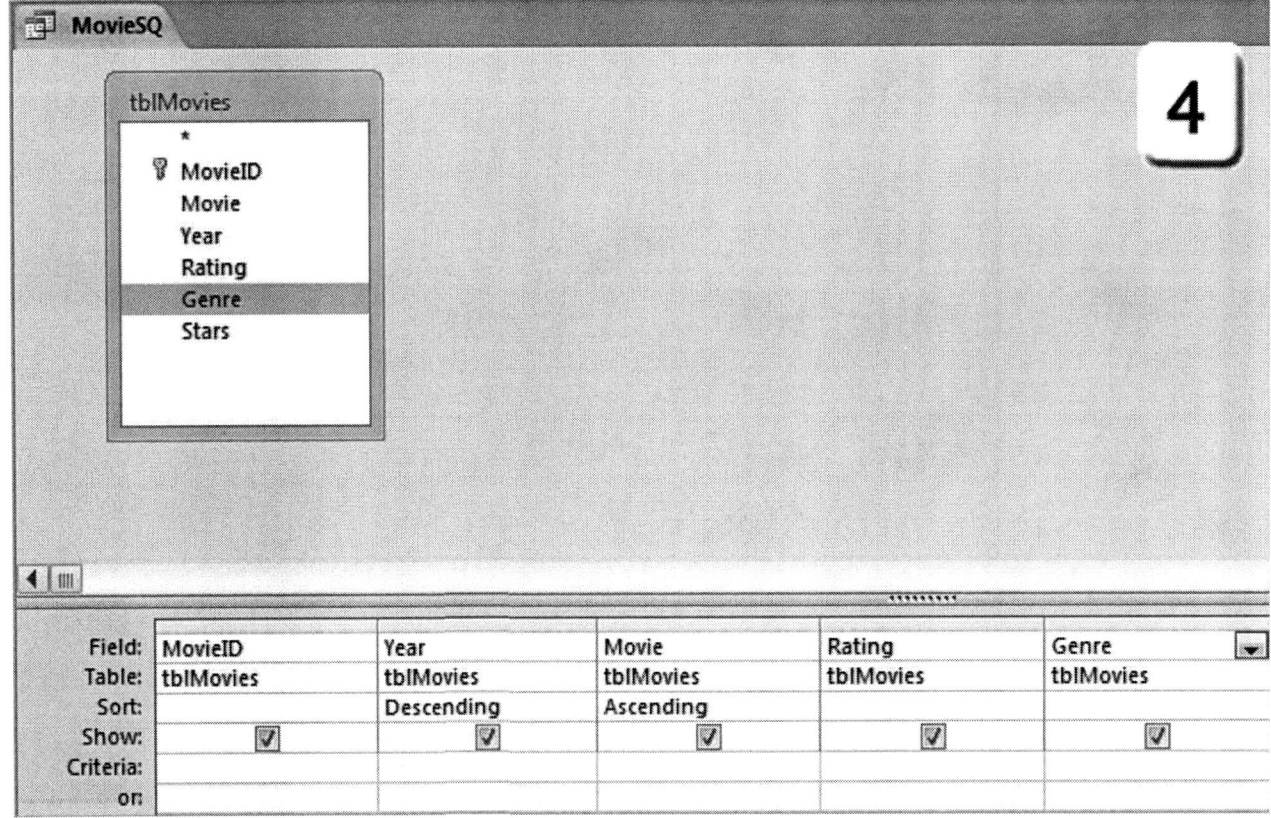

Field:	MovieID	Year	Movie	Rating	Genre	
Table:	tblMovies	tblMovies	tblMovies	tblMovies	tblMovies	
Sort:		Descending	Ascending			
Show:	☑	☑	☑	☑	☑	
Criteria:						
or:						

Exam 77-885: Microsoft Access 2010
4. Creating and Managing Queries
4.3. Manipulate fields: Add Fields to a Query

Run This Query, Too

5. Try it: Run the Query, Yet Again
Go to **Query Tools ->Design->Results.**
Click on **Run.**

What Do You See? The MovieSQ should open in Datasheet View. The Genre Field should be included in the results.

Do This, Too: Save the Query
Go to **File->Save.**

MovieSQ

MovieID	Year	Movie	Rating	Genre
2	2012	21 Jump Street (2011)	R	Action
203	2012	Kahaani (2012)		Thriller
348	2012	The Hunger Games (2012)	PG13	Action
401	2012	Titanic 3D	PG	Romance
3	2011	50/50 (2011)	R	Comedy
4	2011	A Separation (2011)	PG13	Drama
98	2011	Drive (2011)	R	Drama
157	2011	Harry Potter and the Deathly Hallows	PG13	Drama

Exam 77-885: Microsoft Access 2010
4. Creating and Managing Queries
4.1. Construct queries: Create a Select Query

Summary

This discussion begins by creating a Select Query with the Query Wizard. We had an opportunity to play with the Query in Design View as well.

This lesson also introduced our approach to programming: make a change, test the change.

You done good.
You get the cookie.

Or the red gum balls if you wish.

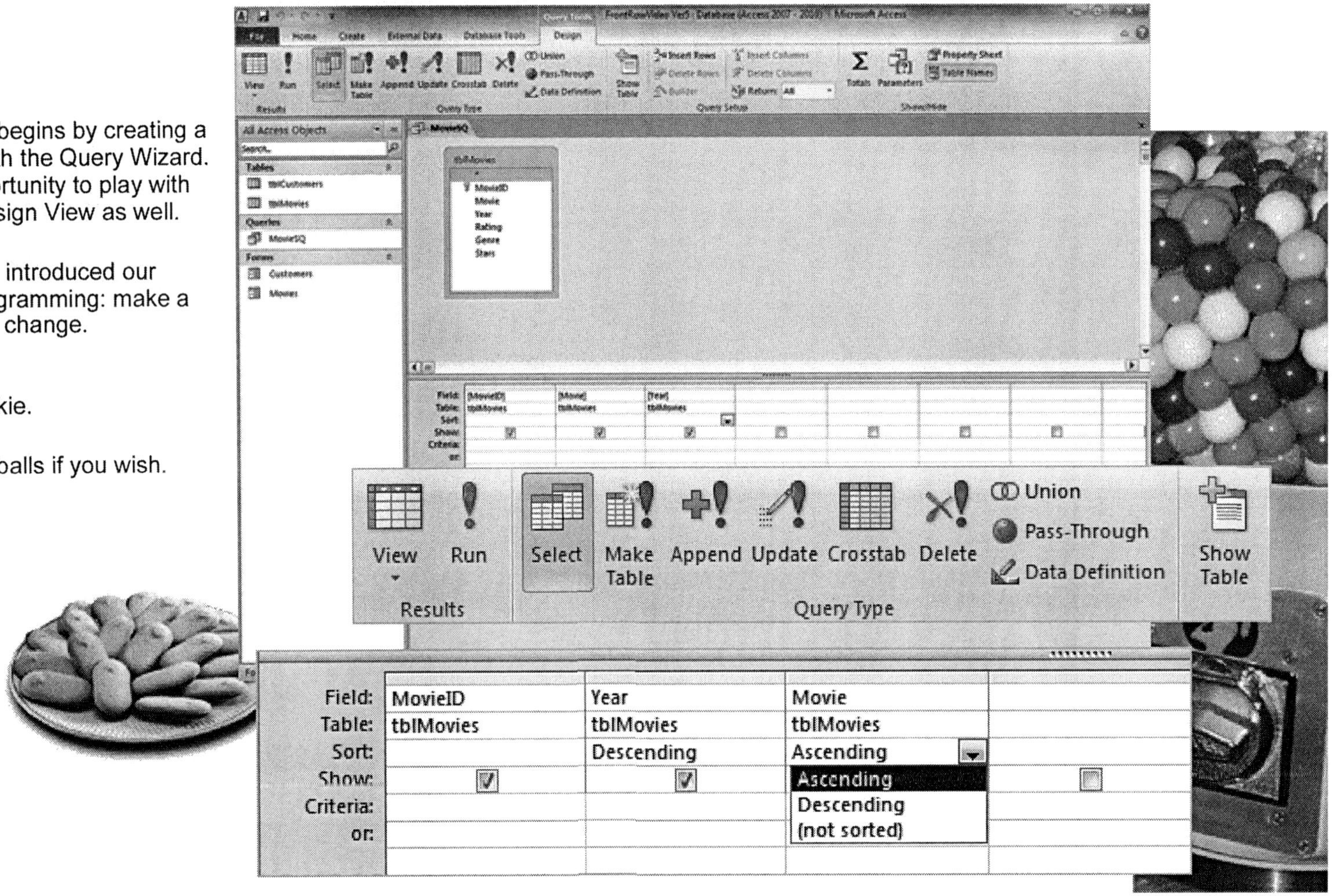

Field:	MovieID	Year	Movie	
Table:	tblMovies	tblMovies	tblMovies	
Sort:		Descending	Ascending	
Show:	☑	☑		☐
Criteria:				
or:				

Ascending
Descending
(not sorted)

Practice Activities

Lesson 7: Query Design
Try This: Do the following steps

1. Open the Brown Bag Lunch database you have been programming. Or you may download the sample database **Brown Bag Lunch ver7.accdb** online.

2. Use the Query Wizard to create a Select Query with tblProducts as the Record Source.

3. Select the following Fields in the Query Wizard,: ProductID, Type, Item, and Specialty.

4. Name the Query ItemSQ and Finish the Wizard.

5. Open the ItemSQ Query in Design View. Use the QBE grid to set the Sort Order for the Specialty Field as Descending. Run the Query to verify that is Sorts with Vegetarian on the top.

6. Return to Design View. In the QBE grid, enter the Criteria "Gluten Free" to the Specialty Field. Run the Query to test that only Gluten Free items are displayed.

7. Return to Design View. In the QBE grid, add a new Field: Type. Set the Sort Order as Ascending. Run the Query to test it, again.

8. Return to Design View. Remove the Criteria "Gluten Free" from the Specialty Field.

9. Rearrange the fields in the QBE grid so that Specialty is to the left of Type. Run the Query to test it one more time. The Query should Sort by Specialty in Descending order (with vegetarian on top) and then by Type in Ascending order (with breakfast first.)

10. Save the ItemSQ Query.

11. Close your Mighty Access dartabase,

Test Yourself

1. Which are templates in the Query Wizard?
(Give all correct answers.)
A. Simple Query Wizard
B. Crosstab Query Wizard
C. Find Duplicates Query Wizard
D. Find Unmatched Query Wizard
Tip: Beginning Access, page 157

2. Queries have which of the following views?
(Give all correct answers.)
A. Datasheet
B. PivotTable
C. PivotChart
D. SQL View
E. Design View
Tip: Beginning Access, page 163

3. Which Query commands show data?
(Give all correct answers.)
A. Select
B. Cross Tab
C. Append
D. Update
E. Delete
Tip: Beginning Access, 165

4. Which Query commands change the data?
(Give all correct answers.)
A. Select
B. Cross Tab
C. Append
D. Update
E. Delete
Tip: Beginning Access, page 165

5. To add a field in Query Design mode, double-click the Field name in the Data Source box above the QBE Grid.
A. True
B. False
Tip: Beginning Access, page 172

6. When you Run a Query, it displays the results based on the fields and any criteria programmed.
A. True
B. False
Tip: Beginning Access, page 167, 170

7. Any change to a Query should be tested to make sure it works as desired.
A. True
B. False
Tip: Beginning Access, page 176

8. What is QBE?
A. Quick Blank Example: a quick new template
B. Query Back Empty: returns any blank fields
C. Question Bank Effect: creates sample question to help in designing a Query
D: Query By Example: a visual format for programming
Tip: Beginning Access, page 164

Access 2010: Questions
More Questions, More Queries

Beginning Access Objectives
In this lesson, you will learn how to:

1. Create a Query in Design View and use the Show Table command to add a Record Source.

2. Add Fields to the QBE Grid.

3. Create a Field that combines (Concatenates) two or more Fields together.

4. Create a Parameter Query that prompts the User to enter more information when the Query runs.

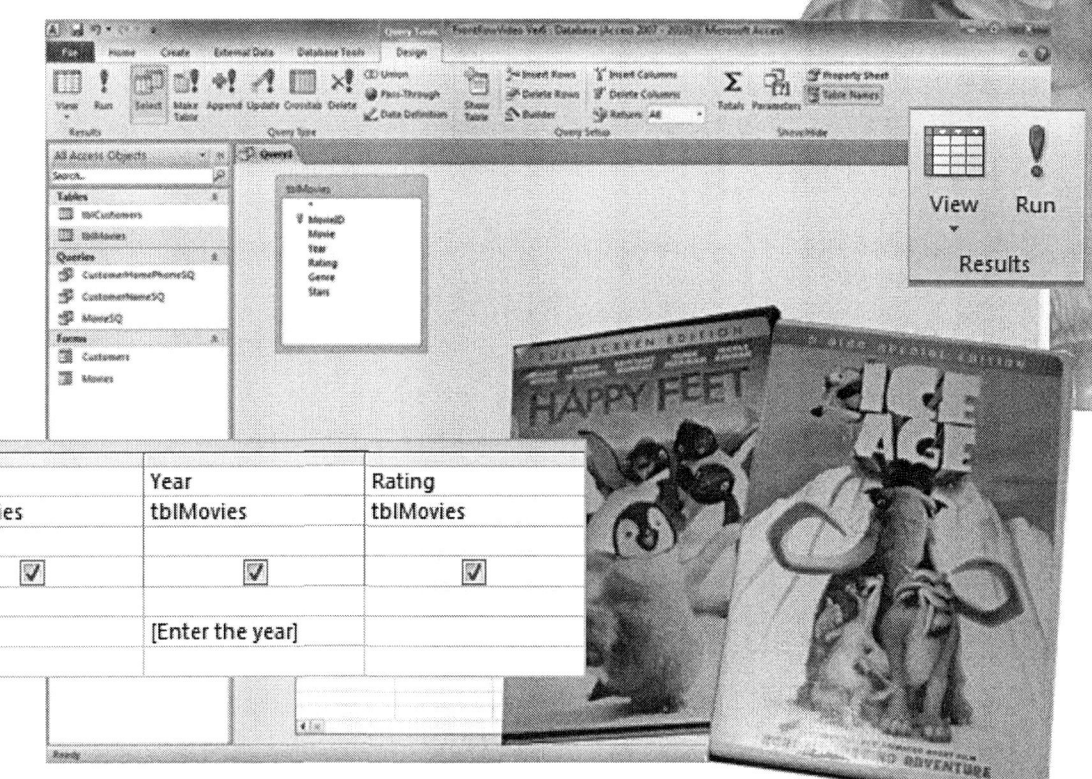

© 2012 Comma Productions, LLC

Field:	MovieID	Movie	Year	Rating
Table:	tblMovies	tblMovies	tblMovies	tblMovies
Sort:				
Show:	☑	☑	☑	☑
Criteria:				
or:			[Enter the year]	

Lesson 8 : More Questions, More Queries

1. Readings

Read Lesson 8 in the Beginning Access guide, page 179-202.

Project

Parameter Queries with calculated Fields from the customer and movie Tables.

Downloads

FrontRowVideo Begin8.accdb
popcorn1.gif, popcorn2.gif,
popcorn3.gif, popcorn4.gif, movies1.gif.

Brown Bag Lunch ver8.accdb
BB Customers Logo.jpg
Brown Bag Logo.jpg
Lunch1.gif, Lunch2.gif, Lunch3.gif,
Lunch4.gif

2. Practice

Do the Practice Activity on page 203.

3. Assessment

Review the Test questions on page 204.

Create

Query Tools->Design

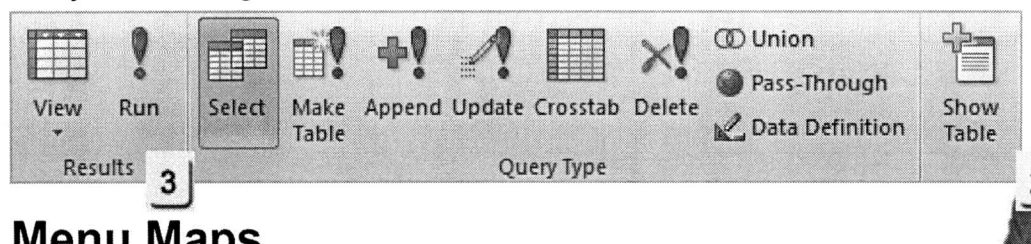

Menu Maps

From the **Create Ribbon**.
1. Create ->Queries-> Query Design, page 184

From the **Query Tools->Design Ribbon**.
2. Query Tools->Design->Show Table, page 184
3. Query Tools ->Design->Results->Run, page 187

More Questions, More Queries

OK, a **Select Query** asks questions. Sometimes, how you ask a question can return a better answer. This lesson will look at ways to use a Query to find the answer. The first example works with the customer data: combining the Fields for reports and printouts. The second example will create a **Parameter Query** that asks the User for more information, say the customer's phone number.

This lesson will create several Select Queries in Design View using the Show Table options.

Microsoft Office Access 2010: Example of a Parameter Query and the results, below

Field:	LastNameFirst: [LastName] & ", " & [FirstName]	CityStateZip: [City] & ", " & [State] & " " & [Zip]
Table:		
Sort:		
Show:	☑	☑
Criteria:		
or:		

Query1

CustomerID	FirstName	LastName	FullName	LastNameFirst	CityStateZip
2	Deeter	Poohbah	Deeter Poohbah	Poohbah, Deeter	Brighton, MI 48116
3	Mary	Contrary	Mary Contrary	Contrary, Mary	Pinckney, MI 48169
4	Timothy	Allen	Timothy Allen	Allen, Timothy	Ann Arbor, MI 48103
5	Alpha	Beta	Alpha Beta	Beta, Alpha	MyTown, MI
6	Sage	Young	Sage Young	Young, Sage	Brighton, MI 48116
*	(New)				

Microsoft Access 2010

Before You Begin

This lesson uses the Front Row Video database. You can continue with the database you have been programming. You can also download the sample Access database at the beginning of this lesson.

1. Try it: Open the Sample Database
Go to the Documents folder.
Open the sample database:
FrontRowVideo Begin8.accdb

What Do You See? In All Access Objects
There are two Tables:
tblCustomers has 5 records.
tblMovies has 401 records.
There are two Forms:
Customers
Movies
And a Query: MoviesSQ

What Else Do You See? This database may have a Security Warning. In order to edit the objects and save your work, you need to click on **Enable Content**.

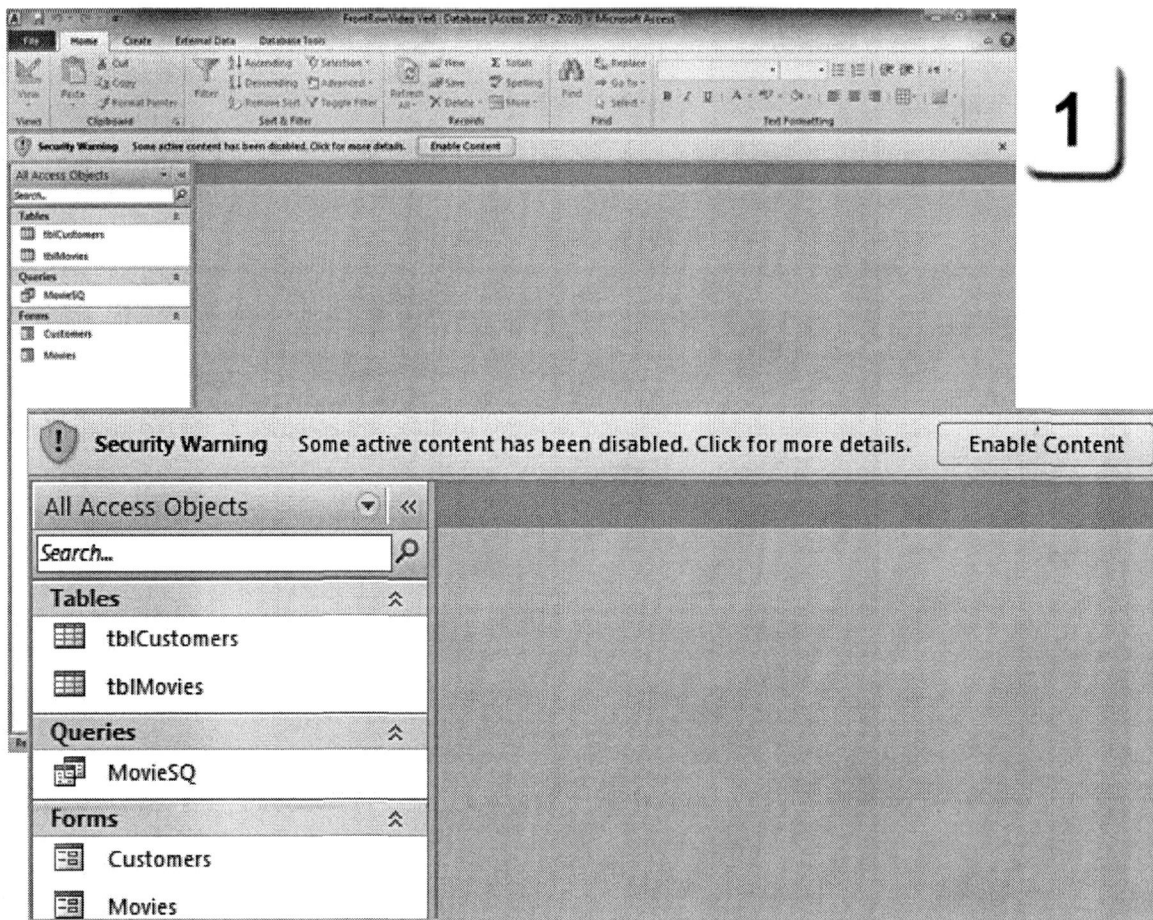

Review the Customer Table

The goal of this lesson is to create a Query that can fill in the information for a customer receipt or report. This Query will use a calculated Field to combine several Fields together to create a mailing label.

This Query will use tblCustomers for the Record Source. Know your data...

2. Try it: Review the Customer Table
Go to **All Access Objects**.
Double click tblCustomers to open it in Datasheet View.

What Do You See? The Customer Table has 5 customers. The Table includes the name and address Fields.

Close tblCustomers. Keep going...

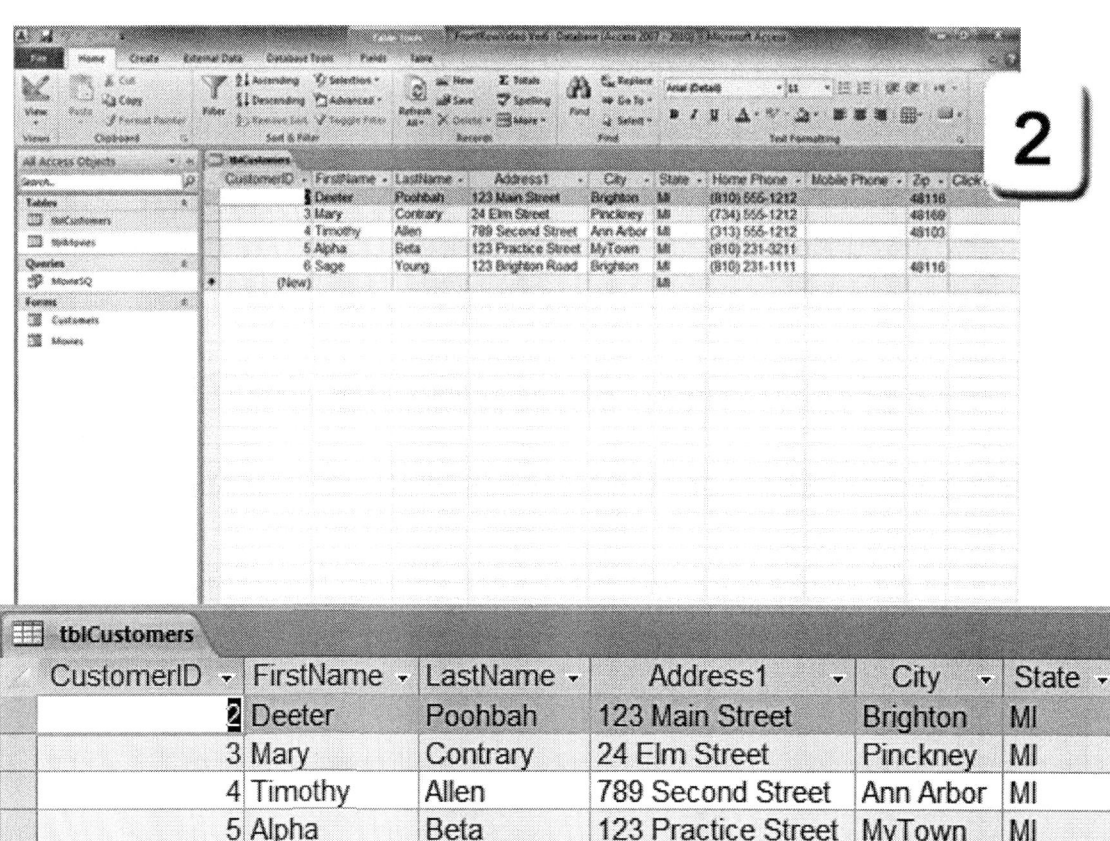

CustomerID	FirstName	LastName	Address1	City	State
2	Deeter	Poohbah	123 Main Street	Brighton	MI
3	Mary	Contrary	24 Elm Street	Pinckney	MI
4	Timothy	Allen	789 Second Street	Ann Arbor	MI
5	Alpha	Beta	123 Practice Street	MyTown	MI
6	Sage	Young	123 Brighton Road	Brighton	MI
*	(New)				MI

Exam 77-885: Microsoft Access 2010
4. Creating and Managing Queries
4.3. Manipulate fields: Create Calculated Fields

Query the Customer Table

This lesson creates a Select Query in Design View. The first step is to select a Record Source when you are prompted by a **ShowTable** window.

Before You Begin: All of the Tables, Forms and Queries are closed.

1. Try it: Create a Select Query
Go to **Create ->Queries-> Query Design.**

What Do You See? A blank query will open. The **Show Table** window will prompt you to choose a Table or Query for the Record Source.

Select a Table: tblCustomers
Click **Add**.

Click **Close**. Keep going...

Create ->Queries-> Query Design

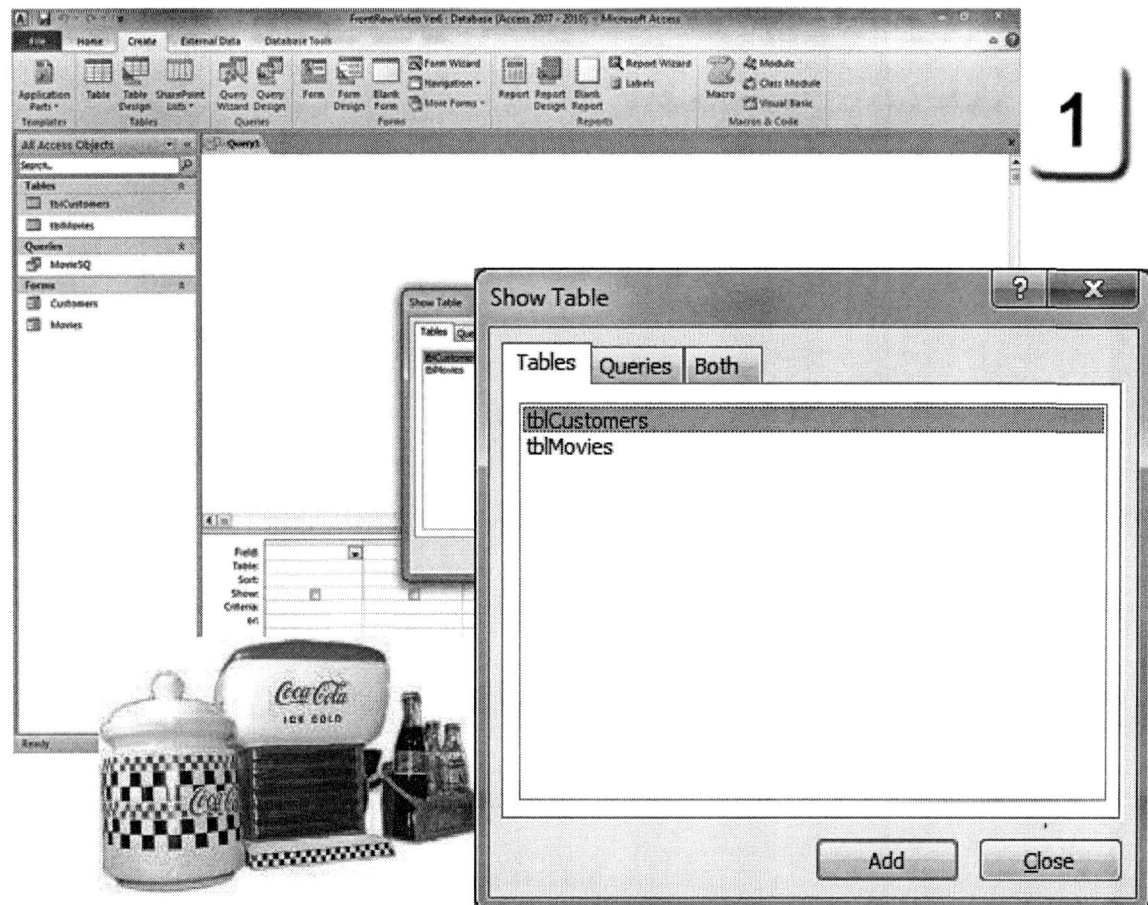

Exam 77-885: Microsoft Access 2010
4. Creating and Managing Queries
4.2. Manage source tables and relationships: Use Show/Table Command

Add Fields to the Query

There is a Table at the top of the Query: tblCustomers. However, the QBE grid is still blank. Let's add the names.

2. Try it: Add Fields to the Query
Go to tblCustomers.
Double click to select the following Fields:
CustomerID
FirstName
LastName

What Do You See? By default, all of these Fields has a check mark for **Show**. That means they will be visible when you Run the Query.

It's a start. Keep going...

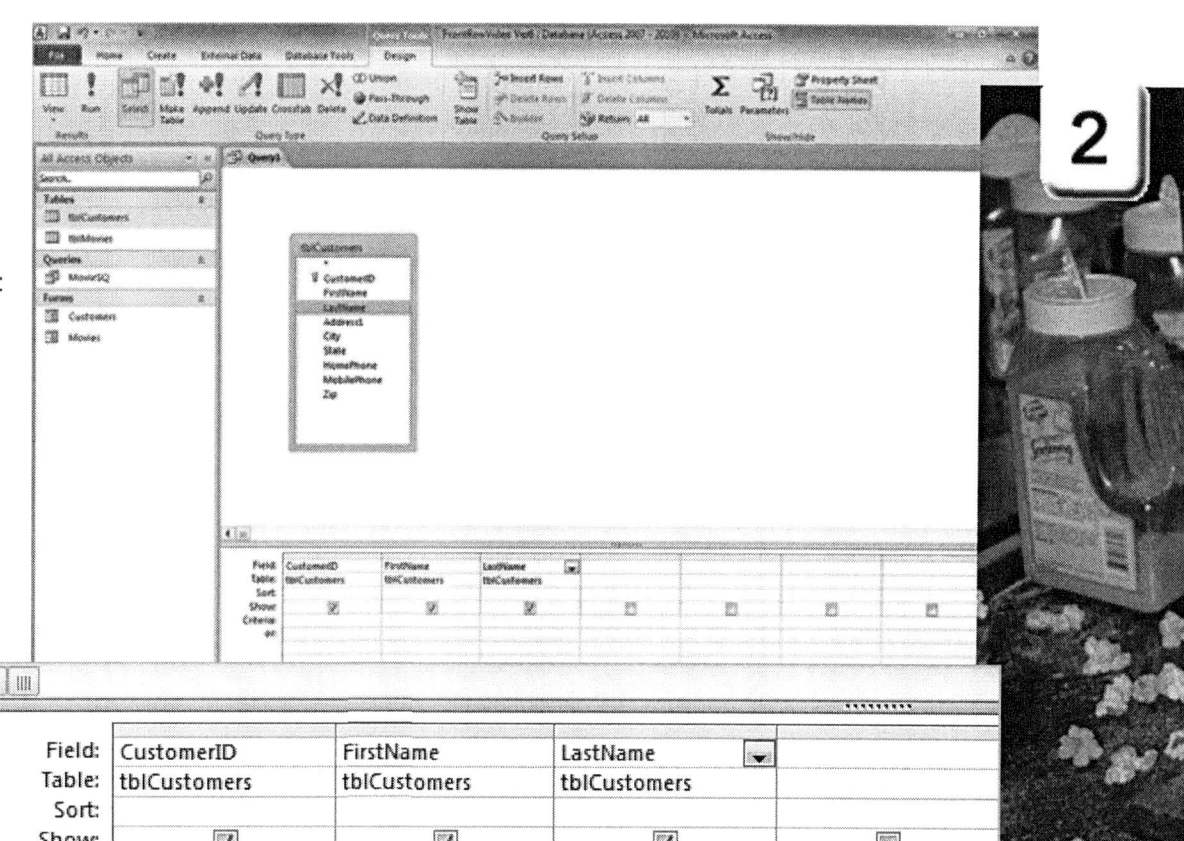

Field:	CustomerID	FirstName	LastName	
Table:	tblCustomers	tblCustomers	tblCustomers	
Sort:				
Show:	✓	✓	✓	☐
Criteria:				
or:				

Exam 77-885: Microsoft Access 2010
4. Creating and Managing Queries
4.3. Manipulate fields: Add a Field

Concatenation

Business envelopes, letters and customer receipts usually display the First Name and Last Name Fields together. You can use a Query to combine both Fields into one. The command is called **concatenation**. Here is how it works.

3. Try it: Concatenate Two Name Fields

Place your cursor at the top of the next blank Column in the QBE Grid.
Type: FullName:[FirstName]&" "&[LastName]

Fullname is the label, or **alias**, for the new field.

[FirstName] and [LastName] are Fields from tblCustomer.

The two **quotes** have a space between them. Whatever is inside the quotes will be placed between the fields.

The two & signs are the glue that sticks the two fields together.

Query Tools ->Design

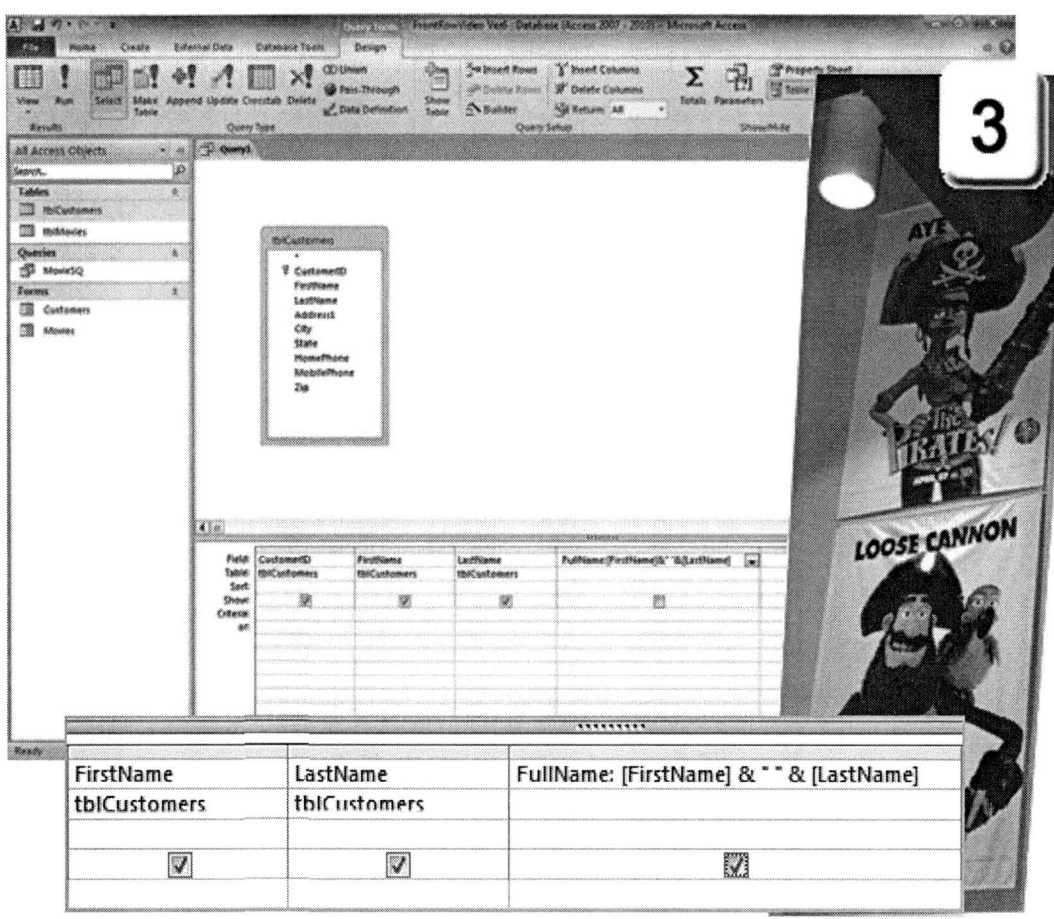

FirstName	LastName	FullName: [FirstName] & " " & [LastName]
tblCustomers	tblCustomers	
☑	☑	☑

Exam 77-885: Microsoft Access 2010
4. Creating and Managing Queries
4.3. Calculated Fields: Concatenation

Test the Query

How does this look when you Run the Query and see the Customers' Names?

4. Try it: Test the Query
The Query is open in Design View.
Go to **Query Tools ->Design->Results->Run.**

What Do You See? The Query Results will open in Datasheet View. There should be a new Field called FullName that combines the First Name and Last Name Fields.

Try This, Too: Return to the Design View
Go to **Home->Views->View.**
Choose a View: **Design View.**

Keep going...

Query Tools ->Design->Results->Run

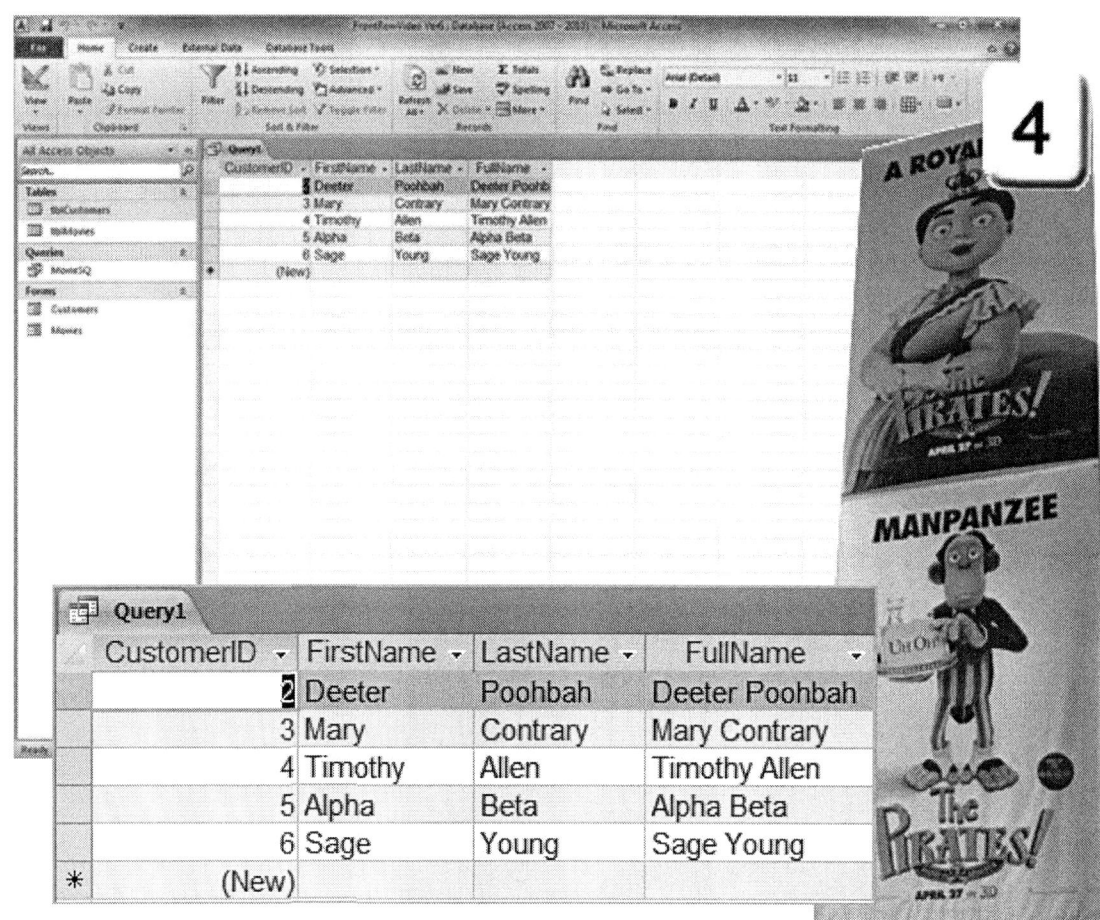

CustomerID	FirstName	LastName	FullName
2	Deeter	Poohbah	Deeter Poohbah
3	Mary	Contrary	Mary Contrary
4	Timothy	Allen	Timothy Allen
5	Alpha	Beta	Alpha Beta
6	Sage	Young	Sage Young
*	(New)		

Exam 77-885: Microsoft Access 2010
4. Creating and Managing Queries
4.3. Calculated Fields: Concatenation

HOME

Take Two

More Concatenations

5. Try it: More Concatenations

If you wanted to display Last Name, First Name your concatenation would look like this:

LastNameFirst:[LastName]&", "&[FirstName]

Another useful concatenation is:

CityStateZip:[City]&", "&[State]&" "&[Zip]

Now, when you create a report or mail merge, the fields will be evenly spaced, without ugly gaps between short and long names.

Enter these examples into the Query.
Keep going...

Query Tools ->Design

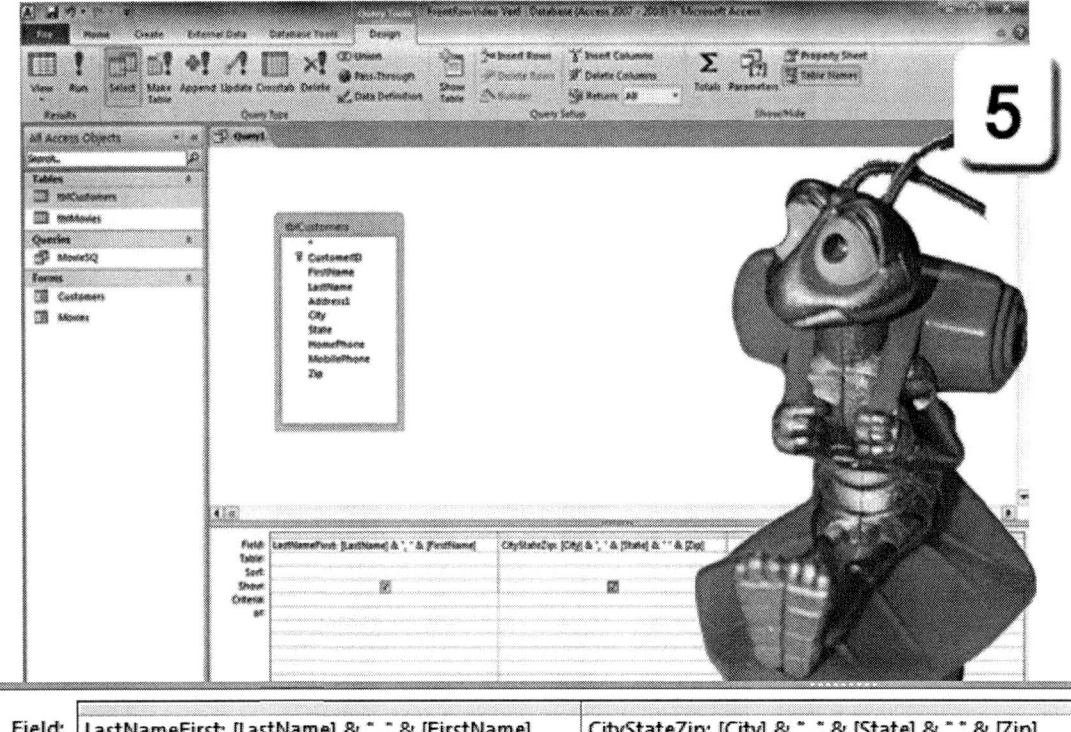

Field:	LastNameFirst: [LastName] & ", " & [FirstName]	CityStateZip: [City] & ", " & [State] & " " & [Zip]
Table:		
Sort:		
Show:	☑	☑
Criteria:		
or:		

Exam 77-885: Microsoft Access 2010
4. Creating and Managing Queries
4.3. Calculated Fields: Concatenation

Test These Changes, Too

6. Try it: Test the Query, Again
The Query is still open in Design View.
Go to **Query Tools ->Design->Results->Run.**

What Do You See? The Query Results will open in Datasheet View. There should be two new concatenated Fields:
LastNameFirst and CityStateZip.

Try This, Too: Return to the Design View
Go to **Home->Views->View.**
Choose a View: **Design View.**

Keep going...

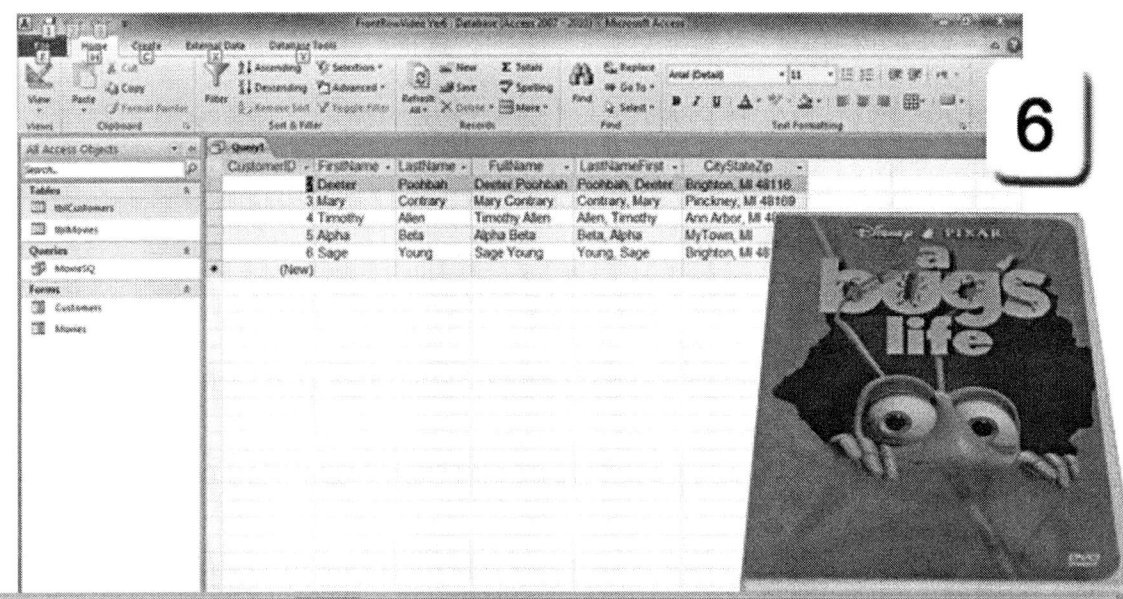

Query1

CustomerID	FirstName	LastName	FullName	LastNameFirst	CityStateZip
2	Deeter	Poohbah	Deeter Poohbah	Poohbah, Deeter	Brighton, MI 48116
3	Mary	Contrary	Mary Contrary	Contrary, Mary	Pinckney, MI 48169
4	Timothy	Allen	Timothy Allen	Allen, Timothy	Ann Arbor, MI 48103
5	Alpha	Beta	Alpha Beta	Beta, Alpha	MyTown, MI
6	Sage	Young	Sage Young	Young, Sage	Brighton, MI 48116
*	(New)				

Exam 77-885: Microsoft Access 2010
4. Creating and Managing Queries
4.3. Calculated Fields: Concatenation

Zoom Into the Code

Typing Code in the little Cells seems like it is the "hard way." You can Zoom into the Code and see it much, much bigger.

1. Try it: Zoom Into the Code
Right Click the FullName Field.
Select **Zoom** from the options.

Keep going...

Query Tools ->Design

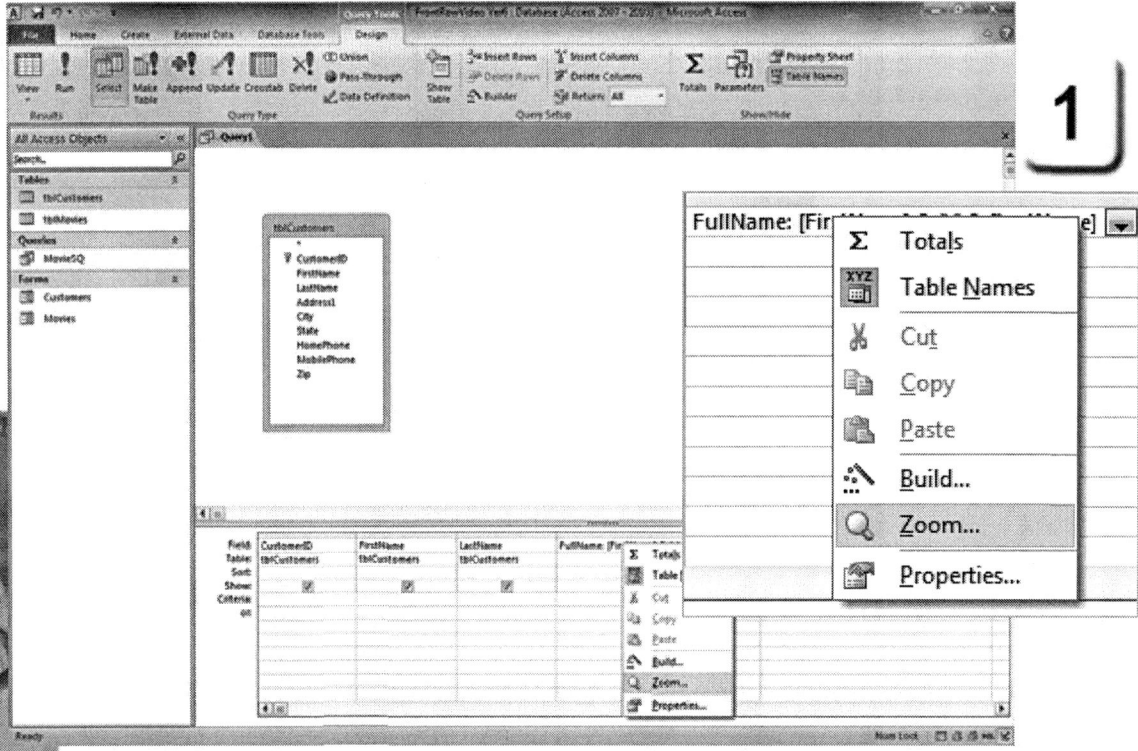

Exam 77-885: Microsoft Access 2010
4. Creating and Managing Queries
4.3. Manipulate fields: Zoom into the Code

Really See the Code

When the Zoom Window opens, the Code may still be small, 6 pt type. Too small is still too small. However, we can change this. We're Access programmers!

2. Try it: Increase the Font Size
The Zoom Window is open.
Click on **Font..**
Edit the **Size**: 14
Click **OK**.

What Do You See? The image on this page shows the Code in 14 pt type. It is easy to see the spaces and punctuation.

Very Good. Click **OK** to close the Zoom.

Query Tools ->Design

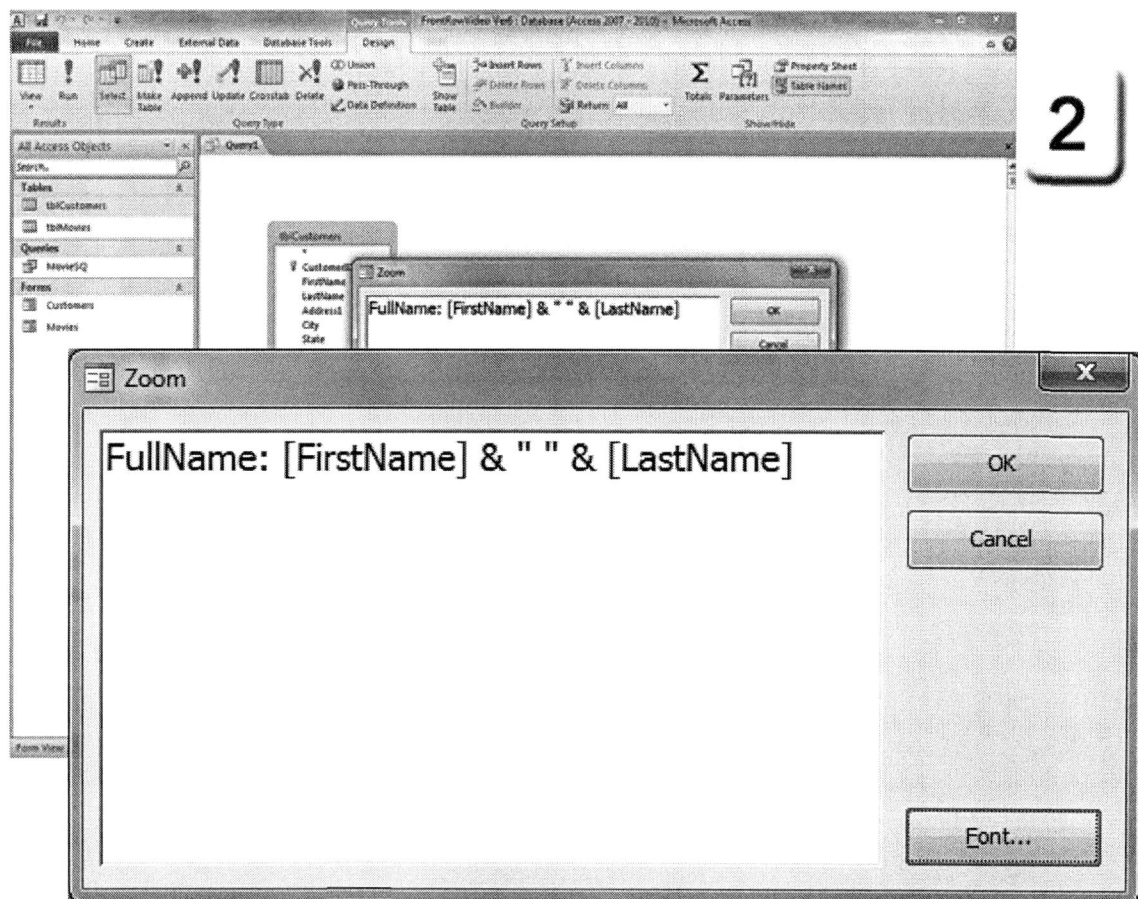

FullName: [FirstName] & " " & [LastName]

Exam 77-885: Microsoft Access 2010
4. Creating and Managing Queries
4.3. Manipulate fields: Zoom into the Code

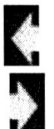

Save the Query

This is a good time to **Save** the Query.

Try This: Save the Query
Go to **File->Save.**

Enter the Query Name:
CustomerNameSQ

Customer because Record Source is
tblCustomers and **Name** because that is
the Field that we manipulated with this
Query. **SQ** because this is a Select
Query.

Click **OK**. Close this Query.

So, we have a useful Customer Query.

File ->Save

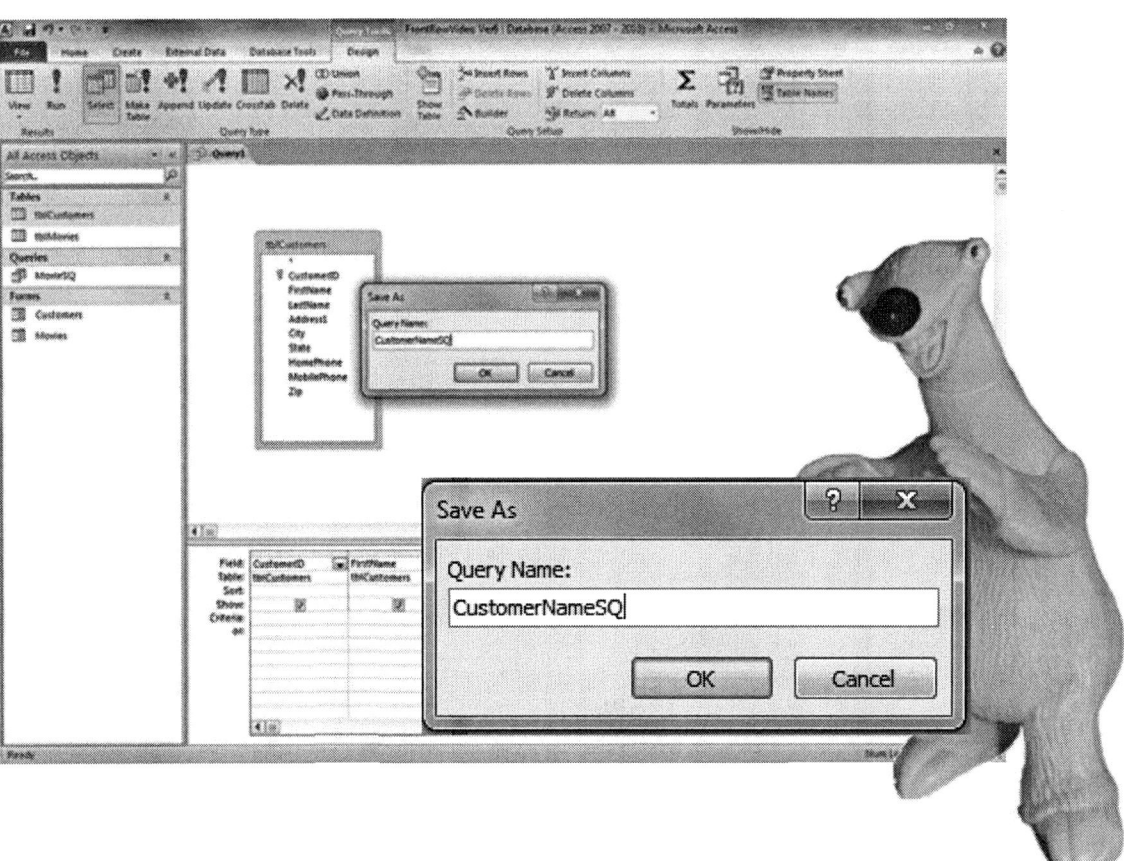

Exam 77-885: Microsoft Access 2010
4. Creating and Managing Queries
4.3. Manipulate fields: Create Calculated Fields

Parameter Queries

Parameter Queries prompt you to answer a question before the Query runs.

Before You Begin: All of the Tables, Forms and Queries are closed.

1. Try it: Create a Parameter Query
Go to **Create ->Queries-> Query Design**.

What Do You See? A new, blank query will open. The Show Table will prompt you to choose a Table or Query for the Record Source.

Select a Table: tblCustomers
Click **Add**.

Click **Close**. Keep going...

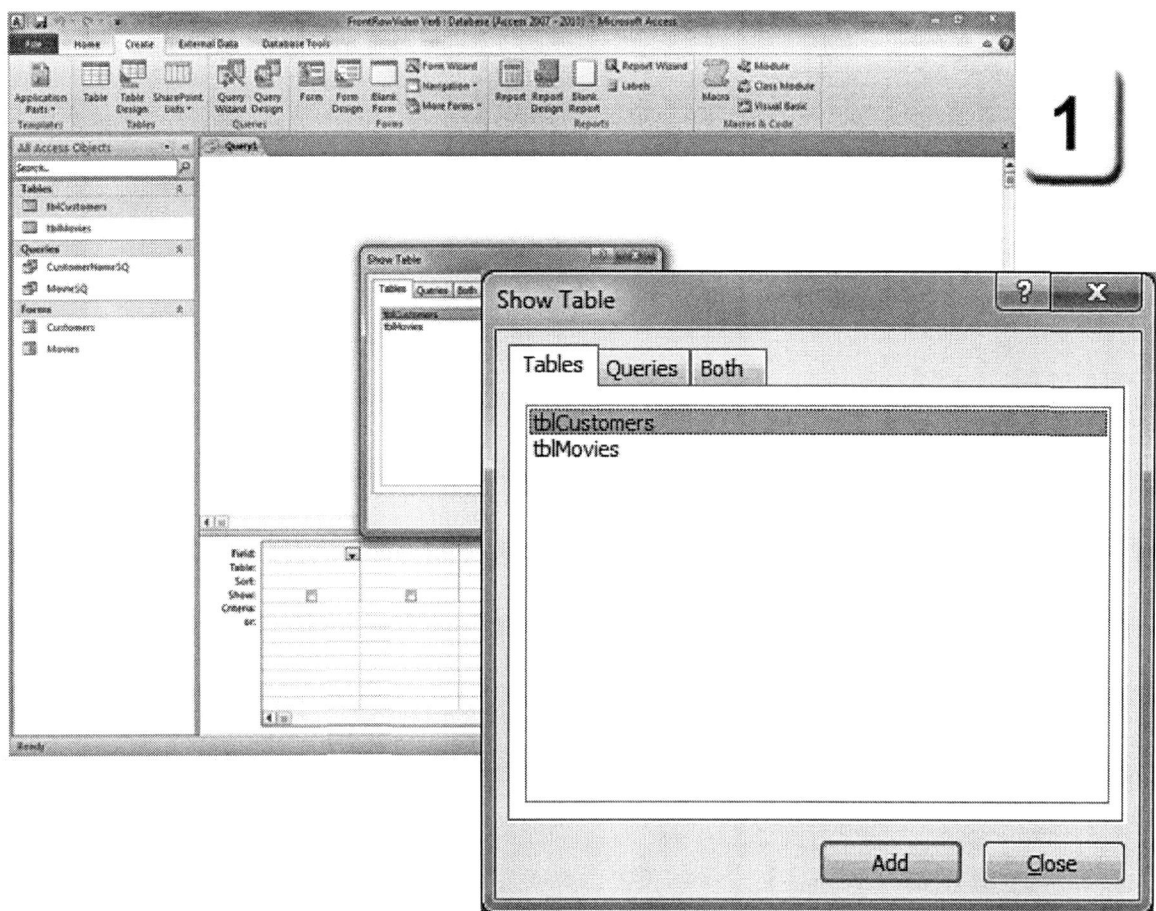

Exam 77-885: Microsoft Access 2010
4. Creating and Managing Queries
4.2. Manage source tables and relationships: Use the Show/Table Command

Query Tools ->Design

Add the Fields

When a customer goes to check out some movies, the clerk at the register asks for a phone number. Our Parameter Query can do the same thing.

2. Try it: Add Fields to the Query
Go to **tblCustomer.**
Double click to select the following Fields:
CustomerID
FirstName
LastName
HomePhone

Keep going...

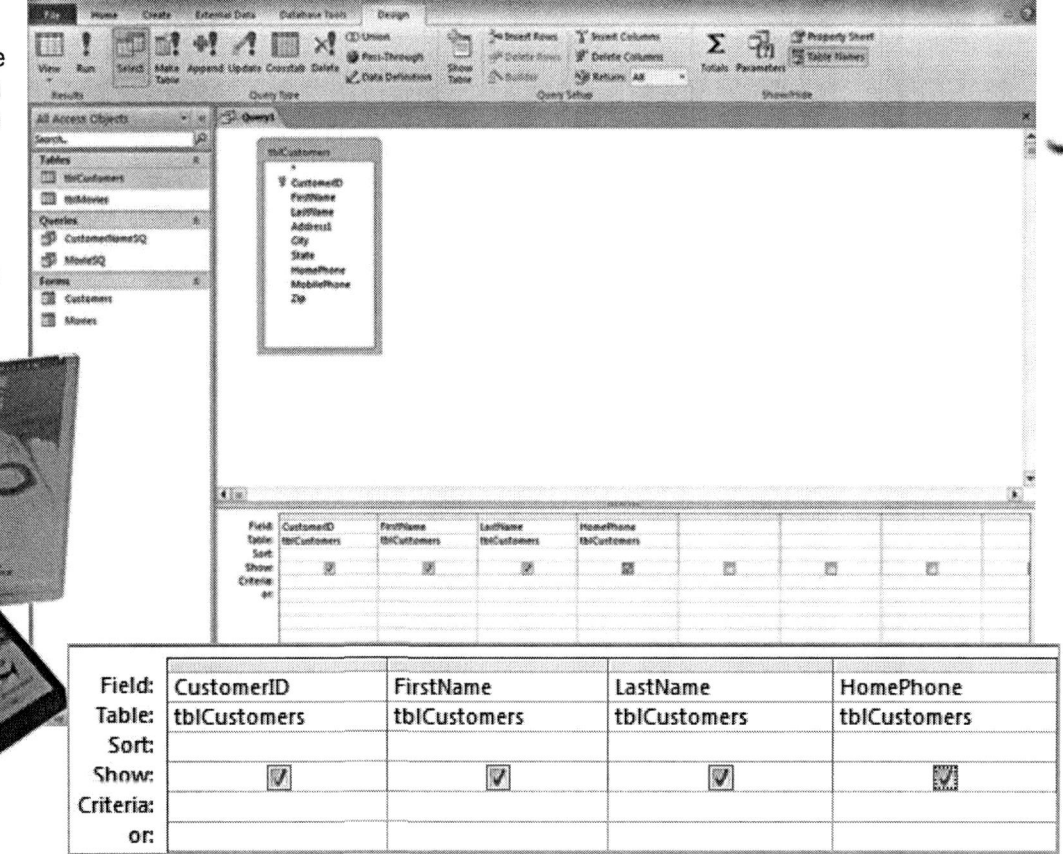

Field:	CustomerID	FirstName	LastName	HomePhone
Table:	tblCustomers	tblCustomers	tblCustomers	tblCustomers
Sort:				
Show:	☑	☑	☑	☑
Criteria:				
or:				

Exam 77-885: Microsoft Access 2010
4. Creating and Managing Queries
4.3. Manipulate fields: Create a Parameter Query

Query Tools ->Design

Add a Parameter
3. Try it: Edit the Criteria
Go to the HomePhone Field.
Enter the following **Criteria**:

[Enter the phone number]

That's it. This is what the User will see
when the Query runs.

Keep going..

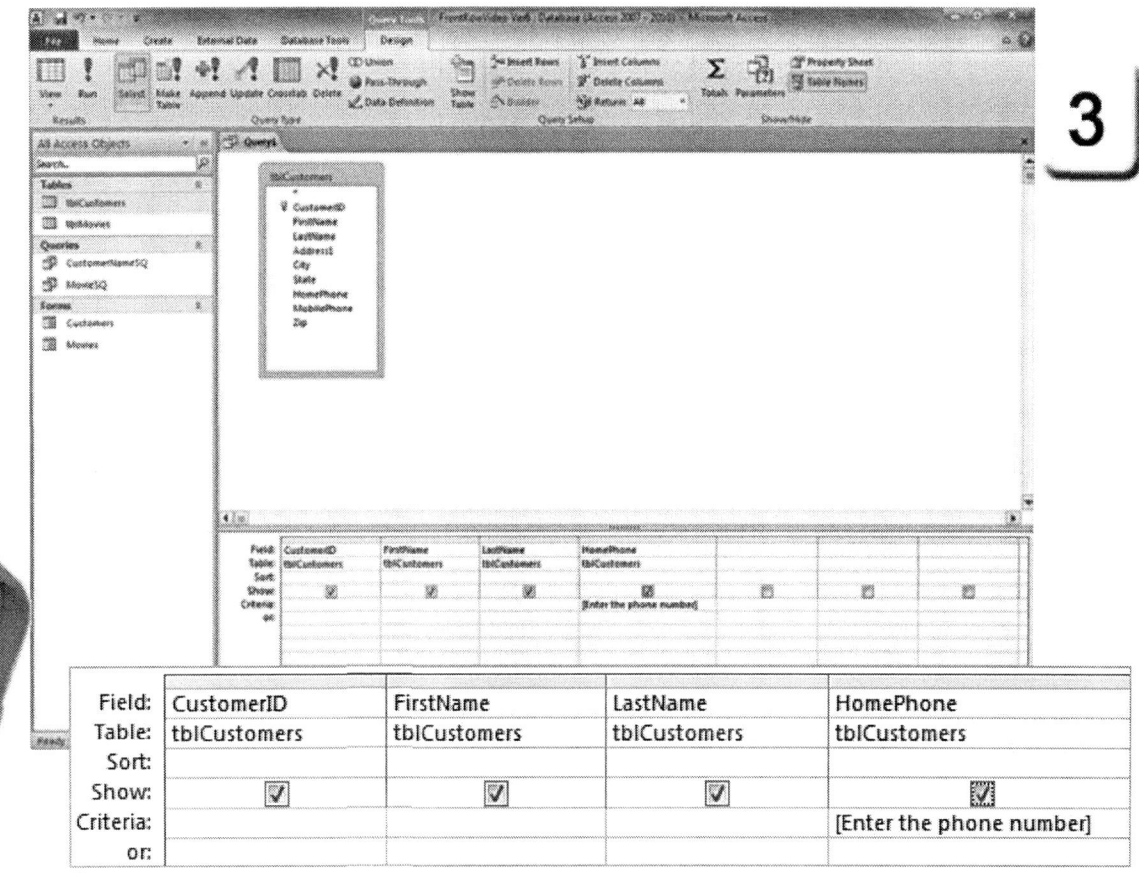

Field:	CustomerID	FirstName	LastName	HomePhone
Table:	tblCustomers	tblCustomers	tblCustomers	tblCustomers
Sort:				
Show:	☑	☑	☑	☑
Criteria:				[Enter the phone number]
or:				

Exam 77-885: Microsoft Access 2010
4. Creating and Managing Queries
4.3. Manipulate fields: Create a Parameter Query

Run the Parameter Query

4. Try it: Run the Parameter Query
Go to **Query Tools ->Design->Results- >Run.**

What Do You See? You will be prompted to Enter the phone number.

Type: 8105551212
Click **OK.**

Now What Do You See? The Parameter Query found the right phone number as well as the customer's name.

Memo to Self: The HomePhone Field was formatted with the Input Mask Wizard. The last question in the Wizard asked if the phone number should be saved with or without the punctuation. We elected to save the data as just numbers...

So, this Parameter Query works if you type in just the numbers, no punctuation.

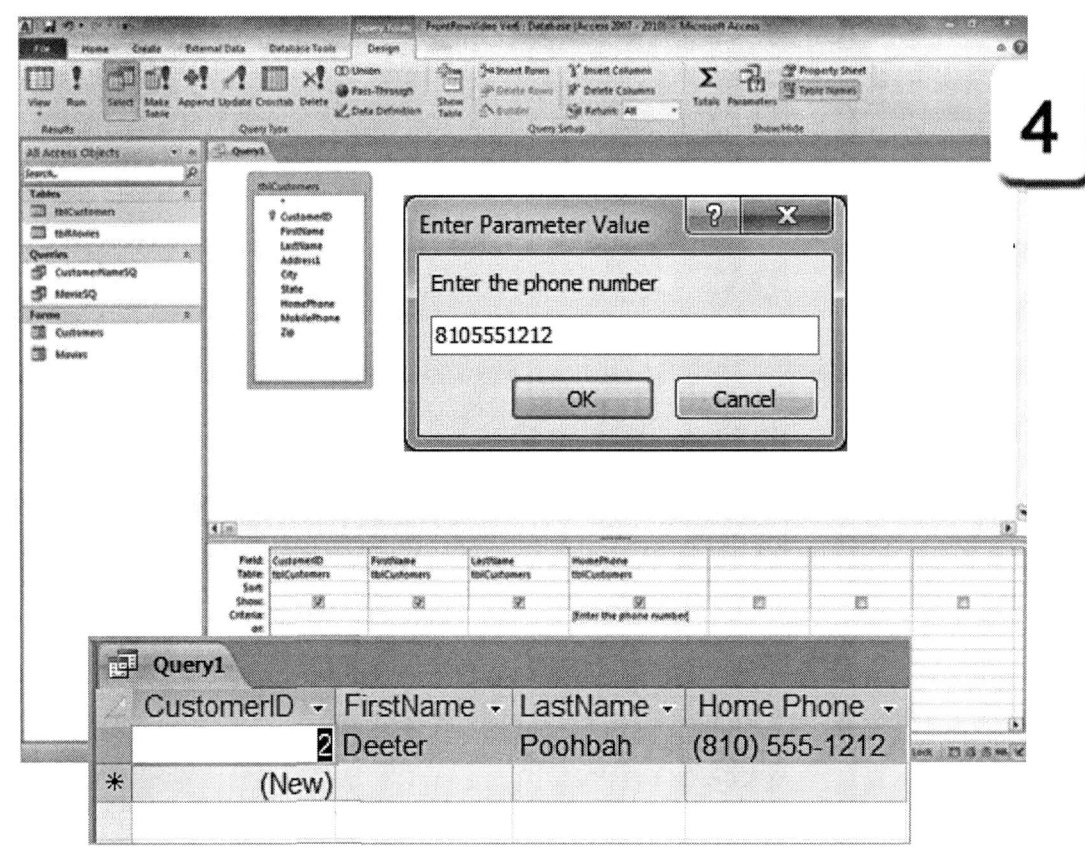

Exam 77-885: Microsoft Access 2010
4. Creating and Managing Queries
4.3. Manipulate fields: Create a Parameter Query

Save the Parameter Query
If it works, it's worth saving, isn't it?

5. Try it: Save the Parameter Query
Go to **File ->Save.**
Enter the Query Name:
CustomerHomePhoneSQ.
Click **OK**.

Close the Query.

File ->Save

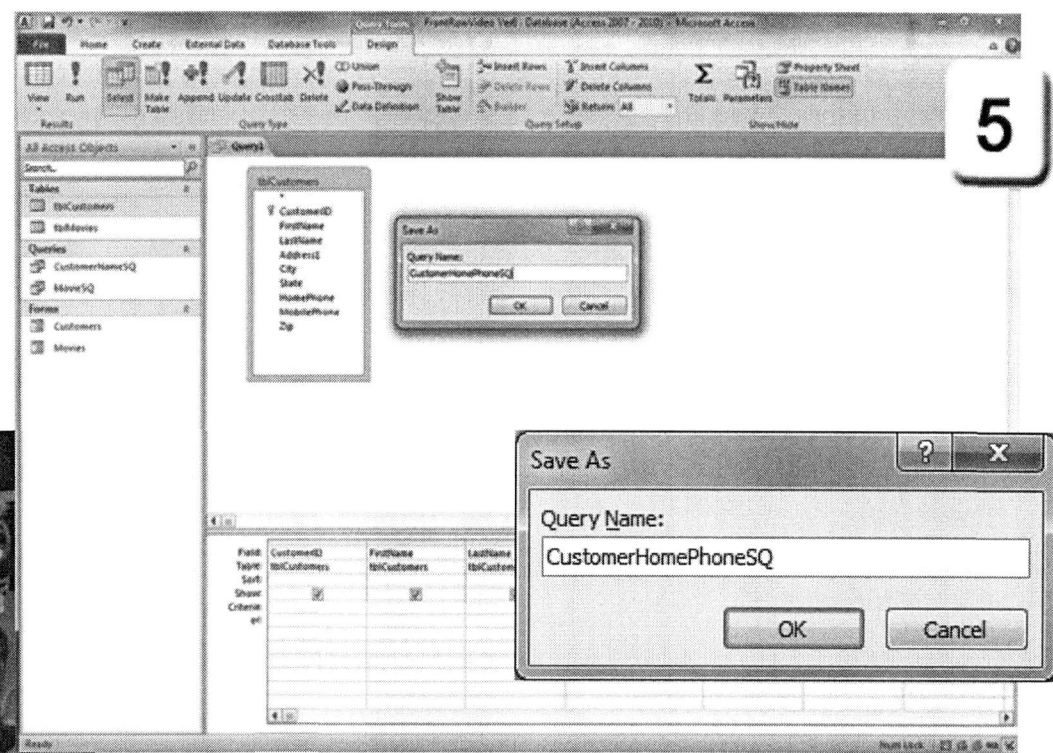

Save As

Query Name:

CustomerHomePhoneSQ

OK   Cancel

Exam 77-885: Microsoft Access 2010
4. Creating and Managing Queries
4.3. Manipulate fields: Create a Parameter Query

One More Query...
In the first lesson on Queries we used the **Query Criteria** to find all of the movies that matched the Year we entered. In order to change the search, we had to return to the Design View and edit the Criteria under the Year from say 2012 to 2011.

This Parameter Query will be more flexible.

Before You Begin: All of the Tables, Forms and Queries are closed.

1. Try it: Create a Parameter Query
Go to **Create ->Queries-> Query Design.**

What Do You See? A new, blank query will open. The Show Table will prompt you to choose a Table or Query for the Record Source.

Select a Table: **tblMovies**
Click **Add.**

Click **Close.** Keep going...

Create ->Queries-> Query Design

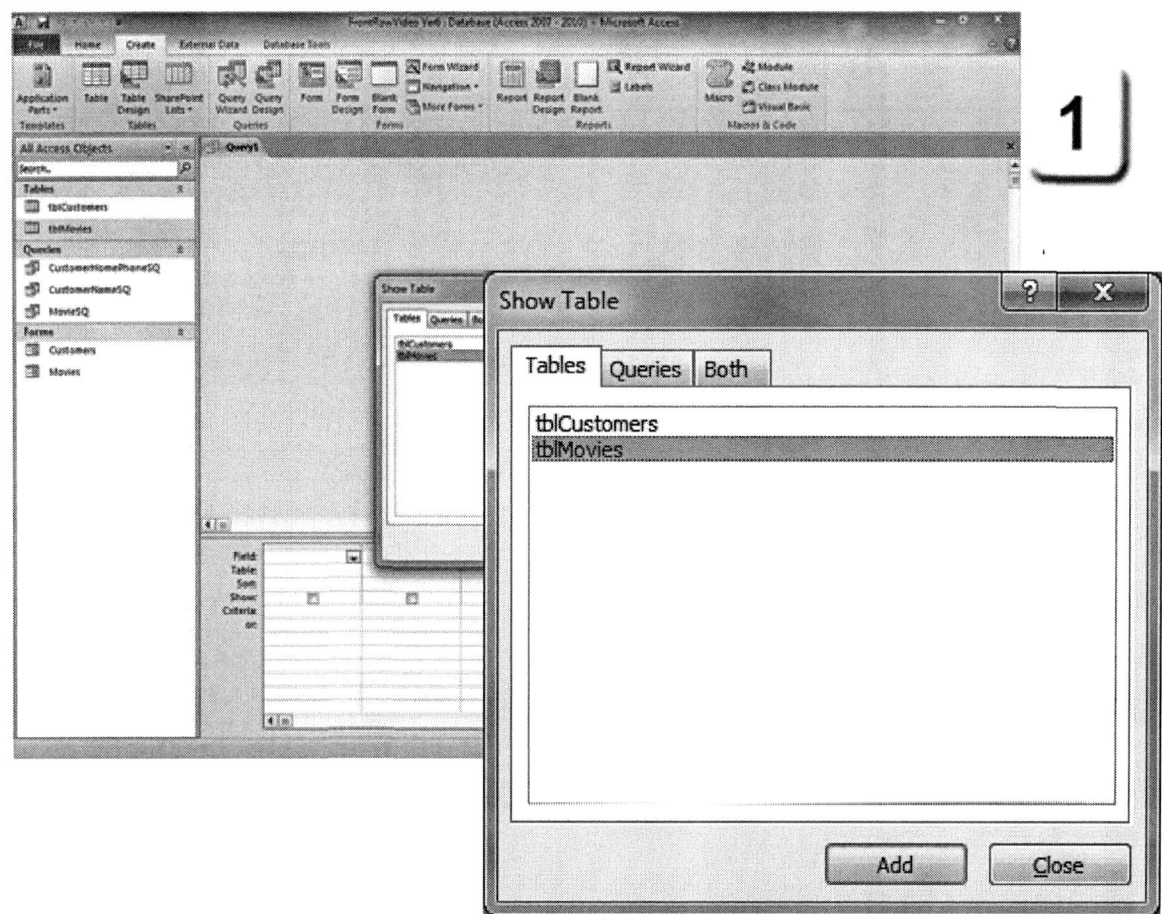

Add All of the Fields

There are two methods for selecting all of the Fields from the Table and adding them to the QBE Grid on the bottom of the query: the Wildcard (*) or double-click.

If you double-click the Wildcard(*) you should see one Field on the Grid that says *tblMovies, where * means "select everything."

If you double-click each Field separately, you will see the Field names lined up on the QBE Grid. This method works great for Parameter Queries because each Field can have a different Criteria if you wish.

2. Try it: Add Fields to the Query
Go to tblMovies.
Double click to select the following Fields:
MovieID
Movie
Year
Rating
Genre
Stars
Keep going, please...

Query Tools ->Design

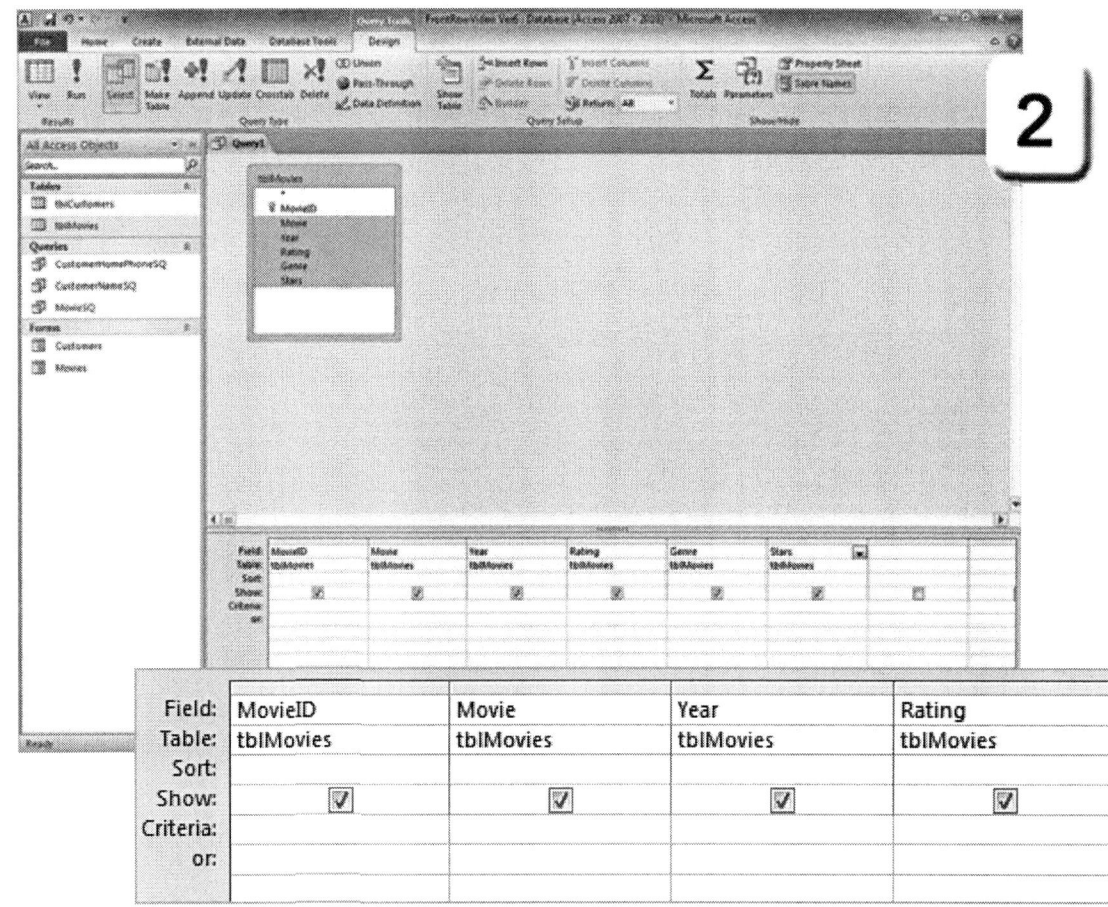

Field:	MovieID	Movie	Year	Rating
Table:	tblMovies	tblMovies	tblMovies	tblMovies
Sort:				
Show:	☑	☑	☑	☑
Criteria:				
or:				

Exam 77-885: Microsoft Access 2010
4. Creating and Managing Queries
4.1. Construct queries: Select All Fields

Take Two

Query Tools ->Design

Add a Parameter
3. Try it: Add a Parameter
Select a Field: Year
Type the following in the **Criteria**:

[Enter the year]

Keep going...

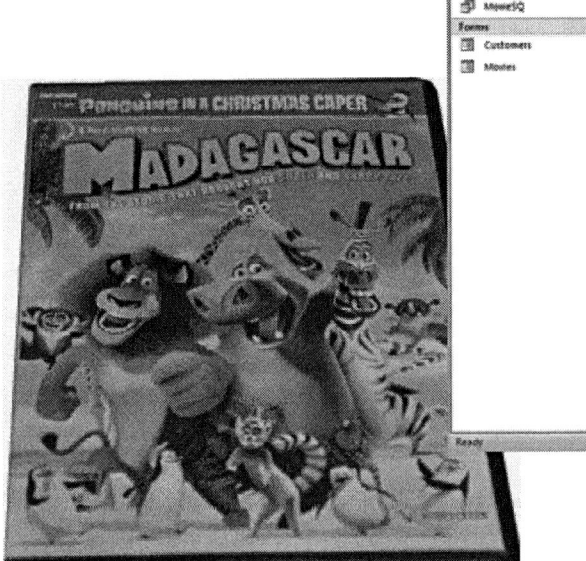

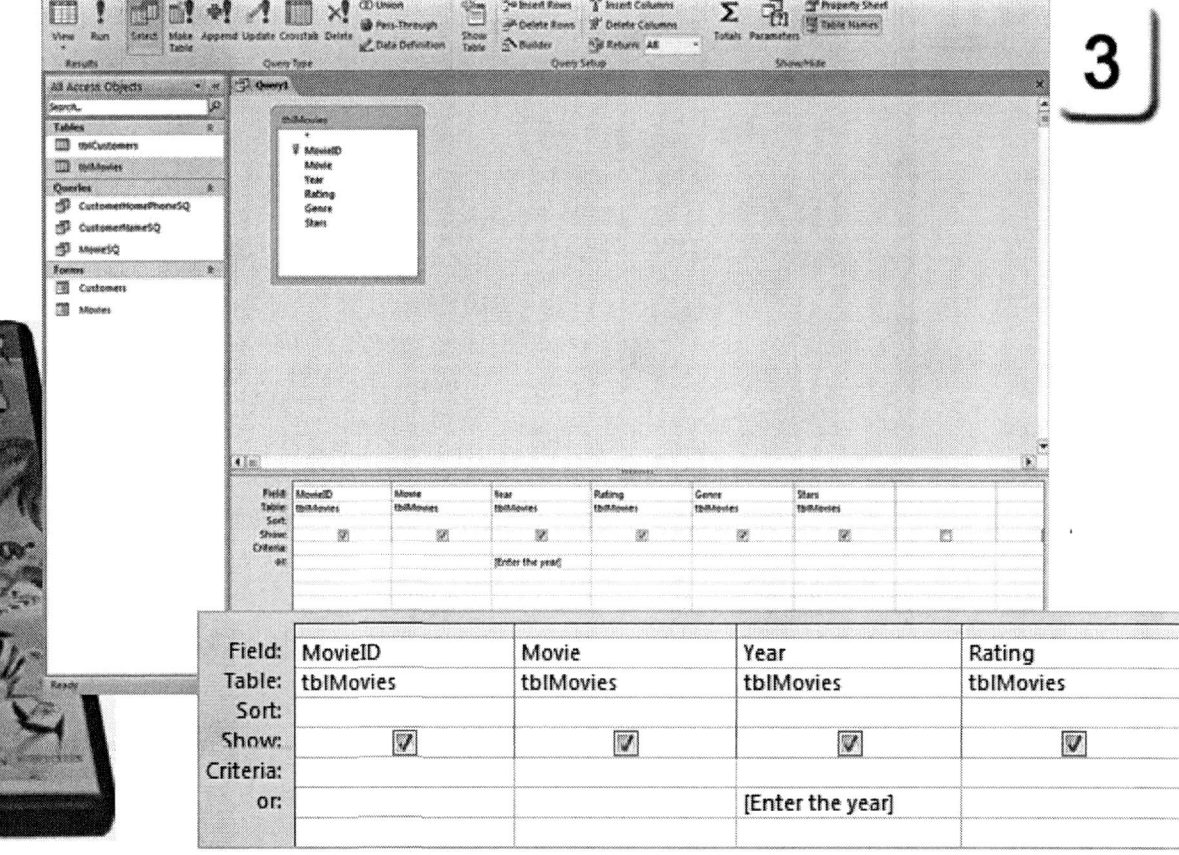

Field:	MovieID	Movie	Year	Rating
Table:	tblMovies	tblMovies	tblMovies	tblMovies
Sort:				
Show:	☑	☑	☑	☑
Criteria:				
or:			[Enter the year]	

Exam 77-885: Microsoft Access 2010
4. Creating and Managing Queries
4.3. Manipulate fields: Create a Parameter Query

Test the Parameter Query

4. Try it: Run the Parameter Query
Go to **Query Tools ->Design->Results->Run.**

What Do You See? You will be prompted to Enter the Year.

Type: 2012
Click **OK.**

Now What Do You See? The Parameter Query found all of the movies that match the year that we typed in.

Do This, Too: Save the Query
Go to **File->Save.**
Enter the Query Name: MoviesByYearSQ.
Click **OK.**

Close the Query.

Query Tools ->Design->Results->Run

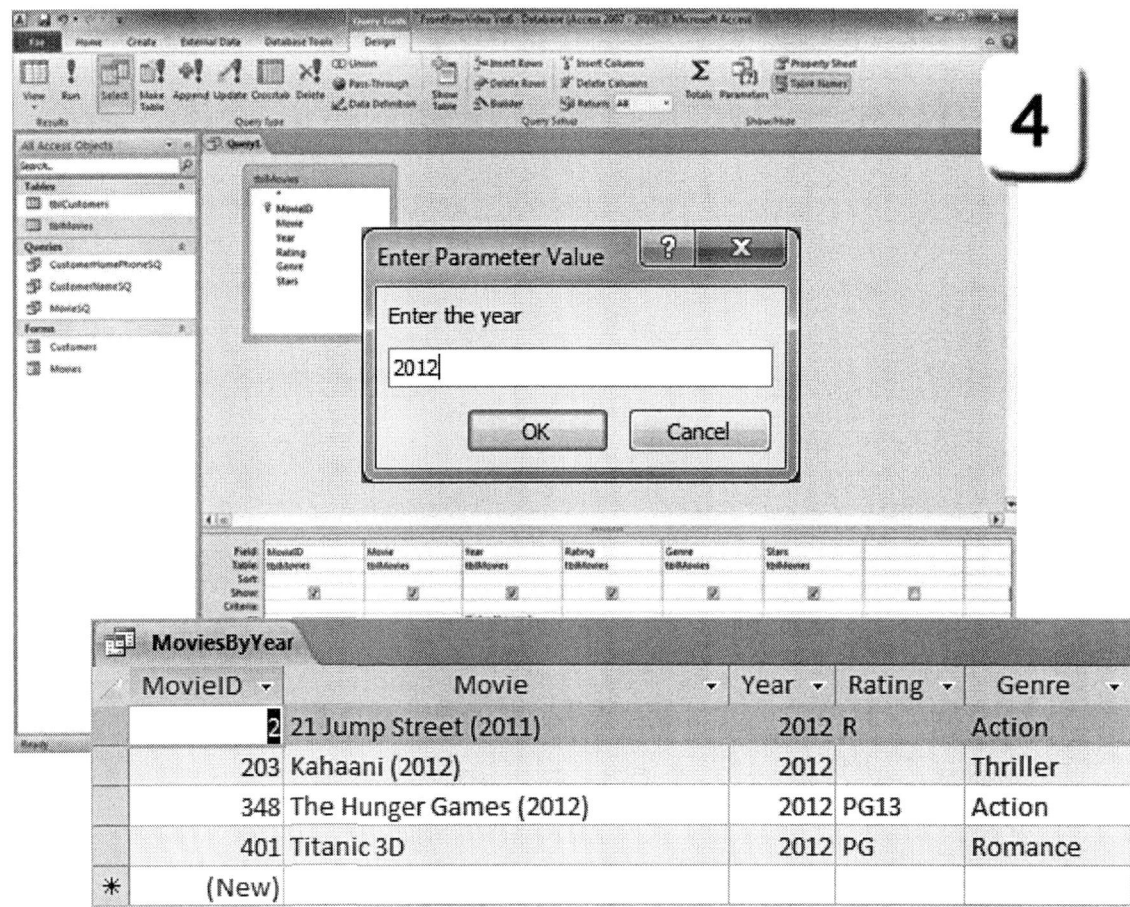

MovieID ▼	Movie ▼	Year ▼	Rating ▼	Genre ▼
2	21 Jump Street (2011)	2012	R	Action
203	Kahaani (2012)	2012		Thriller
348	The Hunger Games (2012)	2012	PG13	Action
401	Titanic 3D	2012	PG	Romance
* (New)				

Exam 77-885: Microsoft Access 2010
4. Creating and Managing Queries
4.3. Manipulate fields: Create a Parameter Query

Summary

This lesson demonstrated how to create a Query in Design View. We used the Criteria to find answers to our questions.

The Parameter Query was interesting because it asks the User for more input, say the year a movie was released.

Allez, Allez in Free.
The movie's starting!

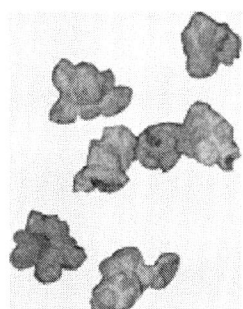

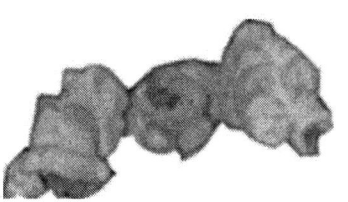

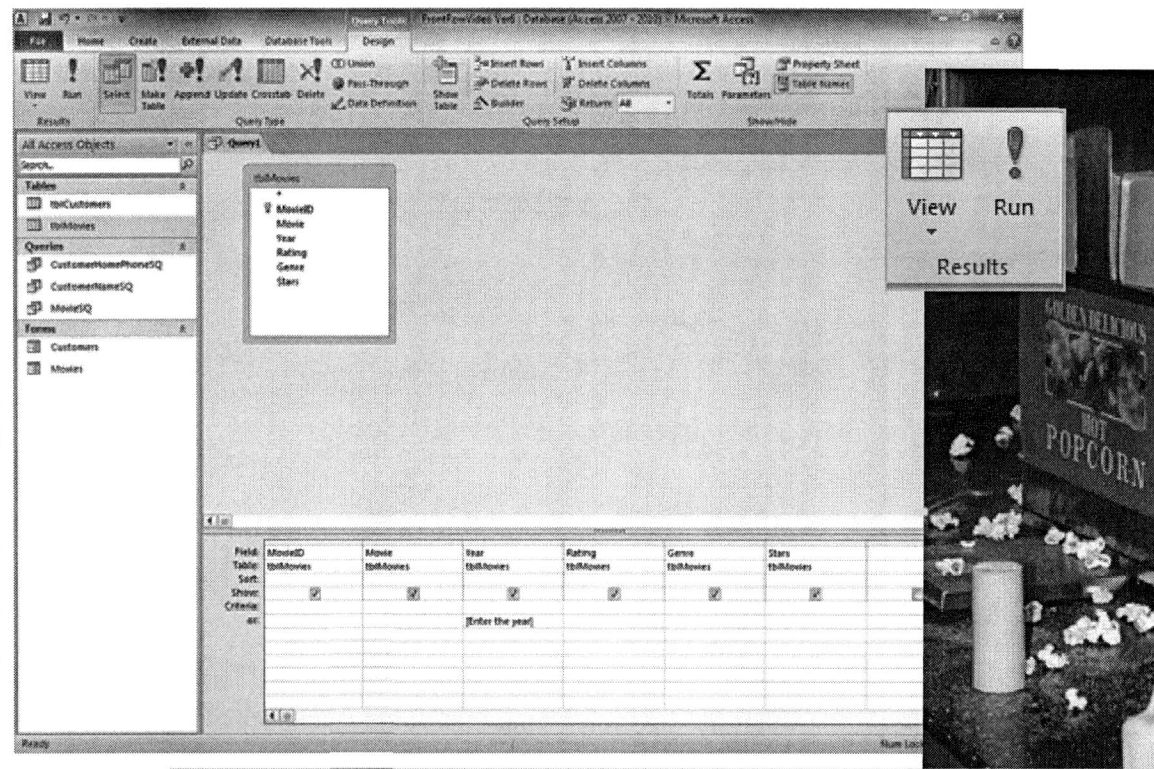

Field:	MovieID	Movie	Year	Rating
Table:	tblMovies	tblMovies	tblMovies	tblMovies
Sort:				
Show:	☑	☑	☑	☑
Criteria:				
or:			[Enter the year]	

Practice Activities

Lesson 8: More Query Design

Try This: Do the following steps

1. Open the Brown Bag Lunch database you have been programming. Or you may download the sample database **Brown Bag Lunch ver8.accdb** online.

2. Use the command **Create->Query->Query Design** to make a Select Query using the Table tblCustomers.

3. Add the following Fields to the QBE grid: CustomerID, Company, and Phone.

4. Add a new Concatenated field as follows:
FullName: [FirstName] & " " & [LastName]

5. Add the following Criteria for the Company Field: [Enter the Company Name]

6. Run the Query. When prompted for a Company enter: Wordnation.

7. Save the Query as CustomerCompanySQ.

8. Close all Tables and Queries.

9. Create a new Query with the command Create->Query->Query Design using the Table tblProducts.

10. Select the following Fields: ProductID, Type, Item, Specialty, and Description.

11. Add the following Criteria for the Type field: [Enter a Product Type].

12. Test the Query. When prompted for a Type enter: Snacks.

13. Save the Query as ProductsbyTypeSQ.

14. Close the Brown Bag database, please.

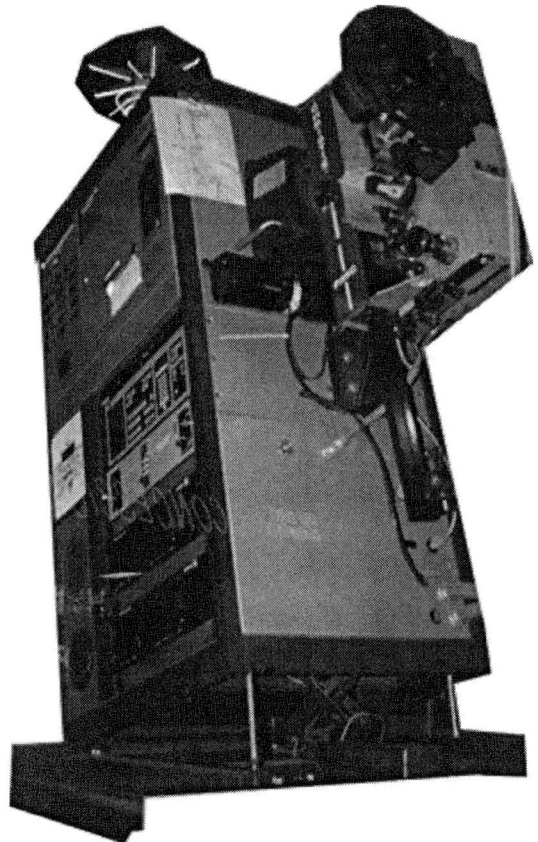

Test Yourself

1. What does Concatenation do?
A. Merges 2 or more cells in a form into one
B. Concentrates the data into just the first part of each field
C. Combines 2 or more fields into a single, new field
Tip: Beginning Access, page 186

2. Which is true about Concatenating Fields?
(Give all correct answers.)
A. Anything, such as a space, in quotes is put between the Fields
B. The Field name is in Brackets, ie [First Name]
C. The new Field needs a label, or alias
Tip: Beginning Access, page 186

3. What command opens a new window where font size can be adjusted to better view and work with the code displayed?
A. Zoom Into Code
B. Edit Code
C. Manipulate Code
D. View Code
Tip: Beginning Access, page 191

4. Which is true about Queries?
A. A Parameter Query asks a question before running the query, such as a phone number.
B. A Select Query asks a question before running the query, such as a phone number.
Tip: Beginning Access, page 194

5. Which of the following is true about the Data Source in Query Design view?
(Give all correct answers.)
A. Double-clicking the wildcard (*) results in adding one "everything" field to the QBE grid.
B. Double-clicking the wildcard (*) adds a new, separate field for each field in the Data Source
C. Double-clicking an individual Field in the Data Source adds that Field being added to the QBE grid as a separate new Field.
Tip: Beginning Access, page 199

Access 2010: Answer

Reports and Report Design

Beginning Access Objectives
In this lesson, you will learn how to:

1. Use the Report Wizard to create a Report based on a Table.

2. Modify a Report in Report Layout View.

3. Apply a Theme and edit the Report Header to include a Logo.

4. Add Page Numbers to the Report Footer.

5. Use the Report Sort and Filter options.

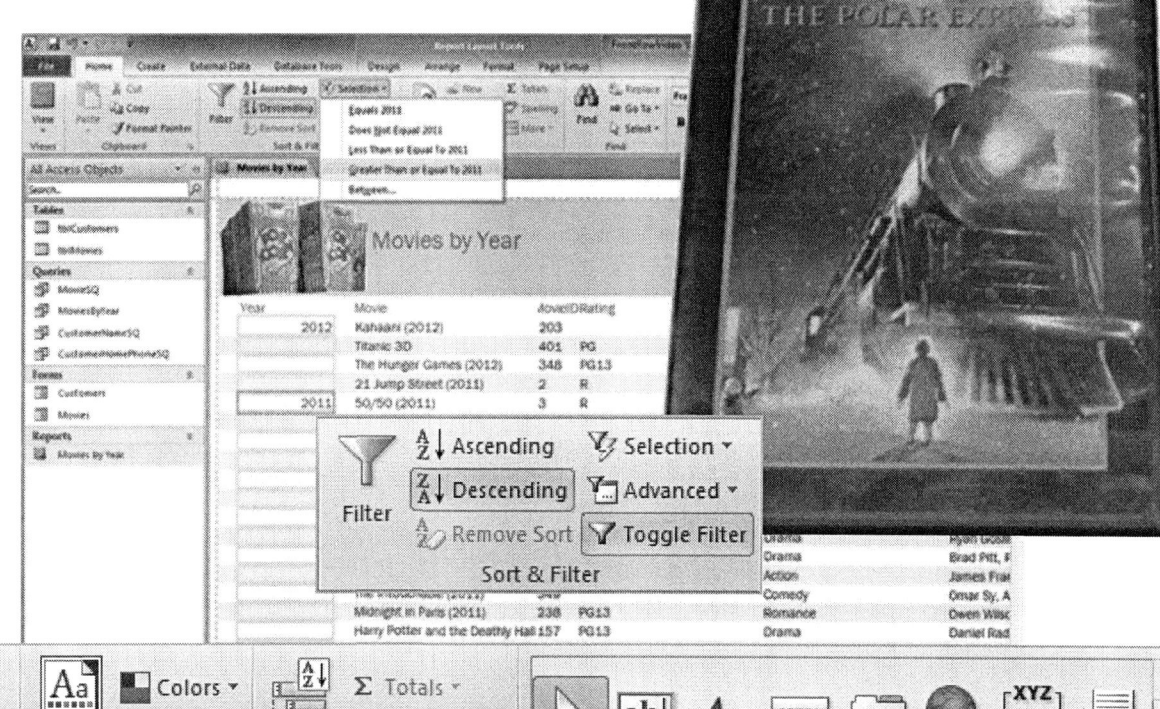

© 2012 Comma Productions, LLC

Take One

Lesson 9 : Report Designs

1. Readings
Read Lesson 9 in the Beginning Access
guide, page 205-231.

Project
A Report created with the Report Wizard
and formatted with a Theme..

Downloads
FrontRowVideo Begin9.accdb
popcorn1.gif, popcorn2.gif,
popcorn3.gif,
popcorn4.gif, movies1.gif.

Brown Bag Lunch ver9.accdb
BB Customers Logo.jpg
Brown Bag Logo.jpg
Lunch1.gif, Lunch2.gif, Lunch3.gif,
Lunch4.gif

2. Practice
Complete the Practice Activity on page 232

3. Assessment
Review the Test questions on page 232.

Report Layout Tools->Design Ribbon

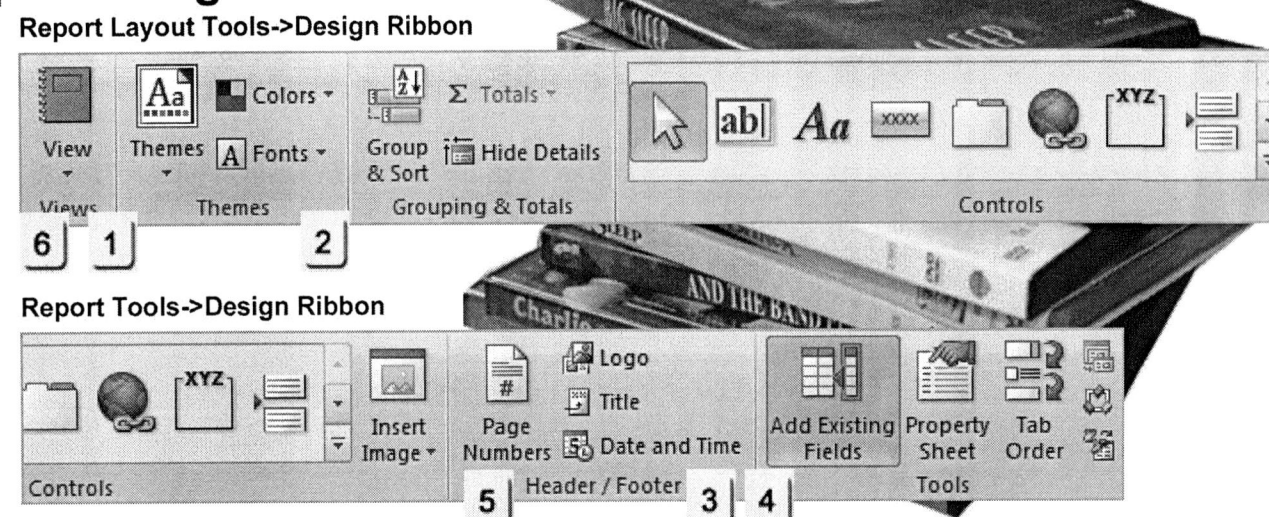

Report Tools->Design Ribbon

Menu Maps
From the **Create Ribbon**
Create ->Reports->Report Wizard, page 210

From the **Report Layout Tools->Design Ribbon**
1. Report Layout Tools, page 217
2. Design->Themes, page 218
3. Design->Header/Footer->Logo, page 220
4. Design->Header/Footer->Date, page 221
5. Header/Footer->Page Numbers, page 222
6. Report Layout Tools->View->Print Preview, page 223

More Menu Maps
From the **Print Preview Ribbon**
Print Preview, page 215

From the **Home Ribbon**
Home ->Views->View->Layout View, page 216
Home->Find->Find, page 225
Home->Sort&Filter->Descending, page 227
Home->Sort&Filter->Filter, page 228
Home->Sort&Filter->Selection, page 230

Reports and Report Design

Technically, a database designer should begin with the Reports, first. Reports printout the answers. Often, an entire database may be designed to fill in the information for a particular government report. The Front Row Video database needs to print customer reports: a receipt or statement of accounts. Our mighty Access database also has to print business reports. We'll begin with a simple report first: a list of all the movies in the Front Row Video collection.

This lesson will use the Report Wizard to create a Report based on the Movie Table. This lesson uses the sample Front Row Video database. You can continue with the database you have been programming. You can also download the sample Access database if you wish.

Sample Microsoft Access 2010 Report

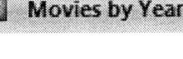

Movies by Year

Year	Movie	MovieID	Rating
2012	Kahaani (2012)	203	
	Titanic 3D	401	PG
	The Hunger Games (2012)	348	PG13
	21 Jump Street (2011)	2	R

Before You Begin

1. Try it: Open the Sample Database
Go to the Documents folder.
Open the sample database:
Brown Bag Lunch ver9.accdb

What Do You See? There are two Tables:
tblCustomers has 5 records.
tblMovies has 401 records.

There are two Forms:
Customers
Movies

There are four Queries:
CustomerHomePhoneSQ
CustomerNameSQ
MoviesByYearSQ
MoviesSQ

What Else Do You See? This database may have a Security Warning. In order to edit the objects and save your work, you need to click on **Enable Content**.

Microsoft Access 2010

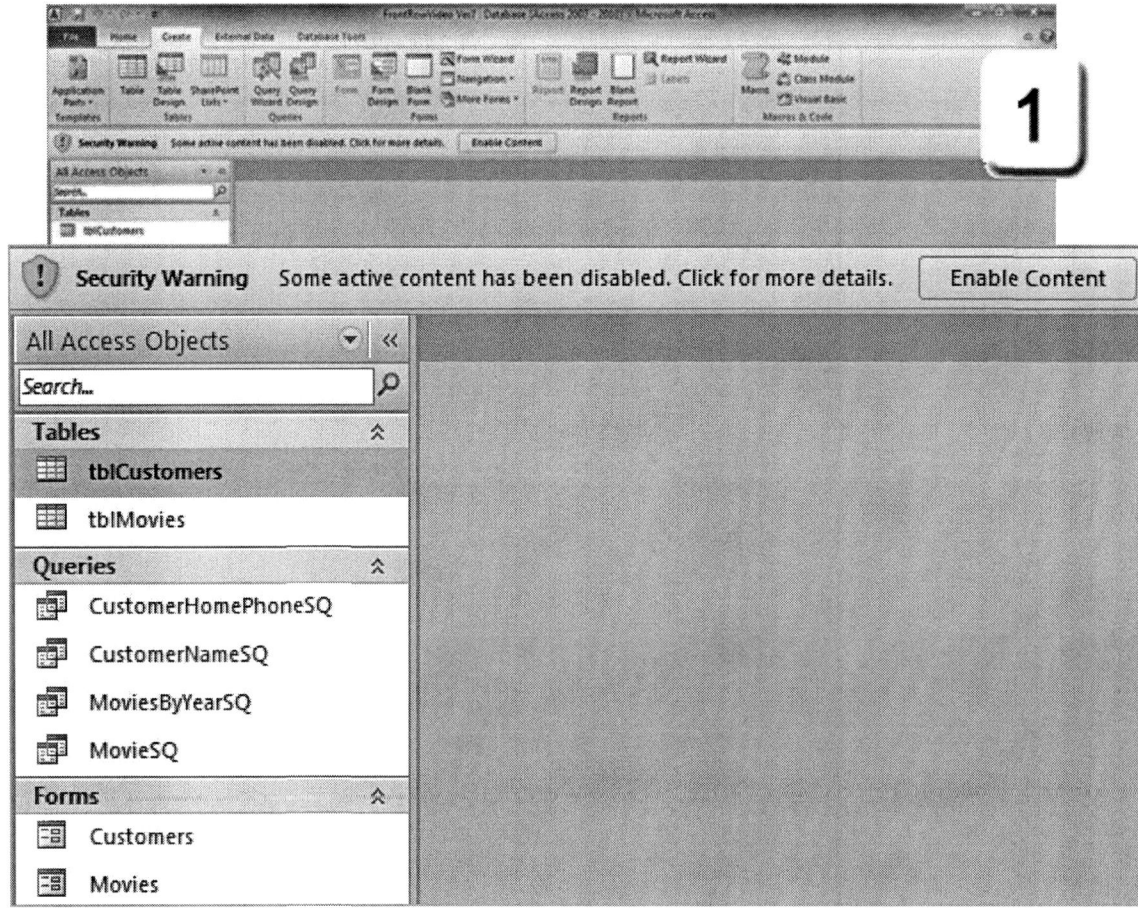

Take One

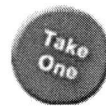

Review the Movie Table

The goal of this lesson is to create a list of the movies in this database, sorted alphabetically and grouped by year.

2. Try it: Review the Movie Table
Go to **All Access Objects->Tables.**
Double click tblMovies to open it in Datasheet View.

What Do You See? The Movie Table has 401 records. The Table includes the name, rating, genre, year and stars.

Close tblMovies. Keep going...

All Access Objects->Tables.

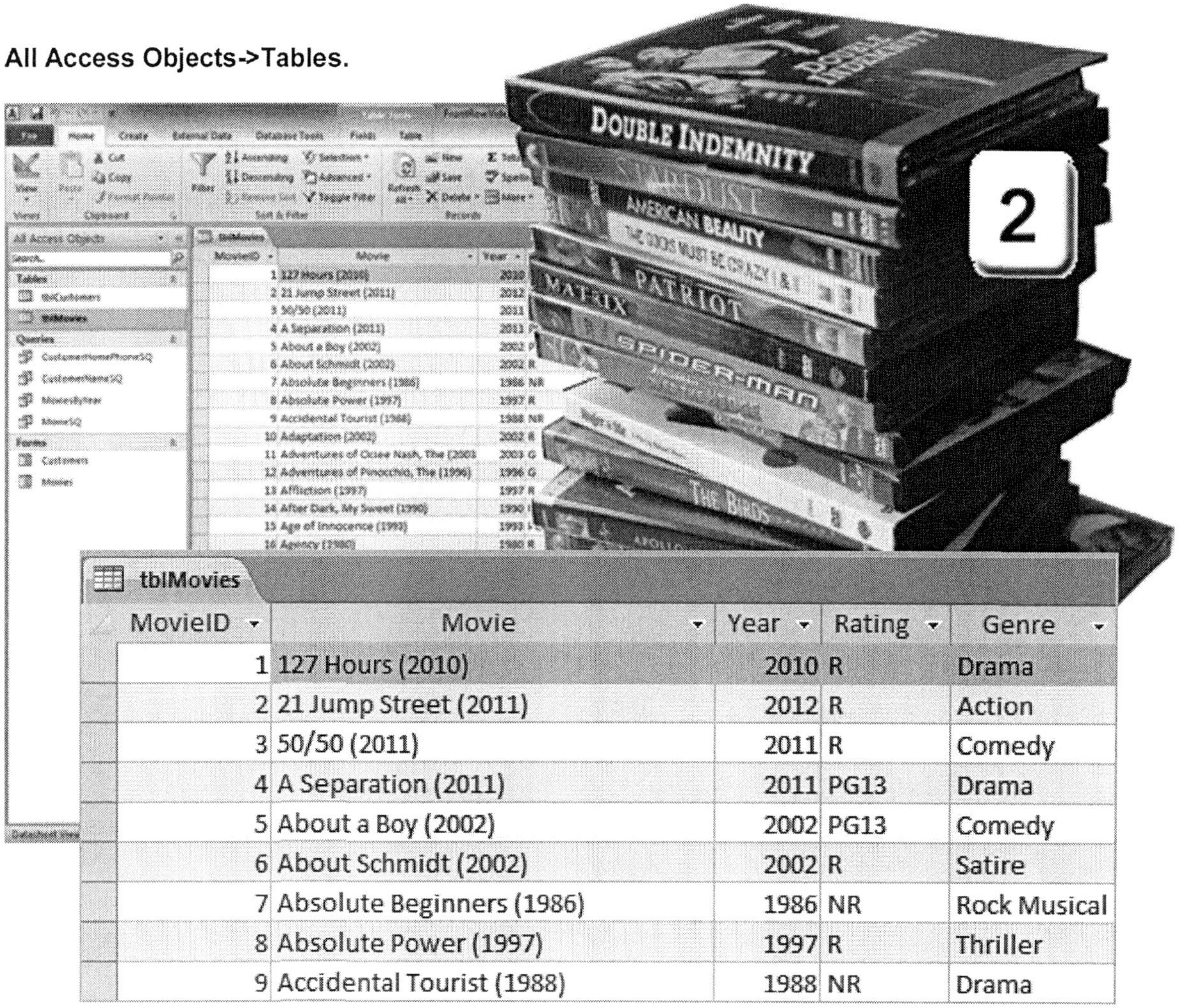

MovieID	Movie	Year	Rating	Genre
1	127 Hours (2010)	2010	R	Drama
2	21 Jump Street (2011)	2012	R	Action
3	50/50 (2011)	2011	R	Comedy
4	A Separation (2011)	2011	PG13	Drama
5	About a Boy (2002)	2002	PG13	Comedy
6	About Schmidt (2002)	2002	R	Satire
7	Absolute Beginners (1986)	1986	NR	Rock Musical
8	Absolute Power (1997)	1997	R	Thriller
9	Accidental Tourist (1988)	1988	NR	Drama

Exam 77-885: Microsoft Access 2010
5. Designing Reports
5.1. Create reports: Use the Report Wizard

Create ->Reports->Report Wizard

Begin the Report Wizard

This example uses the **Report Wizard**. The steps are similar to the Form Design Wizard that we walked through in an earlier lesson. The Wizard will prompt you to select a Record Source and choose the Grouping, Sorting, Layout, and Totals.

1. Try it: Begin the Report Wizard
Go to **Create ->Reports->Report Wizard.**
Choose a **Table/Query**: tblMovies
Select: All Available Fields.

Click **Next**. Keep going...

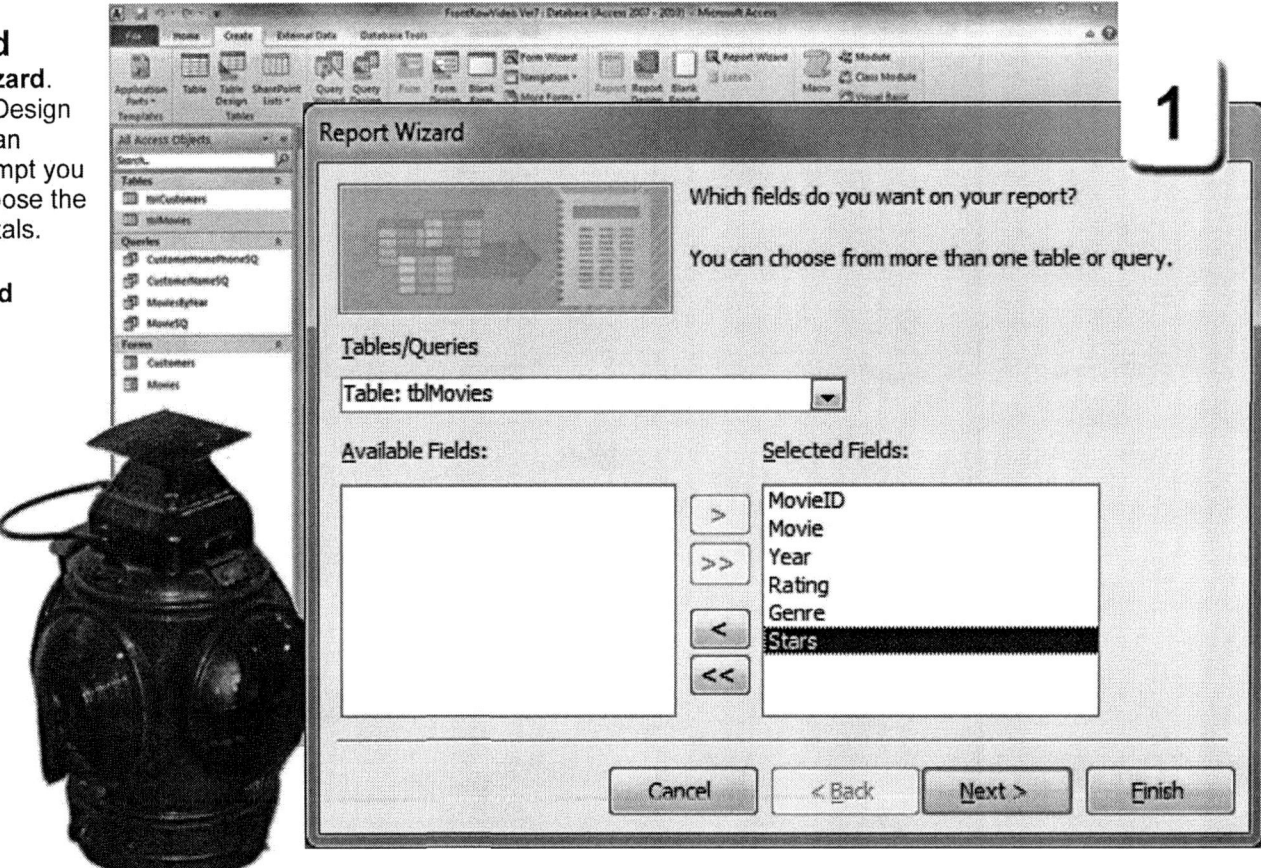

Exam 77-885: Microsoft Access 2010
5. Designing Reports
5.1. Create reports: Use the Report Wizard

Report Wizard: Grouping

Grouping levels organize the Report by Fields. You can have one or more Group Levels. In this Report, the movies will be grouped by year.

On the left side of the Wizard is the list of the Fields available in tblMovies. On the right is a preview of the Report Grouping.

2. Try This: Add a Group Level
Select a **Group Field**: Year

Click **Next**. Keep going...

Create ->Reports->Report Wizard

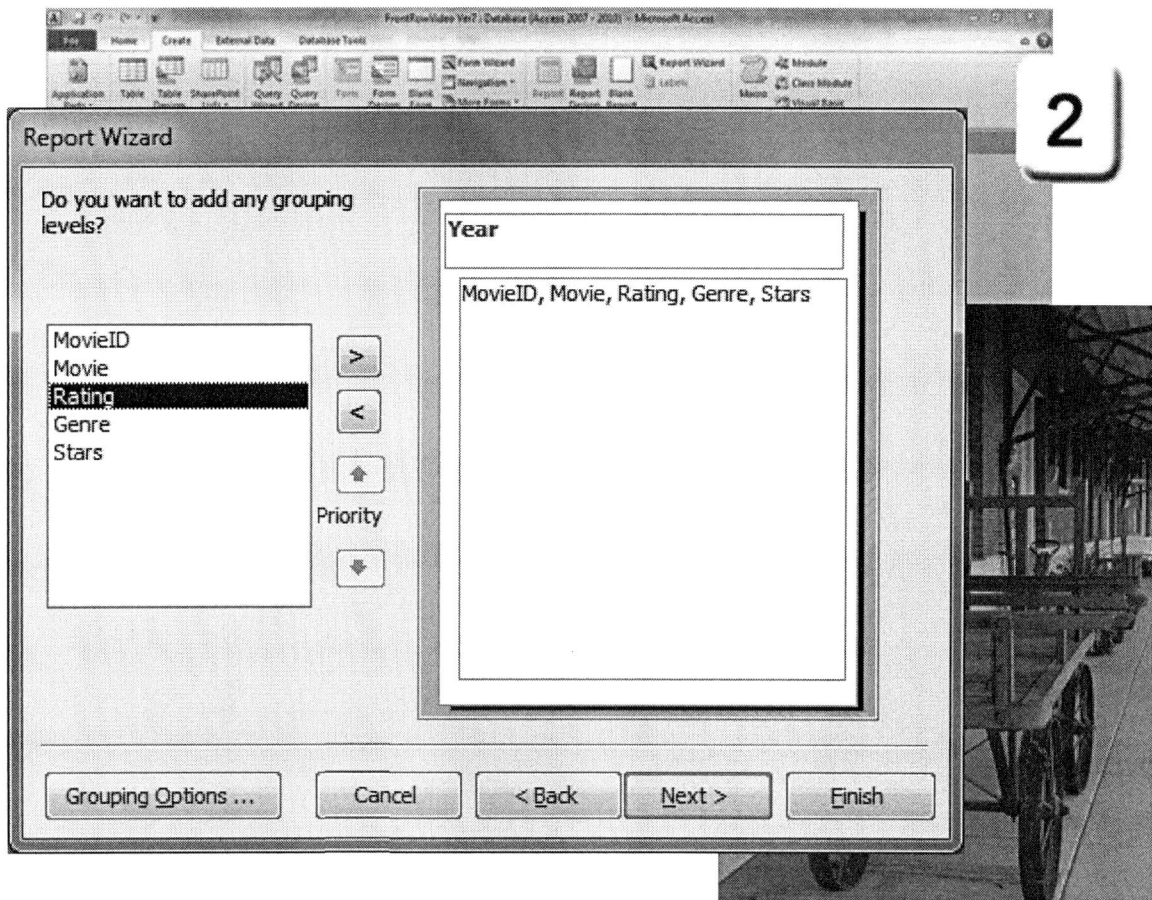

Exam 77-885: Microsoft Access 2010
5. Designing Reports
5.1. Create reports: Use the Report Wizard

Report Wizard: Sort

This step in the Report Wizard will **Sort** the movies alphabetically in each Group.

3. Try it: Sort the Records
Click on the Sort Combo.
Select a Field from the list: Movie

What Do You See? You can add up to four Fields to the Sort order if you wish.

Click **Next**. Keep going...

Report Wizard

What sort order do you want for detail records?

You can sort records by up to four fields, in either ascending or descending order.

1	Movie	Ascending
2		Ascending
3		Ascending
4		Ascending

Cancel   < Back   Next >   Finish

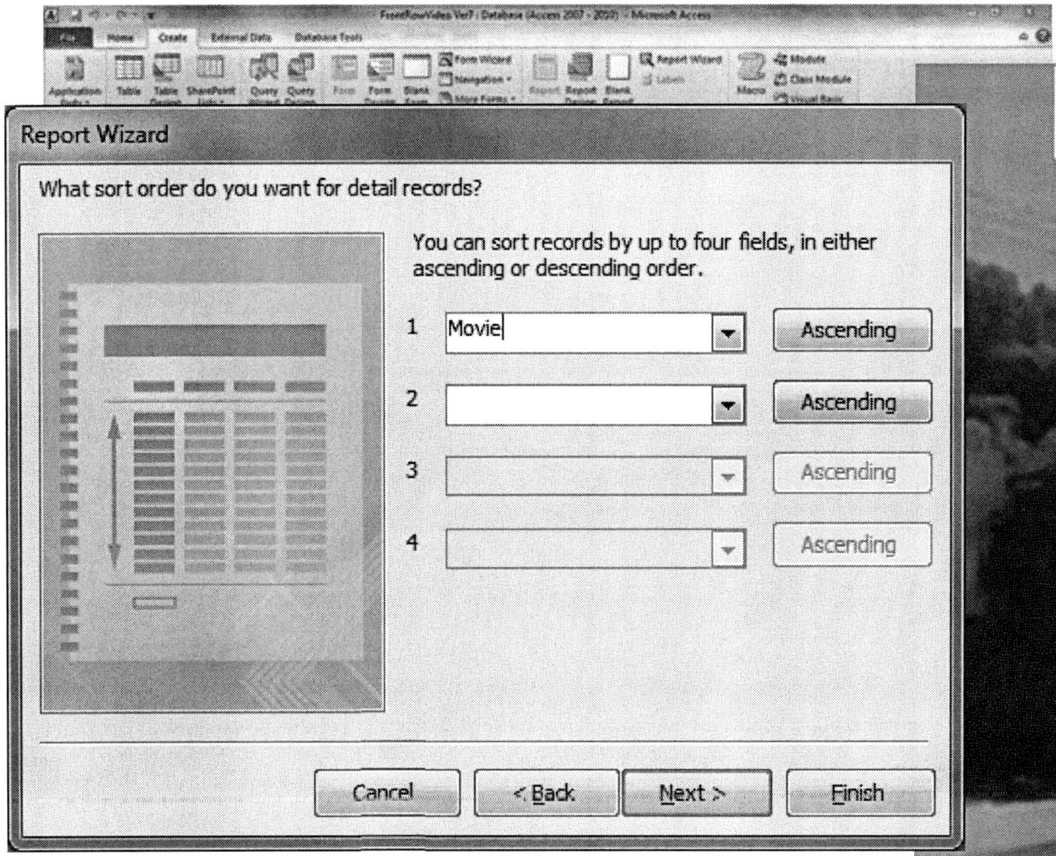

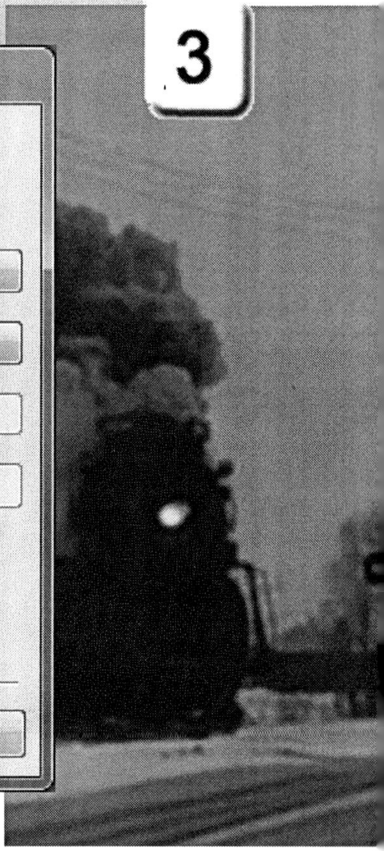

Exam 77-885: Microsoft Access 2010
5. Designing Reports
5.1. Create reports: Use the Report Wizard

Report Wizard: Layout

This step in the Report Wizard asks you to select the Layout options.

4. Try it: Edit the Report Layout
Edit the following options:
Layout: Block
Orientation: Landscape

What Do You See? By default, the Report Wizard will adjust the width of the Fields so that all of them will fit on one page.

Click **Next**. Keep going...

Create ->Reports->Report Wizard

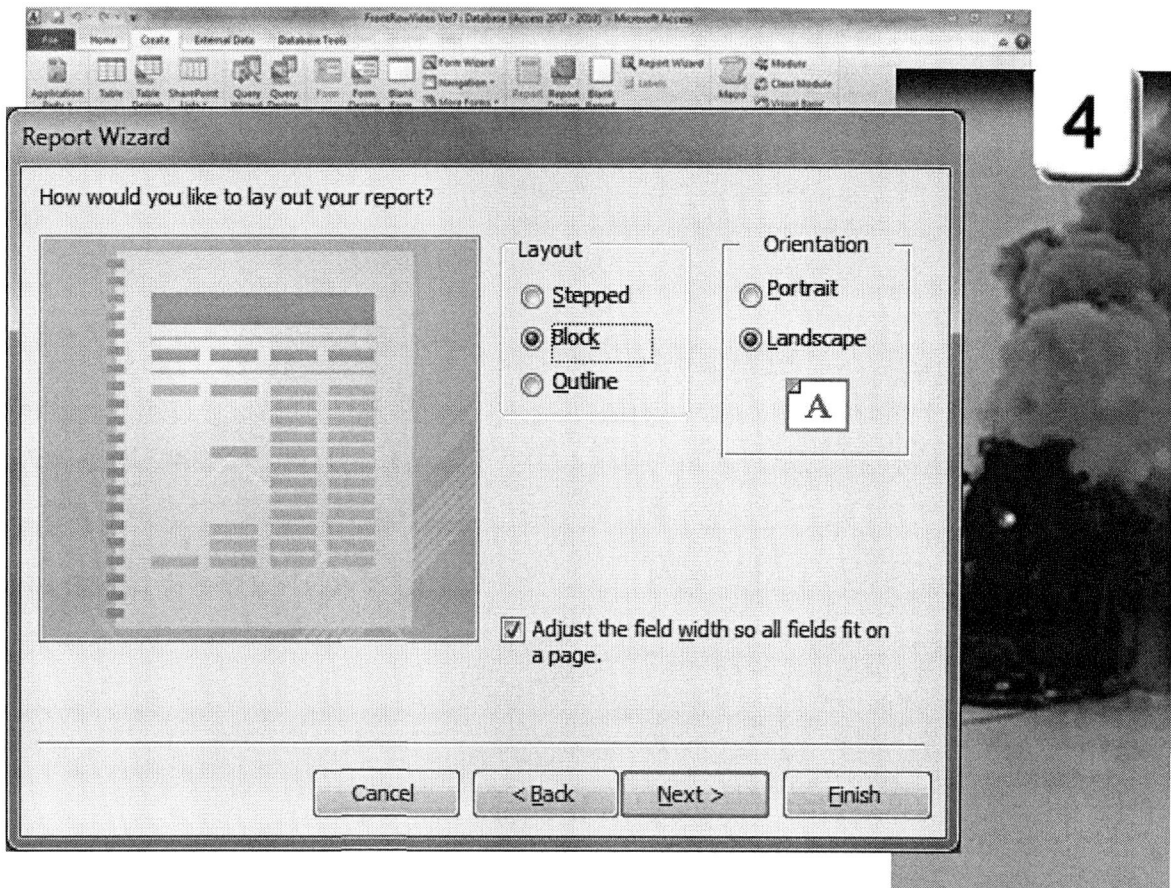

Exam 77-885: Microsoft Access 2010
5. Designing Reports
5.1. Create reports: Use the Report Wizard

Report Wizard: Report Title

This last step names the Report. The name will appear at the top of the Report in the Report Title. It will also be the name of the Report in the Access Objects.

5. Try it: Add a Title
Enter the **Title**: Movies by Year.

What Do You See? There are two options when you click Finish: Preview or Modify.

Select an option: Preview the report.

Click **Finish**.

Turn to the next page to see the report...

Create ->Reports->Report Wizard

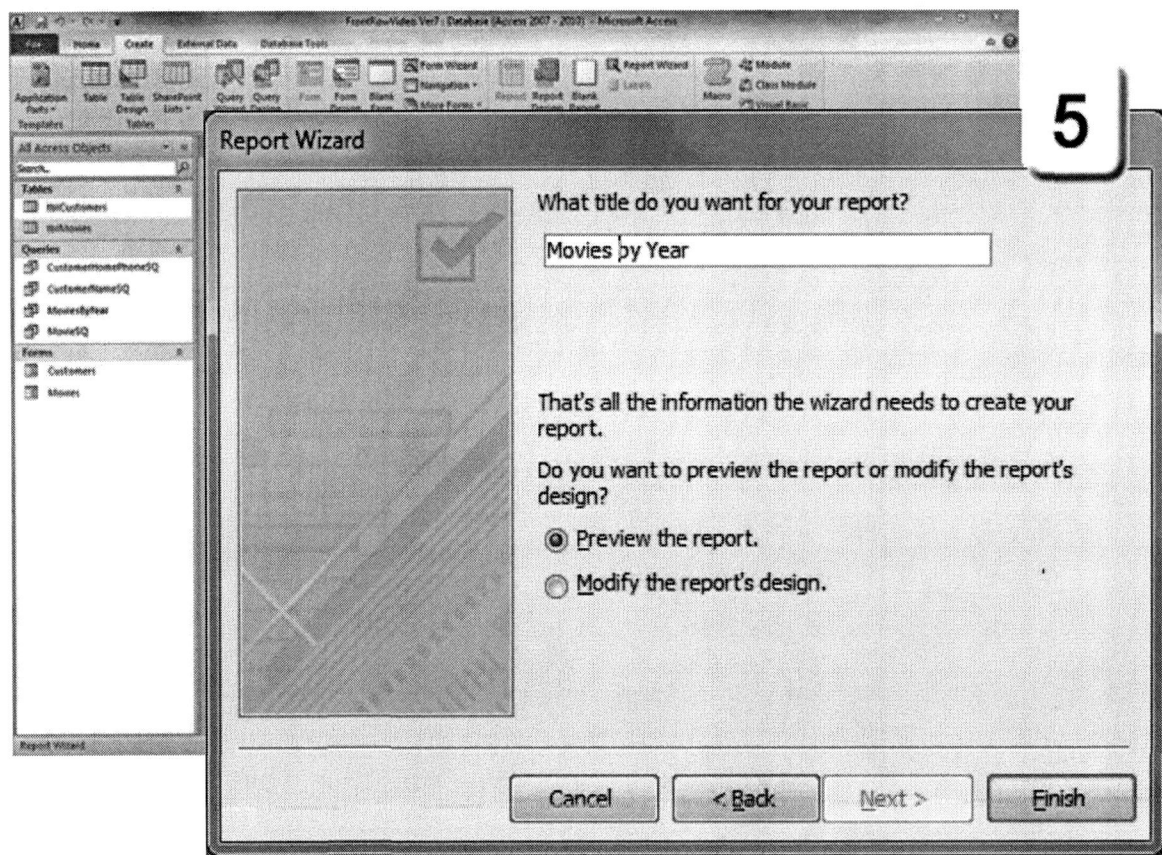

Exam 77-885: Microsoft Access 2010
5. Designing Reports
5.1. Create reports: Use the Report Wizard

Hello, Report!

6. Try it: Review the Print Preview
The Report opened in Print Preview.

The Report Header has the **Title** we added to the Wizard: Movies by Year.

The movies are grouped by year. Some groups have many records, some have only one. For example, there are many movies that have the year 1980.

What Do You See? The Print Preview Ribbon has many print options:
Print
Page Size
Page Layout
Zoom
Data

What Else Do You See? This Report Layout is good, but it needs some editing.

Close Print Preview. The Movies by Year Report will close. Keep going...

Print Preview

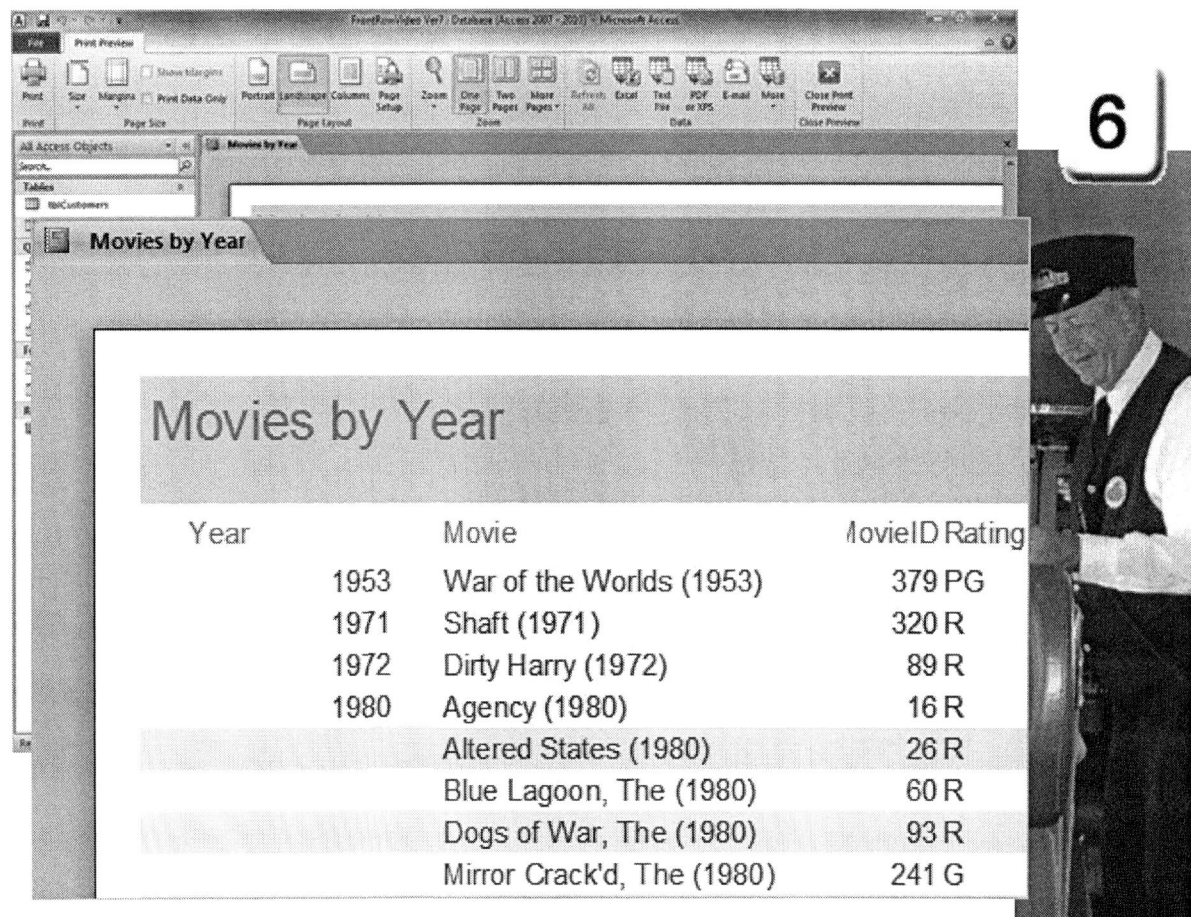

Exam 77-885: Microsoft Access 2010
5. Designing Reports
5.1. Create reports: Use the Report Wizard

Home ->Views->View->Layout View

Open the Report in Layout View

Reports have several Views. The Views include:
Report View
Print Preview
Layout View
Design View

1. Try it: Open the Report in Layout View
Go to All Access Objects
Right-Click the Report: Movies by Year.
Select an option: **Layout View**.

Keep going...

Memo to Self: The same View can be found on
the Home Ribbon. Here are the steps:

Go to All Access Objects
Double-Click the Report: Movies by Year.
The Report should open in Report View.
Go to **Home ->Views->View->Layout View**.

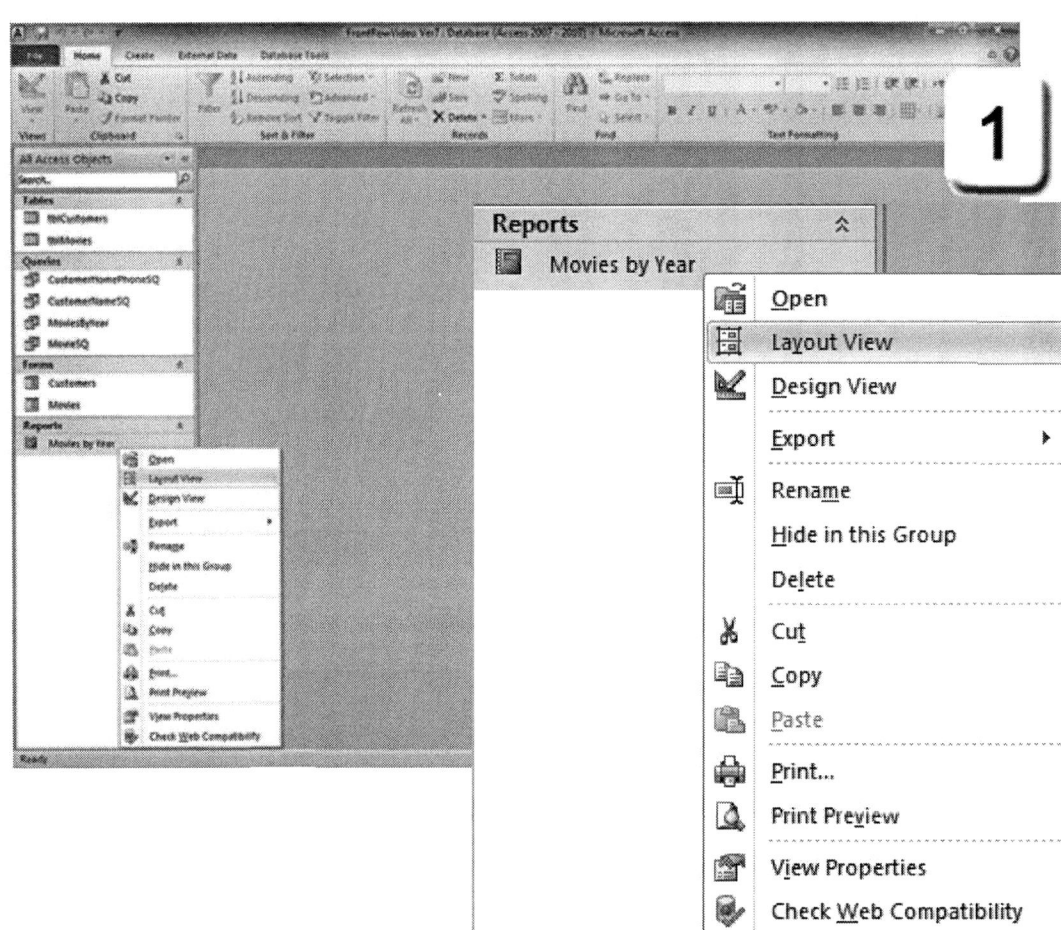

Exam 77-885: Microsoft Access 2010
5. Designing Reports
5.1. Create reports: Use the Report Layout Tools

Hello, Report Layout Tools

2. Try it: Review the Report Layout Tools
The Report is open in Layout View.
There are four Ribbons in the **Layout Tools**.
Design
Arrange
Format
Page Setup

This lesson will focus on the Design Ribbon.
The **Design** Ribbon includes these Groups:
Views
Themes
Grouping & Totals
Controls
Header & Footer
Tools

Keep going...

Report Layout Tools

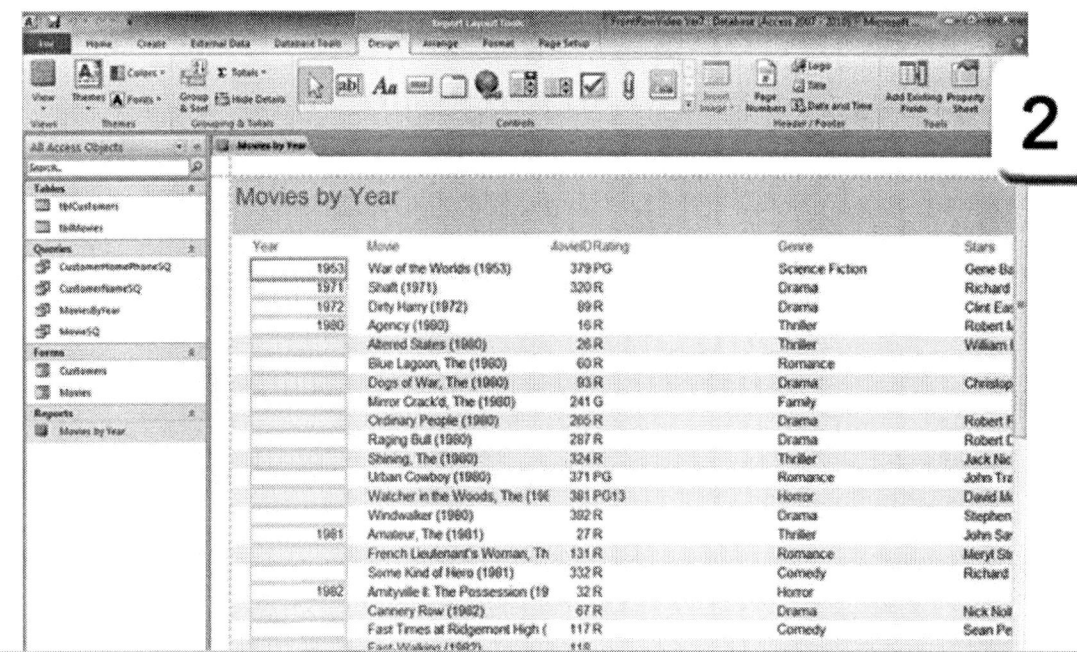

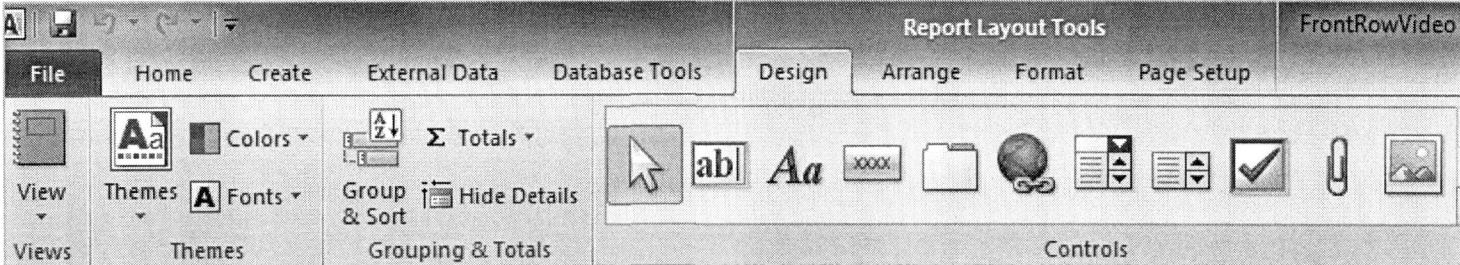

Exam 77-885: Microsoft Access 2010
5. Designing Reports
5.1. Create reports: Use the Report Layout Tools

Apply a Theme to a Report

Report Layout Tools->Design->Themes

Themes format a Report quickly and elegantly. The **Themes** in Microsoft Access match the ones found in Word, Excel, PowerPoint and Outlook. The options for Reports are similar to the ones for Forms that we reviewed in an earlier lesson.

3. Try it: Apply a Theme to a Report
The Report is open in Layout View.
Go to **Report Layout Tools->Design->Themes**.
Click on **Theme**.

Select a Theme from the Gallery: Pushpin.

What Do You See? The Theme formatted the Report **Colors** and **Fonts**.

Keep going...

Exam 77-885: Microsoft Access 2010
5. Designing Reports
5.2. Apply Report Design options: Apply a Theme

Headers/Footers: Logo

This Report has Headers and Footers.
The **Header** can include a Logo, Title and
the Date and Time.

4. Try it: Add a Logo to the Header
The Report is open in Layout View.
Go to **Report Layout Tools->Design**.
Go to **Header/Footer->Logo**.

You will be prompted to **Browse** to your
Documents folder to find a picture.

Select a picture: popcorn1.jpg
Click **OK**. Keep going...

Report Layout Tools->Design->Header/Footer->Logo

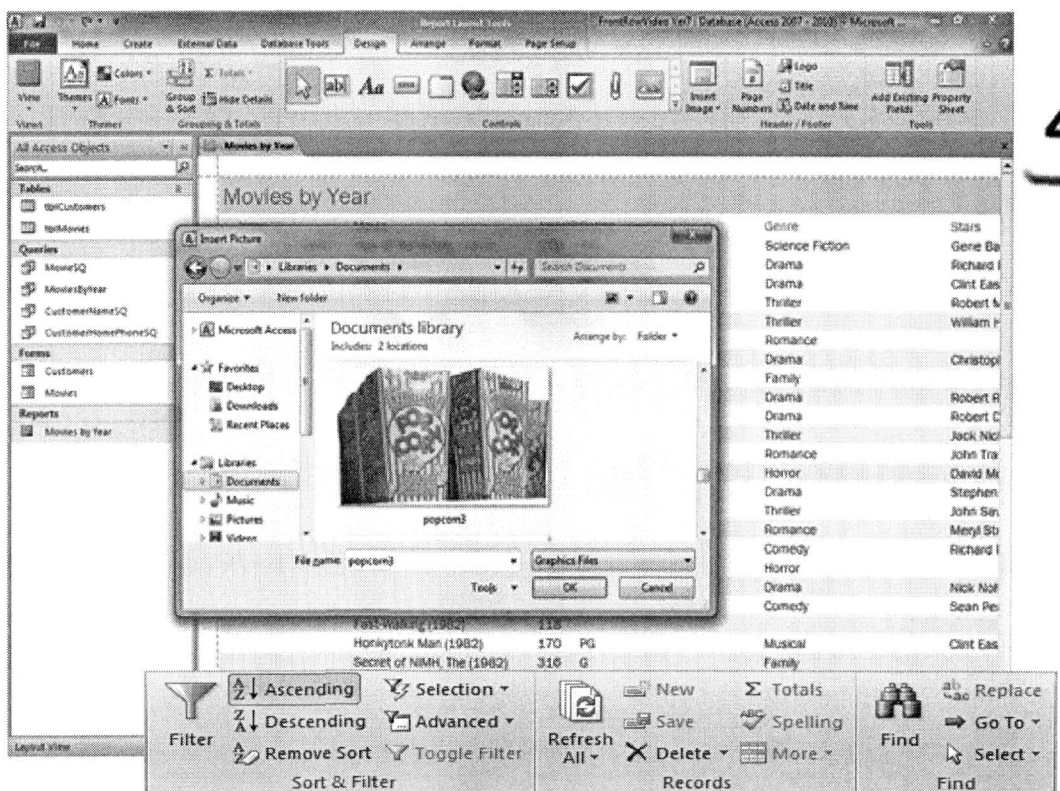

Exam 77-885: Microsoft Access 2010
5. Designing Reports
5.2. Apply Report Design options: Add a Logo to the Header/Footer

Headers/Footers: Logo

The Logo that you added to the Header, may be too small. That is easy to fix.

5. Try it: Format the Logo
Click once on the Logo to select it.

The Logo should have a bold outline with handles. Use the handle to resize the logo. As you make the logo bigger, the height of the Report Header will increase as well.

Try This, Too: Move the Title
Click once on the Title to select it.

Run your mouse over the border until you see a four-headed arrow. Drag the Title to a better position in the Header.

Keep going.

Report Layout Tools->Design->Header/Footer->Logo

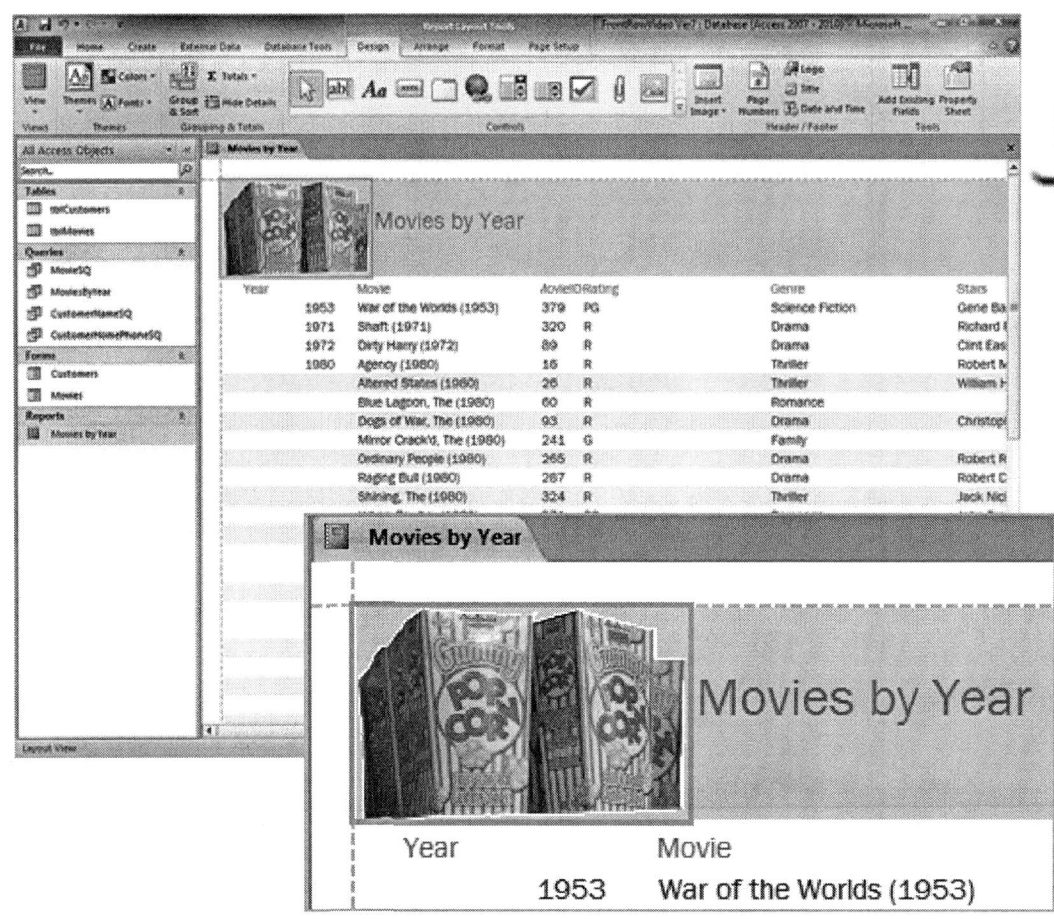

Exam 77-885: Microsoft Access 2010
5. Designing Reports
5.2. Apply Report Design options: Add a Logo to the Header/Footer

Headers/Footers: Date

You can use the Header/Footer options to add the Date and Time to the Report.

6. Try it: Add the Date and Time
The Report is open in Layout View.
Go to **Report Layout Tools->Design**.
Go to **Header/Footer->Date and Time.**

What Do You See? By default both Date and Time are included. The long Date Format and Time are selected.

Select: Include Date
Format: Short (5/9/2012)
Do NOT include the Time.
Click **OK**.

Now, What Do You See? The Date will be placed on the right side of the Report.

Keep going, please.

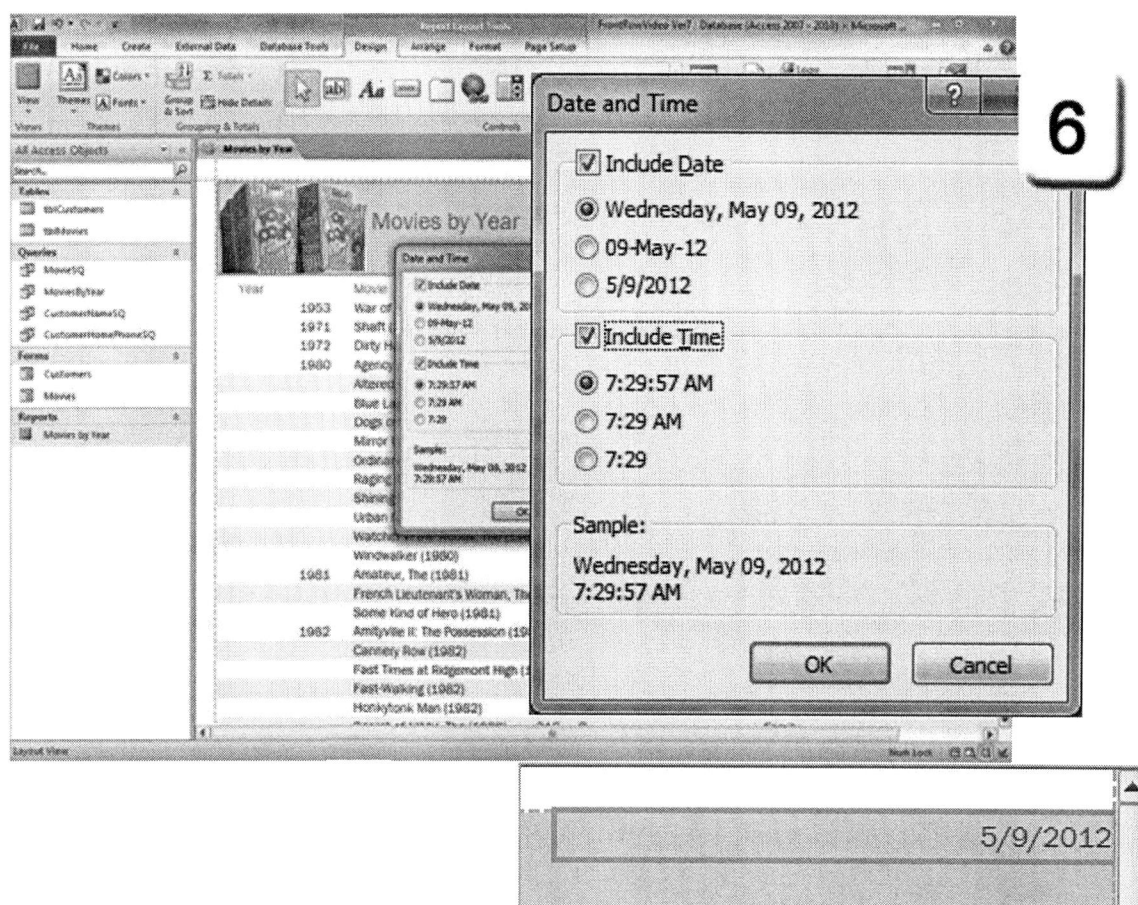

Exam 77-885: Microsoft Access 2010
5. Designing Reports
5.2. Apply Report Design options: Add the Date and Time to the Header/Footer

Footers: Page Numbers

Page Numbers are usually placed in the Report Footer. Let's consider the options.

7. Try it: Add Page Numbers
The Report is still open in Layout View.
Go to **Report Layout Tools->Design**.
Go to **Header/Footer->Page Numbers**.

What Do You See? You will be prompted to select the Page Number Format, Position and Alignment.

Format: Page N of M
Position: Bottom of Page (Footer)
Alignment: Center
Yes, Show Number on First Page.

Click **OK**. Keep going...

Exam 77-885: Microsoft Access 2010
5. Designing Reports
5.2. Apply Report Design options: Add Page Numbers to the Header/Footer

Footers: Page Numbers

We have been working with the Report in Layout View. You can see the page numbers in Print Preview.

8. Try it: Review the Page Numbers
The Report is open in Layout View.
Go to **Report Layout Tools->View**
Click on **Print Preview**.

What Do You See? Look at the Footer at the bottom of the Report. The Page Numbers, Page N of M, are centered.

What Else Do You See? There is another Date/Time Control in the Footer that was added as we walked through the Report Design Wizard.

Do This, Now: Save the Report
Go to **File->Save**.
Done and Done.

Report Layout Tools->View->Print Preview

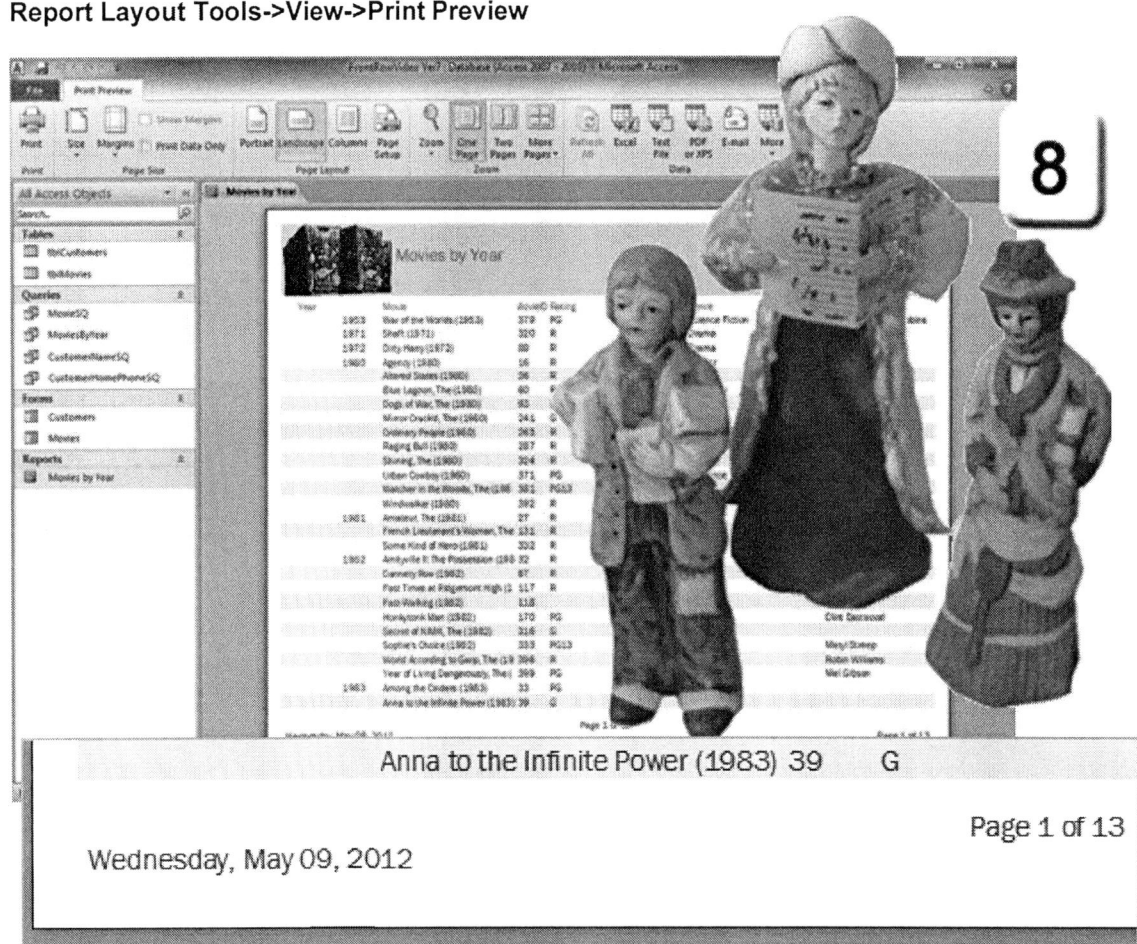

Anna to the Infinite Power (1983) 39 G

Page 1 of 13

Wednesday, May 09, 2012

Exam 77-885: Microsoft Access 2010
5. Designing Reports
5.2. Apply Report Design options: Add Page Numbers to the Header/Footer

Using the Report

There are several useful options available when you open a Report in **Layout View**. Let's review the choices available for **Sort** and **Filter**

1. Try it: Go to the Report View
The Report is open in **Print Preview**.
Go to **Print Preview->Close Print Preview.**
Click on **Close Print Preview**.

When you close the Print Preview, you may return to the **Report View.**
Go to **Home->Views->View->Layout View.**

Try This, Too: Review the Home Menu
The **Home** Menu includes these Groups:
Views
Clipboard
Sort & Filter
Records
Find
Text Formatting

Keep going...

Home->Views->View->Layout View

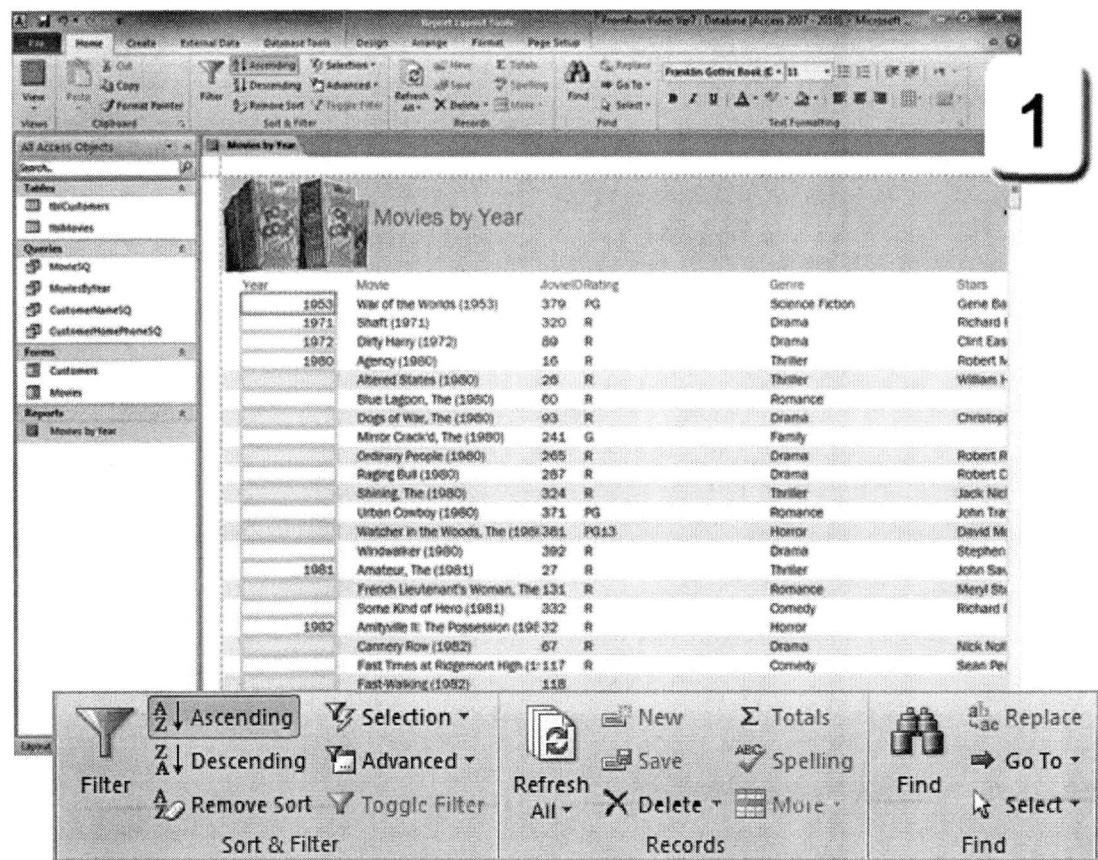

Exam 77-885: Microsoft Access 2010
5. Designing Reports
5.6. Sort and filter records for reporting

Use the Report: Find

You can learn a lot about the data in a Report by using the commands on the **Home** Ribbon. The following pages will show the **Find**, **Sort** and **Filter** options.

2. Try it: Find Data in a Report
The Report is opened in Layout View.
Select a Column: Stars.
Go to **Home->Find->Find**.

You will be prompted to enter the criteria.
Find What: Depp.
Match: Any Part of Field.
Search: All.
Click on **Find Next**.

What Do You See? Each time you click Find Next, Access will go to the next record that matches your criteria.

Keep going...

Home->Find->Find

2

Exam 77-885: Microsoft Access 2010
5. Designing Reports
5.6. Sort and filter records for reporting: Use the Find command

Find Options

3. Try it: Review the Find Options
There are three options for matching the criteria in Microsoft Access:
Whole Field
Any Part of Field
Start of Field

If you select **Whole Field**, Access will search for an exact match.

If you select **Any Part of Field**, Access will parse the data and look for whatever includes the criteria, whether it is in the beginning, middle or end of the data.

If you select **Start of Field**, then the Find search will only return records that include the criteria at the beginning.

Click **Cancel**. Keep going...

Exam 77-885: Microsoft Access 2010
5. Designing Reports
5.6. Sort and filter records for reporting: Use the Find command

Use the Report: Sort

4. Try it: Sort the Records in a Report
Let's begin with **Sort**.

The Report is still opened in Layout View.
Select a Column: Years.
Go to **Home->Sort&Filter.**
Click on **Descending**.

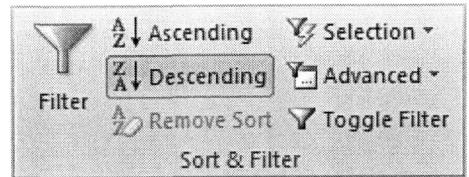

What Do You See? The records should
be sorted descending by Year, from
newest to oldest. The movie titles are not
sorted alphabetically within each group.

Keep going...

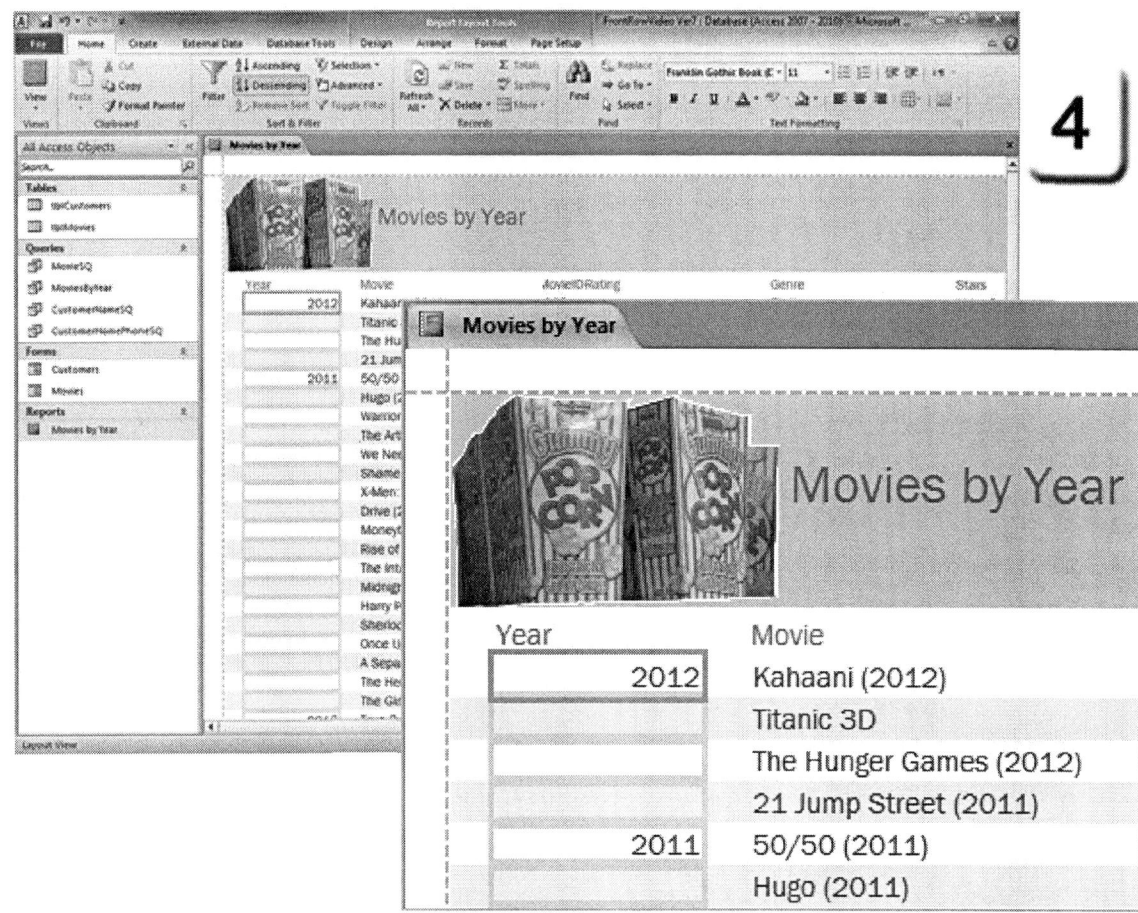

Exam 77-885: Microsoft Access 2010
5. Designing Reports
5.6. Sort and filter records for reporting: Use the Sort Command

Use the Report: Filter

A **Filter** narrows the focus of a Report and only returns the records that meet the criteria. This example uses the data to select only the movies that were released in a particular year, not all years.

5. Try it: Filter the Records in a Report
The Report is still opened in Layout View.
Select a Column: Years.
Go to **Home->Sort&Filter**.
Click on **Filter**.

What Do You See? The Filter should be available by the Field for Year.

Try This, Too: Select Only One Filter
By default, there should be check mark in **Select All**. Clear that check mark and all of the Filters will be cleared as well.

Select a Filter: 2000.
Click **OK**. Keep going..

Home->Sort&Filter->Filter

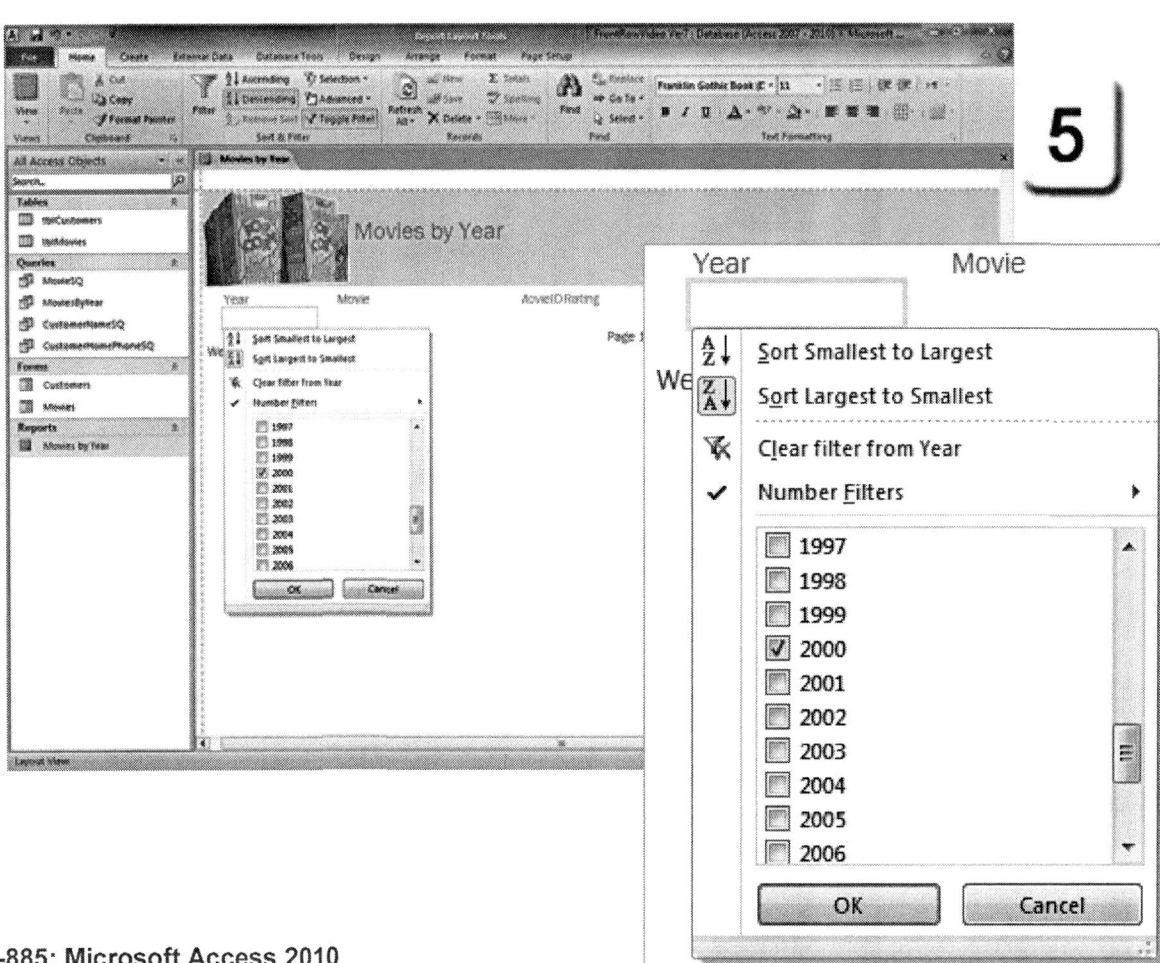

Exam 77-885: Microsoft Access 2010
5. Designing Reports
5.6. Sort and filter records for reporting: Use the Filter Command

Review the Filtered Report

6. Try it: Review the Filtered Report
This Report displays 17 out of 401 records in tblMovies when the Filter is set for 2000.

Made You Look: In the Sort&Filter Group there is a button that will **Toggle** the Filter. Toggle means that it will turn the Filter on or off so that you can see the data with or without the Filter.

In this example, there are 17 records that match the Filter criteria 2000. There are 401 records when the Filter is toggled off.

Try This, Too: Clear the Filters
Go to **Home->Sort&Filter->Advanced**.
Click on **Clear All Filters**.

Keep going...

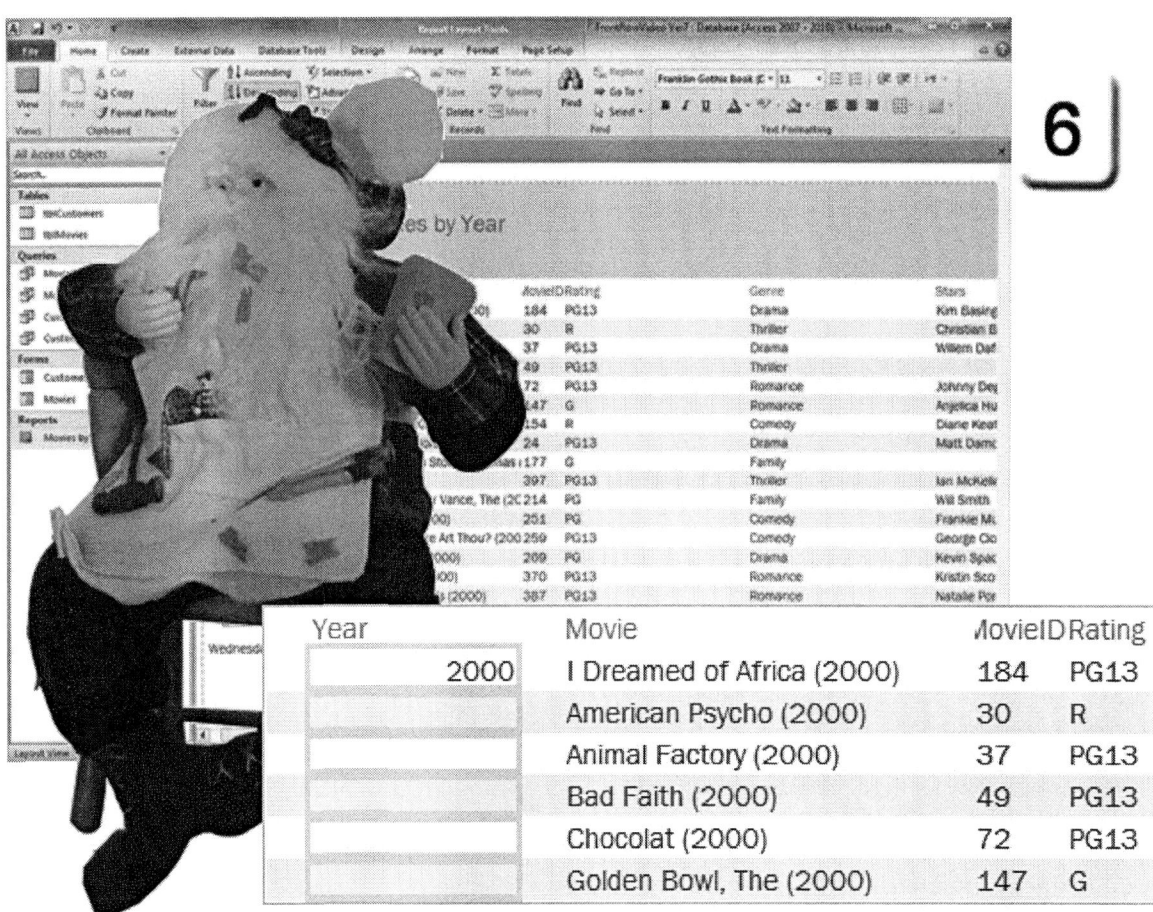

Year	Movie	MovieID	Rating
2000	I Dreamed of Africa (2000)	184	PG13
	American Psycho (2000)	30	R
	Animal Factory (2000)	37	PG13
	Bad Faith (2000)	49	PG13
	Chocolat (2000)	72	PG13
	Golden Bowl, The (2000)	147	G

Exam 77-885: Microsoft Access 2010
5. Designing Reports
5.6. Sort and filter records for reporting: Use the Filter Command

Filter by Selection

A Filter limits the Report to records that match your criteria. Here is a different method for selecting the data you want.

7. Try it: Filter by Selection
The Report is still open in Layout View.
All of the Filters have been cleared.

Select the Year: 2011.
Go to **Home->Sort&Filter->Selection.**

What Do You See? The Selections include:
Equals
Does Not Equal
Less Than or Equal To
Greater Than or Equal To
Between...

Hmmm, math stuff.
Do not select a Filter at this time.

OK, that's enough for now.
Save the Report.

Home->Sort&Filter->Selection

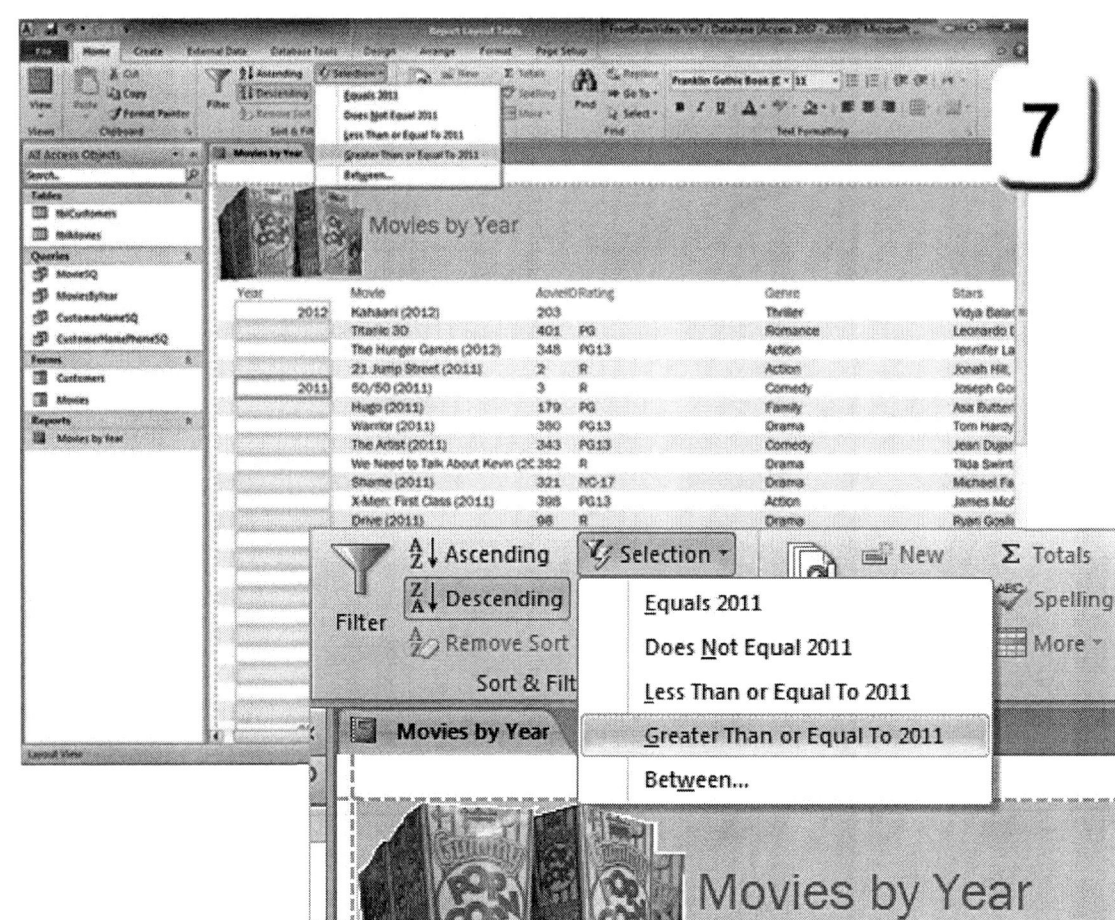

Exam 77-885: Microsoft Access 2010
5. Designing Reports
5.6. Sort and filter records for reporting: Use the Filter Command

Summary

This lesson created a Report by using the Report Wizard. The Wizard walked through the process of selecting a Record Source, tblMovies, as well as the Grouping, Sorting, and Layout.

We investigated the Report Layout Tools, particularly the options available on the Design Ribbon. The Report was formatted with a Theme.

Allez allez in Free.
You get the cookie.

Practice Activities

Lesson 9: Reports and Report Design

Try This: Do the following steps

1. Open the Brown Bag Lunch database you have been working on. Or you may download the sample database **Brown Bag Lunch ver9.accdb** online.

2. Create a Report using the Report Wizard.

3. Select the Query ProductsByTypeSQ as the Record Source. Select all available Fields.

4. Group by Type.

5. Sort the Item Field in Ascending order.

6. Set the Layout to Block.

7. Name the Report as Products by Type. Finish the Report Wizard and Close the Print Preview.

8. Modify the Report design in Layout View. Apply the Theme Apothecary.

9. Add a Logo in the Header. Add the image **Brown Bag Logo.jpg**,. Resize the logo to make it just larger than the Header Label text. Move the Logo to the far left of the Header.

10. Move the Header Label so that it is just to the right of the Logo.

11. Use the Insert Date/ Time command to add a short date with no time to the Header.

12. Add a page number to the Footer. Format the page number to be page N of M with alignment left. Show the number on the first page.

13. Save the Products by Type Report.

14. Close the Brown Bag database.

Test Yourself

1. Which is true about Report Grouping? (Give all correct answers.)
A. Grouping levels organizes the Report by Fields
B. You can only have one Group level
Tip: Beginning Access, page 211

2. What is the maximum number of Grouping levels that can be applied in the Report Wizard?
A. 2
B. 4
C. 6
D. Unlimited
Tip: Beginning Access, page 212

3. By default, the Report Wizard adjusts the Field widths so all the Fields fit on the page, if possible.
A. True
B. False
Tip: Beginning Access, page 213

4. Which of the following are Report Views? (Give all correct answers.)
A. Report View
B. Layout View
C. Print Preview
D. Design View
Tip: Beginning Access, page 216

5. Report Layout Tools includes which Ribbons? (Give all correct answers.)
A. Design
B. Arrange
C. Format
D. Page Setup
Tip: Beginning Access, page 217

6. Which is the correct way to resize a logo on a Report?
A. Click the image to select it and use the handles to resize it
B. Click the image and use the Property Sheet to chance the image height and width
Tip: Beginning Access, page 220

Access 2010: Answers
Reports and More Reports

Beginning Access Objectives
In this lesson, you will learn how to:

1. Create a Report that uses a Parameter Query for the Record Source.

2. Modify the Report with the Report Layout Tools.

3. Create a Table with the Report Arrange options.

4. Use the Table functions to Move and Merge Cells.

© 2012 Comma Productions, LLC

Enter Parameter Value

Enter the phone number

8102313211

OK   Cancel

Front Row Video

Where our customers have the best seat in the house

Beta   5

8102313211   Alpha Beta

Friday, May 18, 2012

Lesson 10 : Reports and More Reports

1. Readings

Read Lesson 10 in the Beginning Access guide, page 233-258.

Project

A Report that uses a Parameter Query for the Record Source.

Downloads

FrontRowVideo Begin10.accdb
popcorn1.gif, popcorn2.gif,
popcorn3.gif,
popcorn4.gif, movies1.gif

Brown Bag Lunch ver10.accdb
BB Customers Logo.jpg
Brown Bag Logo.jpg
Lunch1.gif, Lunch2.gif, Lunch3.gif,
Lunch4.gif

2. Practice

Do the Practice Activity on page 259.

3. Assessment

Review the Test questions

Report Layout Tools->Design

Report Layout Tools->Arrange

Menu Maps

From the **Create Ribbon**
Create ->Reports->Report Wizard, page 243

More Menu Maps

From **Report Layout Tools->Design**
1. Report Design Tools ->Design, page 248
2. Report Design Tools ->Design->Views, page 249

From **Report Layout Tools->Arrange**
3. Report Design Tools ->Arrange, page 250
4. Report Design Tools ->Arrange->Tabular, page 251
5. Report Design Tools ->Arrange->Move, page 252
6. Report Design Tools ->Arrange->Merge/Spilt, page 253
7. Arrange->Rows & Columns, page 254
8. Arrange->Table->Gridlines, page 257

More Questions, More Answers

In the previous lesson we created a simple Report based on a Table. Both **Reports** and **Forms** can also use a Query as the Record Source. Queries ask questions. Reports show answers. When the questions are asked right, the answers come easy.

Microsoft Office Access 2010: Example of a Parameter Query and the Report, below

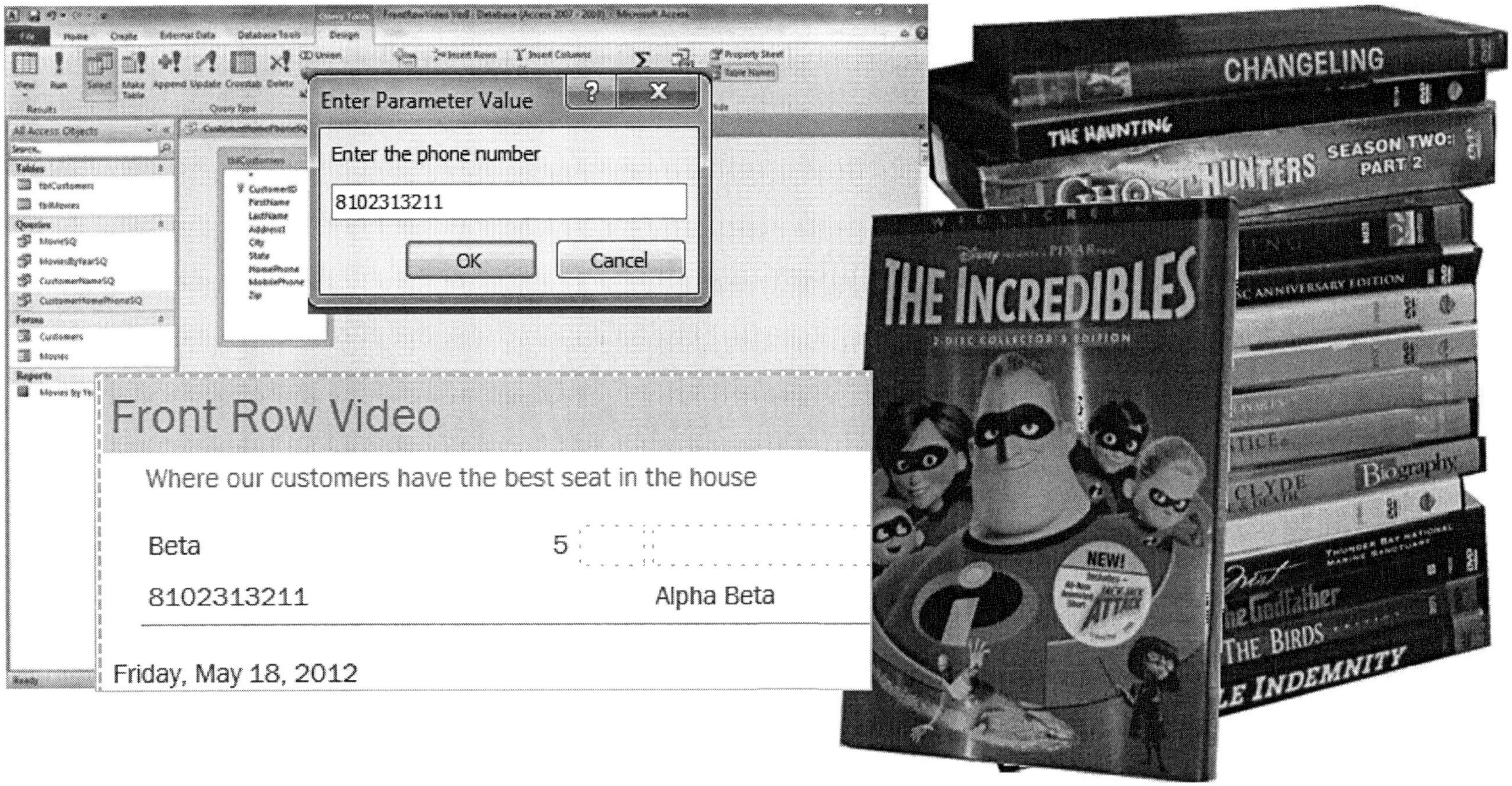

Enter Parameter Value

Enter the phone number

8102313211

OK   Cancel

Front Row Video

Where our customers have the best seat in the house

Beta   5

8102313211   Alpha Beta

Friday, May 18, 2012

Before You Begin

1. Try it: Open the Sample Database
Go to the Documents folder.
Open the sample database:
FrontRowVideo Begin10.accdb

What Do You See? Two Tables:
tblCustomers has 5 records.
tblMovies has 401 records.

There are two Forms:
Customers
Movies

There are four Queries:
CustomerHomePhoneSQ
CustomerNameSQ
MoviesByYearSQ
MoviesSQ

There is one Report: Movies by Year

What Else Do You See? This database
may have a Security Warning. In order
to edit the objects and save your work,
you need to click on **Enable Content**.

Microsoft Access 2010

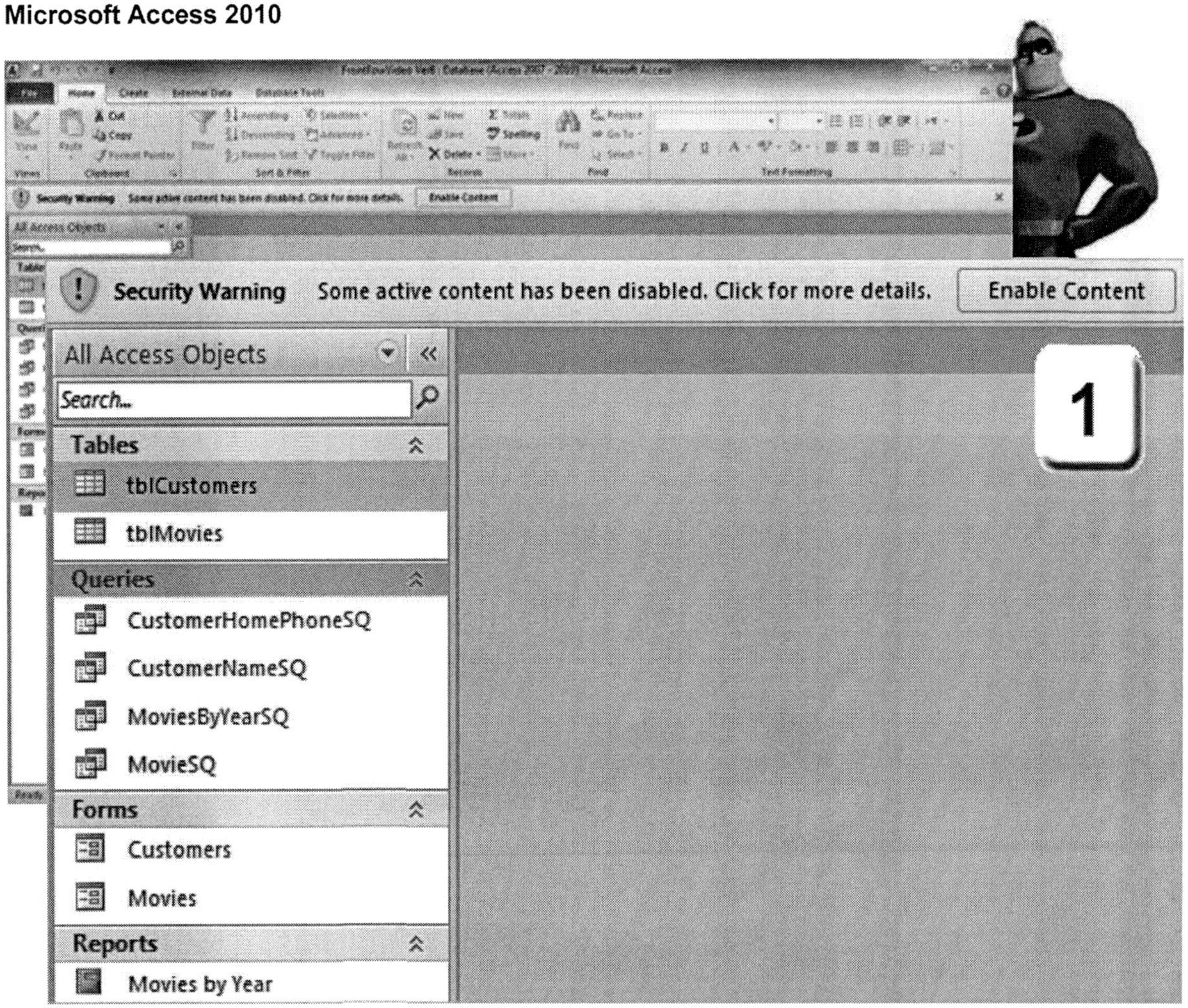

Security Warning   Some active content has been disabled. Click for more details. | Enable Content |

All Access Objects

Search...

Tables
- tblCustomers
- tblMovies

Queries
- CustomerHomePhoneSQ
- CustomerNameSQ
- MoviesByYearSQ
- MovieSQ

Forms
- Customers
- Movies

Reports
- Movies by Year

1

Know Your Data

This Report will print the name, address and phone number for our customers. So, the first step is to review the data in tblCustomers. A Form, Query or Report is only as good as the information in the Table.

2. Try it: Review the Customer Data
Go to **All Access Objects ->Tables.**
Double click: tblCustomers.

What Do You See? There are 5 customers. Each customer has a home phone number.

Close tblCustomers. Keep going...

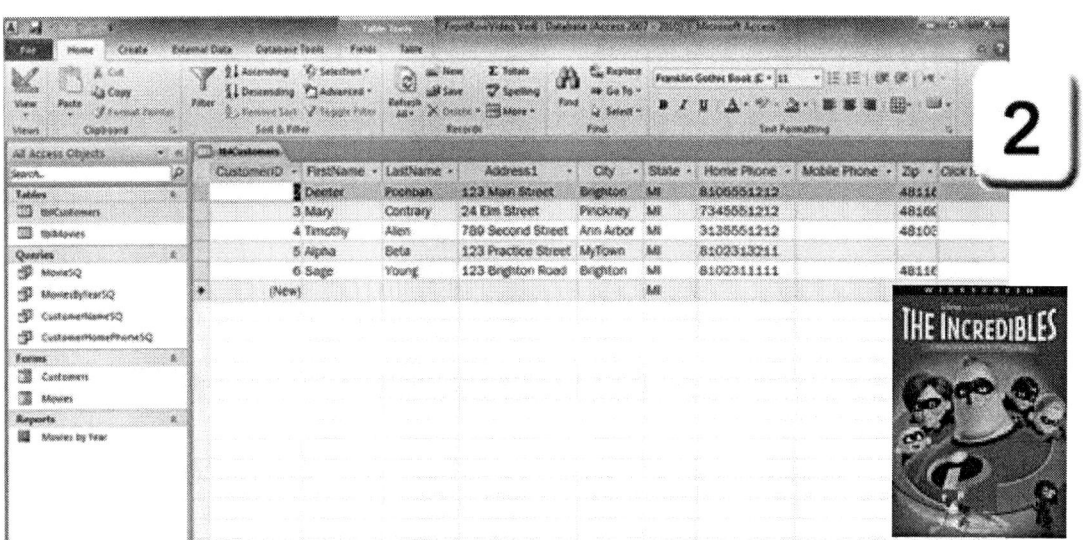

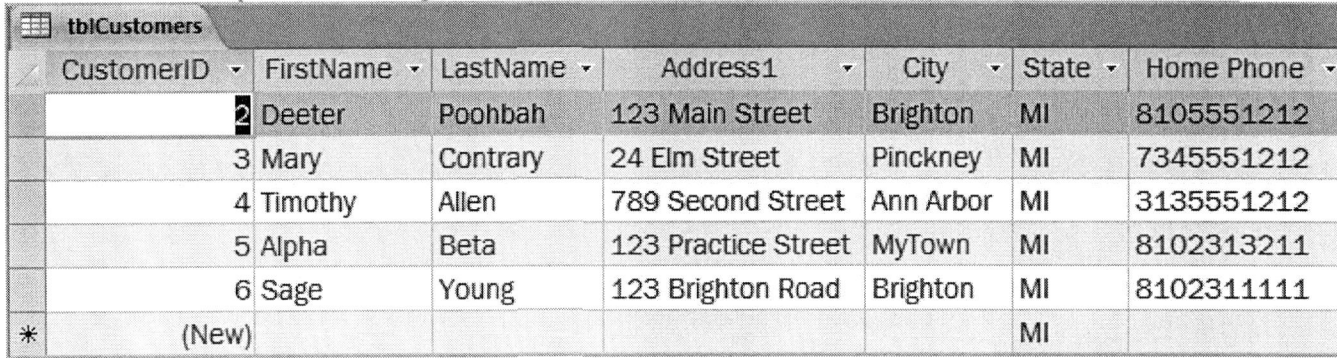

CustomerID	FirstName	LastName	Address1	City	State	Home Phone
2	Deeter	Poohbah	123 Main Street	Brighton	MI	8105551212
3	Mary	Contrary	24 Elm Street	Pinckney	MI	7345551212
4	Timothy	Allen	789 Second Street	Ann Arbor	MI	3135551212
5	Alpha	Beta	123 Practice Street	MyTown	MI	8102313211
6	Sage	Young	123 Brighton Road	Brighton	MI	8102311111
*	(New)				MI	

Queries Ask Questions

This lesson will use a Parameter Query to ask the user to select a customer by entering the customer's phone number.

Our Access database has two **Parameter Queries** that ask users to enter data:

MoviesByYearSQ asks for the Year.
CustomerHomePhoneSQ asks for the Phone.

3. Try it: Run the Parameter Query
Go to **All Access Objects ->Queries.**
Double click: CustomerHomePhoneSQ.

You will be prompted to enter the phone number.
Type: 8102313211

What Do You See? The Query will show one record that matches the number you entered.

Keep going...

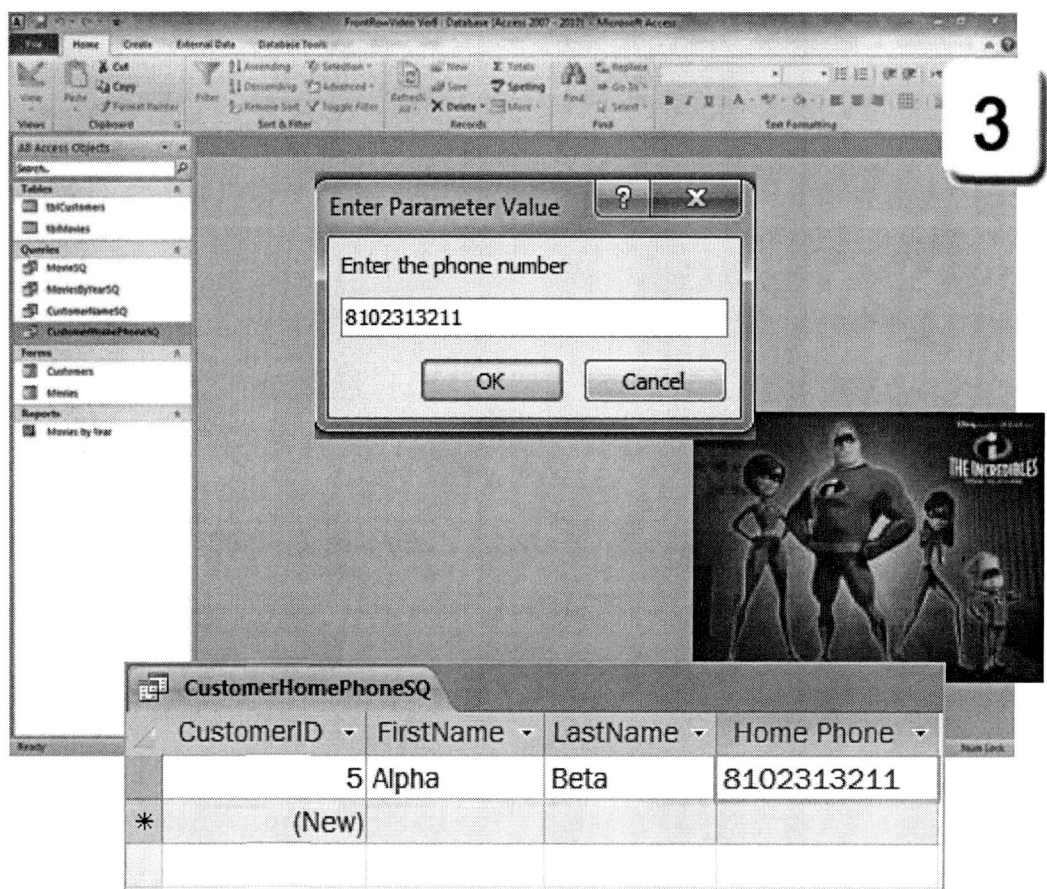

More Questions, More Fields

This Report needs the customer's address as well as the name and phone number. Please take this Query into Design View and add two new Fields.

4. Try it: Go to Design View
The Query is still open in Datasheet View.
Go to **Home ->Views->View.**
Select a View: **Design View.**

What Do You See? There is one table at the top: tblCustomers. There are 4 Fields in the QBE Grid on the bottom:
CustomerID
FirstName
LastName
HomePhone

The HomePhone Field has a Parameter in the Criteria Row: [Enter the phone number].

Keep going...

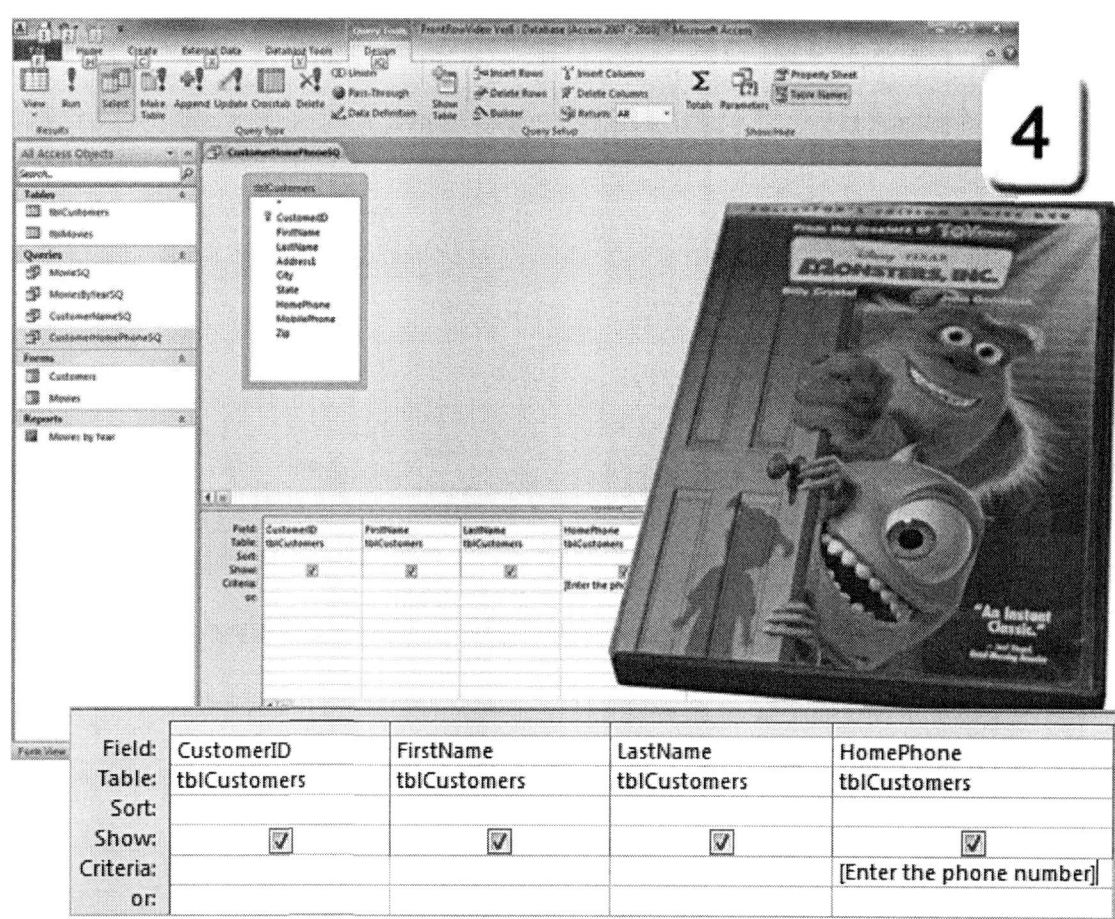

Field:	CustomerID	FirstName	LastName	HomePhone
Table:	tblCustomers	tblCustomers	tblCustomers	tblCustomers
Sort:				
Show:	☑	☑	☑	☑
Criteria:				[Enter the phone number]
or:				

Concatenate Two Fields

Here are the steps to **Concatenate** (combine) the first and last names together into one Field.

5. Try it: Concatenate the Name
The Query is open in Design View.
Place your cursor in Column 6.
Right Click->Zoom.
Type: FullName:[FirstName]&" "&[LastName]

Fullname is the label, or alias, for the new Field.

[FirstName] and [LastName] are Fields from tblCustomer.

The two quotes have a space between them. Whatever is inside the quotes will be placed between the Fields.

The two & signs are the glue that sticks the two Fields together.

Click **OK**. Keep going...

Query Tools ->Design

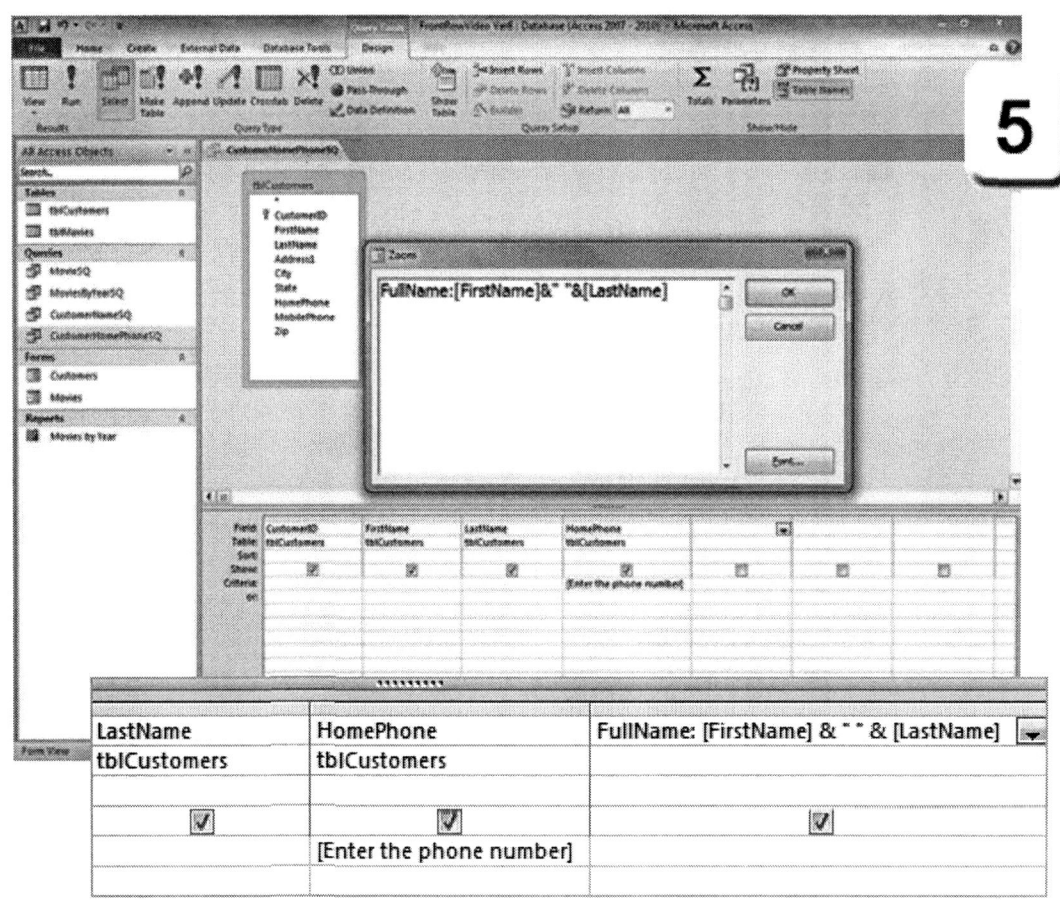

LastName	HomePhone	FullName: [FirstName] & " " & [LastName]
tblCustomers	tblCustomers	
☑	☑	☑
	[Enter the phone number]	

Exam 77-885: Microsoft Access 2010
4. Creating and Managing Queries
4.3. Manipulate fields: Concatenate (combine) Fields

Concatenate Three Fields

Here are the steps to **Concatenate** (combine) the city, state and zip fields for a Mail Merge.

6. Try it: Run the Query
The Query is still open in Design View.
Place your cursor in Column 6.
Right Click->Zoom.
Type: CityStateZip:[City]&", "&[State]&" "&[Zip]

CityStateZip is the alias, for the new Field.

[City], [State] and [Zip] are Fields from tblCustomer.

The two quotes have a space between them. Whatever is inside the quotes, say a comma, will be placed between the Fields.

The two & signs are the glue that sticks the two Fields together.

Click **OK**. Keep going...

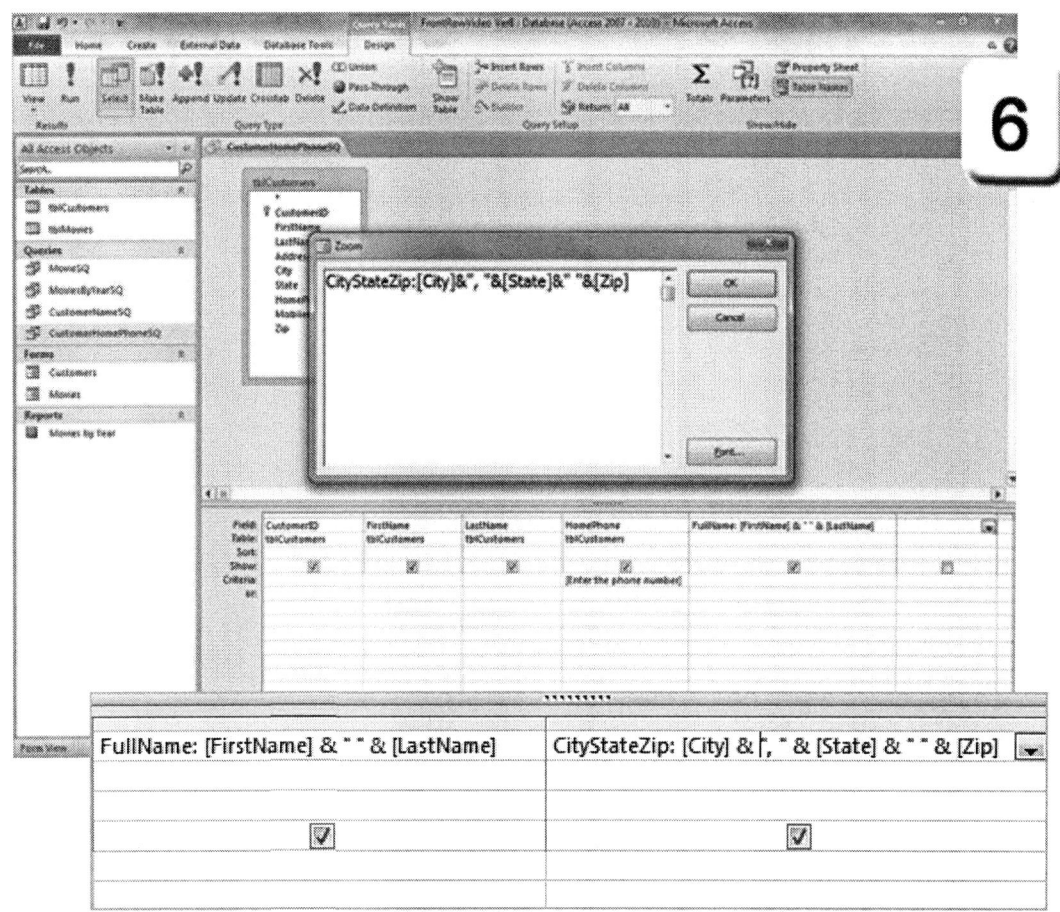

FullName: [FirstName] & " " & [LastName]	CityStateZip: [City] & ", " & [State] & " " & [Zip]	
☑	☑	

Exam 77-885: Microsoft Access 2010
4. Creating and Managing Queries
4.3. Manipulate fields: Concatenate (combine) Fields

Run the Query
This Query needs to be tested because it has been changed. Let's Run the Query and see if the new Concatenated Fields work.

7. Try it: Run the Query
The Query is still open in Design View.
Go to **Query Tools ->Design->Results->Run**.
Enter the phone number: 8102313211.

What Do You See? The Query Results will open in Datasheet View. There should be two new concatenated Fields:
FullName and CityStateZip.

Try This, Too: Return to the Design View
Go to **Home->Views->View**.
Choose a View: **Design View**.

Do This, Now: Save the Query
Go to **File->Save**.

So far, so good. **Close** the Query.

Query Tools ->Design->Results->Run

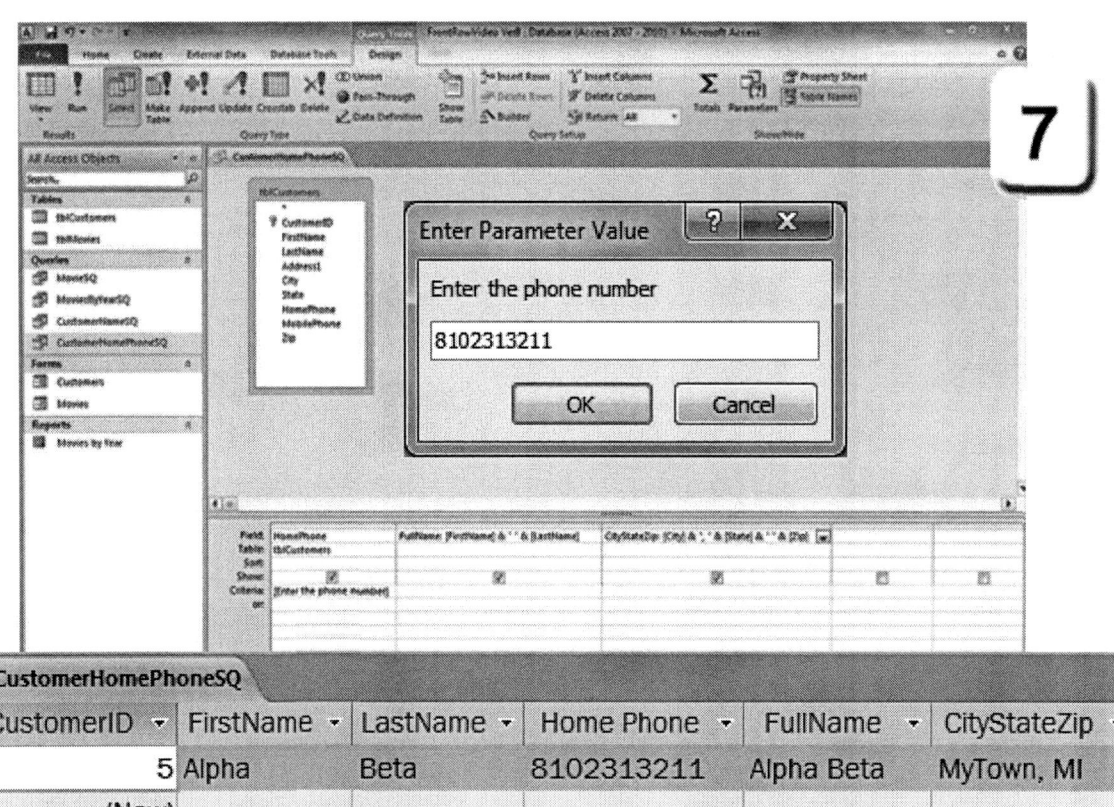

CustomerID ▾	FirstName ▾	LastName ▾	Home Phone ▾	FullName ▾	CityStateZip ▾
5	Alpha	Beta	8102313211	Alpha Beta	MyTown, MI
* (New)					

Exam 77-885: Microsoft Access 2010
4. Creating and Managing Queries
4.3. Manipulate fields: Concatenate (combine) Fields

Create a New Report

Let's walk through the Report Wizard to create a new Report that uses a Parameter Query, **CustomerHomePhoneSQ**, as the Record Source.

1. Try it: Use the Report Wizard
Go to **Create ->Reports->Report Wizard.**

What Do You See? The Report Wizard should open. Please answer the prompts.

Select a Table/Query:
CustomerHomePhoneSQ

Select the following Fields:
CustomerID
LastName
HomePhone
FullName
CistyStateZip

Click **Next**. Keep going...

Create ->Reports->Report Wizard

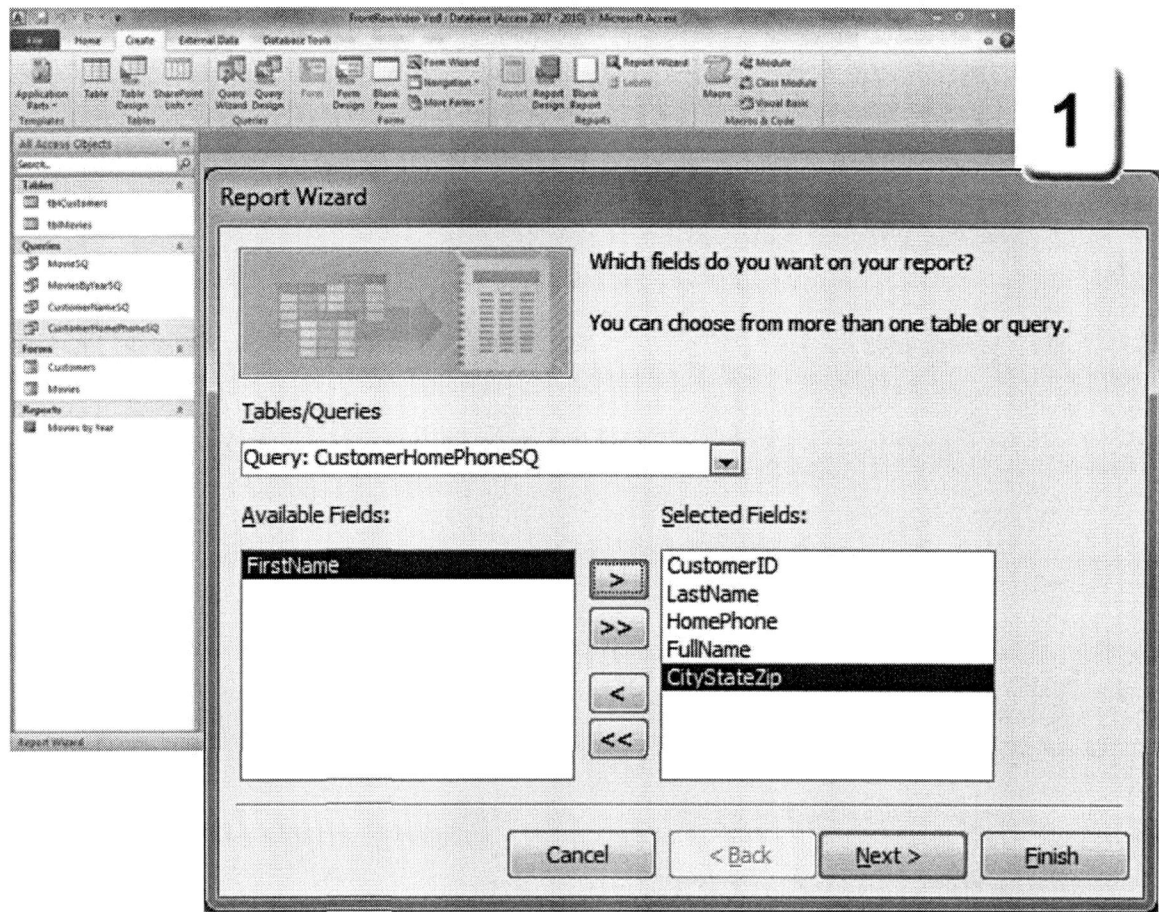

Exam 77-885: Microsoft Access 2010
5. Designing Reports
5.1. Create reports: Use the Report Wizard

HOME

Report Wizard: Grouping
2. Try it: Add a Grouping Level
Select a Field: LastName.
Add LastName to the Group Header.

Click **Next**. Keep going...

Create ->Reports->Report Wizard

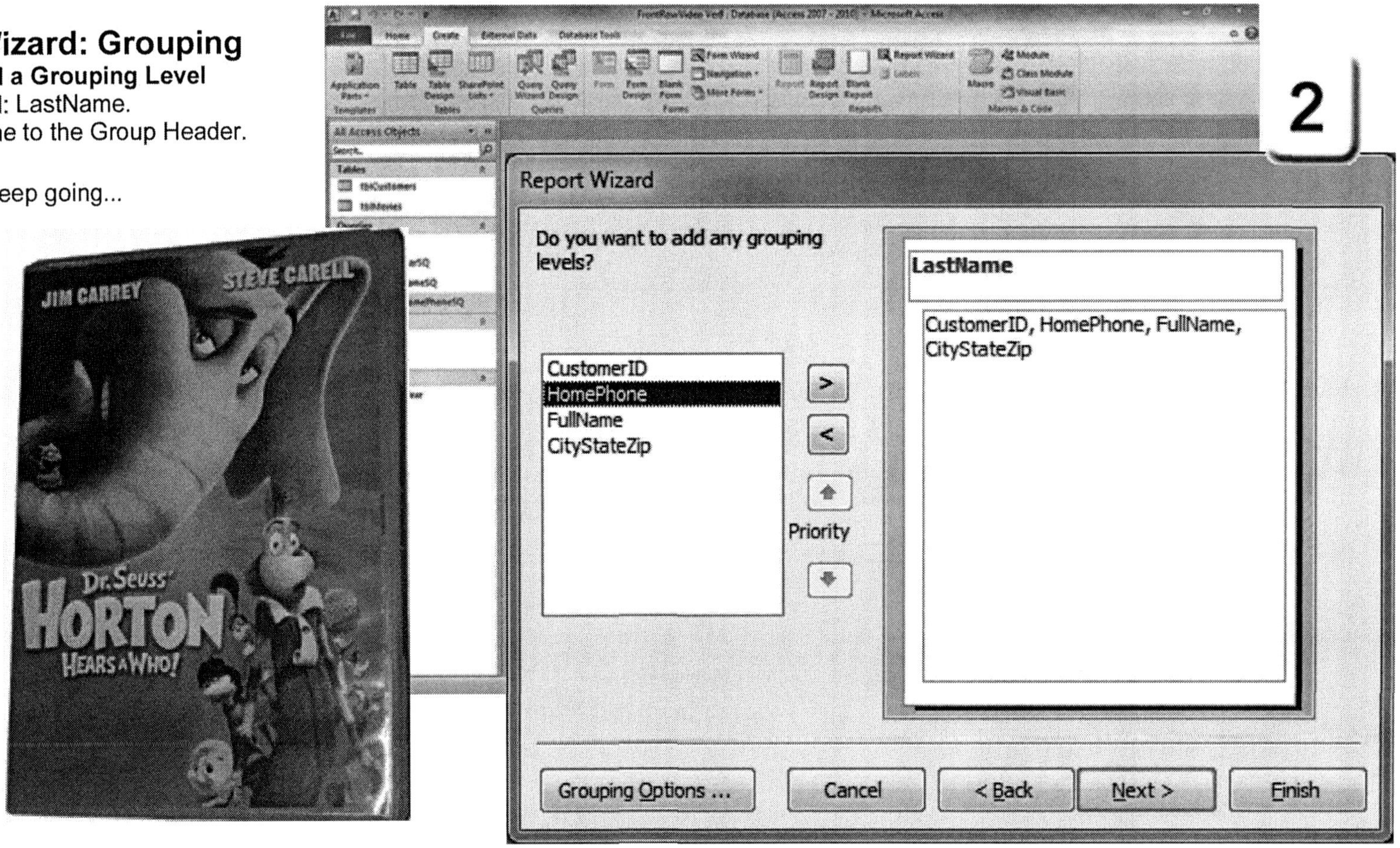

Report Wizard

Do you want to add any grouping levels?

LastName

CustomerID, HomePhone, FullName, CityStateZip

CustomerID
HomePhone
FullName
CityStateZip

> <
Priority

Grouping Options ...   Cancel   < Back   Next >   Finish

2

Exam 77-885: Microsoft Access 2010
5. Designing Reports
5.1. Create reports: Use the Report Wizard

Create ->Reports->Report Wizard

Report Wizard: Sorting

3. Try it: Consider the Sorting

There is nothing to Sort in this Report. It is based on a Parameter Query that results in one customer record.

Click **Next**. Keep going...

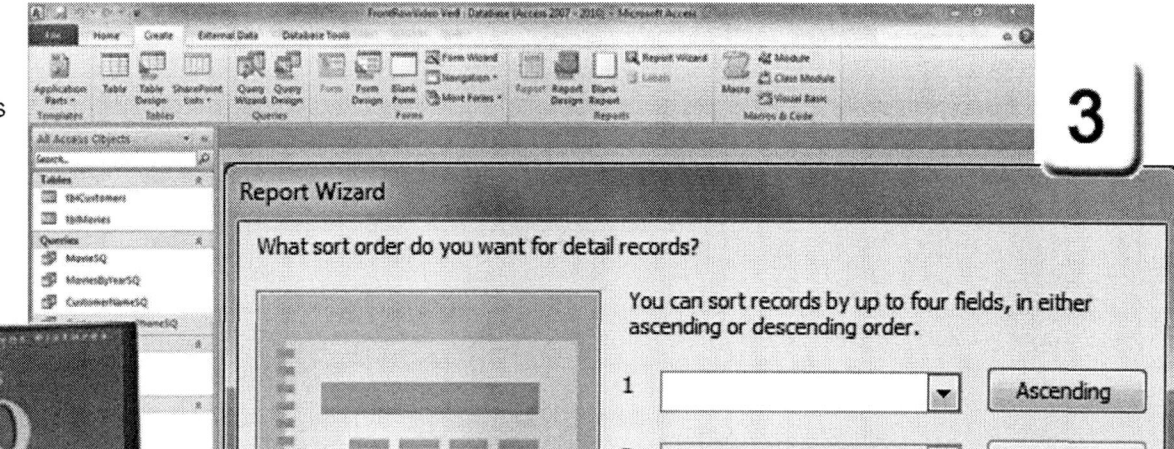

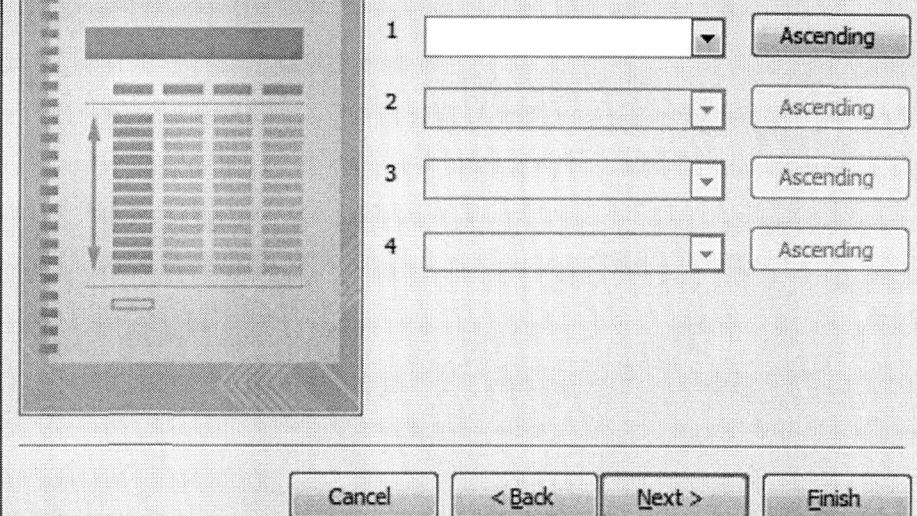

Exam 77-885: Microsoft Access 2010
5. Designing Reports
5.1. Create reports: Use the Report Wizard

Report Wizard: Layout

4. Try it: Choose a Report Layout
Select a **Layout**: Block.
Choose the **Orientation**: Portrait.

What Do You See? By default, the Report Wizard will adjust the Field width so that all of the Fields should fit on the page.

Click **Next**. Keep going...

Create ->Reports->Report Wizard

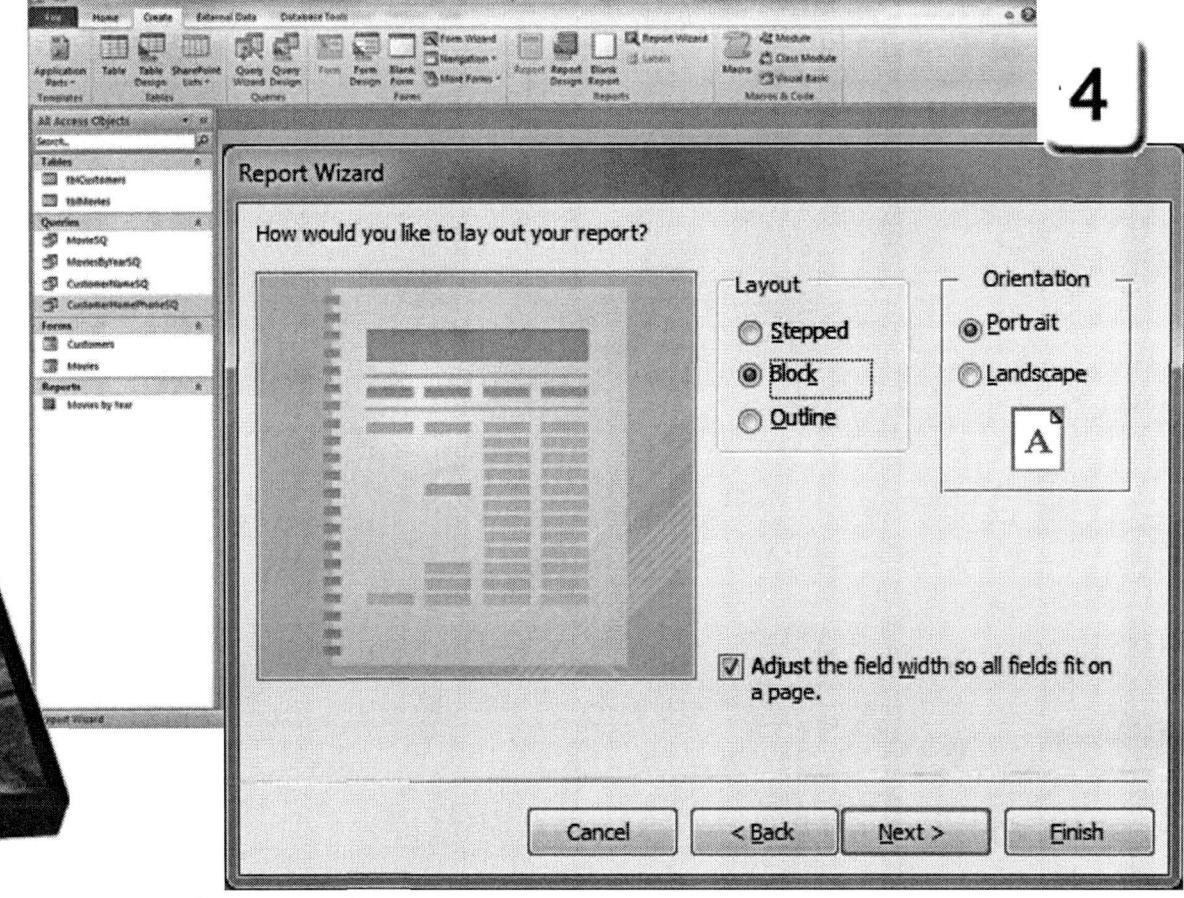

Exam 77-885: Microsoft Access 2010
5. Designing Reports
5.1. Create reports: Use the Report Wizard

Create ->Reports->Report Wizard

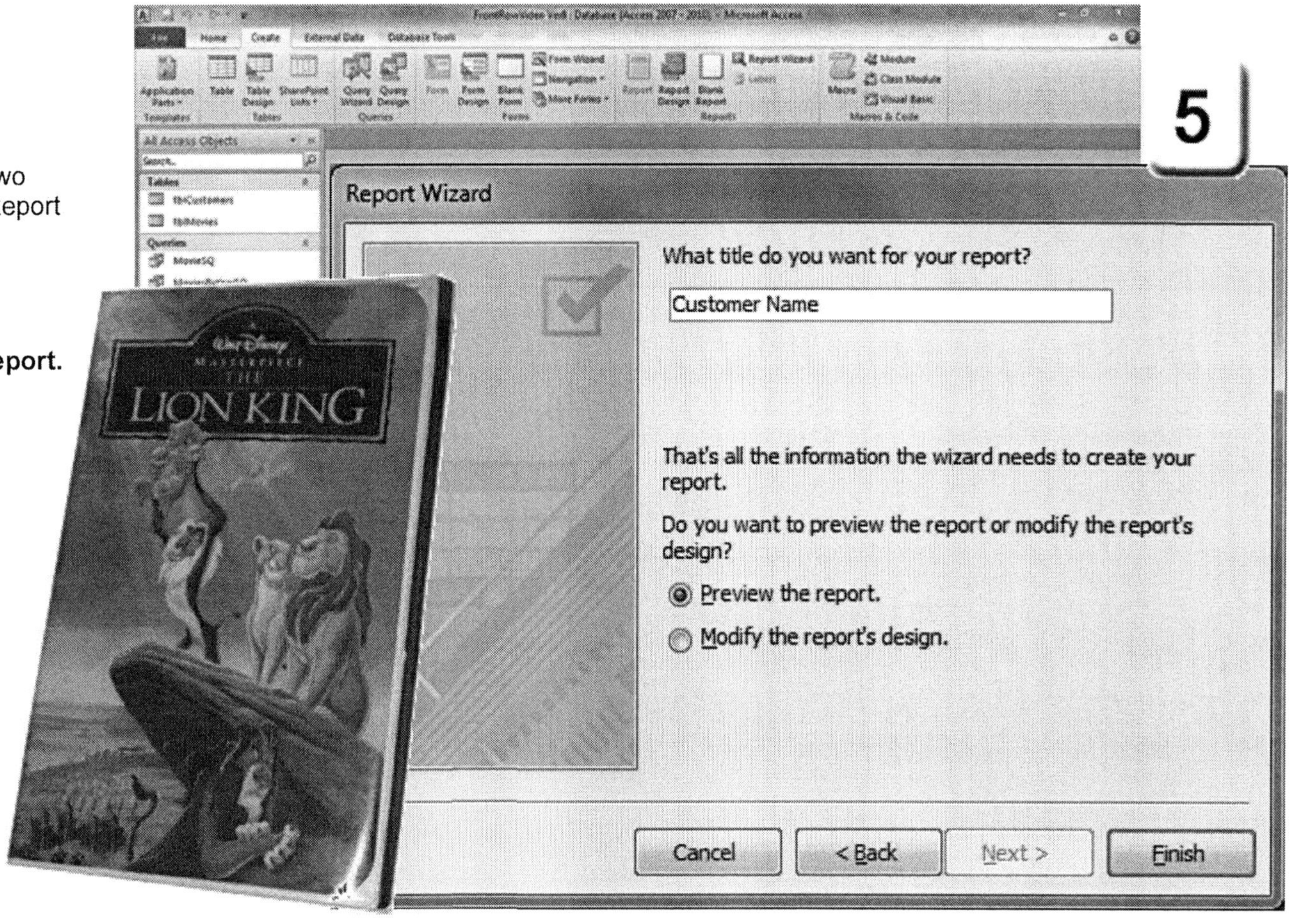

Report Wizard: Title
5. Try it: Enter a Report Title
Enter a **Title**: Customer Name

What Do You See? There are two options after you complete the Report Wizard:
Preview the report
Modify the Report's design

Select an option: **Preview the report.**

Click **Finish**. Keep going...!

Report Wizard

What title do you want for your report?

Customer Name

That's all the information the wizard needs to create your report.

Do you want to preview the report or modify the report's design?

◉ Preview the report.

◯ Modify the report's design.

| Cancel | < Back | Next > | Finish |

Exam 77-885: Microsoft Access 2010
5. Designing Reports
5.1. Create reports: Use the Report Wizard

Report Design Tools ->Design

Hello, Customer Report

This Report is based on a Parameter Query. When the Customer Name Report opens in Print Preview, the **CustomerHomePhoneSQ** Query will Run and ask for information. So, you will be prompted to enter a value.

6. Try it: Enter Parameter Value
Enter the phone number: 8102313211
Click **OK**.

What Do You See? The Report will open in Print Preview and show one customer record that matches the number you entered.

OK, OK. This Layout needs some work.

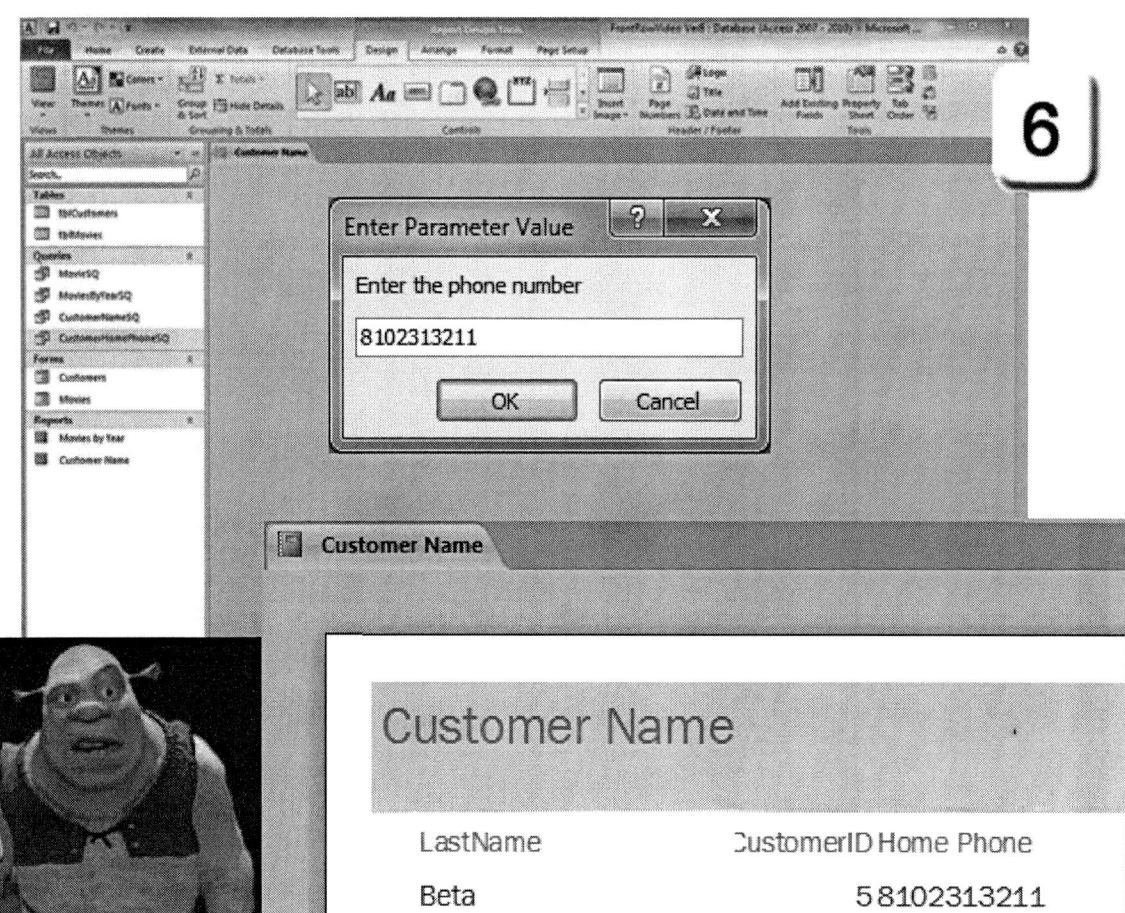

Exam 77-885: Microsoft Access 2010
5. Designing Reports
5.1. Create reports: Use the Report Wizard

Change the Report View

This little Report opened in Print Preview. We need to go to **Layout View** in order to edit the Report. The Report Layout View has excellent tools on the **Arrange** Ribbon.

Before You Begin: Close the Print Preview
Go to **Print Preview->Close Print Preview**.
Click on **Print Preview**.

What Do You See? The Report may be open in Design View. The Report Design Tools should be available.

1. Try it: Go to Layout View
Go to **Report Design Tools ->Design->Views**.
Select a View: **Layout View.**

This is a Parameter Query. You will be prompted. Enter the phone number: 8102313211

Keep going, please.

Exam 77-885: Microsoft Access 2010
5. Designing Reports
5.1. Create reports: Use Report Design Tools-Arrange

Change the Report Layout
Please Review the Report Tools
The Report is open in Layout View. There are four Ribbons in the Report Design Tools:
Design
Arrange
Format
Page Setup

This Report has a very simple Layout. If you change the Report to a Table Layout, there will be a lot more options available.

2. Try This: Select The Report Controls
Select all of the **Report Controls.**
Keep going...

Here is one way to select all of the Controls:
Click on the first Control: LastName.
Hold the **Ctrl** key on the keyboard as you click the other Controls: CustomerID, HomePhone, FullName and CityStateZip.

Release the **Ctrl** key. The Controls that are selected should be highlighted.

Report Design Tools ->Arrange

Exam 77-885: Microsoft Access 2010
5. Designing Reports
5.3. Apply Report Arrange options: Use the Table Functions

Create the Table

3. Try it: Create the Table
The Report Controls are still selected.
Go to **Report Design Tools ->Arrange.**
Go to **Table->Tabular.**

What Do You See? The **Arrange** Ribbon now has the following Groups available:
Table
Rows & Columns
Merge/Split
Move
Position

What Else Do You See? The Fields are arranged in a Table: Rows and Columns.

Keep going...

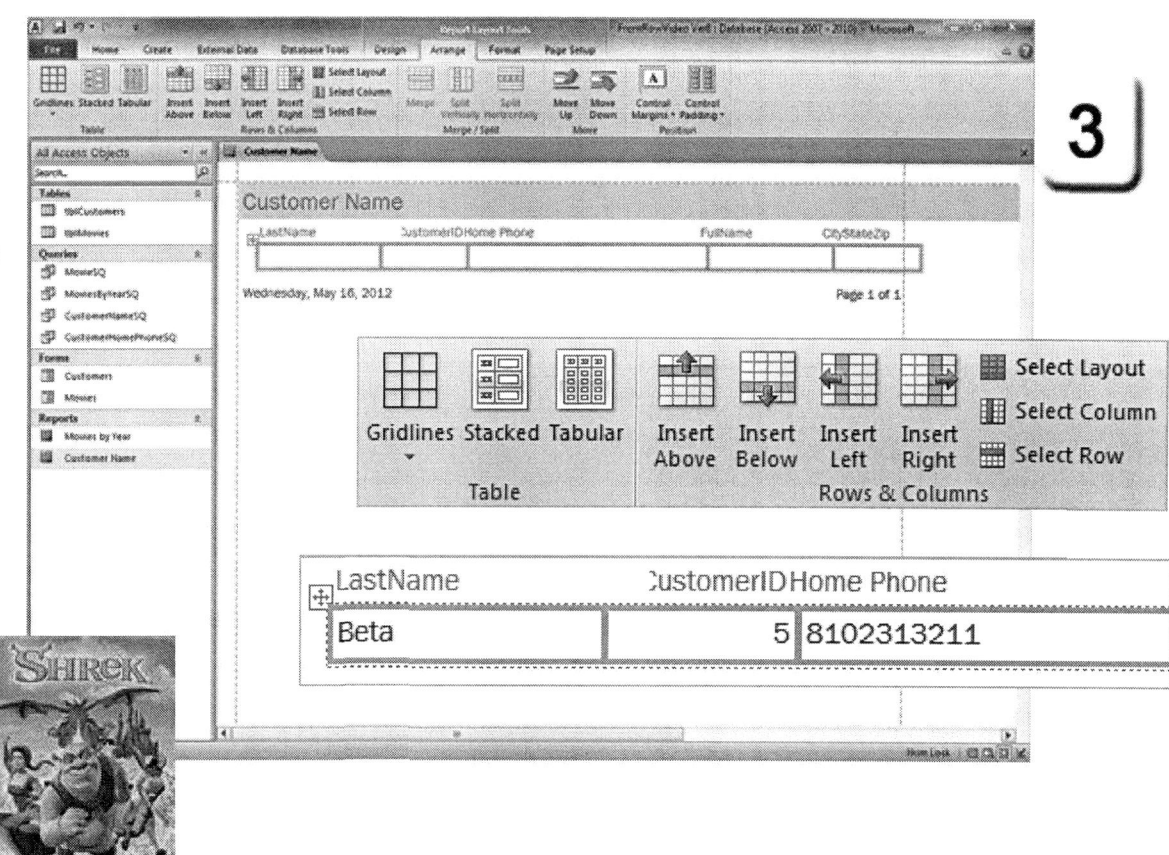

Exam 77-885: Microsoft Access 2010
5. Designing Reports
5.1. Create reports: Use Report Design Tools: Arrange

Take Two

Arrange: Move Up

Let's work with the **Report Design Tools**.
Looking at the Arrange Ribbon: The Rows
& Columns are similar to the ones on the
Ribbons in Microsoft Excel and Word.

Here is something different. You can use
the **Move** commands to change the
layout.

4. Try it: Move the Report Control
The Report is still open in Layout View.
Select a Control: LastName.
Go to **Report Design Tools ->Arrange**.
Go to **Move->Move Up**.

Try it, Again: Move Another Control
Select a Control: CustomerID.
Go to **Report Design Tools ->Arrange**.
Go to **Move->Move Up**.

What Do You See? The Table has two
Rows, now. Row 1 has two Controls:
LastName and CustomerID. The rest of
the Controls are on Row 2.

Keep going..

Report Design Tools ->Arrange->Move->Move Up

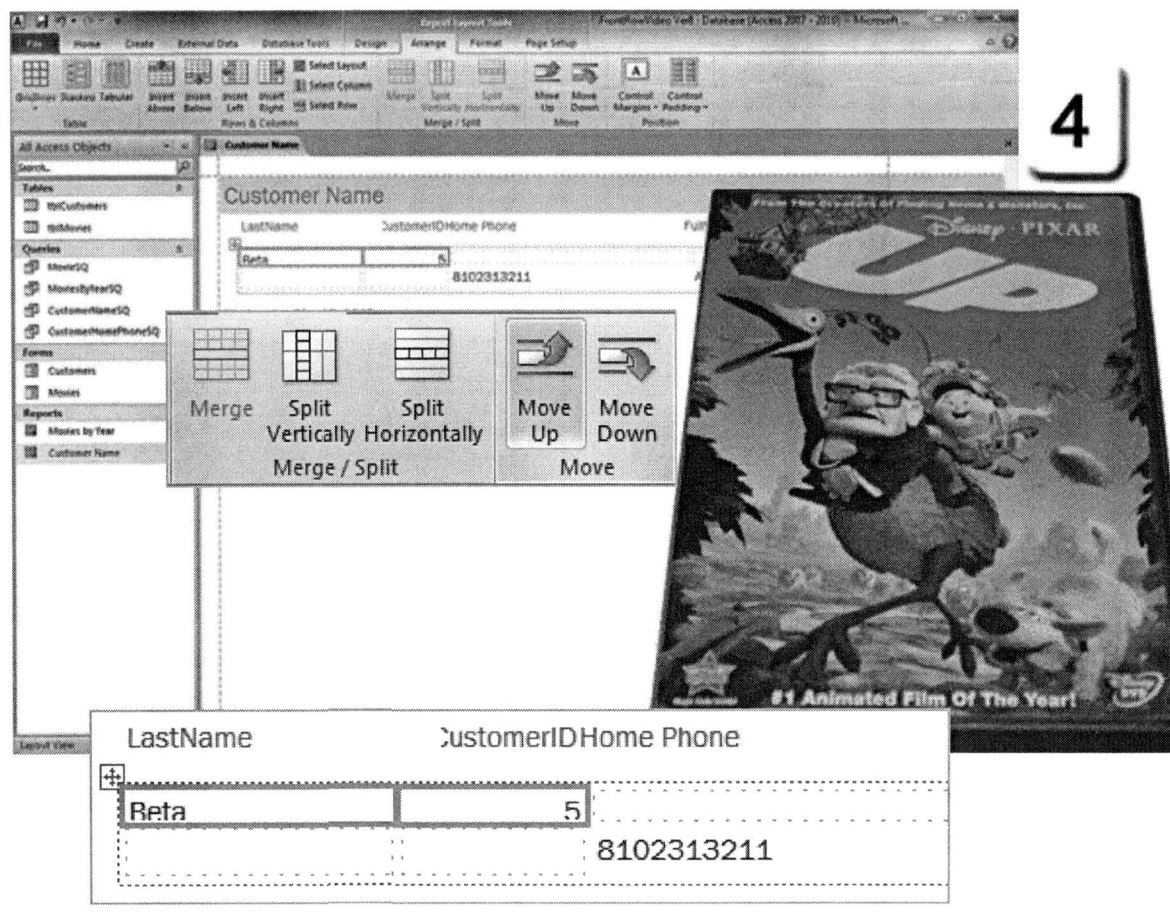

Exam 77-885: Microsoft Access 2010
5. Designing Reports
5.3. Apply Report Arrange options: Use the Table Functions: Move

Arrange: Merge Cells

There are two blank Cells in Row 2. Here are the steps to Merge those Cells with the Home Phone Control.

5. Try it: Merge the Cells
The Report is still open in Layout View.
Select the first three Cells in Row 2.
Go to **Report Design Tools ->Arrange.**
Go to **Merge/Spilt->Merge.**

What Do You See? All three Cells have been merged into one.

Keep going...

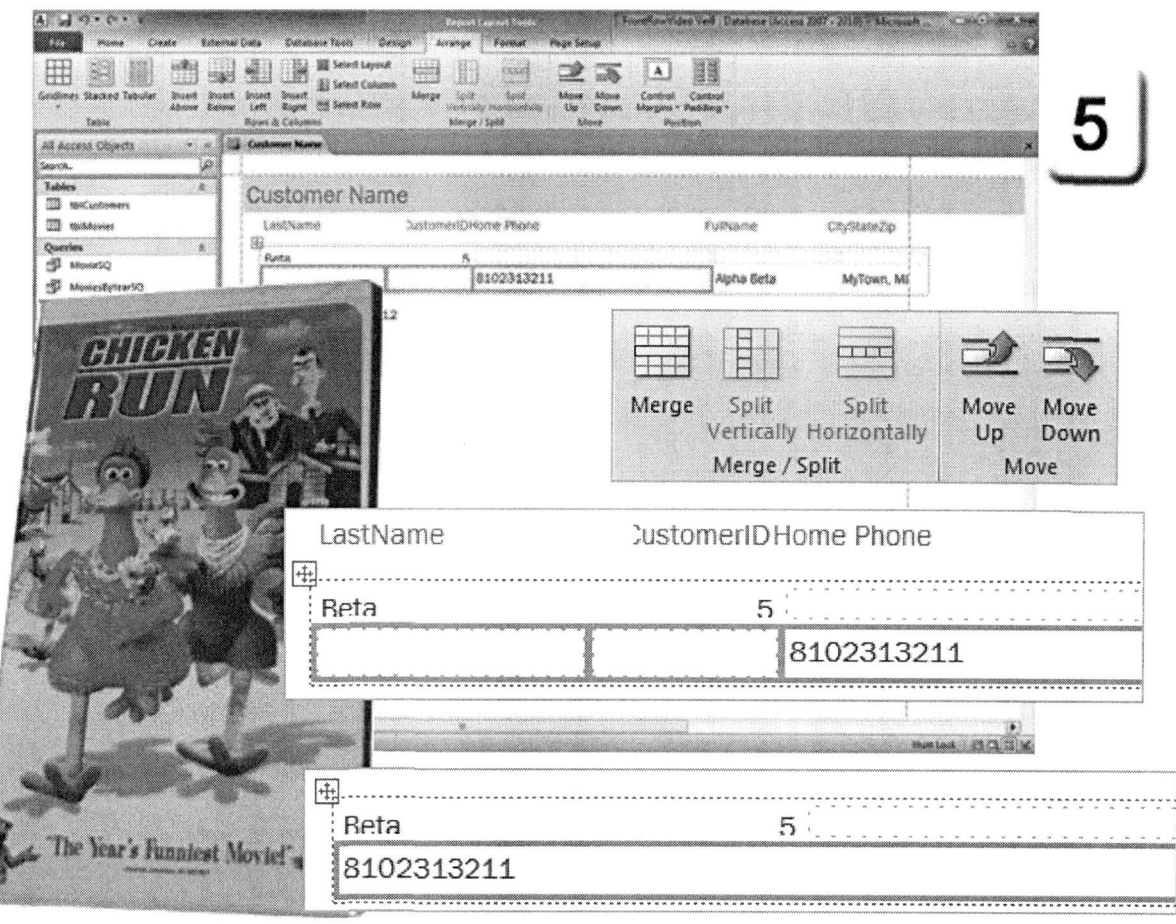

Exam 77-885: Microsoft Access 2010
5. Designing Reports
5.3. Apply Report Arrange options: Use the Table Functions: Merge

Arrange: Resize the Cells

The Cells in this Table can be resized. Before you begin, use the **Rows & Columns** options to select what you need.

6. Try it: Resize the Cells
Select a Control: FullName.
Go to **Report Design Tools ->Arrange.**
Go to **Rows & Columns->Select Column.**

What Do You See? The Column should be highlighted. Run your cursor over the Column border. Now, you can use a double-arrow to resize the Controls. The HomePhone Control can be smaller (it is only 10 numbers). The FullName and CityStateZip should be larger.

Keep going...

Report Design Tools ->Arrange->Rows & Columns->Select Column

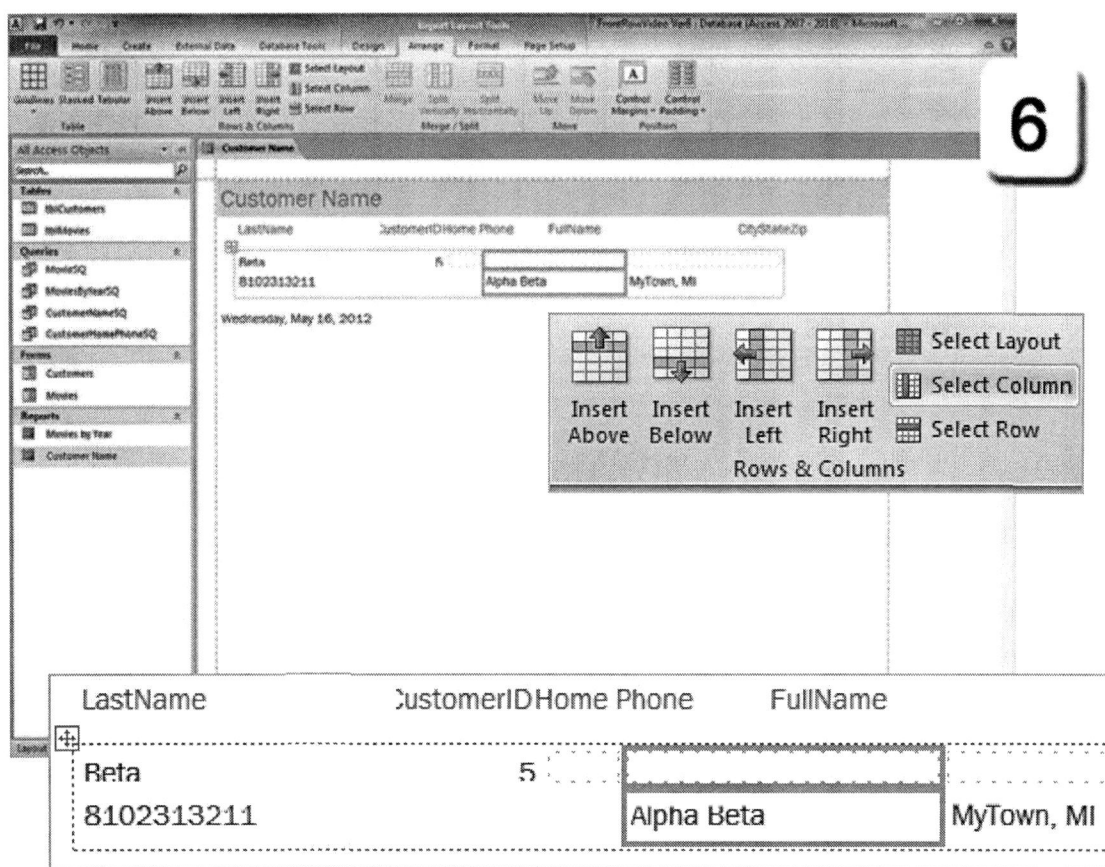

Exam 77-885: Microsoft Access 2010
5. Designing Reports
5.3. Apply Report Arrange options: Use the Table Functions: Rows & Columns

Delete the Control Labels

Each Control has a Label in the Report Page Header. The Labels in this report do not add anything. In fact, the Page Header looks cluttered with too much information.

7. Try it: Select the Control Labels
Select the following labels:
CustomerID
HomePhone
FullName
CityStateZip

Try This, Too: Delete the Control Labels
Type **Delete** on the keyboard.

There should be one Label left in the Page Header. Keep going, please.

Report Design Tools

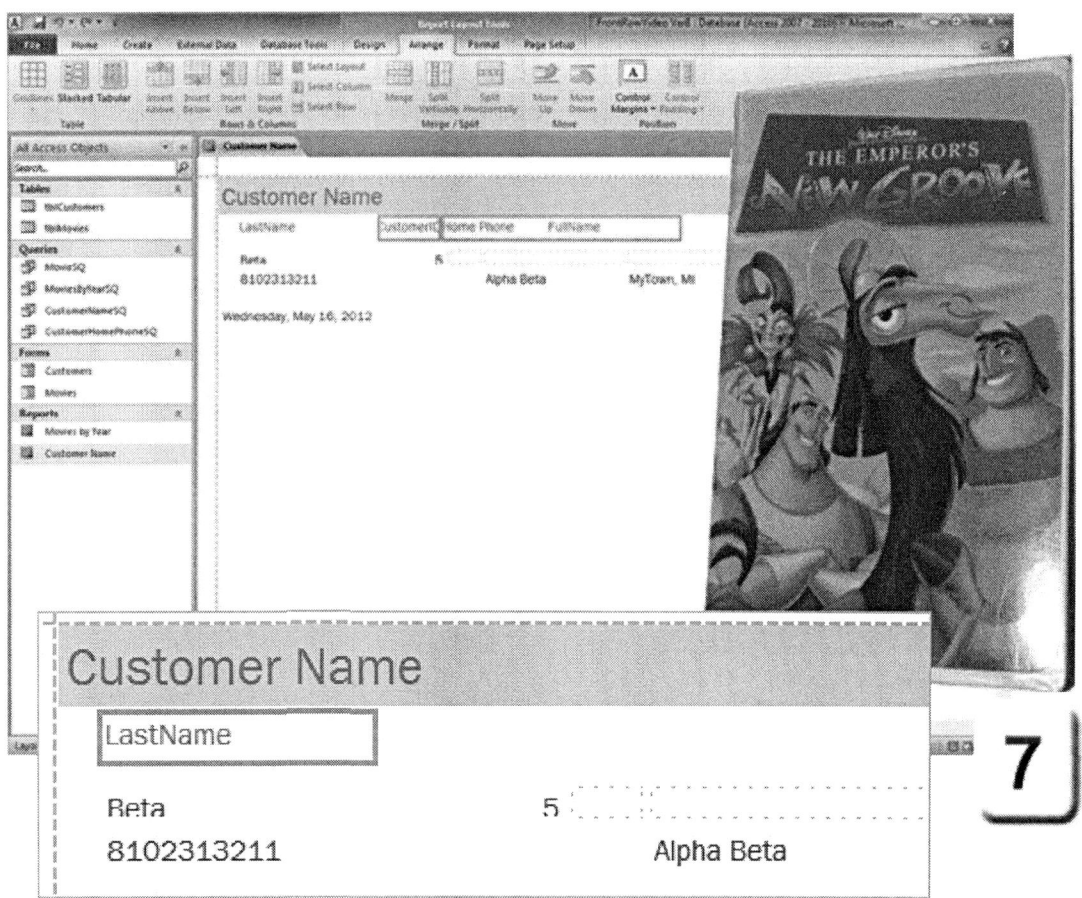

Exam 77-885: Microsoft Access 2010
5. Designing Reports
5.3. Apply Report Arrange options: Use the Table Functions: Rows & Columns

Edit the Label

The Report may be called "Customer Name." However, this is the Front Row Video store and that is the brand that should be presented to the customer.

8. Try it: Edit the Label
Select the Label in the Report Header.
Type: Front Row Video

Select the Label in the Page Header.
Type: Where our customers have the best seat in the house

Keep going...almost done.

Report Design Tools

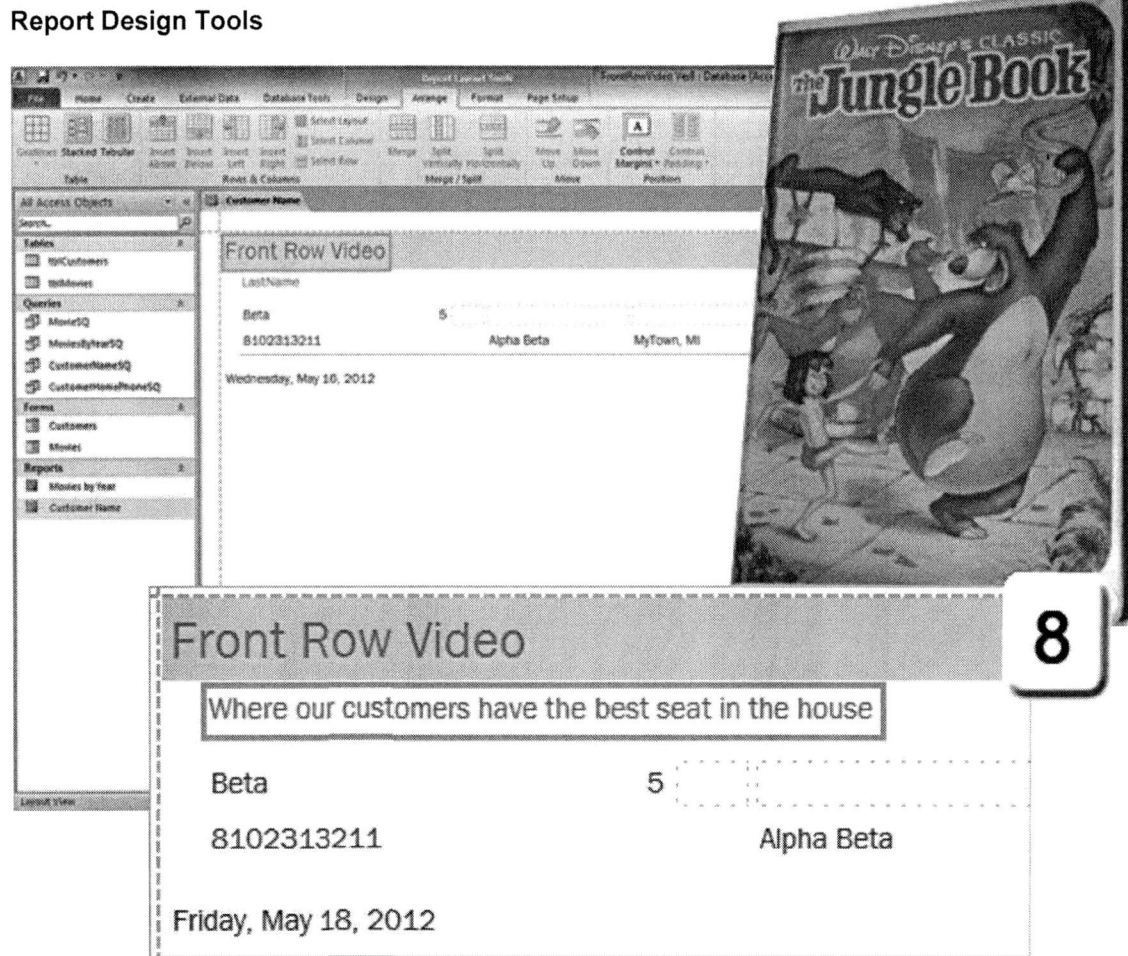

Arrange: Gridlines

9. Try it: Add Gridlines to the Table
Select the following Controls in Row 2:
HomePhone
FullName
CityStateZip

Go to **Report Design Tools ->Arrange.**
Go to **Table->Gridlines.**
Select an option: Bottom

What Do You See? The Controls should be formatted with a line on the bottom.

Do This, Now: Save the Report
Go to **File->Save.**

That looks good.

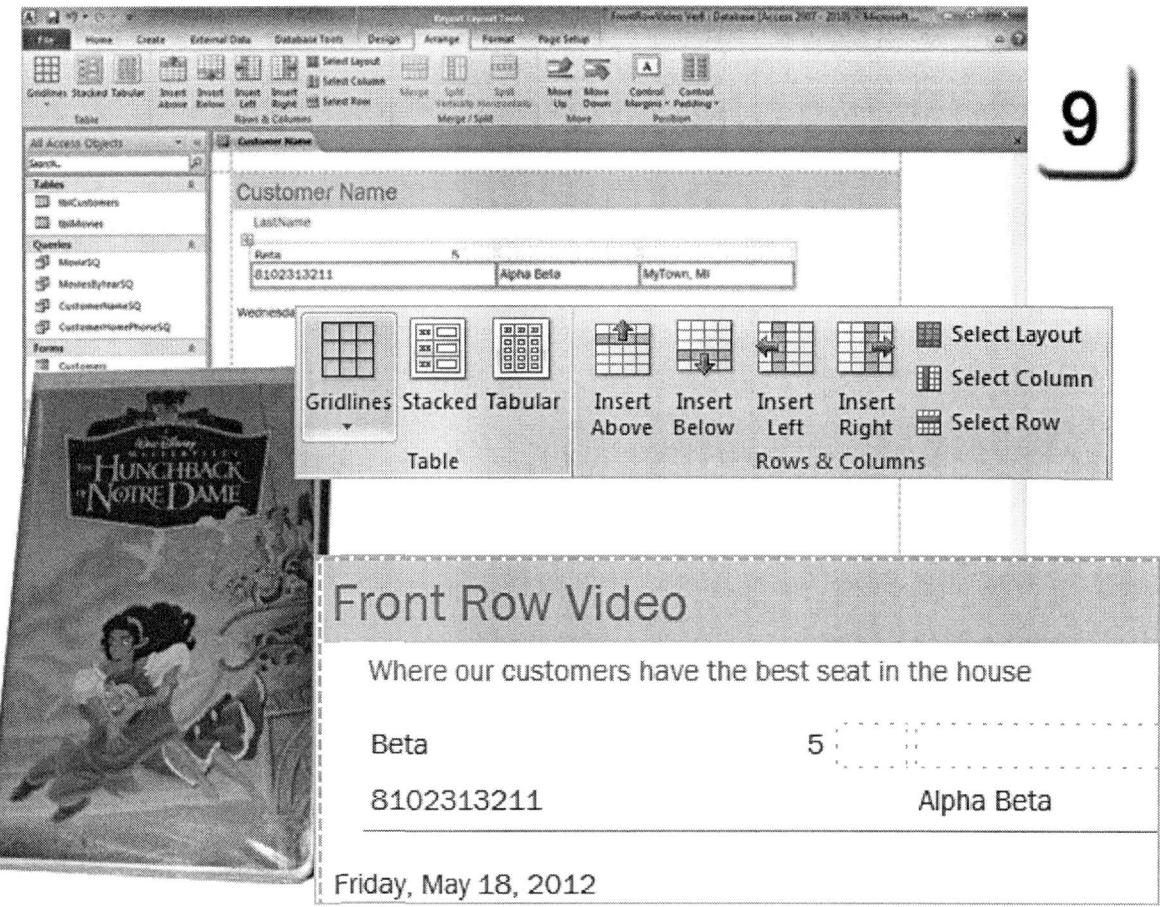

Exam 77-885: Microsoft Access 2010
5. Designing Reports
5.3. Apply Report Arrange options: Use the Table Functions: Gridlines

Summary

This lesson began by modifying a Parameter Query. We used the Report Wizard to create a new Report based on the Parameter Query. Finally, we modified that Report in Layout View.

This concludes the Beginning Guide to Microsoft Access 2010.

Well, you done good.
You earned all of the cookies.

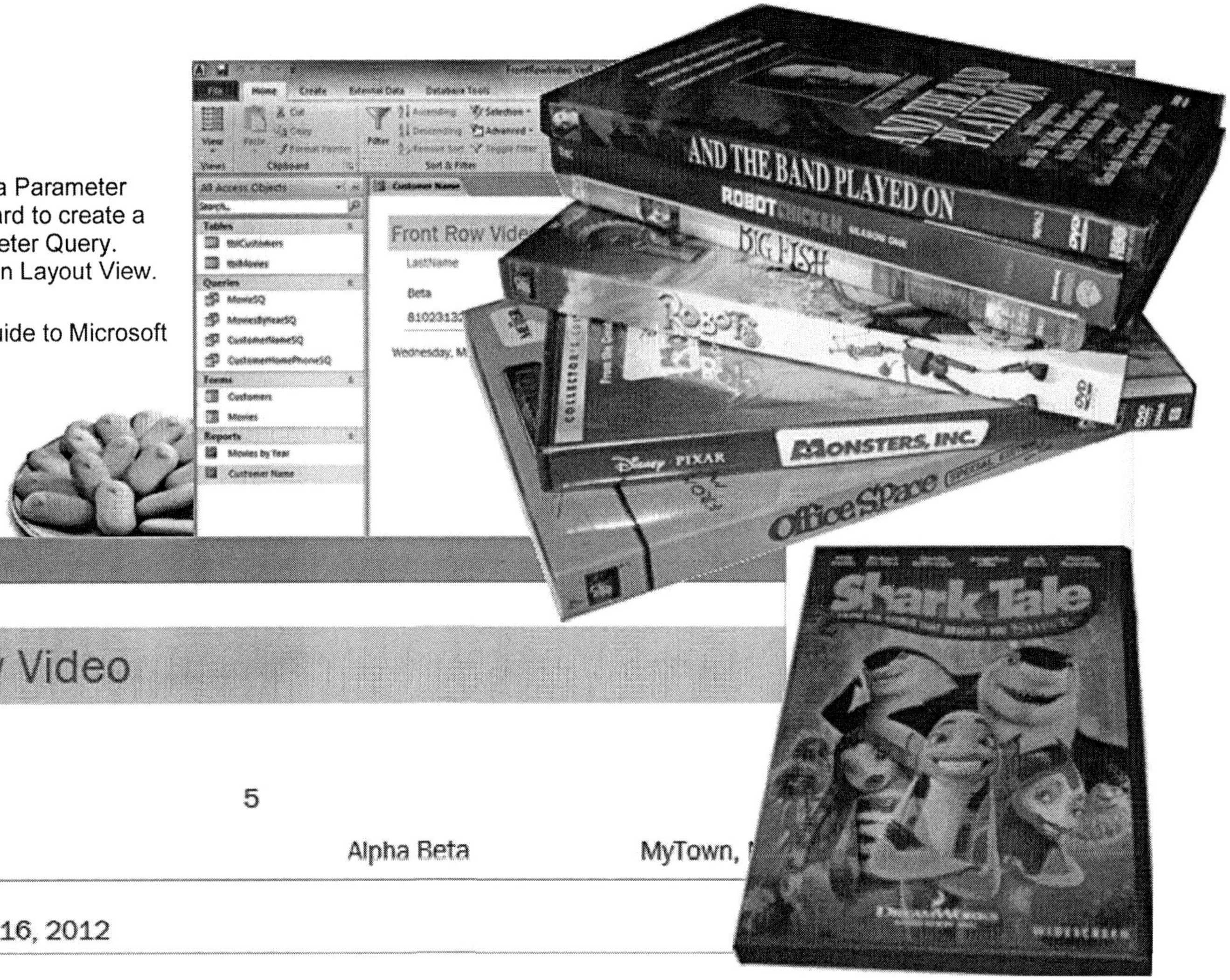

Front Row Video

LastName

Beta   5

8102313211   Alpha Beta   MyTown,

Wednesday, May 16, 2012

Practice Activities

Lesson 10: More Report Design

Try This: Do the following steps

1. Open the Brown Bag Lunch database you have been programming. Or you may download the sample database **Brown Bag Lunch ver10.accdb** online.
2. Open the CustomerCompanySQ Query. When prompted, enter the company Wordnation.
3. Open the Query in Design View.
4. Add a new field. Add the following Concatentation:
   Location: [City]&", "&[State]
5. Run the Query to test the new field. Use the Parameter WordNation when prompted.
6. Create a new Report using the Report Wizard. Use the Query CustomerCompanySQ as the Record Source. Select all available fields.
7. Add a Grouping level: Company. Select a layout: Stepped.
8. Name the Report: Customer Name. Select Preview and Finish the Wizard.
Use the Parameter Wordnation when prompted.
9. Close Print Preview. Open the Report in Design View.
10. Select all the Fields in the Detail Section. Change the arrangement to Tabular.
11. Go to Arrange Rows & Columns and Insert 2 new Rows above.
12. Select the CustomerID Control in the Table. Use the Move Up command to place the Field in the top Row.
13. Move these Fields up to the second Row: Phone Number and Location.
14. Use the Table Tools to Merge the Cells.
Select Cells A2:A4. Merge them.
Select Cells A3:A4. Merge them.
15. Go to the Page Header and Delete the Labels EXCEPT the Label for Company. Change Company to "The taste of eating out, the price of brown bagging it."
16. Go to the Report Header. Change Customer Name to Brown Bag Lunch Co.
17. Select the second Row, with the company name Wordnation and apply a top gridline.
18. Save the Customer Name Report. Please close the Brown Bag database.

Test Yourself

1. Which is the acceptable way to Concatenate 2 fields with a space between them?
A. (FirstName)&" "&(LastName)
B. [FirstName]&"space"&[LastName]
C. [FirstName]&" "&[LastName]
Tip: Beginning Access, page 240

2. What Ribbon has the command for the Report Wizard?
A. Home
B. Insert
C. Create
D. Wizards
Tip: Beginning Access, page 243

3. When switching to Design View on a Report that includes a Parameter Query, you need to enter a parameter before proceeding.
A. True
B. False
Tip: Beginning Access, page 249

4. Refer to the Concatenation code: FullName: [FirstName]&" "&[LastName]. What is the label of the new Field created?
A. FullName
B. New Field
C. Unnamed Field
D. Concatenated Name Field
Tip: Beginning Access, page 240

5. Refer to the new field LastNameFirst with the record Smith, Bill. Which Concatenation will create this field?
A. [LastName]&" "&[FirstName]
B. [LastName]&","&[FirstName]
C. [LastName]&"comma"&[FirstName]
Tip: Beginning Access, page 241

Access 2010: Appendix

Working with Databases

Beginning Access Objectives
In this lesson, you will learn how to:

1. Create a copy of an Microsoft Access Objects with Save Object As.

2. Use Copy and Paste to create a new copy of a Table and review the options.

3. Rename an Access Object.

4. Delete an Access Table and confirm.

5. Use Save Database As to make a backup version of a database.

© 2012 Comma Productions, LLC

HOME

Lesson 11 : Working with Databases

1. Readings

Read Lesson 11 in the Intermediate Access guide, page 261-284.

Project

A sample Table that is not saved.

Downloads

FrontRowVideo Begin11.accdb
Brown Bag Lunch ver11.accdb

2. Practice

There is no Practice Activity for this lesson.

3. Assessment

There is no test for this lesson.

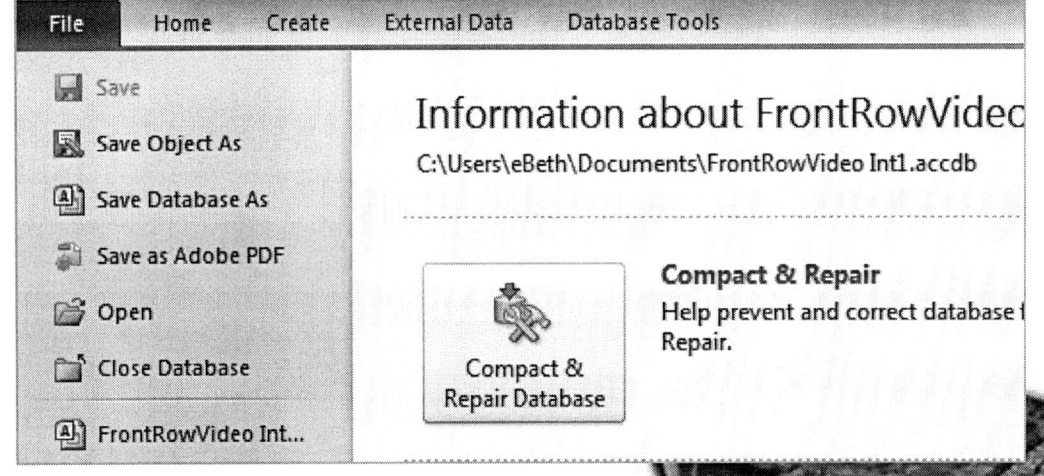

Menu Maps

From the **File Ribbon**.
1. File->Open, page 264
2. File->Save Object As, page 267
3. File ->Save Database As, page 273
4. File ->Save and Publish->Save Database As, page 276

From the **Right Click**
1. Right-Click ->Rename, page 268
2. Right-Click ->Copy, page 269
3. Right Click->Delete, page 270

Working with Databases

A **Database Administrator** has one key objective: save the data. The rest--Queries, Reports, better Forms--come next. The last lesson in this Beginning Guide to Microsoft Access 2010 teaches how to manage your Mighty Access databases. Good Database Administrators never DELETE an object or record. The best practice is to make a copy. We will practice creating a copy of a Table and renaming it. This lesson also includes how to create a backup copy of a database and offers suggestions for managing version control.

Sample Microsoft Office Access 2010 Database

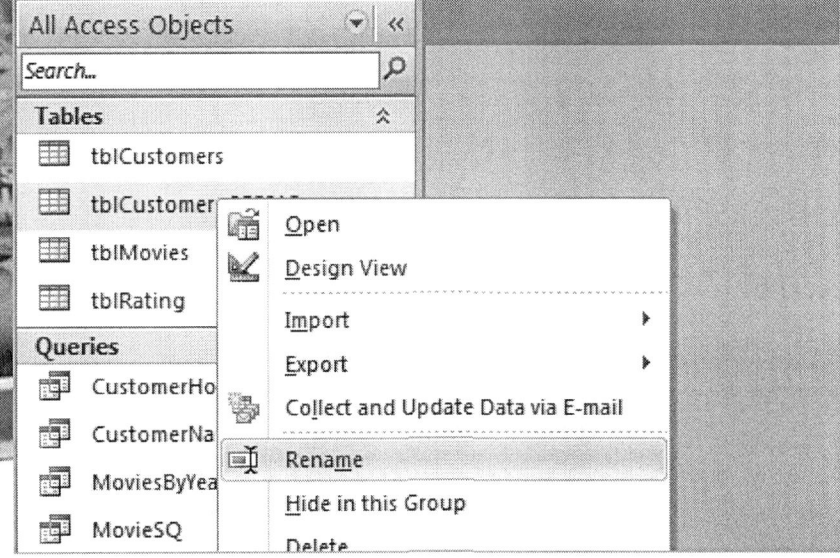

Getting Started

1. Try it: Start Microsoft Access 2010
Go to **Start ->All Programs.**
Go to the **Microsoft Office** folder.
Click on **Microsoft Access 2010.**

What Do You See? Welcome to the Microsoft Access Backstage. There are several options for getting started including templates or even a blank database.

Click **Open.** Keep going...

Memo to Self: The steps to start the Microsoft Access 2010 software program may not MATCH the ones in this lesson. Your steps may be different depending on which operating system you are using. That is OK.

Start ->All Programs->Microsoft Office->Microsoft Access 2010

Exam 77-885: Microsoft Access 2010
1. Managing the Access Environment
1.1. Create and manage a database: Open a Database

Open a Database

2. Try it: Open a Database

When you click **Open** you will be prompted to Browse for a Microsoft Access Database.

Browse to your Documents folder.
Select a database: <u>FrontRowVideo Begin11.accdb</u>
Click **Open**. Keep going...

Exam 77-885: Microsoft Access 2010
1. Managing the Access Environment
1.1. Create and manage a database: Open a Database

Start ->All Programs->Microsoft Access 2010->Open

Enable the Database

A database needs read/write permissions so that it can update the Tables when a User enters new information. However, when you open a database it may be disabled as a security check. You need to **Enable Content** in order to edit and save your programming. Here are the steps.

3. Try it: Enable the Database
If the database opens with a Security Warning: Click on **Enable Content.**

FrontRowVideo Begin11.accdb has:

Two Tables: tblCustomers, tblMovies

Four Queries: MovieSQ, MoviesByYearSQ, CustomerNameSQ and CustomerHomePhoneSQ

Two Forms: Customers, Movies

Two Reports: Movies by Year, Customer Name

Keep going....

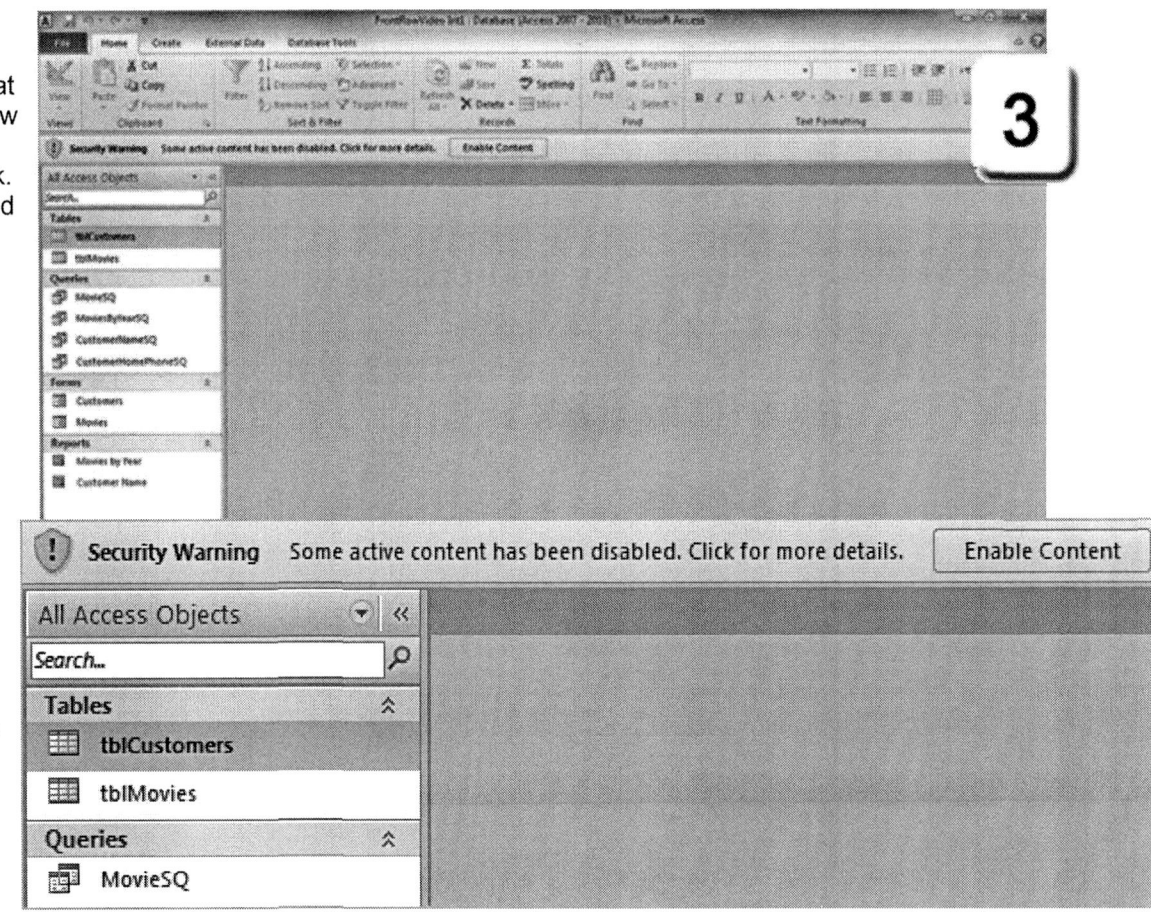

Exam 77-885: Microsoft Access 2010
1. Managing the Access Environment
1.1. Create and manage a database: Open a Database

Save Object As

Before manipulating any data in the Tables, it is a wise precaution to create a COPY of the Table. So, a word to the wise!

Before You Begin: Select an Object
Go to **All Access Objects->Tables**.
Select a Table: tblCustomers

1. Try it: Save Object As
Go to **File->Save Object As.**
The Microsoft Access 2010 Backstage will open and you will be prompted to enter a **name** for the new Customer Table.
The default name is: Copy of tblCustomers.

Save As: Table.
Click **OK**. Keep going...

File->Save Object As

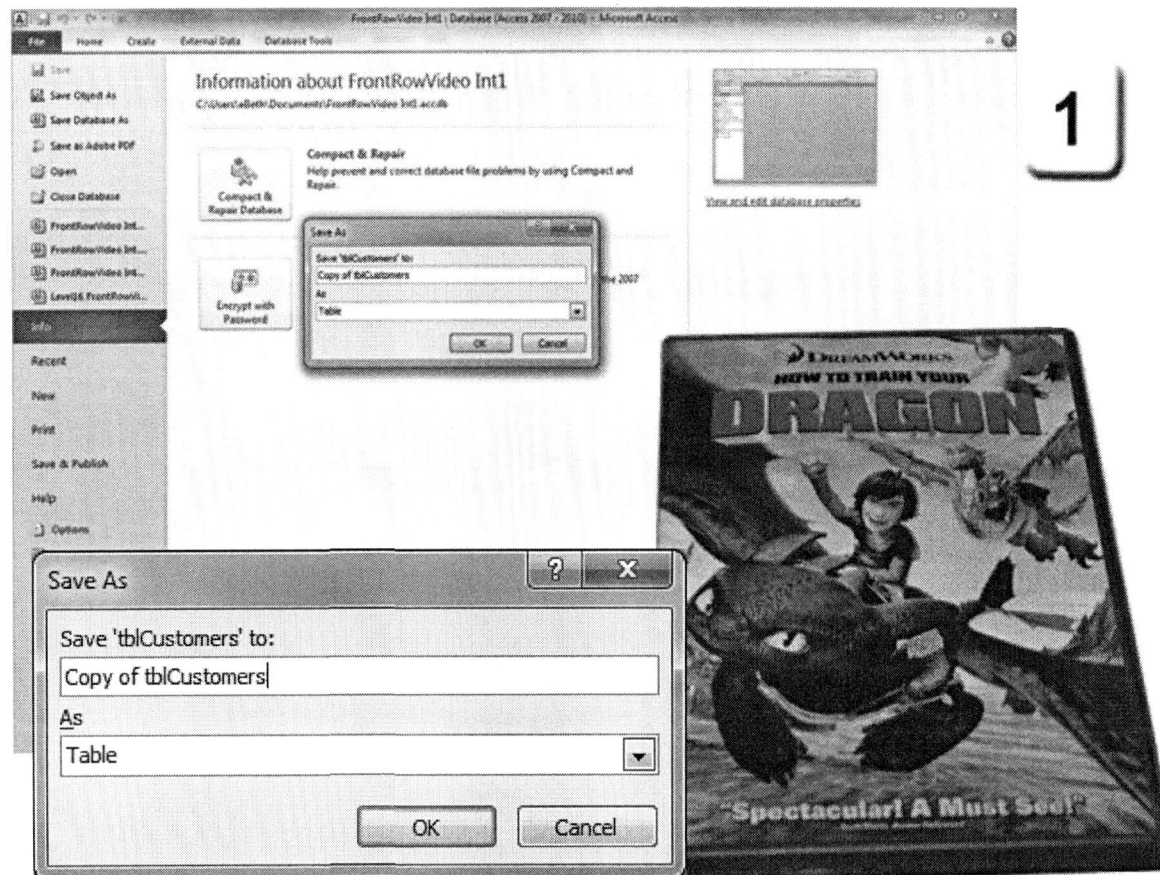

Exam 77-885: Microsoft Access 2010
1. Managing the Access Environment
1.1. Create and manage a database: Use Save Object As

Rename the Table
2. Try it: Rename the Table
Select a Table: Copy of tblCustomers

Right-Click the Table: Copy of tblCustomers.
Click **Rename**.
Enter a new name: tblCustomers 052012,
where 052012 is the current date.

Click the **ENTER** key to finish. Keep going...

Right-Click ->Rename

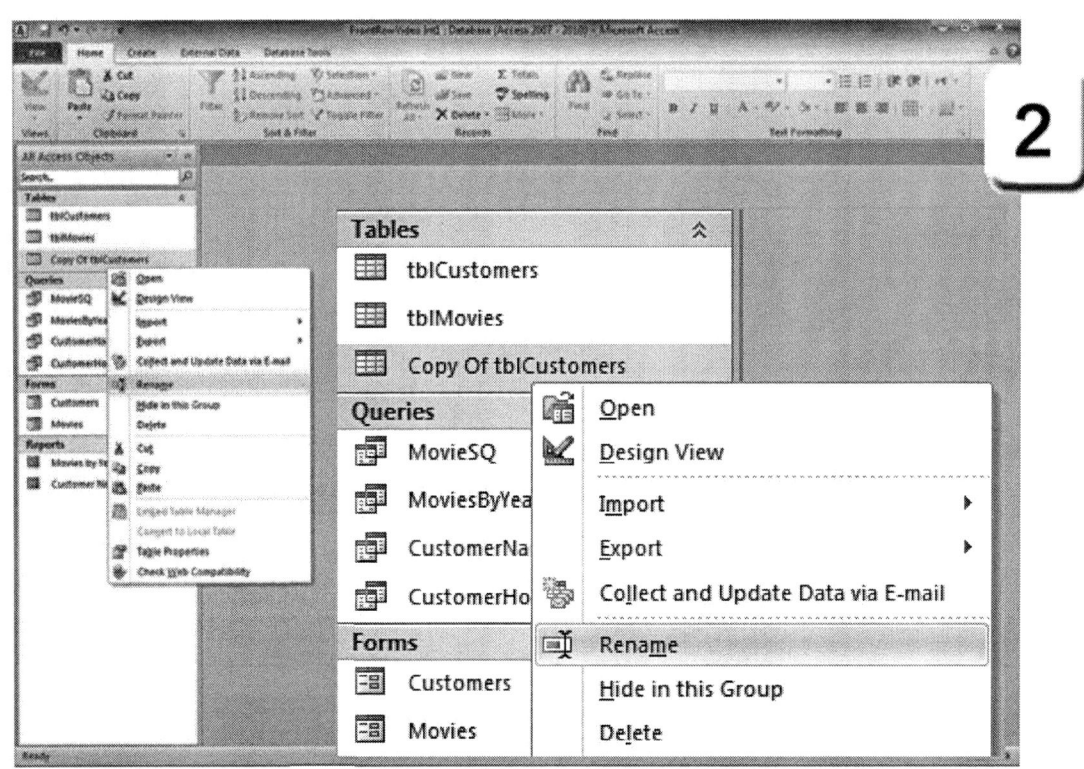

Exam 77-885: Microsoft Access 2010
1. Managing the Access Environment
1.2. Configure the Navigation Pane: Rename an Object

Copy and Paste a Table

The previous pages demonstrated how to create a duplicate Table by using the **Save Object As** command.

Microsoft Access can **Copy and Paste** Objects as well. There are interesting options when you Paste a Table.

3. Try it: Copy a Table
Select a Table: tblCustomers
Right click the Table: tblCustomers.
Click **Copy**.

Try This, Too: Paste the Table
Right click the Table Group.
Select an option: Paste.

You will be prompted to enter the following:
Table Name: Copy of tblCustomers
Paste Options: Structure and Data

What Do You See? You can choose to keep the Table **Structure only,** without the Data if you wish. This is a good way to purge any sample records. Keep going...

Right-Click ->Copy

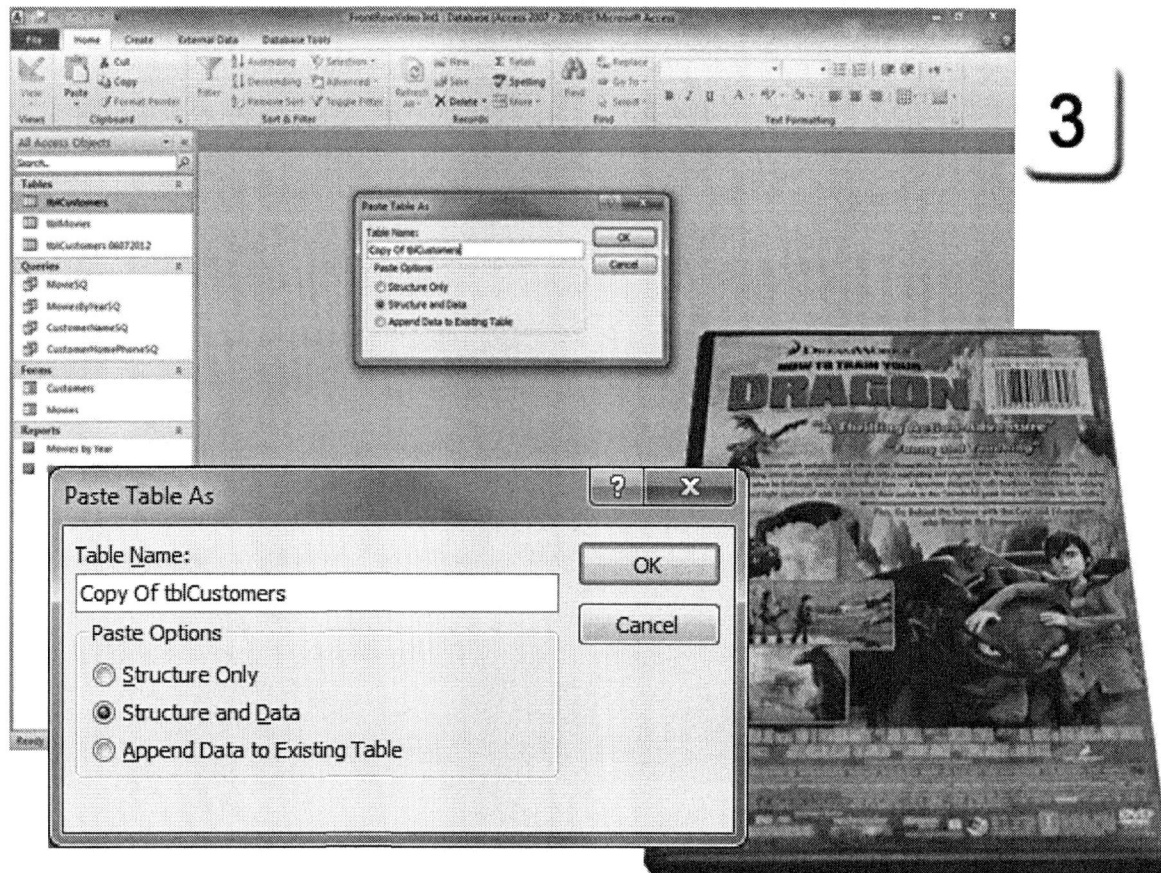

Exam 77-885: Microsoft Access 2010
1. Managing the Access Environment
1.2. Configure the Navigation Pane: Copy and Paste Objects

HOME

Delete a Table

The purpose of a database is to save the data. So, when a Table is deleted, the database asks if this is really something you want to do.

4. Try it: Delete a Table
Select a Table: Copy of tblCustomers.
Right click the Table: Copy of tblCustomers.
Click on **DELETE**.

What Do You See? You will be told that deleting this object will remove it from the database...That means: **There is No UNDO!!**.

Click **Yes**. The Copy of tblCustomers Table will be permanently deleted from the database.

Keep going...

Right Click->Delete

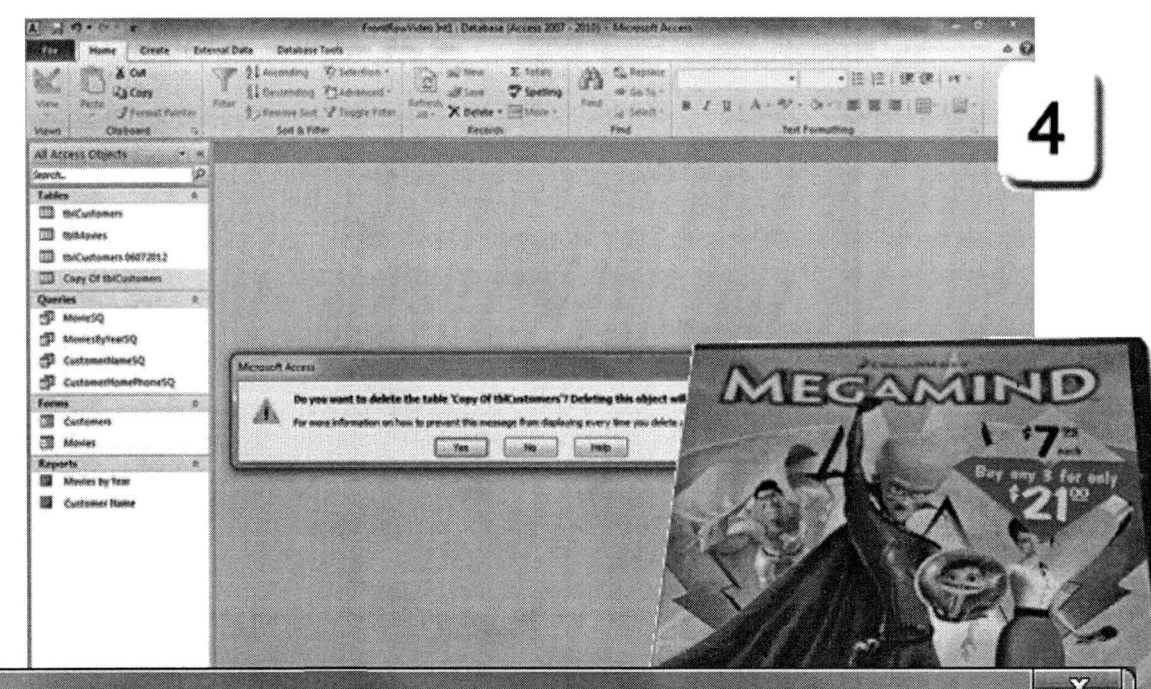

4

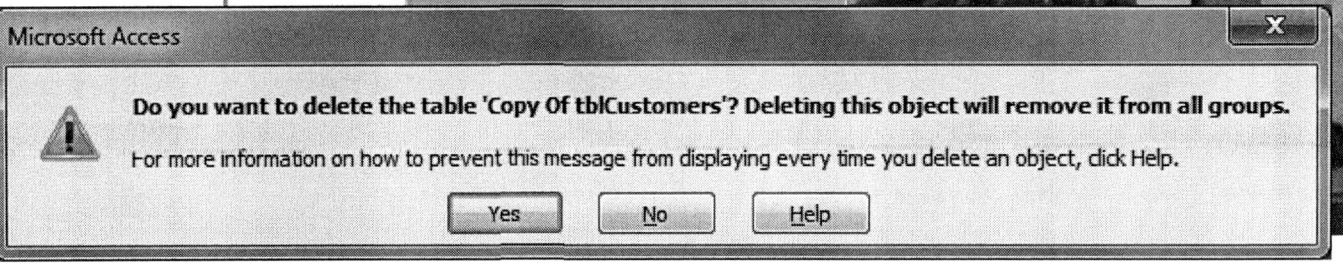

Microsoft Access

⚠ **Do you want to delete the table 'Copy Of tblCustomers'? Deleting this object will remove it from all groups.**

For more information on how to prevent this message from displaying every time you delete an object, click Help.

[Yes]   [No]   [Help]

Exam 77-885: Microsoft Access 2010
1. Managing the Access Environment
1.2. Configure the Navigation Pane: Delete Objects

Find the Navigation Options

As you work with your database, you may accumulate many copies of the Tables. Which one is the current data and not the backup? It can become very confusing.

Save As What? When you create a copy or Save As, you will be prompted to enter a name for the backup. If you include the date as part of the name, it makes it easy to identify when the backup was created. For example: tblCustomers 052012.

Use the Navigation Pane By default, the Navigation Pane displays All Access Objects. The Objects are Grouped and Sorted. You can change the Navigation Pane if you wish. What are the options?

1. Try it: Find the Navigation Pane Options
Go to **All Access Objects**.
Click on the **Option arrow**.

What Do You See? The Access Objects are grouped by Type (Table, Chairs).
Keep going...

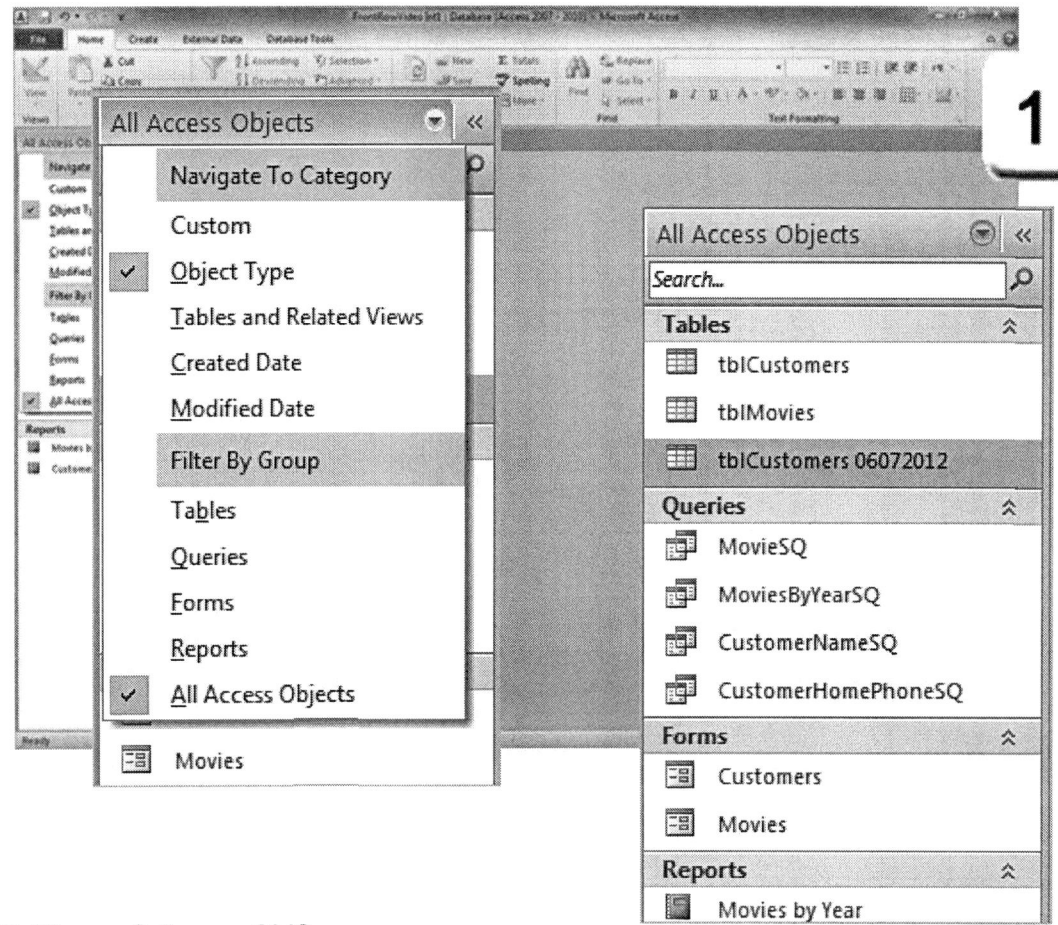

Exam 77-885: Microsoft Access 2010
1. Managing the Access Environment
1.2. Configure the Navigation Pane: Copy and Paste Objects

Set the Navigation Pane
2. Try it: Set the Navigation Pane
Go to **All Access Objects.**
Click on the **Option arrow.**
Select: **Modified Date.**

What Do You See? The Access Objects are sorted by Date. The Sort Order is Descending (newest to oldest): the object that was saved last is first on the list.

What Else Do You See? The Navigation Pane uses the Date to Filter by Group, too.

Try This, Too: Return to the Default View
Go to **All Access Objects.**
Click on the **Option arrow.**
Select: **Object Type.**

Very Good.

Set Navigation Pane Options

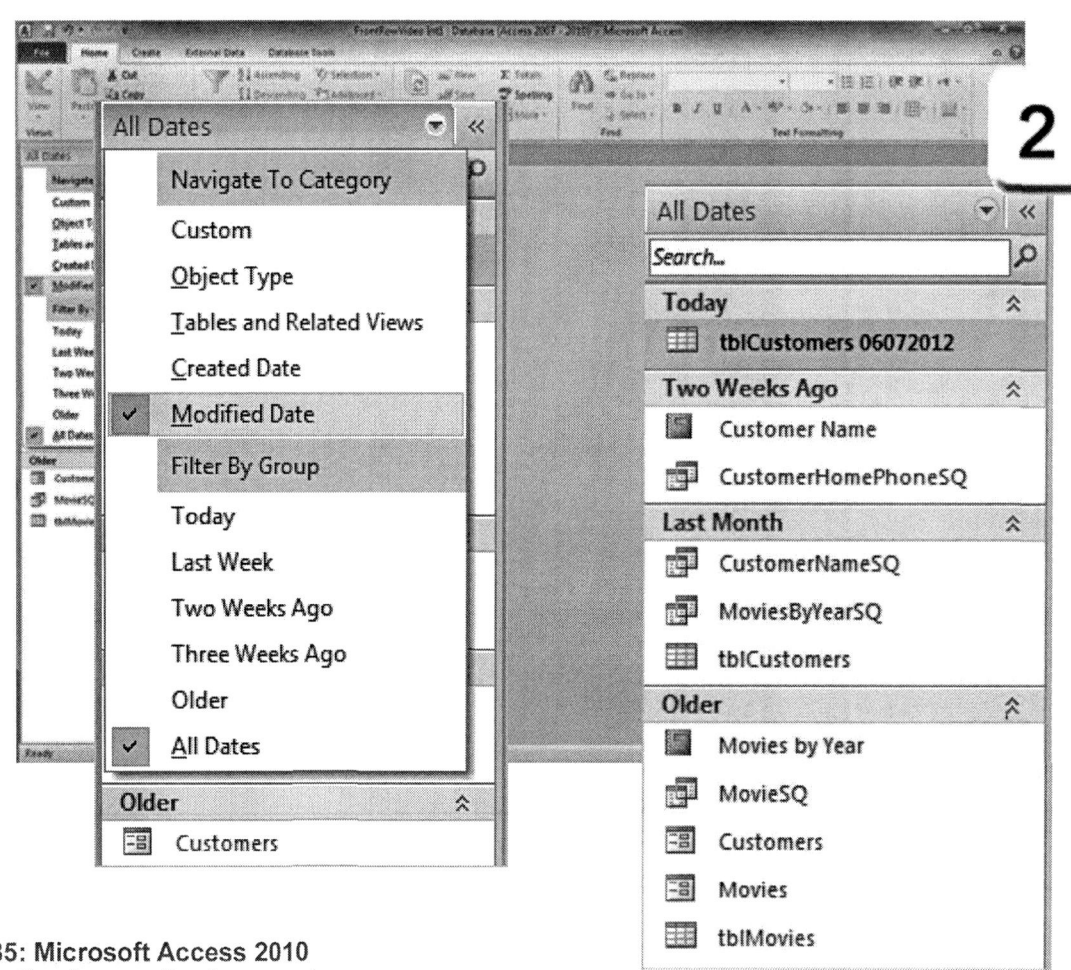

Exam 77-885: Microsoft Access 2010
1. Managing the Access Environment
1.2. Configure the Navigation Pane: Set Navigation Pane Options

Save a Copy of the Database

The preceding pages showed how to make copies of the Access Objects. You can create another copy of your database as well.

1. Try it: Save Database As
<u>FrontRowVideo Begin11.accdb</u> is still open. Go to **File ->Save Database As.**

What Do You See? If a Table, Form, Query or Report is left open, Microsoft Access will close all open objects. You will be prompted to Save anything that you were working on.

Click **Yes**. Keep going...

File ->Save Database As

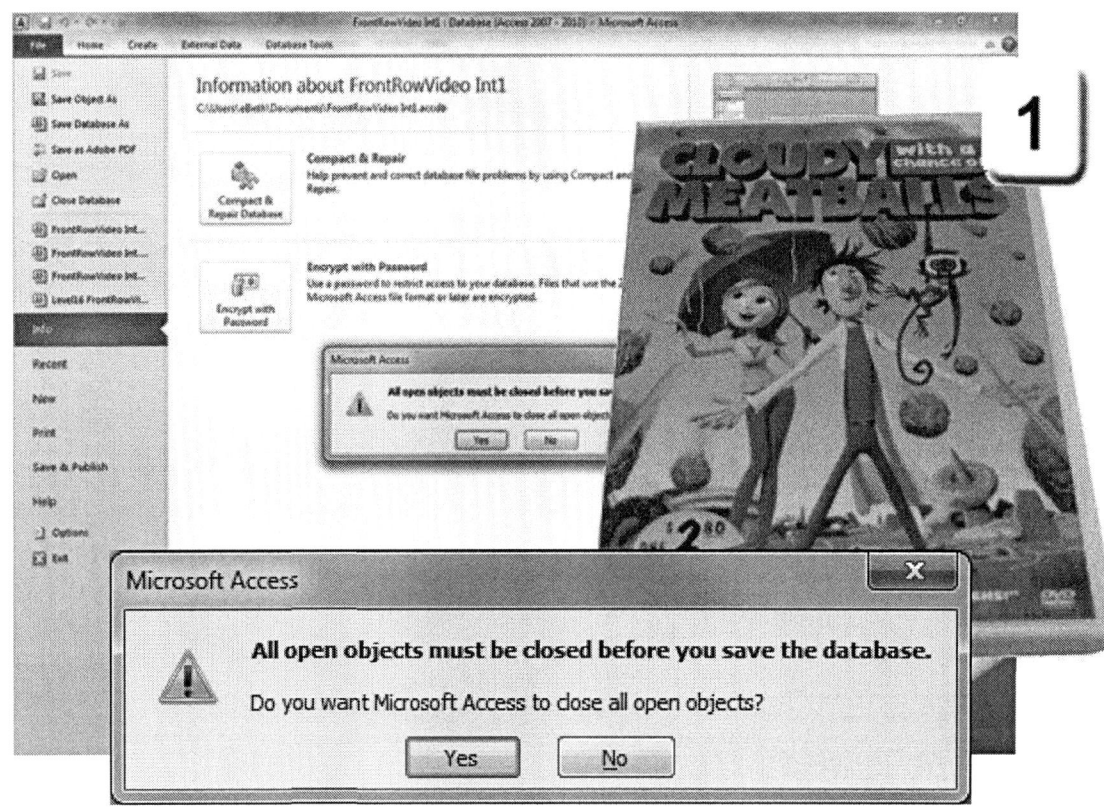

Exam 77-885: Microsoft Access 2010
1. Managing the Access Environment
1.1. Create and manage a database: Save a Database As

 Take One

File ->Save Database As

Save A Copy: Options
2. Try This: File ->Save Database As
Browse to your Documents folder.

Enter the following:
File name: FrontRowVideo Int EAN 052012

Where "EAN" are your initials.
and "052012" is the current month and year.

Click **Save**. Keep going...

File name:	FrontRowVideo Int EAN 052012
Save as type:	Microsoft Access Database

Hide Folders   Tools ▾   Save

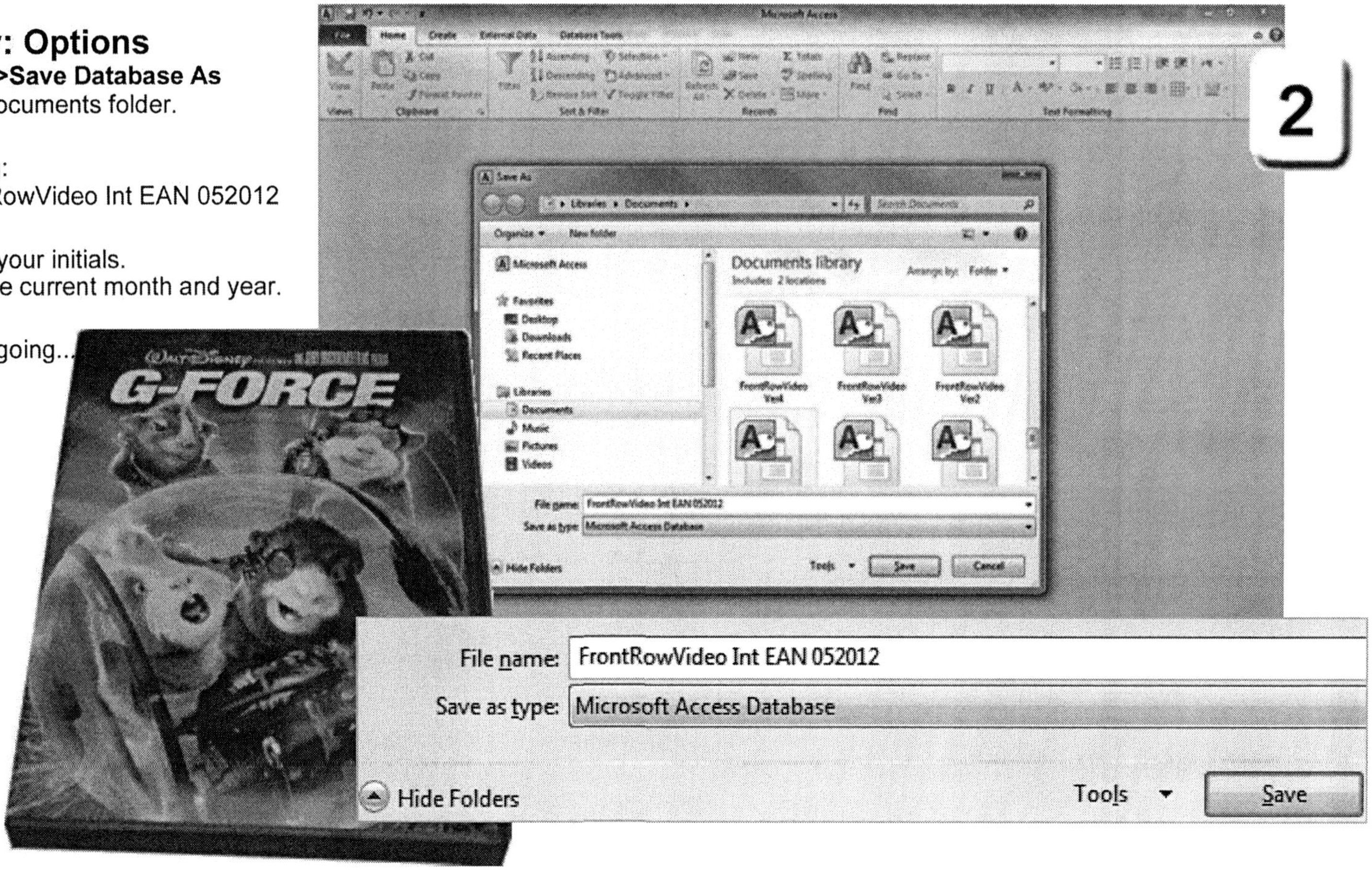

Exam 77-885: Microsoft Access 2010
1. Managing the Access Environment
1.1. Create and manage a database: Save a Database As

Find the Database Copy

3. Try it: Trust, But Verify
Go to the Documents Folder and confirm that there is a new copy of the database.

Try This, Too: Open the Database
Double click the database copy, **FrontRowVideo Int EAN 052012** in this example, to open it in Access 2010.

Return to the Documents Folder while the database is still open.

What Do You See, Now? There should be a little laccsb file. Whenever a database is open, this **locking file** keeps track of which records are open to make sure two people don't edit the same record at the same time.

Close the Documents Folder.
Return to Microsoft Access, please.

Sample Documents Folder

3

FrontRowVideo Int EAN 052012

FrontRowVideo Int EAN 052012

Save and Publish

There are several different versions of Microsoft Access. Each version has a unique file format.

You can use the **Save and Publish** options in the Backstage to make copies of the database that are compatible with Microsoft Access 2000 or Access 2002-2003.

1. Try it: Save and Publish
A COPY of the database is still open.
Go to **File ->Save and Publish.**
Click on **Save Database As.**

What Do You See? The Default Access database format is *.accdb, The File Type for Access 2000 (*.mdb) is different than the File Type for Access 2002-2003.

Keep going...

File ->Save and Publish->Save Database As

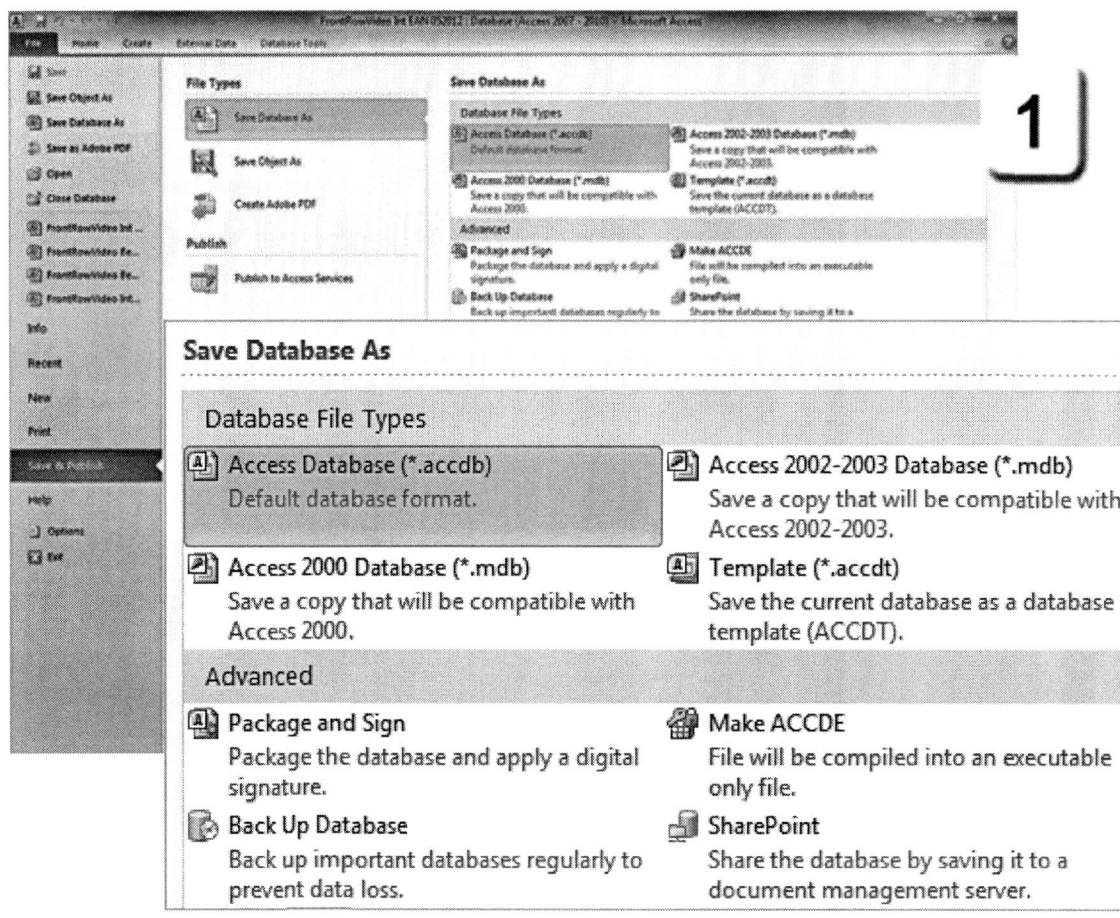

Save Database As

Database File Types

Access Database (*.accdb) Default database format.	**Access 2002-2003 Database (*.mdb)** Save a copy that will be compatible with Access 2002-2003.
Access 2000 Database (*.mdb) Save a copy that will be compatible with Access 2000.	**Template (*.accdt)** Save the current database as a database template (ACCDT).

Advanced

Package and Sign Package the database and apply a digital signature.	**Make ACCDE** File will be compiled into an executable only file.
Back Up Database Back up important databases regularly to prevent data loss.	**SharePoint** Share the database by saving it to a document management server.

Exam 77-885: Microsoft Access 2010
1. Managing the Access Environment
1.1. Create and manage a database: Save and Publish

Save and Publish:
Save as a Template

In Microsoft Word, Excel, Outlook and PowerPoint you can save a file as a Template if you wish. Microsoft Access has the same option.

This Mighty Access database can be saved as a Template and used to make a another application. There are many advantages to using a Template: The Forms are complete with logos and User Controls, such as the Combo Boxes.

2. Try it: Save as a Template

A COPY of the database is still open.
Go to **File ->Save and Publish.**
Go to **Save Database As->Template.**
Enter the following:
Name: Front Row Video Template.
Description: a movie rental database with four Tables and four Queries.
Category: User Templates
Include Data in Template: check Yes.

Click **OK.**
Keep going...

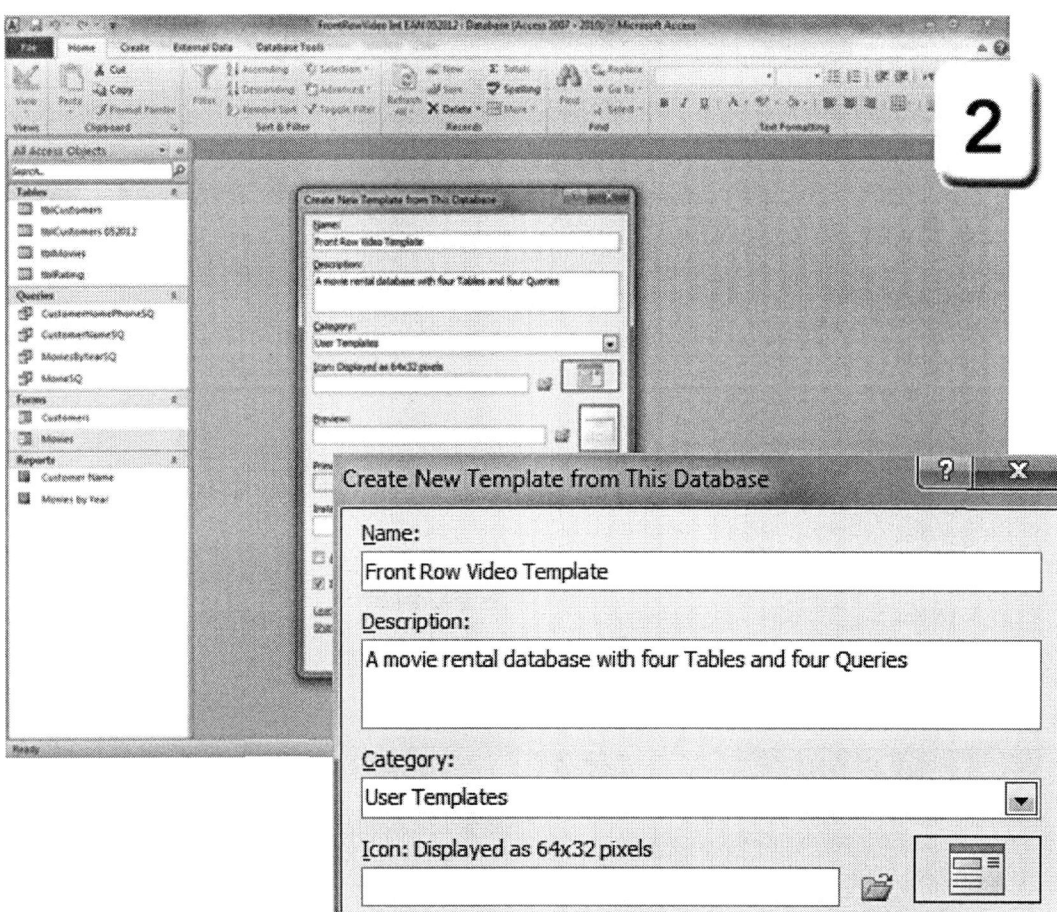

Exam 77-885: Microsoft Access 2010
1. Managing the Access Environment
1.1. Create and manage a database: Save and Publish Save as Template

User Templates

After the Template is created you will be notified that it is Saved in the User Templates folder. Here are the steps to open a User Template.

3. Try it: Find the User Templates
A COPY of the database is still open.
Go **File ->New->Available Templates.**
Click on **My Templates.**

What Do You See? The From Row Video Template should be listed in the Available Templates folder.

Create a Database from a User Template
Select a Template: Front Row Video Template.
Click **Create.**

Keep going...

File ->New->Available Templates->My Templates

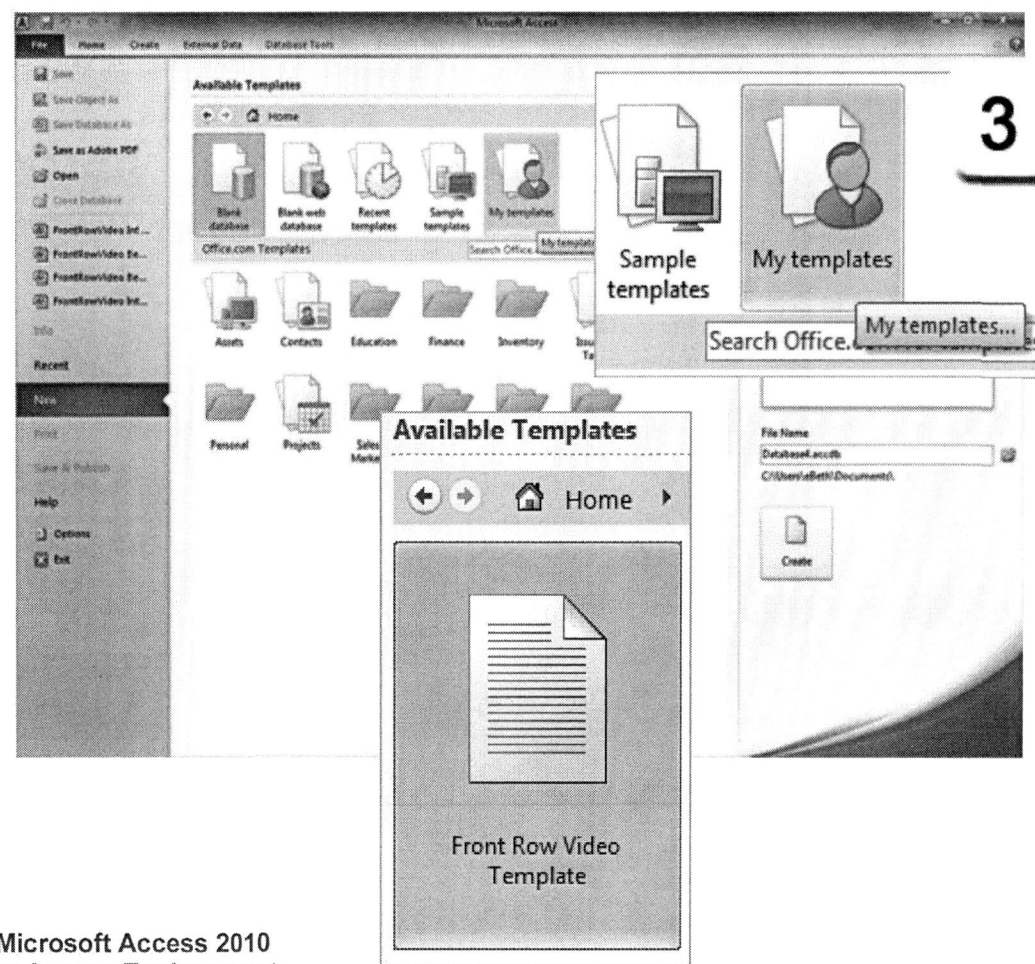

Exam 77-885: Microsoft Access 2010
1. Managing the Access Environment
1.1. Create and manage a database: Create a Database from a Template

All Access Objects

Hello, Database from Template
4. Try it: Review the Database
This sample database, a copy of
__FrontRowVideo Begin11.accdb__ has the
following Objects:

Four Tables: tblCustomers,
tblCustomers052012, tblMovies, and tblRating.

Four Queries: CustomerHomePhoneSQ,
CustomerNameSQ, MoviesByYearSQ,
MovieSQ.

Two Forms: Customers, Movies.

Two Reports: Customer Name, Movies by Year.
Keep going...

Memo to Self: Click **Enable Content** if you see
the Security Warning.

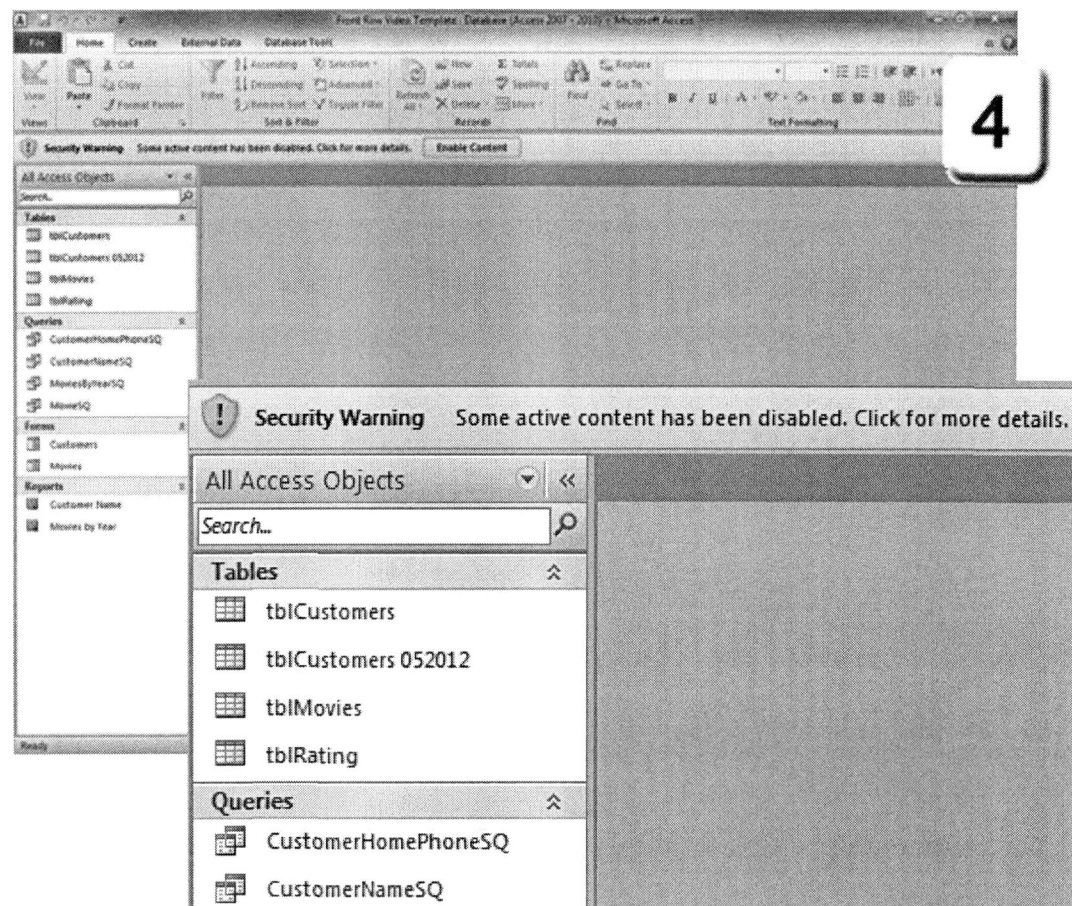

Exam 77-885: Microsoft Access 2010
1. Managing the Access Environment
1.1. Create and manage a database: Create a Database from a Template

Create ->Templates->Application Parts->Quick Start->Tasks

Use a Quick Start Template

Quick Start allows you to quickly add to your Access database. Quick Start templates create a Table and companion Form with one click.

The Quick Start templates can be found in the Application Parts.

5. Try it: Use a Quick Start Template
The Front Row Video Template is open.
Go to **Create ->Templates->Application Parts.**
Select a **Quick Start** Template: Tasks.

Keep going...

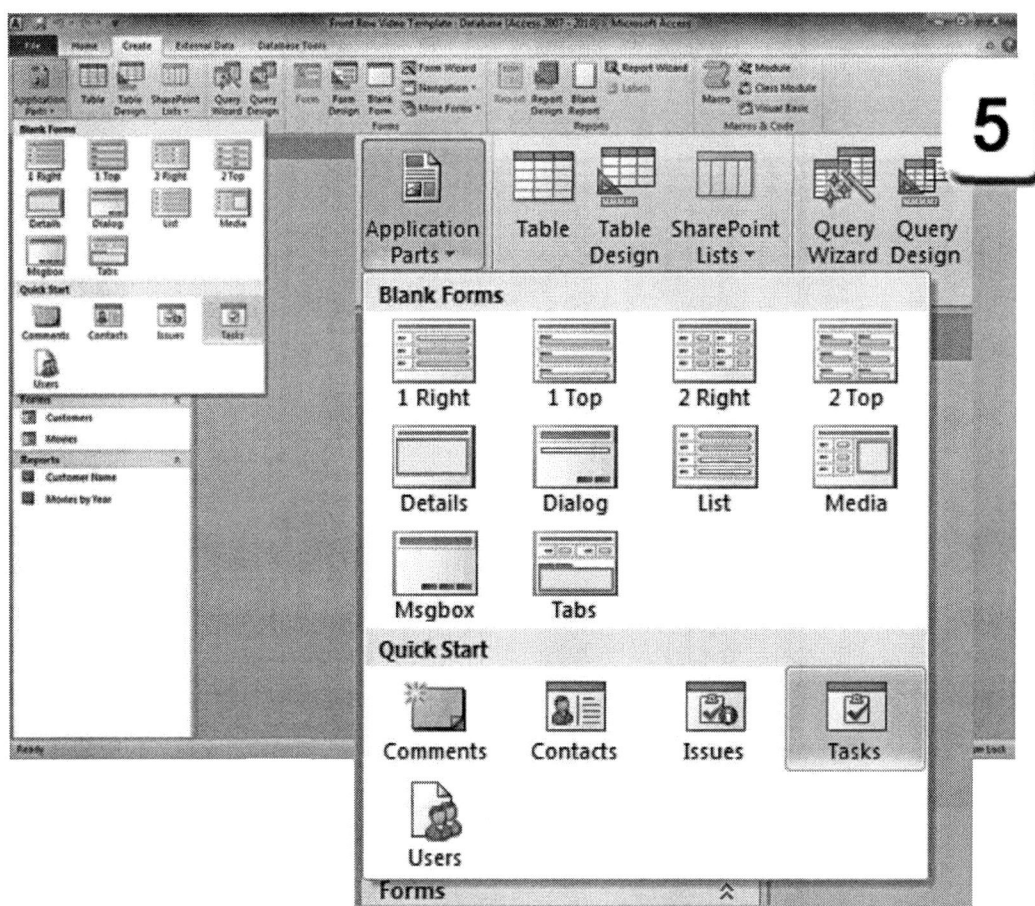

Exam 77-885: Microsoft Access 2010
1. Managing the Access Environment
1.2. Configure the Navigation Pane: Use Quick Start Application Parts

The Quick Start Wizard

6. Try it: The Quick Start Wizard

The Quick Start Wizard will prompt you to create a simple Relationship. The example given is tblCustomers: One customer may have many Tasks. The other example is that one Tasks may fix a complaint from many customers. The third option is that there is no relationship between Tasks and tblCustomers, or perhaps any other Table in the database.

Select: There is no relationship.
Click **Create**. Keep going...

Memo to Self: There is a discussion on why Tables should be related and what that means in the Advanced Guide to Microsoft Access. You can skip ahead and read the lesson on database design if you wish.

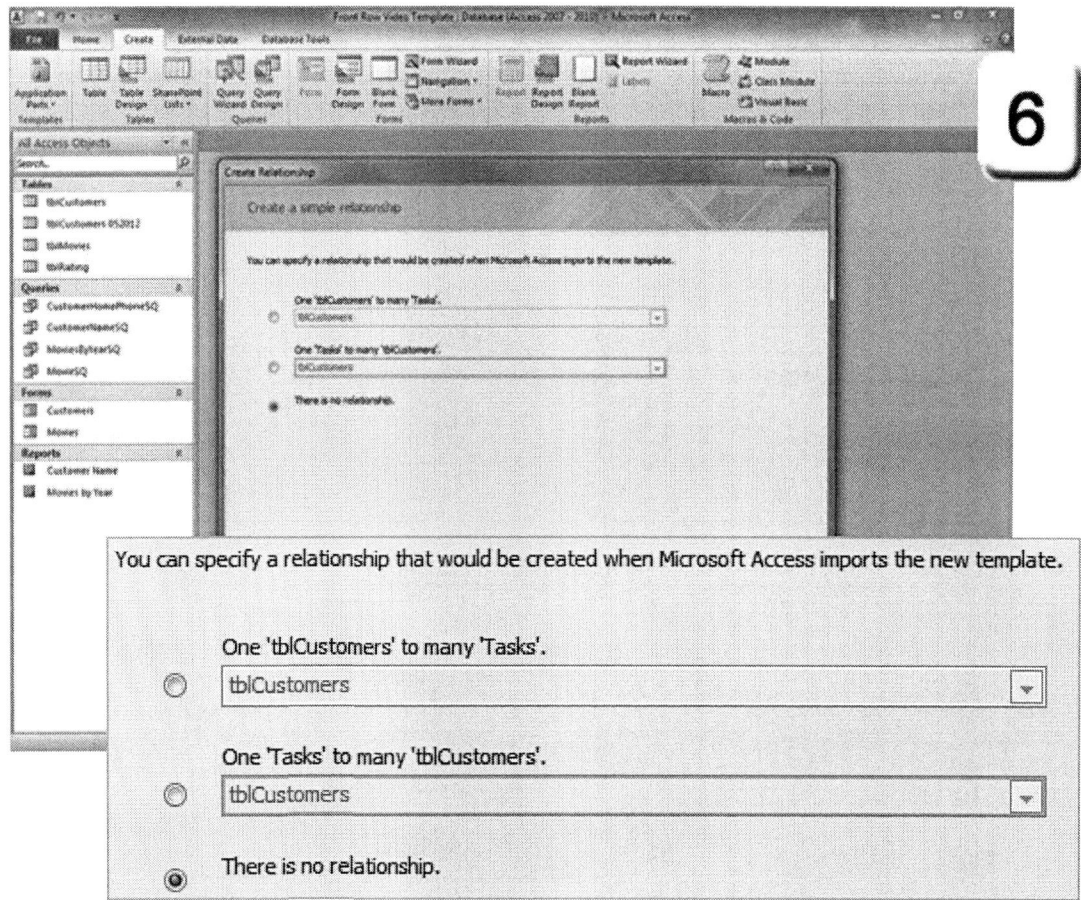

You can specify a relationship that would be created when Microsoft Access imports the new template.

One 'tblCustomers' to many 'Tasks'.
⊙ tblCustomers ▾

One 'Tasks' to many 'tblCustomers'.
⊙ tblCustomers ▾

⦿ There is no relationship.

Exam 77-885: Microsoft Access 2010
1. Managing the Access Environment
1.2. Configure the Navigation Pane: Use Quick Start Application Parts

Hello, Quick Start Parts

There are two new Forms in the Access database: TaskDetails and TaskDS. TaskDetails is a Form View. TaskDS is a Datasheet View.

7. Try it: Open the Task Form
Go to **All Access Objects->Forms**.
Double-click to open a Form: TaskDetails.

What Do You See: The new Form has Text Fields to enter the Task. There are several Combo Box Controls for the Priority, Date and % Complete. There are also two command buttons for Save & New and Save & Close.

Try This, Too: Test the Task Form
Enter the following:
Task: Finish Database.
Priority (1) High.
Start Date: Please select today from the Date Picker.

Click **Save & Close.** One more thought...

All Access Objects ->Forms

Exam 77-885: Microsoft Access 2010
1. Managing the Access Environment
1.2. Configure the Navigation Pane: Use Quick Start Application Parts

Where's the Data?

When we created the two Task Forms with
the Quick Start Application Parts, the Wizard
also created a Table to store the Data. Last,
but not least, please review the Task Table
and the data in it.

8. Try it: Review the Task Table
Go to **All Access Objects->Tables.**
Double-click to open a Table: Tasks.

What Do You See: The Task Table saved
the data we entered into the TaskDetail
Form.
Done and Done! **Close** the Tasks. Table.

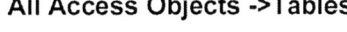
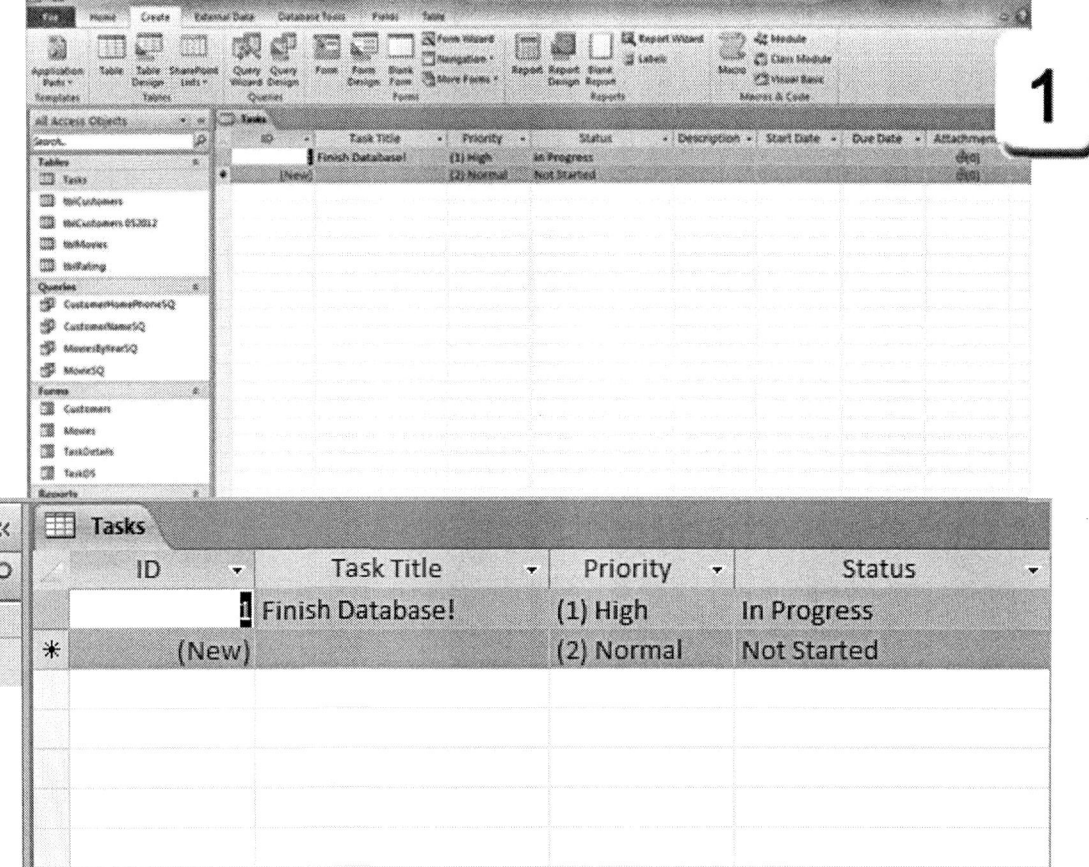

ID	Task Title	Priority	Status
1	Finish Database!	(1) High	In Progress
* (New)		(2) Normal	Not Started

Exam 77-885: Microsoft Access 2010
1. Managing the Access Environment
1.2. Configure the Navigation Pane: Use Quick Start Application Parts

Summary

This lesson offered several methods for making copies of the Access Database Objects. We also walked through the steps to save a copy of the database, as well.

All of these steps should be part of your backup program. Imagine how angry you would be if you lost a Form that took hours to design and proof? Save your work and use descriptive names so that others can understand which version is which.

We also looked at creating Templates and using Quick Start Forms. Join us in the Intermediate and Advanced Guide to Microsoft Access 2010: we'll make our own Forms with Command Buttons!

Short, but sweet. You get the cookie.

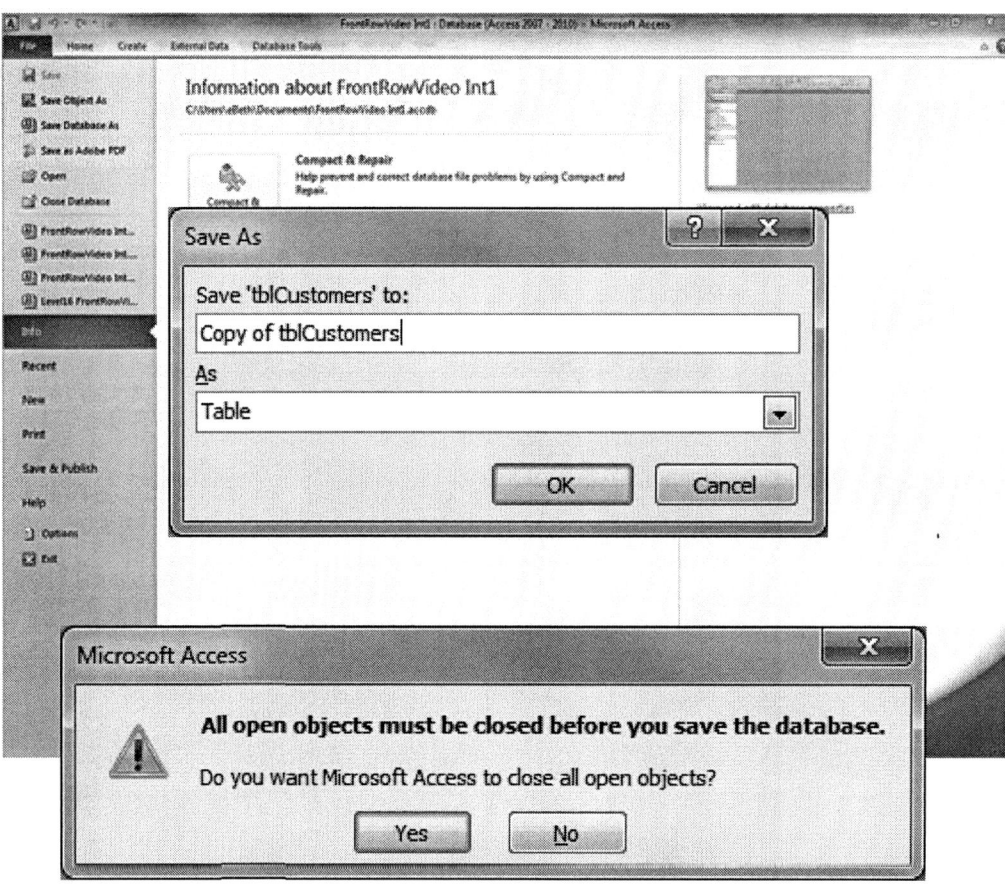

Beginning Access Skill Test

Before You Begin: Download and open the sample database:
Beginning Access Skill Test.accdb

1. Create a Form with the Form Wizard.
Use tblCustomers as the Record Source.
Select all available Fields for the Form.
Select the Columnar Layout.
Name the Title Customers. Finish the Wizard

2. Open the Customers Form in Design View.
In the Form Header use the Property Sheet to edit the position of the
Label: Left 1.25" and top 0.25".
Format the Label Font: 48pt, White, Bold.
Resize the Label to fit if needed.

3. Add the image Lunch4.gif to the Header.
Resize the image: Width 1" and Height 1".
Format the color of the Header with a Shape Fill Color: Dark Blue 2.

4. Select ALL the Form Controls & Labels (except the Header Label).
Change the Width to 2.5" and the Height to 0.25"

5. Resize each of the Labels so that they are as wide as the text.
Move the Controls next to the Labels, with minimal space between.
Move the Controls and their Labels:
   Place Company below Last Name.
   Place Phone below Company

6. Select the Form and change the Tab Order to Auto Order.

7. Select the Form and set the Cycle Properties to Current Record.

8. Format the Form with a Quick Style: Pushpin.

9. Save the Customers Form and test the Form in Normal View.

10. Close the Beginning Access Skill Test.accdb.
Submit this database online.

Microsoft Access 2010 Study Guide

Microsoft Office Specialist (MOS): Exam 77-885 for Access 2010

Microsoft Access 2010 Study Guide
Microsoft Office Specialist (MOS): Exam 77-885 for Access 2010

Beginning Microsoft Access 2010: Glossary

Microsoft Office Specialist (MOS): Exam 77-885 for Access 2010

Concatenation: combines multiple Fields into a new, single Field. p186

Control: where users enter and change data on a Form. Attached to a Label. p141

Cycle: refers to what happens after you Tab to the last Form Field. You either remain on the current record, returning to the first Field, or you advance to the next record. p145

Datasheet View: this view of an Access Table looks like an Excel spreadsheet, complete with a Header Row. p29

Data Validation: verifying or limited data to ensure accuracy of data entry. p46

External Data: data retrieved from other programs, such as QuickBooks or Microsoft Excel. p85

Field: where the record of data is stored. p37

Field Properties: programmable options attached to a selected database field. p59

QBE/ Query By Example: a visual format for programming Query objects

Queries: function that looks up or manipulates data by asking questions of a Table.p30   See also: *Select Queries* and *Action Queries*

Real Users: the people who have to use the database to get their job done. p131

Record: holds all of the information about a specific item or entry in the database. p39

Reports: Access data in printed form, such as a receipt or an inventory. p32

Select Query: asks questions and returns the appropriate data as an answer. p164

Tab: using the keyboard key Tab to move from one form field to another. p111

Tab Order: sequence of Form Fields selected when pressing the Tab key on the keyboard. p145

Table: Access databases store all data in Tables. p29

Theme: specifies colors and fonts applied to the current Access object. p114

Toggle: switch a command from on to off, or off to on, such as with a Filter. p96

Wizard (Form, Query, etc): a step-by-step guide that walks you through creating or using a complex function. p86, 105

Worksheet: section of an Excel workbook (or file), used when importing data from Excel. p85

Beginning Microsoft Access 2010: Index
Microsoft Office Specialist (MOS): Exam 77-885 for Access 2010